# ROUTLEDGE LIBRARY EDITIONS: WW2

Volume 48

# THE YANKEE MARLBOROUGH

# THE YANKEE MARLBOROUGH

R.W. THOMPSON

LONDON AND NEW YORK

First published in 1963 by George Allen & Unwin Ltd

This edition first published in 2022
by Routledge
2 Park Square, Milton Park, Abingdon, Oxon OX14 4RN

and by Routledge
605 Third Avenue, New York, NY 10158

*Routledge is an imprint of the Taylor & Francis Group, an informa business*

© 1963 George Allen & Unwin Ltd

All rights reserved. No part of this book may be reprinted or reproduced or utilised in any form or by any electronic, mechanical, or other means, now known or hereafter invented, including photocopying and recording, or in any information storage or retrieval system, without permission in writing from the publishers.

*Trademark notice*: Product or corporate names may be trademarks or registered trademarks, and are used only for identification and explanation without intent to infringe.

*British Library Cataloguing in Publication Data*
A catalogue record for this book is available from the British Library

ISBN: 978-1-03-201217-9 (Set)
ISBN: 978-1-00-319367-8 (Set) (ebk)
ISBN: 978-1-03-204643-3 (Volume 48) (hbk)
ISBN: 978-1-03-204645-7 (Volume 48) (pbk)
ISBN: 978-1-00-319405-7 (Volume 48) (ebk)

DOI: 10.4324/9781003194057

**Publisher's Note**
The publisher has gone to great lengths to ensure the quality of this reprint but points out that some imperfections in the original copies may be apparent.

**Disclaimer**
The publisher has made every effort to trace copyright holders and would welcome correspondence from those they have been unable to trace.

# THE YANKEE
# MARLBOROUGH

BY

R. W. THOMPSON

LONDON
GEORGE ALLEN & UNWIN LTD
RUSKIN HOUSE  MUSEUM STREET

FIRST PUBLISHED 1963

*This book is copyright under the Berne Convention. Apart from any fair dealing for the purpose of private study, research, criticism or review, as permitted under the Copyright Act 1956, no portion may be reproduced by any process without written permission. Enquiry should be made to the publishers.*

© George Allen & Unwin Ltd, 1963

PRINTED IN GREAT BRITAIN
in 11 on 12 point Juliana type
BY SIMSON SHAND LTD
LONDON, HERTFORD AND HARLOW

# PREFACE

This book is a personal search for one of the greatest and most enigmatic personalities of our time. It was, I have no doubt, a rash undertaking, but not lightly undertaken. As long ago as 1924 I was deeply impressed by the two monumental volumes of *These Eventful Years*, edited by J. L. Garvin. In his introduction Garvin wrote:

'Man has amazed himself by the revelation of his powers and appalled himself by the disclosure of the primeval terrors that slept in his heart.'

It is devastatingly clear that man was not sufficiently amazed, nor appalled; moreover, Garvin's further warning was unheeded: 'It never was more important,' he wrote, 'for men in general to study the recent past in order to be prepared for the future.'

In that recent past Churchill was already an important figure, and it was clear by the end of the 1920s that he had observed it brilliantly. The future turned out to be more terrible than anything Garvin, or even Churchill, is likely to have imagined at that time, but it grew inexorably out of the pattern of history, gathering momentum far too rapidly for the political, economic, social and philosophical skills of men.

Even before 1945 the present, and inevitably the future, was getting out of control, and it was certain after Hiroshima and Nagasaki—if not before—that new and bold attitudes of mind would be necessary if the world was to be preserved as a decent habitation of men, or even preserved at all. These things invested life with a new and dreadful urgency, and were reflected in the social behaviour of the generations inheriting a present that at first seemed bankrupt, and presently bereft, it might be, of a future.

It has been and remains an exciting world to live in, and one offering unique and awe inspiring opportunities. Curiously, it may be also one of the ages in which the vast majority of men prefer to submerge themselves in a new mass type of society, leaving the handling of their affairs to a handful of supremely powerful individuals. In Britain the institution of Parliament is in danger of withering away, its members having little or no say in major affairs of State. What John P. Mackintosh calls 'The retreat from democracy' is already well advanced, and in his book, *The British Cabinet System*, he discusses the remarkable powers of present-day Prime Ministers.

Churchill was the first in this new pattern, enabled to take supreme command by the urgencies of war. His personality is so closely woven through the texture of England's story in the twentieth century that I felt compelled to try to discover him on my own account, not, as John Raymond[1] warns, quoting Oakeshott in his exquisitely modulated essay on Rosebery, to wrest 'a complete figure from a complex setting, seeking to epitomize history in the far too simple terms of the individual', and thus to arouse the anger of historians and biographers, but to gain, perhaps, a clearer insight into the recent past. Events which seem meaningless, quixotic, irresponsible or stupid, may become meaningful in the light of the character, ambitions, personal experiences, and even the physical nature and health of an individual.

I was halfway through writing *The Price of Victory* when Churchill's shadow began to stand between me and my work. 'Facts' were not enough, and I had to try to gain some vantage point from which I might hope to see him more clearly. For he had become a myth, and his deeds legend, and I feared that the mid-twentieth century being what it is, commanding communications and all the apparatus of brain-washing beyond the most extravagant imaginings of our fathers and forefathers, the myth and the legend might harden; and that great man might become a kind of 'idol', never to be known as the creature of flesh and blood, of hopes and fears, of triumphs and disasters, of reason and unreason, which, of course, he was.

And thereby, the loss might prove incalculable, for the events in which he had played a dominant, or major, rôle would be inevitably blurred, distorted; even lost.

If these are axes these and these alone have I ground. This is simply a study of a man, a personal interpretation of one of the most vividly alive human beings with whom it has been our fortune to share more than half a century.

Before I was ten years old I was very much aware of Churchill as the kind of a man to make dreams come true, a living proof that fascinating personalities of the stature of Marlborough and Clive had once been 'real'. Above all, as a child, I was fascinated

[1] *The Doge of Dover.*

by war and peace, and it occurs to me to wonder (at this late hour) whether too much may have been made of Churchill's addiction to toy soldiers. In a modest way I was at least equally addicted. Lead soldiers were cheap and colourful, and these with forts and artillery in considerable variety must have furnished a great many Edwardian, as well as Victorian, nurseries. Besides, war was not yet the shockingly lethal business it was so soon to become. The Boer War, as I understood it, had been something of a disgrace, and was still hotly debated in my childhood. I tended to pass it by in favour of more heroic episodes. Tshaka was one of my secret heroes, and I was shocked by Dingaan's treachery. More seriously I had read good accounts compiled from the reports of official observers of the Russo- Turkish War, the Russo-Japanese War, and the Crimea. In 1914 I saw the review of the Grand Fleet in the Solent from a pinnace, and watched the searchlight display that night from the dormitory windows of my preparatory school on the mainland shore of the Solent. I had no idea then that I should pursue a life of adventure, war and writing on my own account.

Doubtless I have been influenced in my attitude to Churchill by the radical liberalism of my father and grandfather, their frequent exasperation with what they called 'his antics', and their admiration for Asquith and Lloyd George. But I did not, and do not, share my father's distaste for flamboyance and rhetoric, which made it difficult for him to view objectively, not only the words and deeds of Churchill, especially on such occasions as 'Sydney Street', but deprived him of pleasure in the artistry of such men as C. B. Fry on the cricket field.

For my part I liked Churchill's escapades, and was fascinated by the aura he diffused. He was the only living character remotely comparable with characters in books by Dumas and Baroness Orczy. He made their heroes credible.

It will be clear, I hope, that I may be properly regarded as one of those 'men in general' to whom Garvin addressed his warning after the first world war.

II

Churchill's immense production of autobiographical writing has been a joy in the reading, and must remain the principal source of information about his personality, and his deeds. I have, I believe, consulted most of the important political and military biographies and autobiographies of the last one hundred years, and without the kindness and co-operation of Brigadier John Stephenson, Librarian of the Royal United Services Institution, and of Lieut. Commander Peter Kemp, editor of the *Journal*, the task would have been infinitely more laborious and difficult.

Nevertheless, without the constant help of three friends, all closely connected in various ways with the events of the last fifty years, and with the man I have sought to discover, I doubt whether I should have made much headway in this contest. The letters exchanged between us on each and every aspect of the subject would make at least three books as big as this one. Their readiness to discuss my wildest thoughts and ideas, their patience, their candour, their labour in being always, as it were, at my service, is beyond all ordinary thanks. And through this main correspondence I have had the benefit of criticism and comment from some of those who had been directly concerned in particular events under discussion.

Throughout all the period of research and writing the letters of Major-General Eric Dorman O'Gowan have been immensely stimulating upon a wide variety of strategic matters, and especially in regard to India and the Middle East.

My most diligent correspondent, my guide and friend through many years of great difficulty, a rock in time of trouble, a man with a mind and heart alien to malice, and dedicated to service, must remain anonymous.

My debt to Capt. B. H. Liddell Hart is no less. The range of his activities, the urgencies of his own life and work, his unique devotion to military history, and his untiring efforts to illumine strategic thinking, make it remarkable that he should find time to help so many of those plodding along behind. Over the last five years he has furnished me with personal notes, copies of correspondence, lectures and so forth, relevant to my tasks, and now, for the second time, he has done me the inestimable service of reading my manuscript, annotating with great care, and saving me from many blunders.

I am also deeply indebted to Mr R. T. Clarke for his most careful, sympathetic and valuable reading on behalf of the publisher.

To all those who have borne with me, and especially to my wife, my grateful thanks.

In the brief bibliography to this volume I have included only those books from which I have quoted, or thought it necessary to possess and to have constantly at hand. I have not, for example, included fringe reading, nor the greater part of my Second World War reading, much of which is listed in the bibliographies of my books directly concerned with that war. This book, far more than any that have gone before, is the product of my own life and experience.

*Belchamp Walter*
*March 1962*

ACKNOWLEDGEMENTS

I wish to make particular acknowledgement of the value of *The Fabulous Leonard Jerome* by Anita Leslie, in regard to the Jerome family and the early background of Lady Randolph Churchill. Christopher Hassall's biography of Edward Marsh sheds a gentle and indispensable light upon the whole middle period of Churchill's literary life. In the political sphere I found the three volumes of L. S. Amery's *My Political Life* an intensely readable and reliable guide, a rare combination in political autobiography. Robert Sherwood's *White House Papers* remain invaluable in regard to the Second World War, and especially, in this instance, for Sherwood's own assessment of the character of President Roosevelt. Margaret Coit's *Mr Baruch* was also helpful, and for its rare insight into a particular phase of the conferences of the Second World War I found James Gould Cozzens's *Guard of Honour* unique.

# CONTENTS

| | |
|---|---|
| **PREFACE** | 7 |
| **PART ONE**<br>THE YANKEE MARLBOROUGH | 19 |
| **PART TWO**<br>WRITER AND POLITICIAN | 115 |
| **PART THREE**<br>THE APPRENTICESHIP TO POWER | 181 |
| **PART FOUR**<br>THE WARRIOR | 255 |
| **BIBLIOGRAPHY** | 355 |
| **INDEX** | 358 |

It is a mistaken view of history to assume that its episodes were entirely due to fundamental causes which could not be averted, and that they were not precipitated or postponed by the intervention of personality The appearance of one dominating individual in a critical position at a decisive moment has often altered the course of events for years and even generations.
*David Lloyd George*


The scales wherein he was weighed are broken. The years to come bring weights and measures of their own.
*Winston S. Churchill*
on Lord Randolph Churchill

# PART ONE

# THE YANKEE MARLBOROUGH

# CHAPTER I

※ ❀ ※

CHURCHILL was a Yankee and a Marlborough, a child of two worlds, the old world of Britain and Europe; the new world of the United States of America. It was a dual heritage of immense significance. It combined in him the possibilities of two kinds of power. It accounts for his tremendous impact upon his times, for it became his single vision to unite the old and the new, not merely as allies, but in indissoluble union, and thus in a sense to unite himself.

A lesser man, had he been capable of such a vision, would have dismissed it as impossible, even absurd, and concentrated upon a single heritage. A man of greater emotional stability, or of greater intellectual depth, would have made a choice. Churchill was the victim, not only of his birth and breeding, but of his total egocentricity. He came to regard himself as above competition with ordinary men, and destined for power. It is as important to understand this as to know that Henry VIII—whom he resembles —was a King.

Churchill was born at the hub of society and in the main stream of politics, an inheritor of an aristocratic and warlike tradition, of unquestioned privilege and position, a member of the inner circle of the ruling class of the wealthiest nation in the world. At the time of his birth the British Empire, at its zenith, embraced one quarter of the world's peoples, and girdled the earth.

Yet these things in themselves were rapidly becoming doubtful assets, and no longer certain passports to power for those who had regarded power as their prerogative. Most of those who ruled were born in palaces; many of those who were destined to rule would be born in hovels, or in humble circumstances.

'Emperors and kings and princes who in their differing ways supposed they held the fate of Europe and the world in their hands,' wrote a correspondent of *The Times* of the Congress of

Vienna, still held their 'glittering parades of power', unaware of their impending doom.

Karl Marx and the seventh Duke of Marlborough, Churchill's grandfather, were contemporaries. John Stuart Mill, Darwin, Huxley and a score of others, were filling the nineteenth century with new thinking, but its impact upon the ruling class was slight. 'The mighty still sat proudly in their seats, but a storm was gathering out of the darkness, and already there was lightning in the sky,'[1] wrote Lytton Strachey of the year 1821, when the liberal mind strove to ensure the succession to the British throne to the young Princess Victoria, and thus to save themselves and the nation from the bloody and terrible Duke of Cumberland.

Fifty-three years later, at the time of Churchill's fortuitous and premature birth in Blenheim Palace, Queen Victoria still occupied the throne her mother and the liberals had won for her. The nation had waxed fat, but the greatest revolution in the history of the world had steadily gathered momentum, and was moving inexorably to its climacteric, promising chaos. The storm, thunderous and terrible over all Europe, had not yet loosed its torrents, and in Blenheim Palace its echoes were no more than a distant murmur. From the eastern escarpment of the Cotswolds beyond the boundaries of the great park, the spires of Oxford could be seen rising out of the valley mists. The heavy palls of smoke thickening above the new industrial towns, and the angry glare of the blast furnaces in the night sky, were afar off.

The victories of Wellington and Nelson at Waterloo and Trafalgar had opened vast new markets for the products beginning to pour out from British workshops. Within the span of a century the peasantry of Britain had become an industrial proletariat, enormously multiplied and multiplying, and inhabiting slums in conditions of gross squalor. Grim, squat rows of dwellings, seeming cut from dingy strips with giant scissors, reached out from the growing towns to strangle the green countryside. Industrial waste began to pollute rivers and streams. Sanitation was primitive or non-existent, and the decencies and humanities lagged far behind the enormous demand.

The swift development of steam power allied to the Bessemer method of processing steel in a country rich in coal were prime factors in giving Britain a lead over the rest of the world in the race for wealth. Railways veined the land, hauling the products

[1] Lytton Strachey, *Queen Victoria*.

of the mills, mines and workshops to the ports. Ships of iron and steel driven by steam power carried British goods to the ends of the earth with speed and safety. The world was expanding and contracting at the same time, presently to burst at the seams.

Women with chains between their legs were harnessed to haul trucks through the narrow tunnels of the mines. Safety precautions were costly and therefore remained primitive. Disasters were frequent. Children worked in factories until they curled to sleep in corners on bare boards, and on the foundation of a new slavery, devoid of dignity, but not of hope, a new world was building.

Very few were able to look dispassionately at the new world in the making, and most rationalized a situation they considered themselves powerless to change. Those with 'nothing to lose but their chains' proclaimed a new gospel; those who had inherited the earth, and the newcomers who were busily inheriting it at breakneck speed, began to entrench themselves to resist the devil's creeds of change. Social reformers, observing that money was spreading into new hands, and that the basis of political power was broadening, consoled themselves. The workers were becoming emancipated. All would be well.

But it was a revolution destined to spread outwards from Europe and the United States of America to the whole world, changing the faces of societies that had endured in a recognizable image for centuries. In the economic and social fields Marx and Engels researched and speculated, providing charts by which millions would choose to steer through the economic and social upheavals of the new century. These researches, speculations and conclusions, meriting the profound attention of those in power, provoked the extremes of hate, fear and rage in the ruling classes, and especially in those to whom wealth and power were new, while bringing hope to the masses of the proletariat.

A new pattern of politics was nurtured, on the right and on the left, from which would spring fascist and communist revolution, revolution and counter-revolution. Princes still ruled. In 1870 France had suffered humiliating defeat at the hands of Germany. The wounds would fester. Prince von Bismarck, still able to manipulate the pieces on the European stage with a sure hand, had nurtured new dreams of Empire in his Imperial master. The decaying Austro-Hungarian and Turkish Empires still had the power on the one hand to precipitate disaster in Europe, and on the other to inflict terrible wounds upon the tragic peoples of a derelict empire. In Russia a Tsar and his secret police maintained the splendours of a decadent aristocracy upon a dungheap of serfdom, while on the fringes of these great powers little kings held violent and passionate peoples in subjection.

When Churchill was born on November 30, 1874, this world was doomed. Eighty-five years later, with his remarkable performance on the world stage already ten years in the past, Britain, its people and all that they possessed, could be wiped off the face of the earth in fifteen minutes by either one of two great powers. The atlases used in boyhood by middle-aged men had become obsolete twice in a lifetime. Not only the map of Europe, but the map of the world, had been redrawn. Empires had disappeared; kingdoms engulfed. New empires of a power, previously unimaginable, had arisen, and nearly all the pawns and minor pieces had been swept off the board.

In the mid-twentieth century two great powers confronted each other grinding like millstones, threatening to crush mankind out of existence. Greed and envy were seen to be the outstanding characteristics of the human race, and materialism had become the new religion. The vital resources of the world were plundered and squandered with demoniac and deadly energies which seemed to have lost a basis of reason or morality. A new and infinitely more terrible revolution threatened total disaster to the world. Man, always his only enemy, had discovered the means of his own destruction, and was jettisoning his hopes of survival.

## II

In the first half of the nineteenth century the rapid expansion of a fundamentally primitive economy into the bewildering complexities of the new industrialization burst upon the squirearchy of England like a flood of boundless and unpredictable magnitude. Nothing comparable had ever happened anywhere in the world. Local councils and the means of local government did not exist. Country squires and landowners serving as local magistrates, and accustomed to administer the simple affairs of rural areas in leisurely manner, were overwhelmed. Remedies, as Caesar had observed of the conflicts threatening Rome, always followed too slowly upon diseases.

Industrial progress had followed steadily upon invention from the seventeenth and eighteenth centuries, when the military and political genius of Marlborough had stabilized Europe and checked decisively the ambitions of Louis XIV. Yet in the early days the genius of Vaucanson and Jacquard had put France in the van of the simple industrial expansion of the eighteenth century, and it is probable that if France had kept the frontiers agreed by the Treaty of Amiens, giving her access to the Belgian coalfields, she would have won and held the leadership in the Industrial Revolution she foresaw and named. It was to be, in its fashion, a new renaissance.

Coal allied to steam was the essential key to the kingdoms of vast wealth beginning to excite the imaginations and insatiable appetites of men. James Watts's triumphant mastery of the early steam engines developed by Savery and Newcomen at once put a servant of immense strength into England's hands. The simple days of water power and charcoal fuel were over, with all their beneficial limitations upon the growths of societies and economies. In England the abundance of coal, and the short haul to her growing ports, opened the floodgates of wealth and power. New rivalries were born and new weapons.

As early as 1800 England produced ten million tons of coal. Fifty years later, while the French toiled for an annual output of five million tons, England had increased the yield of her mines to nearly forty million tons. In the last half of the century Germany became Britain's bitter and most potent rival ready to claim the coming century as her own.

The seeds of the startling growths of the nineteenth century had been gently sown one hundred years earlier. The eighteenth century had been not only the age of reason, but the age of invention, and had seen also a brief flowering of elegance and gracious living. Within the span of the middle fifty years of the eighteenth century, while Watt worked on perfecting his engine, men like Kay, Arkwright and Hargreaves developed means of spinning yarns which were to put Lancashire and the West Riding of Yorkshire in the forefront of textile manufacture. The production of pig-iron in England, multiplying by three in leisurely fashion, was suddenly multiplied by twenty soon after the nineteenth century dawned.

As the staggering process gathered momentum, the patterns of rivalries were taking shape. In the latter half of the nineteenth century England, as a country, had a virtual licence to manufacture 'gold'. Such was the alchemy of steam and coal allied to invention. Machines had begun to make machines. It is doubtful if any nation could have reorganized society to keep pace with the expansion of industry and population from the mid-eighteenth century onwards.

### III

None of these grim and tremendous developments which were to provide the thews and sinews of military and political power, and to change thereby the nature of the world, stirred the imagination of Churchill as child, boy or man. His was always the romantic vision. Not by strength alone might men prevail, but by valour and steadfastness.

Churchill was sixty-six years old, a politician of forty years' standing in Britain, before the vast industrial potential of the United States burst the barriers of his defences against the squalid mechanics of war and revealed to him, in a way that facts and figures had failed to do, that manpower and the machine in close alliance were the essential to waging modern warfare.

Thus until industry and war were fused in his imagination and could no longer be denied, he had been blind. It may be that Churchill's extraordinary glamour, and the essence of his myth, arises from the fact that he did not belong in the machine age or the twentieth century. He was a man of the seventeenth and eighteenth centuries, and in this light the nature of his performance becomes unique. His great instrument was his voice, and with it he evoked responses so powerful that he enabled men to impose upon the present, at least for a little while, the simple virtues they imagined had hitherto prevailed. The force of Churchill's personality allied to his powerful imagery and his gift for words invested squalid and fearful facts with overtones of glory.

A phrase of his grandfather's, the Duke of Marlborough, used while unveiling a statue in Dublin, stuck in Churchill's memory: 'And with a withering volley he shattered the enemy's line.'

He walked often, in those days of his father's 'exile', in Phoenix Park, Dublin, accompanied always by his nurse, Mrs Everest, and enjoying the sights and sounds of the soldiers on parade and at rifle practice. It seems probable that even in those early years the names of Blenheim and Marlborough were woven in his mind to evoke dreams of glory. He, too, was a Marlborough, unaware that the accident of his premature birth had enabled him to make his entrance into the world at Blenheim Palace. Years later he would remark, 'I chose it!'

Omens both good and bad abound for those who seek them, and this was one, for boy and man, a most potent and glorious omen. On his nursery floor he had learned to set out his toy soldiers with unusual skill, and to fight over old British battles. He was not alone in contemplation of such scenes. With him, his constant aide and audience, grave but smiling, severe, yet deeply loving and capable of compassion, was that unique phenomenon the British nanny, occupying a position hard to define, a servant uniquely privileged, the arbiter and often the sole disciplinarian of the early lives of the British ruling classes, curiously involved in the hidden intimacies of body and mind, a vital figure of Victorian and Edwardian England.

It would be at least as revealing and just to speak of the England in which Churchill lived and rose to power, as a 'Nanny-archy', as it is to refer to the United States of America as a 'Matriarchy' or Germany as a 'Patriarchy'.

The echoes of those early years are hushed only with the grave. A monarch might have his Fool to fulfil some similar function throughout his adult years, and a companion fulfilling comparable service might become a necessity to one so reared. But for Mrs Everest, his nurse, Churchill's childhood was peculiarly alone, even for his class. His parents were deeply involved in the whirl of politics and the exacting demands of society. His beautiful mother was engraved upon his memory forever, shining for him 'like the evening star'. But his father was always remote, difficult to approach, inspiring deep respect tinged with reverence, stirring compassion, and not without awe.

While the house in St James's rented by Churchill's parents in 1880 hummed with politics, intrigue and the gossip of society, Churchill retreated to the nursery, only rarely glimpsed by the guests. His maternal aunts, Clara Frewen and Leonie Leslie, saw him as 'a pale little ghost', lurking in the shadows of the hall as the guests assembled for luncheon, among them Blanche Hozier, whose daughter 'Clemmie' would marry 'poor little Winston'.

Churchill was every inch his mother's son, but Mrs Everest provided the warmth and affection he needed. Above all she was his audience. Such a figure would grow into his life as a necessity, or else loneliness would become at times unbearable. All the burgeoning forces of his powerful personality were concentrated inwards upon himself, and the vivid and romantic dreams of battles and glory, fashioned his egocentricity and nurtured the seeds of his innate desire for power.

Until he was seven years old and sent to the first of the dismal schools he loathed, the nursery was his world. He would not compete with his fellows, as a child, boy or man. He could not tolerate an equal in his own camp, nor would he suffer willingly at close quarters, in private argument or discussion, a mind capable of challenging his personal pre-eminence. If forced to do so, he would slump back in his chair, his lower lip pouting, like a baby.

Churchill lived from infancy in the centre of a stage of his own creation, and as Harry Hopkins said of him in the climactic days of his life, 'Wherever he was, was the vortex.' He regarded himself as a gentleman, a soldier, a general and commander-in-chief by right. His self-confidence, a friend wrote of him, was of an order beyond the understanding of ordinary men, and the common denominator of those seeking and wielding great power.

It is difficult also for an ordinary man to believe that within Churchill, underlying that bold and tremendous exterior, there were not also the seeds of self doubt, of fear that in matching himself with his fellows on equal terms he might be defeated. Surely no man is, or should be, free from devils!

Churchill could not stand alone without that essential support which had never failed him. His world, expanding ten thousand-fold from his nursery floor, did not evolve from the world of 'I' to become the world of 'We'.

He was, above all, the boy who never grew up, the leading character in a romance in the manner of Dumas, which he wrote, produced and acted himself. He perceived swiftly the nature of the world in which he wished to live, the kind of part he was resolved to act. His performance over a period of fifty years in the limelight was one of a sustained virtuosity and zest, probably unique in history.

Churchill wounded many people deeply, often as a child wounds, without malice or thought. He was the slave of his personal likes and dislikes, and would not include among his close advisers and associates any man to whom he was antipathetic, however eminent, however clearly the finest mind available in any particular field. His companions, for the most part, were those of ambitions akin to his own and prepared to hitch their waggons to his star.

Thus he preferred Lindemann to Tizard; Brooke to Dill; Montgomery to Auchinleck. He liked Lindemann, Brooke and Montgomery and disliked Tizard, Dill and Auchinleck. Moreover, Lindemann was ruthless in ambition, and Montgomery, in Churchill's words, was 'on the make'. Brooke had other qualities deeply appealing to a man who remained at heart a child.

Churchill's path to power is strewn with many corpses of brilliant and dedicated men, one of whom, his contemporary, remarked of him: 'No other man who made so great a mark upon his times passed from first to second childhood without maturity intervening.'

The nursery thread, the nurse-child, child-nurse relationship runs through Churchill's life from the cradle to the grave. It is clearly discernible in his personal attitudes to men like Rosebery and Fisher, Lloyd George and Alan Brooke, and obversely in his affectionate, even gentle, dominance over Edward Marsh, Hastings Ismay and Brendan Bracken.

'You are a good little boy, Eddie,' he scribbled in appreciation of some particular service, yet when Edward Marsh finally retired after thirty years of devoted service, Churchill was heard to remark: 'Eddie was never any use to me.' Marsh had at one point sacrificed a brilliant career in the Civil Service to go with Churchill into the political wilderness. He had been personal secretary, literary adviser, the brilliant and meticulous reader of proofs of many books, the careful and loving guardian of his master's speeches and of all his words.

Churchill's attitude to Brendan Bracken was of a more positive kind, carrying with it undertones of a genuine admiration and true affection. It has been said that Bracken was the only man Churchill ever truly trusted, and that he had but four friends in the middle and final phases of his life, Bernard Baruch, Beaverbrook, Brendan Bracken and his wife. In these friendships Churchill's ambivalence arising out of the fundamental split and conflict in his blood is apparent. He is a cross between a nineteenth-century American tycoon and an eighteenth-century English gentleman.

'Nature made you and Winston for each other, and it does you both great good to meet,' Bracken wrote to Baruch early in the

1930s. Throughout all his life Churchill was torn between his love for Britain and Europe and his love for his mother's country, the United States, courting first one and then the other, and finally rejected by both. He was incapable of regarding himself or his nation, which for him was always the hub of a great empire, as second to any man or nation, however exalted. He offered himself and his country in equal partnership at a time when such an offer had become tragic self-delusion.

Even at the peak of his eminence and power, Churchill's rages and tantrums bore the stamp of the child with the giant's strength, yet however terrible his wrath it would quickly expire, and he would be again 'all sweetness and light'. If those invested with authority to serve him as his professional advisers stood firm, they would prevail. It seemed that he accepted, as a kind of balm, that his judgments should be dominated in the last resort, as though he was afraid when confronted with the ultimate solitude of power. Like a wayward monarch he must be served by his favourites, amused by his 'Fool', shriven by his 'Confessor'.

Power was Churchill's goal and his destiny, and the British Parliament his authority, the temple of his gods.

## IV

Until Churchill entered Harrow School in 1887, after having returned a completely blank paper in Latin prose, and little more in mathematics, for his entrance examination, the grim and dreary monotony of his early school days had been leavened mainly by the battles he fought and refought in his imagination. His dreams insulated him from the dull lessons, the real fear of the birch, and the absurdity, as it seemed to him, of the vocative case in Latin.

His classical education had foundered forever upon the first rock of *mensa, mensa*, O table! With less arrogance, but with equal fortitude, he rejected mathematics as unintelligible. He has written that he used to count the days and hours to the end of each term, to the release from 'this hateful servitude', when he would be able once more to 'range his soldiers in line of battle on the nursery floor'. Rorke's Drift and Majuba Hill (for which he would be avenged), Balaclava and Sebastopol, Gordon's murder at the hands of the Mahdi, and Roberts's march from Kandahar, stirred his childhood blood and imagination.

From the miserable preparatory school of St James's he had been rescued at the age of ten to spend three comparatively peaceful years, which included a severe bout of pneumonia, at the school of two kind old ladies at Brighton. By that time *Treasure Island* had begun to broaden his mind and stimulate his love for words.

The least discerning of his teachers shared the views of most members of his family that he was a backward and difficult boy. Others, including his maternal grandfather, Leonard Jerome, had greater but undefined hopes for him. Jerome regretted that his grandson was not 'all American', and wondered whether it might be possible for any man to reconcile the conflict inherent in his blood and to serve two such masters as Great Britain and the United States of America. Reviewing his own turbulent and adventurous life as he lay dying in his darkened rooms at Brighton in the cold and gusty March of 1891, Leonard Jerome doubted it. Yet the boy awoke echoes of hope within him. A racing friend had shocked Clara Jerome by remarking of the marriage of her daughter Jennie to Lord Randolph Churchill:

'Interesting breeding, stamina goes through the dam, and pace through the sire.'

Jennie Jerome had enough stamina and pace for two. Her tremendous vitality allied to Randolph Churchill's high-pitched, nervous nature, with its tendency to burn itself out in flashes of brilliance, was clearly 'interesting', and might establish the ingredients of a tremendous personality.

Churchill at fifteen, a red-headed, freckled boy, standing at his dying grandfather's bedside, stirred Leonard Jerome's last hopes. He had realized that the boy was not merely indulging the normal child's play with his growing armies of soldiers, and that out of it a historical sense was growing. Even Lord Randolph, on his infrequent visits to the nursery, had been impressed by his son's masterly handling of his troops and grasp of tactics.

For better or for worse, Winston Leonard Spencer Churchill carried the last hopes of his grandfather and the ambitions of his mother. The dislike of the English side of the family left them unperturbed. The Dowager Duchess of Marlborough exhorting Consuelo Vanderbilt, the American bride of the ninth Duke, to have a son, would save Winston from the threatened obscurity of a dukedom.

'Your first duty is to have a child,' the old Duchess had warned

Consuelo. 'And it must be a son, because it would be intolerable to have that little upstart Winston become a duke.'[1]

A dukedom was no part of Leonard Jerome's ambitions for his grandson, and the boy himself, with whom such strictures may have rankled, might have brooded, echoing in his heart the words Shakespeare put into the mouth of Richard of Gloucester, 'Well, say there is no kingdom, then, for Richard; what other pleasures can the world afford?'

Assuredly it would be improbable that Churchill should seek or find his pleasure in a lady's lap. Impossible to imagine, in that winter of 1891, the dark and terrible patterns of the future, and his fateful destiny. The past could only be a dangerous guide to those destined for, or seeking, power. The antics of such men as Alexander I, Tsar of all the Russias, and his princely contemporaries, may seem both comic and tragic today, but to look back the short distance on their deeds from 1891 was to reveal how little, outwardly, had changed.

Even the statesmanship of such men as Castlereagh and Talleyrand had failed to prevent the 'emperors, kings and princes' from redrawing the map of Europe for the worse, apportioning the empire of the great Napoleon, ignorant, it seemed, of ethnic frontiers, and leaving the running sore of Poland. Despite that, the Europe shaped by John Churchill, first Duke of Marlborough, was still clearly discernible.

There had been some great disturbances of the peace, most recently the Franco-German tragedy of 1870, and the Russo-Turkish war of 1877-78, but the means and manners of settlements and treaties remained constant. In 1878 Disraeli had returned with Lord Salisbury from the Congress of Berlin bringing, as he phrased it, 'Peace with honour' between Turkey and Russia. The Balkan peninsula seemed to have emerged more stable, and the independence of proud peoples, notably the Montenegrins and the Serbs, was recognized. Limits had been set to Turkish tyranny.

Of such a nature were the immediate facts of history at the time when young Churchill stood at Leonard Jerome's deathbed. Yet in that same year Adolf Hitler, surnamed Schicklegruber, would be born in a little dwellinghouse of Braunau-am-Inn on the Austro-Bavarian border, and destined to be the greatest of Churchill's antagonists.

[1] Consuelo, Duchess of Marlborough, *The Glitter and the Gold.*

In that year also a ten-year-old boy, the son of a poor shoemaker of Gori in Trans-Caucasia, was preparing to enter the Georgian Orthodox Church. His name was Joseph Dzhugashvili. His mother was a washerwoman, the daughter of a serf, to be widowed when her only surviving child was eleven years old. Under the name of Stalin he would become supreme dictator of 'All the Russias', forging on the anvil of Lenin one of the most backward people on earth into an instrument of immense strength and power through more than thirty years of terror, torment and struggle in war and peace.

There were others, among them Tojo, a five-year-old in Japan; Roosevelt, a seven-year-old patrician of the new world; Mussolini, an Italian infant of no great promise. Of them all, Churchill, Hitler and Stalin were destined to be the three protagonists, locked together in mortal combat in the old world, not merely for the fate of nations, or of continents, for balances of power and spheres of influence, but for the destiny of mankind.

Even those with the prescience to be fully aware of the great forces, generating a tremendous head of steam beneath the surface and radically changing the fundamentals of political and military power, could not have predicted the tragic and terrible disasters in store. It is clear now that the 1890s were the crucial years. Old pots were cooking on furnaces of undreamed of power. Wilhelm II succeeded to his father's throne as Emperor of Germany, kicked Bismarck, the skilful 'pilot' of the ship of state, into obscurity, and swiftly revealed his grandiose dreams and vain, distorted visions, wooing Nicholas of Russia with his ridiculous, but dangerous, 'Willy-Nicky' letters.

In the mid-1890s, as Winston Spencer Churchill came to manhood and embarked upon his adventurous career, the First World War was already in the making to defy the wit and wisdom of the statesmen of Europe.

## V

Churchill's life is clearly seen in retrospect as a preparation for the great rôle he was finally called upon to play in the early summer of 1940. He was then in his sixty-sixth year, arrived at that late hour at the supreme moment when all that he had learned, and all that he had become, must be put to the test. He had suffered his hours of despondency, but in all those years his faith that a great destiny awaited him had seldom faltered. The long preliminaries were over; for better or worse the weapon was fully forged and tempered.

Wilful and arrogant, rarely amenable to mental or physical discipline imposed by others, he had taken what he wanted from life, rejecting many of those things the wisdom of his elders attempted to dictate. His education had been a steady growth from the nursery, through youth and slow maturity into middle age, and beyond; at last, complete. Every man's life is the product of its parts, and not one small piece may be added or subtracted, for these are the man. Churchill always thought he knew best what was best for him, and what he needed. Probably he was right. Idle as it may be to speculate, it is at least possible that the mental disciplines of the classical languages might have inhibited and restricted his flare for rhetorical English prose, the free flow of his vivid and romantic thoughts, his brilliant gift for the spoken word, his most potent weapon. He loved words, and was tone deaf to all other forms of music.

Similarly, had he disciplined his mind to grasp the fundamentals of mathematics many of his magnificent ideas, the possible and the impossible, might have been stifled by his awareness of the 'logistics' involved.

Every man is a balance of vice and virtue, and it was Churchill's strength that he enlarged the bounds of the possible, and thereby stimulated ordinary men to deeds beyond their normal limits.

Moreover, it is worth bearing in mind, especially when contemplating past events, that no man knows for what he is preparing, and the everlasting mystery of the next moment is too easy to forget once its content is known. No one knows what will happen next, least of all to himself, and those who aspire to the heights of politics and the supreme command of nations must be, above all, brilliant opportunists, grasping every hand and foothold along the way, capable of swift and bold decisions, of sustained endurance, of supreme self-confidence, and an unfaltering flair for turning the desperate chances of war and peace to advantage.

Strategists and thinkers plot the hoped-for course, but the tactician is at the helm. The supreme commander steers the ship, but he does not know where he is going.

The arts of war and politics had engaged Churchill's powerful imagination almost from the cradle, stimulating his vision and fortifying his spirit, and for these activities he was amply endowed. His education falls into five main parts, first the nursery, imprisoning him in his almost total egocentricity and subjecting him to the only form of discipline to which he was ever amenable, followed at some distance by his years at Harrow, and the first real flowering of his love of language. Then came the period of attempts at self-education, the untutored reading, travel and military adventure, followed by his entry into politics, and the years under his great 'tutor', David Lloyd George, in the arts of politics and war. And finally his long period of scholarship in the wilderness, when he drew the loose ends of his experience together and grew to his full stature.

With the six volumes of his *The World Crisis* he put his financial affairs on a sound basis, purchased and developed his estate at Chartwell, and established a personal headquarters from which he planned for the future.

Balfour described *The World Crisis* as 'Winston's brilliant autobiography disguised as a history of the universe'. It was a major work by any standards, and one of the finest pieces of war reporting in the long history of war. T. E. Lawrence compared its author with Thucydides. It prepared Churchill for the fulfilment of his greatest literary ambition, and in his study of his great ancestor, Marlborough, 'he may have discovered', in Leopold Amery's words, 'that fusion of political and military ideals, as well as the inspiration of family piety, for which all his life he had been groping'.[1]

Throughout the 1930s, surrounded by his personal advisers and friends at Chartwell, Churchill prepared himself for war, but it was above all his work on his *Life of Marlborough* that made it possible for him to take command of the nation.

When at last the task was his he could say: 'I felt as if I were walking with destiny and that all my past life had been but a preparation for this hour and for this trial.'[2]

---

[1] L. S. Amery, *My Political Life*, Vol. III.
[2] Winston S. Churchill, *The Second World War*, Vol. I. 'The Gathering Storm'.

# CHAPTER II

❧❦❧

IN THE KORAN there is a saying: 'Man is justified by the greatness of his acts, but woman through the magnitude of her illusions.'

Churchill is justified as much by the magnitude of his illusions as by the greatness of his acts, for his acts arose often out of his illusions. That he was a consummate actor there cannot be a shadow of doubt, and he cultivated his ability assiduously to a pitch of superb artistry and timing. 'Had his life been conducive to one on the boards of a theatre (not the opera; he did not know one note from another),' wrote an intimate friend, 'he could easily have been as great an actor as ever walked the stage.'

Britain, Europe, the world, was his stage in war and peace for half a century of his adult life. Even in minor rôles he held the limelight, unfailing in his ability to arouse the most powerful emotions in his audiences. But what part did he play? What character, above all, lived in his heart and vision? In what rôle, in what image, did he see himself?

Unquestionably he believed himself destined for power, and in his first novel, *Savrola*, he reveals remarkably the fabric and structure of his dreams. Yet it is much easier to ask than to answer such a question.

In a character of remarkable complexity, certain characteristics remained constant. He did not wonder, even as a child, or boy, or man, how he could fit into any environment, whether people would like him. He looked out upon a great variety of people, places and things, and saw them all in relation to himself, not himself in relation to them. How would they 'fit in' with him? He would have been the last man in the world to whom to address those infuriating words: how is the world using you? He used the world. His manners were abominable, especially to servants, and all those he considered beneath him he treated like flunkeys.

No man ever owed more to woman; to his nurse; to his mother, whom he adored, and who with unflagging energy and ruthless ambition launched him upon the world and his career; to his wife, the loyal, loving, tireless companion of his life. There is a cruel feminine streak in his nature, so infuriating to some that an exasperated general exploded: 'If he were a woman I could put up with him. If he were an Elizabeth I or Cleopatra. But Gloriana with a cigar I cannot stomach.' Few, in fact, could stomach him at the height of his power, and one of those closest to him wrote: 'It was most interesting to see the totally different man—almost a schizophrenic trick—when in power and when out of power. His completely ruthless use of power horrified me. He was the most egocentric man I have ever known.'

H. G. Wells likened Churchill to Gabriele D'Annunzio, that startling and brilliant Prince of Monte Nevoso, soldier, novelist, poet, historian, champion of lost causes. Few comparisons have been equally acute, for there was a man whose exploits must stir the romantic to the roots, arousing envy even in a Churchill.

What more bold than D'Annunzio's march from Ronchi and his occupation of Fiume! What more quixotically exhilarating than his defiance of all Europe!

But there was nothing—or very little—quixotic about Winston Spencer Churchill. He did not tilt at windmills. He did not embrace lost causes, but sought rather the very roots and sources of power, gauging with sure insight the hidden springs. When asked in the early years after his fall from power why he had chosen to be a conservative after his early liberalism, Churchill brooded for many minutes, not only because he was old, but because the question had aroused in him many memories and set many trains of thought in motion. At last his wife urged him to answer:

'The British people are conservative,' he said.

I have seen in him reflections of the personality of Henry VIII, others have seen in him echoes of Napoleon, and even of Cromwell. But Cromwell's great driving force was a simple belief in God, a puritan God. Neither Churchill, nor his great ancestor Marlborough, were ever driven by such a master.

Undoubtedly Churchill found much to admire and even to emulate in such characters, but his guiding star must surely have been Marlborough, a Marlborough of 'many parts', a Marlborough so variously compounded that he becomes a grand illusion, and Churchill plays himself, a tremendous character in his own right, a genuine original creation, a Jerome and a Churchill, with a romantic sense of history, and the indestructibility of a 'tycoon'.

When in 1906 he commented upon the behaviour and qualities of financiers, he was commenting upon himself, as he always did: 'This money-gathering, credit-producing animal cannot only walk —he can run. And when frightened he can fly. If his wings are clipped he can dive or crawl.'

Such qualities are at least as essential to a man who has been called the greatest political acrobat of his times, as to a financier.

Churchill always wrote about himself because he *was* the story, and his books must be always the greatest source of information about him. So much is revealed, so much suppressed or hidden, so much as elusive as an echo, clearly heard yet incomprehensible. Yet to those who give their minds and profoundest sympathies to this strange man and his life some insights may be vouchsafed.

Reviewing Churchill's book, *Great Contemporaries*, a critic wrote: 'Mr Churchill gleams back at us from twenty-five looking glasses, formidable, affectionate and lovable.' Those who knew Churchill well would question his affectionate and lovable qualities, but few would quibble with the rest of the statement. Yet affection warms his portrait of Lawrence of Arabia, and to Lawrence, that magnificent visionary, scholar and man of action, delving into the past and the future, Churchill 'warts 'n' all' was a man to be admired. Lawrence stirred Churchill's imagination, touched his innermost springs, and called forth his admiration in a way that even D'Annunzio could not have done.

Churchill's admiration for men like Rosebery and Morley has something in it of the pious, of acceptance of established standards and judgments rather than a spirit truly felt. It is when he writes of such men as Boris Savinkov and Trotsky, *alias* Bronstein, that there are vivid flashes of himself, of the inner Churchill.

In his portrait of himself through Savinkov is Churchill the adventurer, the brave, the romantic fighter. In his portrait of himself through Trotsky he reveals all the unbalance of his mind, his capacity for hatred, his liability to obsessions which may blind him to reality and mar his judgments. Of such a nature was his final obsessional hatred of Adolf Hitler.

Many among Churchill's contemporaries had far greater intellectual qualities; many were gifted with greater vision and knowledge of the forces at work in the world; many were free from the obsessions and powerful emotions to which Churchill was a prey.

A remark of Asquith's seems especially relevant: 'Our two rhetoricians, Lloyd George and Winston, as it happens, have good brains of different types. But they can only think talking; just as some people can only think writing. Only the salt of the earth can think inside, and the bulk of mankind cannot think at all."[1]

Thus it is those above all who think talking who too often make indelible marks upon their times in their lifetimes. Those who think writing have a delayed impact. Those who think make their marks often upon a distant future.

Yet the word 'genius', in the definition of General Fuller in his *Alexander*, seems to fit Churchill: 'Genius is a baffling word. It is neither high talent, not outstanding intelligence, nor is it the products of learning, or of discipline or training. It is, so it would seem, a creative gift intuitive and spontaneous in its manifestations, that endows its possessor with a god-like power to achieve ends which reason can seldom fathom. It is neither capable of analysis, nor explicable, it is solely demonstrative. . . .'

No man without some such strange alchemy, able to transmute baser metals into gold, might have hoped to live with a thousand years of history in a single lifetime, and to become the leading actor at a time when most men think of retirement. When the curtain came down on his last performance, which was also his greatest, millions felt that an 'age' had come to an end. And it had. By his genius millions had lived for a little while in a more vivid world, 'lost' in, yet sharing the honours of, the play.

But in a real sense it was not a play at all. It was an *entr'acte* of enormous proportions, spanning the gulf between the major acts, the first of which is history, the last of which is yet to come. The old actors are all dead, along with the sources of their power and strength. The new actors, and the new sources of their power and strength, are not yet clear. We hear the disturbing rumble of their voices and the thunderous undertones of their power. The stage is filled with shadows.

## II

Acutely aware of the immense achievements of his great paternal ancestor, John Churchill, first Duke of Marlborough, Churchill

[1] H. H. Asquith, *Memories and Reflections*.

perceived in late middle age the qualities of political foresight, of strategic and tactical brilliance, upon which Marlborough's victories were built. It must be doubtful if he ever truly understood Marlborough's great capacity for taking pains, his inexhaustible patience, his friendships, his wonderful ability to understand both his allies and his enemies, and to hold men loyal to him.

Churchill's patience was of a different order: it was patience with himself, not with others or with events. The whole force of his nature and his immense energies were concentrated into a single channel, acknowledging no demands upon him but his own. He appears to have been free from sensual or sexual desires, finding his relaxation in painting, or manual tasks, and his orgasm in battle or personal involvement in physical danger. He surrounded himself with men similarly free from the powerful diversions and demands of sex and sensuality, and was extremely fortunate in that very few of these were violently repressed. A serious illness in youth had deprived Edward Marsh of sexual expression, endowing him instead with a remarkable sweetness of disposition and a capacity for devoted friendships with either sex. Lindemann, on the other hand, seethed with repressions, as well as with ambition, and 'enjoyed none of the sensual pleasures'.[1] Women did not interest him.

The list could be lengthened, but it would be an unwarranted intrusion upon the privacy of individuals to do so. Nevertheless, most of those forming Churchill's intimate circle through the long years of his rise to power were free to devote their energies to Churchill's service, without the diversions of wives or mistresses.

But it is difficult, if not impossible, to separate Churchill from the overwhelming shadow of his ancestor, for it is Marlborough allied to the blood of the Jeromes that makes the man. A vacuum of nonentities took the young Churchill at a single stride to his ancestor's side. There was no one to obscure the route, and Churchill absorbed every word any man had written on the subject.

Two centuries before Churchill's birth, Captain John Churchill had distinguished himself as a soldier in the pay of the King of France, first under the leadership of Louis Joseph, Prince of Condé, and then under the brilliant Turenne.

'The Duke of Marlborough, then Captain Churchill,' wrote

---

[1] Christopher Hassall, *Edward Marsh*. C. P. Snow, *Science and Government*.

David Hume, towards the end of the eighteenth century, 'here learned the rudiments of that art which he afterwards practised with such fatal success against France.'

Churchill had passed his fiftieth year when he commented upon that 'fatal success': 'The triumph of the France of Louis XIV would have warped and restricted the development of the freedom we now enjoy, even more than the domination of Napoleon or the Kaiser.'[1]

In the political context of the 1930s the triumphs and tragedies of Louis XIV, Napoleon and the Kaiser had become irrelevant and obsolete. The great forces and undercurrents at work at high pressure throughout the nineteenth century had set up an unbridgeable barrier between Louis and Napoleon and the present, catapulted Kaiser and Tsar to extinction, disrupted the Austro-Hungarian Empire, as though it had never been, yanked Turkey out of the Middle Ages, and spawned Hitler, Stalin and Mussolini.

Churchill did not appear to perceive that Marlborough's victories were decisive precisely because the France of Louis XIV had nothing more to offer until, and unless, her power was curtailed. Persians, Greeks, Romans had suffered like fates. It awaited others in their time.

Bolingbroke, Marlborough's political antagonist, and Creasy, the historian, both highly critical of Marlborough's social behaviour, pay glowing tributes not only to his unsurpassed generalship, but to his equally brilliant statesmanship. Bolingbroke said of him that he was the greatest general and 'the greatest minister that our country, or perhaps any other, has produced....'

Creasy enumerated some of his outstanding qualities: 'Had it not been for his unrivalled patience and sweetness of temper, and his marvellous ability in discerning the character of those with whom he had to act, his intuitive perception of those who were to be thoroughly trusted, and of those who were to be amused with the mere semblance of respect and confidence—had not Marlborough possessed and employed, while at the head of the allied armies, all the qualifications of a polished courtier and a great statesman, he never would have led the allied armies to the Danube.'[2]

[1] Winston S. Churchill, *Marlborough, his Life and Times.*
[2] Sir Edward Creasy, *Fifteen Decisive Battles of the World.*

It might almost be a catalogue of the qualities Churchill lacked, for those who knew him well would find it difficult to imagine a man more opposite in character.

Whereas Marlborough, in the manner of his times, would accept 'gifts' upon which other ages might put different constructions, and was a romantic lover in his youth, Churchill would be beholden to no man, fearing that by accepting any kind of present he would be thereby under an obligation. It is doubtful if Churchill was capable of love, for it was a mental, physical and spiritual expression beyond his comprehension. He loved himself. The emotions of affection and romantic sentiment aroused by his mother, and afterwards by his wife, were as near as he might approach to love.

Yet Marlborough, and his mother, were his guiding stars.

Marlborough's lasting contribution to Britain and to Europe was the fruit of his statesmanship, made possible by his generalship, and his devotion to a cause. Even in the twentieth century a Marlborough might have established a new Europe in a new world to withstand the first awesome impulses and impact of the nuclear revolution.

Winston Churchill was not such a man, yet perhaps no other of his generation could have lived with the revolution of the twentieth century, a match for his dreadful antagonists, as obsessed in his fashion as they in theirs. Had he been pure Churchill in the marrow of his bones, sharing some of the qualities of Marlborough, it is at least conceivable that he might, with his immense energy allied to clear purpose, have preserved Britain and Europe in some semblance of the pattern and purpose he knew so well. But he was unfaithful to both his mistresses in being faithful to himself.

His vigour was relentless; his patience and sweetness of temper, lacking, his judgment of character often disastrous, his megalomania in the field of strategy, ruinous. Thus his triumph was also his tragedy. A comparison with his great contemporary, the American pro-consul, Douglas MacArthur, is hard to avoid. Together they were the greatest showmen of their times. They made the same mistakes in reverse and were confounded. MacArthur, the strategist, interfered in politics; Churchill, the politician, interfered in strategy. Both men pursued unlimited aims with limited means.

But for Churchill, his vision was split, his loyalties to himself in conflict, for Jerome and Marlborough were never wholly reconciled in that restless, far ranging mind and spirit, and blinded always by a vision of power.

To chase Churchill is like chasing a Will o' the Wisp; to capture him perhaps impossible, yet it is almost certain that in the chase one will come to know him better, to see more clearly wherein lies his greatness, and his humanity. He was above all a boy who never grew up, the leading character in a Dumas romance which he wrote, produced and acted himself. To compare him with d'Artagnan is irresistible, but that Gascon, whose ancestry lacked complications, was free, owning no authority save the sword, a law unto himself, a true soldier of fortune. Yet d'Artagnan needs the mystique of Louis XIV to give him relevance.

What mystique does Churchill need? Marlborough is not enough. Britain and the United States of America are too much.

In his great life of Marlborough Churchill reveals that he, too, cannot resist d'Artagnan. He relishes the incident when at the siege of Maestricht John Churchill, Monmouth and d'Artagnan, swords in hand, fought side by side together into the breach.

'There was Monsieur Artagnan with his musketeers who did very bravely' and is 'deathless in Dumas fiction.'

Churchill himself is deathless in fact or fiction. 'Twenty to twenty-five, those are the years,' he wrote, looking back from his middle fifties on the days when he was himself a d'Artagnan of the pen and the sword, a swashbuckling soldier of fortune. Yet d'Artagnan eludes him. He shares his fearlessness, but cannot achieve his splendid isolation. He is not so sure of himself with 'Athos, Porthos and Aramis', his companions. His brother officers are not amused by his antics. The courtesies and behaviour patterns of a gentleman irk him. He cannot cast them aside without loss. He is no Gascon. He is not free. He is the inheritor of a special history, and the chalice of powerful blood.

We must return to the world of his birth, where, 'like to ... an unlicked bear whelp'[1] he carries no impression but the dam.

---

[1] 'Like to a chaos or an unlicked bear whelp, he carries no impression like the dam.'  *Henry VI*, Part III, Act III, Scene II.

# CHAPTER III

CHURCHILL'S filial regard for his father, Lord Randolph, would not have permitted him to echo the remark, attributed to Caesar, that with the notable exception of himself there had been no distinguished member of his family for 200 years. In the middle of the seventeenth century the first Sir Winston Churchill, an impoverished country gentleman of Wootton Glanville in the County of Dorset, had achieved an astonishing *tour de force* of procreation, fathering four children of great distinction. Two hundred years later Winston Leonard Spencer Churchill filled a remarkable 'flush'.

Sir Winston, an ex-royalist cavalry officer and steadfast monarchist, was married to Elizabeth, a daughter of the Drake family of Devon stock, and compelled by adversity to accept the hospitality of his mother-in-law's civil war scarred roof at Ashe. It was an ordeal, not only for Sir Winston, but for his wife and children. Lady Drake, a woman of great force of character, was as passionately dedicated to the Roundhead cause as was her son-in-law to the Royalist. Sons, daughters, and in-laws were bitterly divided by civil war, and under one roof and within walls pock-marked by cannon shot. The family was riven from top to bottom, and it is an astonishing tribute to family strength, or perhaps to a deadly inertia, that they contrived to live together at all. The best that might be said of the situation is that one side or other of the family was certain to be, at all times, on the winning side.

At the Restoration Sir Winston achieved a miserable pecuniary restitution, but improved the blazonry of his coat of arms. He retained his motto: 'Faithful but unfortunate.'

A dozen children had been born to Sir Winston and the faithful Elizabeth through the tedious and dangerous years. Five had survived. The eldest, Arabella Churchill, mistress of the Duke of York, afterwards James II, mothered for him an impressive train of bastards, the first born of whom was James Fitz James, Duke of Berwick, victor of Almanza, king-maker, Marshal of France, Duc de Fitz James, Duke of Liria and Xerica, Lieutenant of Aragon.

John Churchill, Arabella's brother and Winston's eldest surviving son, had become Earl, then Duke of Marlborough, victor of the great battle of Ramillies in the same year that Berwick won Almanza to secure Philip V on the throne of Spain. Marlborough, whose string of honours rivalled those of his magnificent nephew, counted also the decisive battle of Blenheim, as well as Oudenarde and Malplaquet in the list of his triumphs. These two men, excelling in many noble virtues, combining audacity with reasoned caution, and springing at one remove from the same loins, had not exhausted the brilliant seed of their progenitor. Two of Marlborough's younger brothers became, respectively, a general of distinction, and an admiral of the Blue.

The Churchill family thereupon failed in the male line. Marlborough's son Charles died while a student at Cambridge in 1703, and three years later an Act of Parliament assured the succession to the Dukedom through the female line. Meanwhile Anne Churchill, Marlborough's daughter, had married Lord Charles Spencer, presently Earl of Sunderland, and their son Charles Spencer inherited the dukedom of Marlborough in succession to his maiden aunt, Henrietta. The surname of Churchill was lost until restored by Royal Decree in response to a plea of the fourth Duke. Thus Churchill is more truly a Spencer than a Churchill, and has observed that his name under the letter S instead of C came towards the end of the rosters instead of the beginning. Such is the music and mystique of names that it may be difficult for some to imagine Churchill being Churchill had his name remained Spencer.

Until the birth of Winston Leonard Spencer Churchill in 1874 the family males lacked stamina and staying power. Lord Randolph burned himself out to die at the age of forty-six in January 1895, narrowly pre-deceasing his elder brother who died at the age of forty-eight. The other three brothers had not survived childhood. But for these early deaths it is improbable that Winston Churchill would have avoided a dukedom that would, almost certainly, have condemned him to political obscurity.

Churchill's mature study of his ancestor, Marlborough, revealed to him the vital part played by early childhood and upbringing in the development of that remarkable man. 'John Churchill's whole life bears the imprint of his youth,' he wrote. Whereas Churchill's own childhood had been spent in a somewhat unnatural isolation of the nursery, confined with Mrs Everest, his nurse, in a world circumscribed by romance and dream, and divorced from the normal stresses of family life, the young Marlborough had had to discover some means whereby he might live in tolerable peace in the midst of moody and passionate adults holding bitterly opposed views, and riven by ideas incomprehensible to a child.

Moreover, the formidable old Lady Drake, chatelaine of the battered manor of Ashe, and the hand that fed him, was on the opposite side from his father. Before Marlborough emerged from childhood he had learned to keep his own counsel, to exercise discretion, and to value the art of compromise. His patience and tolerance were already notable. Perhaps, above all, knowing the deep ties of blood and even of affection, underlying the bitter feuds and surface currents disturbing the peace of the family, he realized the ephemeral bases of even the most fervently held political beliefs. There were values more permanent than these. Thus he was equipped, like George Monck, first Duke of Albemarle, to serve the State. Life was, perhaps, a see-saw upon which a sane and balanced man must learn to ride.

John Churchill, the young soldier, the dashing courtier, the not unwilling lover of the beautiful Barbara Villiers, Lady Castlemaine, mistress of the King, was early dedicated to success as well as to service.

Thus Marlborough's great qualities of patience and sweetness, tolerance and compromise, which made of him a master of all the arts of the possible and brought to his country the lasting fruits of his statesmanship, had been nurtured in the seventeenth century equivalent of the nursery as surely as Winston Churchill's absorption in the grandeurs and glories of battle, his tactical skills and strategic misconceptions, his tremendous egocentricity and curious personal relationships, were similarly sown and fed. There was no grounding there in statecraft for the young Churchill, no early lessons in patience or discretion, no apprenticeship in the virtues of tolerance of ideas and faiths and interests other than his own.

But while the relationship of Marlborough and Churchill may be rightly emphasized, a comparison must not be drawn too far.

Both men, in their fashions, were incomparable and unique figures. And Churchill was the first bearer of a vital reinforcement of new blood of remarkable potency, the blood of the American Jeromes. This was New England blood allied to the blood of the great Red Indian tribe of the Iroquois.

Thus on his father's side Churchill was the son of ancient European stock traced back to a Courcelle of the Conquest, through Currichills and Chirechiles to Churchill, by that indefatigable genealogist and progenitor, the first Sir Winston. On his mother's side he was a most potent son of the new world with a geneology even more ancient, his immediate and remote ancestors, warriors and hunters, ranging the great plains for buffalo, superlative horsemen, and tribal politicians whose skill might well have made them predominant over the North American continent, but for the coming of the white man.

What a brew was this to run in the veins of a man; what awe inspiring possibilities might it not portend! And old Leonard Jerome, brooding on the future of the ginger-haired fifteen-year-old boy, the firstborn son of his lovely Jenny and Lord Randolph Churchill, was well aware of it. Outwardly the boy wore the looks of his father, but within he was Jerome, just as his young brother Jack, of whom he was at times jealous, bore the handsome markings of his mother and inside was all Spencer Churchill.

Perhaps in boyhood Churchill had some mild grounds for jealousy, but by the time he had won his spurs in the 4th Hussars his mother sensed that in Winston her father might live again, and to a greater purpose. Few men have felt more strongly the hand of destiny upon them. The knowledge that he was half American and that the surname of Churchill had died with the great Duke John, and that he was more truly a Spencer, only served to strengthen his conviction that he was not only a Churchill and a Marlborough, but that the mantle of his great ancestor was his. The accident of his premature birth at Blenheim Palace strengthened his personal myth. The Jeromes, had he known much about them at the time, were the kind of ancestors in whom the young Churchill might have revelled and found sustenance. But Marlborough he venerated, wrapping that glittering cloak round his own shoulders and demanding its immense privileges. Nevertheless, it was the blood of the Jeromes that drove him, and would drive him to his dying day.

## II

It seems unlikely that Churchill knew very much about his mother's family until late in middle age. By that time the knowledge could give him pleasure, but had come too late to do him service. His grandfather, Leonard Jerome, and his grandmother, born Clara Hall, and many of the branches of their two houses, provided the kind of ancestors in whom the young Churchill might have discovered not only much of himself, but also a worthy counterpart to the single fugue of Marlborough, and his concentration upon his father's stock. Thereby his egocentricitiy might have been leavened. He might have seen himself clearly as an Anglo-American, with all the tremendous possibilities that might hold for him, and have recognized those virtues and attributes in his nature which would have enabled him to make America his own.

For me, at any rate, there is no doubt that the America of his lifetime would have provided a stage peculiarly suited to Churchill's great talents. There was the perfect blend of politics and big business, the easy marriage of the political tycoon and diplomacy. Hindsight makes it almost certain that he would have been not only a millionaire, like his grandfather, and his own greatest friends, Baruch and Beaverbrook, but an ornament of Congress and the Senate. It is difficult, given this angle of vision, to deny him The White House.

Undoubtedly there were moments, in the first flush of manhood, and in his age, when his mind recognized and—for a moment—fondly dwelt upon this 'other Eden'. Such speculations may not be irrelevant in any attempt to gain an insight into the nature of the whole man; to see him, perhaps, as he might have been with all his schizophrenic possibilities banished, the conflict early resolved.

When at the pinnacle of his success a friend lent him, dubiously, a somewhat scurrilous account of his grandfather's life and of his associates in the Wall Street Jungle of the 1860s, Churchill was delighted, gloating aloud:

'What a politician! What a man!'

'You to the life,' observed the friend.

Commenting upon his father-in-law to be, Lord Randolph had told his father, the seventh Duke: 'Mr Jerome is a gentleman

THE YANKEE MARLBOROUGH 49

who is obliged to live in New York to look after his business. I do not know what it is."[1]

It is unlikely that either the Duke or his son greatly cared. With their blood they could marry whom they pleased. But the Jeromes considered themselves good enough for anyone, and their daughters much too good for any man not capable of earning a living by his own efforts. Hence, and not the least of the considerations, the need for Lord Randolph to win his seat in parliament before his marriage to Jenny Jerome. Thereafter the demands of English society and a political career claimed the Churchills to the exclusion of almost everything else, and for all her pride in her gay and flamboyant father, Lady Randolph, immensely shrewd and ambitious, may have felt that her American blood was a doubtful asset. The handsome Lord D'Abernon had been quick to note her remarkable feline grace, and observed 'More of the panther than of the woman in her look but with a cultivated intelligence unknown to the jungle.'[2]

These attributes she had from her mother, her inheritance of Red Indian blood, and of which only Leonie of the three Jerome girls was ever heard to boast. It was a subject on which their mother never spoke, a secret of her birth which she treasured with a fierce and sensitive pride, and which sustained her in her hours of solitude.

### III

Jenny Jerome's memories of her family and of her childhood begin in Trieste during her father's Vice-Consulship. With her sister Clarita she learned to speak Italian and French before she could speak American. She remembers the warm beauty of her mother, her inward gravity, and exquisite physical poise, and the high spirits of her father. She remembers the deep snow in the passes when the family crossed the Alps and halted at Mont Cenis on the road to Paris at the end of her father's Consulship. Her parents had tasted the splendours and gaieties of Franz Joseph's Imperial admiration. She must have been a most unusual personage in Court at Vienna, and the 'lovely Clit' had aroused genuine

[1] Quoted by Anita Leslie in *The Fabulous Leonard Jerome*.
[2] Ibid.

such a setting, her sense of taste faultless, knowing exactly where, when and how to wear diamonds or pearls.

Paris stole Clara Hall Jerome's heart. Henceforth she was more a European than an American. For to Clara the Americans must have seemed, at least in part, in alien occupation of her native land, their manners and customs far removed from those which were more in keeping with her sensitive spirit and her deep roots. In Europe she had the admiration she could not command at home. She did not compete. In Europe the ancient past lived with the present, making it whole. In Europe she found peace and a measure of happiness, as well as a fitting background for the upbringing of her daughters. From infancy she trained and watched over them with extraordinary care, fitting them—if it is not too romantic a thought—to be the wives of 'Braves'.

When the family returned to New York in 1854 the raucous and exuberant vulgarity of the turbulent and fast expanding city beat upon her spirit, her dignity, and her sense of style, as the strident blaring of a brass band playing 'Colonel Bogey' at full blast, would beat upon the ears. The dazzle of diamonds and the din of voices at her ever-lengthening dinner table separated her more and more from her husband. This was his world. It could never be hers. Nor did she wish it for her daughters. If she belonged in America, it was in old America, the America of the mountains and forests and plains.

Leonard Jerome's fortunes had suffered a setback during his absence in Trieste, and, with terrific zest, he at once set about the task of restoring them. Yet it is misleading to consider Jerome's 'fortunes' in terms of restoration. It implies a consistency of aim, and the existence of a basic core, even the foundation of some financial edifice. Jerome built nothing but his life.

In a matter of months he won and lost the Pacific Mail Line, and dropped a million. He won and lost control of at least half a dozen railways, not noticing that railways were building to 'nowhere' faster than pioneers could open up land, or crops could grow. He had a large interest in the new Atlantic cable, and lent his yacht, *Clara Clarissa*, for cable salvage operations. He even part owned and joint edited *The New York Times*, defending his premises at the pistol point against Tammany Hall mobs.

It is doubtful if Leonard Jerome ever knew, or cared, what he owned or what he lost. It is said that more than ten million dollars ran through his fingers in a year or two. But always he remembered to settle money on his wife and family, and when he was finally 'ruined' a few millions were easily salvaged from the wreck.

Jenny remembers the family brownstone house on Madison Square draped in black and white in mourning for the death of Abraham Lincoln. She remembers the family villa at the fashionable seaside resort of Newport, pony-races with her sisters, and how it used to bother her mother that Leonard liked the children to 'run wild'. 'Strong women make beautiful women,' Clara Jerome said. But she had her own ideas on the method. Her daughters took cold baths daily, and learned to dance, skate and play the pianoforte. 'Running wild' was no part of her curriculum.

In 1856 Clara had given birth to a third daughter, Camille, the 'loveliest' of them all, and in 1858 to yet a fourth daughter, rather sadly named Leonie after Leonard, for it was improbable that there would be a son for him now. In 1863 Camille died suddenly in Newport, and with that Clara hungered more and more for Europe and especially for Paris. Her health, basically sound, demanded she said the attention of certain physicians in Paris. Her husband's many loves, even though they did not threaten at any time the security of the home or the marriage, none the less gravely disturbed her sense of propriety. It is doubtful if she ever suffered any deep pangs of jealousy. She was all woman and knew her husband too well. But his romantic attachments were often irksome and a social nuisance.

Fanny Ronalds, about whom even the dullest of dullards went into poetic rhapsodies, seemed to have bewitched Leonard, and in 1866 while Wall Street rocked in one of its early crises, and Austria waged war with Italy, Clara surprised her husband by writing a long and warmly phrased letter of congratulation to Admiral Tegethoff at Pola, victor of the sea Battle of Lissa against odds.

'I did not know he was such a friend of yours,' said Leonard, realizing suddenly that Clara had not lacked admirers in European society.

In 1867 Clara Jerome took her daughters to Paris. At forty she was still a woman of great charm and subtle beauty, and her daughters would still further ensure the success of her *salon*.

In Paris they had found a happy setting.

There was no hint in the Paris of 1867 of the tragedy that was soon to overwhelm France and sweep away the Second Empire. Clara established herself and her daughters in a 'charming small house' on the *Champs Elysees*, arranged the education of the younger girls by the best available tutors and governesses in all departments, and launched her eldest girl, Clara, into French society at a Tuileries Ball.

Americans were popular in Paris in the upper reaches of society, well represented by an exclusive and talented set, while still regarded in the stodgier climate of Victorian England as barbarians, or at best *parvenue*. For three years Clara Jerome felt 'at home'.

From the Jerome house on the *Champs Elysees* the girls could watch the gorgeous progress of Eugenie's informal sorties, her carriage adorned with splendid footmen and outriders in brilliant livery, and the scarcely less elegant equipage of the Princess Metternich, whom their mother numbered among her friends. At seventeen Jenny rode in the Bois with the Prince de Sagan, Duc de Talleyrand, and had met many of those whose power and prominence in European politics would continue for a decade.

Fluent in French and Italian, and with a pleasing English-speaking voice, she was well equipped to take her place in European society, and to encounter the young men, one of whom would most certainly ensure such a position for her. Her good looks were already striking, promising beauty of a high order in maturity, a promise endorsed by her still beautiful mother and her handsome father.

And then, almost on the eve of her 'coming out', Bismarck's Germany delivered the tragic blow to France, the harbinger of Armageddon, and the end of an era of comparative peace in Europe. While Napoleon III, sick and utterly dispirited, sat his horse bravely at Sedan through the shot and shell of a disastrous day, and the French armies went down to utter defeat, Eugenie acted as Regent at St Cloud, and the brave words of the Parisians gave way to bewilderment. The Jeromes caught the last train out of Paris for Deauville, there to await the news of the end. A few weeks later they left for England in the wake of Sir John Burgoyne's yacht, carrying the Empress into exile.

There were very few Americans in London in the early 1870s, and the American male was almost unknown. It was an interlude of fog and disappointment for the young Jeromes.

'In England...' wrote Lady Randolph, 'the American woman was looked upon as a strange and abnormal creature, with habits and manners something between a Red Indian and a gaiety girl."

English spring and summer were destined to relieve these first dismal impressions, and a small house at Cowes, in the Isle of Wight, provided a pleasant haven for the family in the exclusive social milieu of the Royal Yacht Squadron Club.

Meanwhile Leonard Jerome, on a mission to Europe, rode blindfolded through the Prussian lines with General Sheridan to the United States Embassy in Paris. From her father Jenny gained an impression of the tragedy. He had watched the Prussian infantry marching down the *Champs Elysees* singing *Der Wacht am Rhein*, and 'most of them wearing spectacles'. The Paris of the Second Empire had gone for ever, and if the Jeromes had any doubts a visit from the Emperor, 'le Comte de Pierrfonds', underlined the truth. 'Even in my young eyes,' wrote Jenny, 'he seemed to have nothing to live for.'

## IV

In the spring of 1873 Miss Jenny Jerome devastated Lord Randolph Churchill at first sight. The occasion was her long delayed 'coming out' party at a Royal Yacht Squadron Ball at Cowes, and Lord Randolph, an otherwise romantic and frivolous young man, hated dancing. For an hour Jenny yielded to his insistence and denied herself a galaxy of partners to sit talking with him. Immediately afterwards he told Colonel Edgecumbe that he intended to marry 'the dark one'. He had had barely time to know her name.

The Prince and Princess of Wales, afterwards Edward VII and Queen Alexandra, had smiled with favour upon the Jeromes, and especially upon the dazzling young woman, flushed with the excitement of her first 'official' dance. That surely was accolade enough.

Clara Jerome consented to the match, although it is probable that she would have preferred a French husband for her daughter. Leonard was induced to give a 'provisional' blessing from New York but this he at once withdrew upon a suspicion of reluctance on the part of the Duke of Marlborough. Leonard Jerome did not entertain a high opinion of the English aristo-

[1] *Reminiscences of Lady Randolph Churchill.*

cracy, and demanded of his daughter's husband-to-be that he should not only love her, but be in a position to support her by his own efforts.

The Duke, it seemed, was only showing a natural caution, anxious to be sure that it was 'true love', and for his son to fight and win the Woodstock seat in the forthcoming Parliamentary Election. A year of waiting could not do harm. Leonard, unable to deny a pretty woman anything, and especially a woman in love and as strikingly beautiful as he observed his daughter to be, again blessed the engagement, and settled £6,000 a year on his daughter, in spite of being 'ruined'.

The Jeromes returned to Paris, and while Lord Randolph prepared for the election and wooed his constituency, Jenny flirted mildly with the young Comte de Fenelon, who aroused Lord Randolph's ire by daring to instruct her in English usage.

'... Hang *le Petit Fenelon* ... little idiot!' he wrote. 'He may be a good authority about his own beastly language but I cannot for a moment submit to him in English.'

Early in 1874 Lord Randolph won his seat in the House, married Jenny, and in May took her to Blenheim for her first considerable encounter with her stodgy old in-laws and the magnificent palace. And there, in a small downstairs room simply furnished, Winston Leonard Spencer Churchill was born in November, 'more than a month before his time'.

*The London Gazette*, No. 28,176 records:

'On the 30th Nov., at Blenheim Palace, the Lady Randolph Churchill, prematurely, of a son.'

Less than two years later an 'unfortunate affair' in which the Marquis of Blandford was implicated, involved Lord Randolph in quarrels with 'Court Society' and the Prince of Wales. In these circumstances of family worries Disraeli offered the Duke of Marlborough the Vice-Royalty of Ireland, and Lord and Lady Randolph, with their infant son, were glad to share the temporary exile. It was a valuable experience, enabling Lord Randolph to visit London to carry out essential Parliamentary duties while serving his father as Private Secretary (unpaid) in Ireland. Finally in 1880 he was able to establish his family in a rented house in St James's Place, and embark fully upon his political career supported by his brilliant wife.

Lady Randolph had shown herself not only an accomplished hostess, but a fearless horsewoman. She wrote that she did not remember meeting a single dull character in all her four years in Ireland, and this is also a tribute to her talents. 'When a panther is married to a gentleman emitting electric sparks,' wrote Anita Leslie, 'their dinner table is likely to be stimulating.'

The years in Ireland had provided a valuable apprenticeship for the serious work at home. Lady Randolph was armed at all points, not only to support her husband's career, but also to lay the foundations of success for her firstborn son, although the direction and nature of that success remained for many years obscure. By the middle 1880s she could count the greatest names in England among her personal friends in her own right. She was equally at ease with men as far apart in birth as Lords Rosebery and Salisbury and Joseph Chamberlain and Dilke. She cultivated friendships wherever they might prove of value. Every door was open to her, and her direct approach was more often refreshing than disconcerting, especially to elder statesmen.

The new reformers, Joseph Chamberlain and Dilke among them, were welcomed at her table in St James's despite the rumbling objections of her father-in-law, who complained: 'How could the influence of such a man (Chamberlain) be anything but pernicious! A man who was a socialist or not far from one....'

One thing was certain: Lord Randolph was an honest man, and soon revealed that he would attempt the impossible and try to be an honest politician. His house became the meeting place of the embryo 'Fourth Party', a small ginger group blessed, but only tentatively, by Balfour. Lord Randolph had all the makings of a Tory rebel. He had visited Canada and the United States with Jennie in 1876, meeting her uncle Lawrence Jerome, whose son William Travers Jerome would be District Attorney of New York. In his travels the sense of change had not escaped him—as it might well have done in the isolation of Blenheim, the Vice-Regal lodge in Dublin, or in the select social circle of his class. It was still possible in England to live on the rim of the volcano without being aware of it. Lord Randolph's American experience was well timed and salutary.

But in England the Reformers had been long on the march, and for many years there had been grave unease in the best minds.

Shaftesbury[1] had fought against the slave labour of children for 15 years until in 1847 he had forced through the ten-hour factory Act. Even the Marquis of Blandford, Lord Randolph's elder brother, was not inactive in his efforts to face new and disturbing facts.

Thus while Winston Spencer Churchill grew from infancy to a freckled red-haired solitary boy of thirteen, ill-equipped to live on equal terms with his fellows, his mother became one of the most influential and forceful women of her day. There was no one worth knowing whom she did not know, no door at which she dared not to knock, no ear she would not claim. As her eldest son said of her a few years later: 'She left no cutlet uncooked for me.'

But young Winston Spencer Churchill had given little comfort to his relations. His birth had carried high hopes, but all that was visible on the eve of his entry into Harrow school, his preliminary 'trials' in a wider world, was disconcerting and unpromising.

How could that sandy-haired little bulldog be the child of her lovely Jennie! his maternal grandmother had wondered. His aunt, Clara Frewen, had felt something akin to pity for the pale little ghost lurking in the shadows, poor little Winston dreaming of his soldiers. Perhaps only Leonie of his close relations, apart from his mother, entertained high hopes for him and loved him. She had grown into a very beautiful woman, some said with even more feline grace than her sister Jennie, and was an even more brilliantly-finished product of the best European—French and German—education.

Aunt Leonie was almost certainly the nearest rival to Mrs Everest in Churchill's wayward and possessive affections. She saw a good deal of him, loving Ireland in the early days, and presently marrying Jack Leslie, a young officer of the Brigade of Guards, who had wooed her from the moment he had set eyes on her at their first dance in Dublin. In those early days Winston was 'copper top' to Leonie, and later on, when he was thirteen and on the eve of his real schooldays, Leonie and Mrs Everest kept him to themselves, taking him the round of the pantomimes and resisting the attempts of the Duchess of Marlborough to have her grandson brought to Blenheim. Surely, she grumbled, the boy hasn't always a cold, and why, she wondered, should Blenheim be worse for colds than London?

[1] When Lord Ashley.

But Leonie and Mrs Everest (that horrid old Everest, the Duchess wrote to Leonie) did not let him go.

His parents saw him seldom. They were often travelling in Europe, Russia and India. At home, life was a turmoil of politics, of entertaining and the exacting social round. The rise of Lord Randolph had been meteoric. At thirty-six he had become Leader of the House and Chancellor of the Exchequer, dedicated and pledged to reduce expenditure on armaments, and pleading a 'sane foreign policy' to make such ever-growing expenditure redundant.

But the race was already on, and the tide flowing against him was to gather ever-increasing momentum, never to be taken at the flood, and the final flood afar off, beyond the vision of any living man—or boy—even of the boy so preoccupied with war in the nursery. And in the wakes of the wars ahead, principles, moral values and faiths would rot in the debris along with the corpses of the youth of the world.

Lord Randolph's fall was as swift and sure—and predictable —as his rise, and utterly devastating. In his heart he knew that he was not a stayer, that he had neither the temperament nor the genuine love of political intrigue that might have led him through to scale new pinnacles. He was too honest a man. Politics—if it had ever been—was no longer a 'gentleman's game'. He had remarked that he did not expect to last more than six months as Chancellor.

'And after that?' a friend enquired.

'Westminster Abbey,' answered Lord Randolph.

In fact he would be buried in the little churchyard on the steep knoll just beyond the bounds of Blenheim Park. And there, too, Jennie would finally join him—and if he had his wish, Winston also.

But all that was far off, save for Lord Randolph. At the age of forty-six, racked by a terrible malady, he had burned himself out, and on January 24, 1895, he died. He had been a Churchill in his own right; in a sense, the last of the Churchills. When he died, his eldest son, Winston, was in the year of his twenty-first birthday, an officer of the 4th Hussars with no taste for regimental duties and the long, patient slog that alone might lead to the top. He had been a constant disappointment to his father, from whom, save for odd moments, he had felt remote, yet moved always by a profound admiration. In his book, *My Early Life*, he records a moment when his father suddenly dropped his usual reserve. It came, as so often happens, in the wake of a reproof, when the emotions are unwillingly, and unwittingly, aroused.

'Do remember things do not always go right with me,' Lord Randolph said to his son. 'My every action is misjudged and every word distorted. . . . So make some allowances.'

At that time Churchill was eighteen. He had recently endangered his life by miscalculating the ability of some slender pine trees to bear his weight, and his own athletic ability to dive from a bridge over a shallow ravine and cushion his fall. He had dropped nearly thirty feet and lay unconscious for three days.

In the period of convalescence following this accident, Churchill met many of the great political figures of the day in his father's house, and perhaps for the first time discovered some of the excitements of politics. But his prospects seemed appalling. He had failed all along the line, in the lower school at Harrow from beginning to end, and crammed into Sandhurst at the third attempt. He was almost a complete stranger to mathematics, and had closed his mind against the classical languages, and yet he was becoming peculiarly equipped to live with, from and by his times in that ablative absolute he had always despised.

v

'The interlude of school makes a sombre grey patch upon the chart of my journey,' Churchill wrote, looking back on his schooldays from middle age. 'I do not want to go there again.'

He was a misfit, and nothing accentuates a misfit more than school. At school there is no escape. Yet Harrow and his time there had not been wasted. If he did not learn to live with and compete with his fellows, he did begin to learn how far it was safe to go, even for one who regarded exceptional personal privilege as an unquestionable, if not divine, right.

The incident in his first term, when he pushed Leo Amery, then a senior boy and champion gymnast, into the swimming pool, has been remarked *ad nauseam*. But what a remarkable and revealing act it was for a 'new boy'—what a try on. And the results were of immediate and lasting value to Churchill. A liaison developed between the senior boy and brilliant classical scholar and the misfit who was not even a rebel. In exchange for

Churchill's great facility at writing English essays, Amery construed Churchill's Latin prose.

Thus, although Churchill never bothered to translate a line of Caesar or Cicero, he did become acutely aware of their forms of language. In after life he echoed them both.

But his greatest piece of fortune was his long school association with his form master, R. Somervell. No good master could possibly ignore a boy occupying his class not only term after term, but year after year. The boy was no fool. What did interest him? The answer was English. Churchill's tastes were typically boyish and romantic. He loved *Treasure Island*, and his aunt Leonie had persuaded Rider Haggard to give her nephew a copy of *Allan Quatermain* on the eve of his departure for Harrow.

'I like A.Q. better than *King Solomon's Mines*; it is more amusing,' he wrote to Haggard. The music of words was the only music he knew, or would ever know.

The result of Somervell's interest in his odd pupil was that under his guidance and care Churchill had a grounding in English, probably unique and otherwise unobtainable in normal school life. It is recorded that he recited twelve hundred lines of Macaulay's *Lays of Ancient Rome* without error, and thereby won a prize. His memory was remarkable, and it was to serve him wonderfully throughout his whole life. He seldom forgot a telling phrase, and stored the memorable against the day, and when the day came, there it was. His great speeches are filled with echoes.

At Harrow also his taste for history grew. He read Macaulay avidly, and soon followed his father's love into Gibbon. He fenced for his school, and swam well, but he did not take part in team games, and regarded the school Rifle Corps with indifference. Perhaps his bravest act during his time at Harrow was to invite his nurse, Mrs Everest, to visit him and to be shown round. He had been teased for his 'Yankee mother', but that was as nothing to the teasing he sustained on account of his nurse. He bore these slings and arrows with stoicism, if not with indifference. It boded well for his political future.

When his father died at the age of forty-six, Winston Leonard Spencer Churchill had almost escaped the dangers of succession to the dukedom, but remained heir presumptive until Consuelo Vanderbilt produced an heir for the ninth Duke. Churchill had gained a most exciting collection of relations through his mother's family. Jennie's eldest sister, Clara, had married Moreton Frewen, a magnificent eccentric and sportsman, a renowned horseman, and first-class shot who had ridden the buffalo trails, and was a blood brother to the *Blackfoot* tribe of Red Indians. While Clara waited at the altar for her groom, she had overheard him arguing fiercely with his best man, Lord Bagot, the merits of *Iroquois*, the horse, not the Indians. For a short time she kept house for her husband in a log cabin, but soon retired to live in one of his manor houses in England.

In spite of her husband's excursions and adventures all over the world, there were some small Frewen cousins in due course. Aunt Leonie and Jack Leslie were also to provide a family of boys.

American blood had become infectious for the Churchills. George Charles, the eighth Duke in succession to Winston's grandfather, married Lily Price of New York after being divorced by Lady Blandford, a daughter of the Duke of Abercorn. They had some difficulty in finding a minister to marry them in the City Hall, New York, but finally found a Methodist.

The ninth Duke followed the new tradition and made good his male line by Consuelo Vanderbilt, the granddaughter of the wicked 'Old Commodore' who had fought for millions side by side with Leonard Jerome. And years later, Consuelo having fulfilled her 'first duty' and had a son, the ninth Duke tried again with Gladys Deacon, of Boston.

But for the tremendous imaginative impact of the great Marlborough upon his mind, and his long-sustained preoccupation with British battles in the nursery, the United States might have claimed Churchill as her own.

# CHAPTER IV

Looking back from the aftermath of the First World War, and striving to discover a pattern in the rubble of the world, historians saw that the last decade of the nineteenth century held the crucial years. In 1895, the year of Churchill's coming-of-age, of his entry into the 4th Hussars, of his father's death—and Mrs Everest's—and his own first sortie into a wider world of people and politics, the seeds of disaster had taken powerful root.

The vain and neurotic Wilhelm II ruled in a Germany whose rapid industrial and maritime expansion demanded 'a place in the sun'. It was not difficult for the Germans, from their geographical viewpoint in the heart of Europe, to imagine themselves 'hemmed in' by jealous powers, and especially by the jealous seas.

In Russia a feeble but well-intentioned Tsar sat on the throne of Peter and Catherine, cushioned by a medieval aristocracy and protected by a savage secret police against the stirrings of an archaic serfdom, no longer to be tolerated in the society of nations calling themselves civilized.

To look back upon those fateful years from the third quarter of the twentieth century is like looking down from the monstrous Gorgonesque branches of some misshapen tree upon the old earth eroding away from the tortured roots. There were some, then, who foresaw conflict on a massive scale, but none who could foresee, and none who could have grasped, the gigantic proportions of the tragedy about to unfold. It unfolds still. The first ominous notes of the overture about to expand inexorably into its terrible and relentless theme, are almost forgotten.

Even now, the life-span of a man later, it seems that this tragedy, which still has mankind in its grip, and may never relinquish him, save to dust and ashes, is unique in that it has thus far failed to enrich human life, and has at the same time degraded death into an obscenity. All the great epochs of history enriched and enlarged the human scene, and added new flourishes and new horizons. New concepts of morality and justice had followed in the wake of war and conquest. Higher ideals had resulted. The arts and literature had been given new impetus. Virtue, as well as barbarity, had been a residue of war.

Those historians who, like Creasy, have seen human progress in terms of the decisive battles of the world, from Marathon to Waterloo, from Tours to Blenheim, must now pause. There have been many decisive battles since Waterloo, but none, I doubt, decisive in that old *genre*.

Morality, principles, faiths, religious and idealistic, have disintegrated in the cauldron of our times, leaving the bitter dregs of rival nationalisms, of barren 'ways of life' dedicated to greed, material wealth and the glorification of the trivial, skilled in depravity and corruption, and believing in the total death of man.

The common peoples of the world have made themselves hostage to a handful of men with the power to make an end of this fair earth and all its promise, and the common people have wished it to be so.

It is a simple matter to select and to parade scapegoats, to heap all the ills of this dread century upon the shoulders of princes, politicians, dictators, power-crazed maniacs and the like. But it seems to me that we, the common people, cannot escape the real blame. All these men rose out of us, supported by us, expressions of us, cheered by us, and their wars clamoured for hysterically by us. It is not a simple problem. Whoever is its expression, a Hitler, a Stalin, a Roosevelt or a Churchill, the people must be its source and its strength.

The problem of power lies at the heart of the matter—of all human affairs. This I believe.

The basic fact of change visible in the 1890s was that the world had become one. It would no longer be possible for any nation, great or small, to isolate itself from the consequences of conflict, or even of change. A stone cast into the pond would spread its ripples to the farthermost banks. A failure to recognize this would be fatal: it was fatal.

Commercial expansion and the search for markets went hand in hand with industrial expansion in Europe and the United States of America, and the rivalries of the great powers extended rapidly deep into Asia. The swift overthrow of ancient China by the upsurge of Japan, followed at once by the rush of the great European powers and the United States of America to the Far East, was decisive for the fate of the world. And perhaps only in that quarter, if the world survives, may man look for that enrichment and renaissance in the pattern of history.

The balances of power in Europe, once skilfully adjusted by Bismarck, would have lost their validity even had he survived at the head of German foreign affairs. In spite of her aching wounds, France joined with Germany in colonial co-operation in Africa directed against Britain, while the Tsar, responding to the sentimental and dangerous letters of the Kaiser, was ready to work with Germany in the Far East.

In 1894 war had flared in Korea, Japan compelling China to an abject peace and the abandonment of Korea to the consternation of the Western powers. Above all, these events were a terrible blow to the ambitions of the Tsar, who saw his dreams of the Trans-Siberian railway shattered. There in the Far East was another 'Turkey' blocking Russia's way to warm water. The fool's alliance of Russia, France and Germany, acting swiftly at the instigation of Germany, vetoed the Treaty of Shimonoseki and forced Japan from her prey, to fume inwardly, biding her time, to build up her sea power 'against the day'.

In 1895 the German Kaiser began to give full tongue to his dreams and ambitions. 'I will not rest until I have brought my navy to the height whereat my army stands!' All operations in these last years revealed that without sea power the vast ambitions of Germany could not be implemented. In 1898 the Spanish-American war added its particular emphasis, and the once great empire of Spain crumbled at a blow. 'In a few months,' wrote Garvin, 'the remnants of the oldest colonial empire in the world, dating from Columbus, had disappeared.'

But, of course, it had not 'disappeared'. The United States of America straddled the isthmus of Panama, dominating the West Indies, and occupying the Philippines far out in the Pacific. By virtue of the Monroe Doctrine the United States resolved to hold the ring round the immense continent of South America.

Some imagined that Germany's naval building programme might be directed against the United States, but this was not so. The famous preamble to the German Navy Bill in 1898 reads:

'In order under existing conditions to protect Germany's maritime trade and Colonies, there is only one means: Germany must possess a battle-fleet so strong that a war would involve dangers of such a kind even for the mightiest of naval antagonists as to bring its own power in question.'

The strategic arguments in the body of the Bill made it clear that Germany intended to dominate the North Sea—the German Ocean—and that Britain, with her naval commitments widespread over the world, would be unable to concentrate her naval power. Germany would seize the strategic initiative, and would inherit the rapidly disintegrating British Empire. South Africa, it was widely believed and hoped, was the fatal challenge to a decadent Britain, and her miserable showing against the Boers seemed to underline the truth.

The pride and power of Germany as the nineteenth century moved to its close would be difficult to exaggerate. Hamburg had become the greatest port in Europe, and the commercial and mercantile expansion of the country was phenomenal.

The end of the century was filled with potent dreams, for while Germany dreamed of her empire, Japan nursed her plans for revenge directed against Russia, and in Europe, Alsace and Lorraine and the memory of her ignominious defeat festered in the soul of France. Britain, the most hated power in Europe, and probably in the world, was singularly unmoved.

The signs and portents of war crowded the years. The Russian seizure of Manchuria made war with Japan a virtual certainty. In the Middle East, France, backed by Germany, appeared to challenge British supremacy on the upper Nile, a challenge that fizzled out when Britain demonstrated at Fashoda that 'sea power was trumps'. In China the 'Boxer Rising' frightened the Great Powers into a momentary show of unity which still further revealed their antagonisms.

Inevitably, world conflict awaited the inevitable spark. The question was when and where? But no one asked or attempted to answer such a question.

## II

The peculiar nature of Anglo-German relations from the last years of the eighteenth century has exercised the minds of many German thinkers and historians, and deserves some emphasis here. Towards the end of the eighteenth century Schiller and Kant had given widespread expression to a wave of Anglophobia in the wake of the American War and the French Revolution. But as the nineteenth century dawned and the Napoleonic Wars dominated the European scene, German attitudes to Britain, manifest particularly in the North German rivalry of Prussia and Hanover, became ambivalent. A remarkable see-saw, and a mixture, of Anglo-philia and phobia was observed. Perhaps a 'love-hate' situation would not convey a false impression.

Throughout the remarkable growths of the nineteenth century in the aftermath of the Napoleonic Wars, the Germans found much to admire in the British handling of her industrial revolution, her avoidance of real revolution in 1848, and above all of her particular blend of liberalism and authority.

Commenting upon some newly issued German histories covering this period, a writer in *The Times Literary Supplement* wrote:

'As the century progressed and social tension increased inside Germany, Britain appeared to men like Gneist, Schmoller, Brentano and Baernreither as a haven of social harmony, while other Germans were still debating whether trade unions should be allowed at all.'

By 1890 these attitudes to Britain had undergone a complete change. Germany had found her own great strength and with it an overwhelming arrogance and belief in her destiny. If there were lessons to be learned, Germany would teach them. 'The German Empire has become a world empire.' 'The twentieth century will belong to Germany.' 'British Empire in decay.' Such was the tone of the slogans shouted in an ominous crescendo from the ramparts of Germany.

Anglophobia was in full spate, and a situation had developed whereby Europe, if not the world, would be challenged to choose between the rival 'ways of life', the civilizations, philosophies and systems, of Germany and Britain. There was not room enough for both to prevail in the same continent; nor possibly in the same world.

In that sense it was a situation comparable with that confronting the world today, with the United States of America and the USSR marshalling the nations of the world into rival camps in support of their differing, but probably converging, 'ways of life'.

C

## III

It may be some reflection of the state of ignorance in high places in Britain that young Mr Winston Churchill, a soldier-subaltern at the outset of his career, could have wished that he had been born a century earlier, with all the glamour and glory of the Napoleonic Wars ahead of him, instead of ... nothing. Or, at best, a few punitive expeditions against tribesmen.

The foreign commitments of Britain in those days were known to less than a handful of men, and foreign affairs were not even the business of the Cabinet. The foreign policy of Britain, in as much as it existed, was the maintenance of peace. It was essential to keep the seas open and safe for her ever-expanding maritime trade, and to maintain her position as a great Indian power. This called for a first-class Indian Army, and the maintenance of well-placed naval bases and fuelling stations. An Englishman could easily travel round the world without setting foot on foreign soil, welcomed from London to Hong Kong and back by his own kith and kin. The long peace and the vast accretions of new wealth had bred a dangerous complacency in the British people, and only France, with her long Atlantic and Mediterranean seaboards, and her colonial possessions, could offer even the smallest of threats to British supremacy at sea.

In the Britain of 1895 there were very few fears, and very little awareness even in the highest places, of the nature of the dire and terrible threats accumulating in the danger spots of the world, and burgeoning in the hearts of the German people. The wars the boy Churchill had fought over his nursery floor, and which engaged his powerful imagination, had become obsolete and would never repeat their patterns. Years later, still with a bitter sense of disappointment, and even of amazement that he, a Churchill, should have been so cruelly cheated, Churchill wrote:

'War, which used to be cruel and magnificent, has now become cruel and squalid. In fact it has been completely spoilt.'

He resented bitterly the 'spoiling' of war by that accursed combination of 'democracy and science' in which it was difficult to detect a single ray of 'magnificence'. War had been a 'gentleman's game', dangerous withal. In 1895, as Churchill observed, 'The Dragoon, the Lancer and, above all, as we believed, the Hussar, still claimed their time-honoured place upon the battlefield.'

In the year that Churchill girded on his sword it was difficult to discover young officers who had heard shots fired in anger, or had thrilled to the thunder of the charge and the clash of sabres. The 'shop' talked in mess or wardroom seldom concerned anything more warlike than 'spit and polish'. Tactical exercises for officers, men or ships were rare, and where they existed at all had little relevance to the conditions of warfare likely to obtain. Strategical studies were the sole concern of the Admiralty and War Office, if indeed they were a concern at all. When in 1899 Fisher assumed the naval command in the Mediterranean, long-range gunnery practice was unheard of, and its institution brought a storm of fury about his ears from old-fashioned entrenched admirals and captains. When he ordered his ships to steam at full speed, scarcely a chief engineer in the fleet but believed that his ship would shake to pieces. The condition of the army was even worse. It provided a playground for young gentlemen in elaborate fancy dress, and a background for the fading memories of the ageing. It was virtually impossible for an officer (and a gentleman) serving in a first-class regiment to live on his pay.

Lord Randolph Churchill had died before he had had the time or opportunity to lay even the foundations of a modest fortune, and Lady Randolph allowed her son £500 a year to eke out his meagre pay, and to help him to maintain the ponies without which his life as a Hussar would be both empty and ridiculous. Churchill had suffered gladly the extreme rigours of training in horsemanship demanded by the instructors of the 4th Hussars, and had delighted in the eccentricities, the memories, and the extremes of individuality displayed by his commanding officer, Colonel Brabazon. The duties of a subaltern were not arduous, and five months each year were devoted to 'leave'. The problem confronting most of Churchill's brother officers was how best to fill in the time satisfactorily, in the social round, the hunting field, polo, shooting and travel.

War had receded so far into the background as to have ceased to be a real hazard of soldiering. It was thus robbed of its element of danger, an element vital to Churchill's spirit and nature. An egocentric is compelled to find expression in his own person for almost all the passions of man. There is no other outlet, such as, for example, a woman provides for many, for with a woman the highest experiences must be shared, and the ego must, if only for an instant, become one with another's. The impossibility of such a sharing for an egocentric robs him of that exquisite rapture of which men are wont to dream, and only in the personal challenge to death may such a man discover a comparable experience and a momentary release from the bonds of self. Churchill's great emotional forces and energies were never dissipated. He was his own man.

In the year of his father's death Churchill began to take his place at his mother's side in the select circle of society to which he belonged, but it was not until his return from a visit to Cuba and the United States in 1896 that he began to feel sure of himself in that company, and to observe those about him with a shrewdness uncommon in so young a man. Mrs Everest had died in the summer of 1895, severing, as it seemed, his last powerful link with childhood. At last he had emerged from the grey tunnel of his boyhood into the adult world for which he had longed.

Churchill's great and immediate joy in his new status was the obvious pleasure his mother derived from his company. They had need of each other, and in some ways the death of Lord Randolph had marked the moment of release for them both. Churchill had admired his mother from the cradle, but she had seemed an unattainable vision, infinitely remote, and impossible to clasp. He had also suffered some pangs of jealousy, fearing that his young brother Jack, with all the Jerome looks allied to a straightforward Spencer-Churchill nature, might be expected to have a far greater appeal. But Jenny Jerome soon showed that she pinned her hopes upon her American son. Here, emerging rapidly from the unprepossessing chrysalis of boyhood, was a young man of spirit and dash, of remarkable and disturbing bearing, with an enormous zest and enthusiasm for life, a bold direct eye, and a not unpleasing countenance. The eyes were level and well set, lacking the excessive prominence of his father's, but capable of a disconcerting stare, and with an arrogance not unusual in a young man of his background and breeding. His chin showed signs of pugnacity and obstinacy, and perhaps the mouth alone revealed his capacities for emotion, generosity and humour, and his powerful sentimentality.

All signs of that 'pale little ghost', that 'poor little Winston', observed by his aunt, Clara Frewen, lurking in the shadows of the hall at St James's Place and watching shyly the arrivals and departures of the guests, had vanished.

In a very short time mother and son developed an easy relationship frequently described by them both as 'brother and sister' in quality. Lady Randolph was still a very attractive and beautiful woman, immensely active and soon even more fiercely dedicated to her eldest son's advancement than she had ever been to her husband's. Winston was her expression. Together they lunched or dined alone in perfect harmony in the comparatively modest circumstances of their home, served at table by three liveried servants. The point may be worth noting because Churchill, throughout his life, treated all persons he considered socially inferior, or even of little use to him, as flunkeys. It did not occur to him to do otherwise. The race was to the swift.

Churchill's relationship with his mother, and earlier with Mrs Everest, is important because it reveals his attitude to women. His romantic nature and tremendous zest for life, his great emotional capacities, were aroused and fulfilled by the excitement of living. Life offered a challenge to be accepted avidly. What did it offer a man? What did he want of it? He would find out.

But he was not sufficient unto himself. He needed the kind of service and sustenance of the spirit that only love would give. Incapable of love, he demanded it from others. His mother would help him as his loyal and devoted ally in blood, as Mrs Everest had helped him after her fashion from infancy to adolescence, as Clementine Hozier would help him with devotion, humour and sustained affection throughout the entire cycle of his adult life.

That three such women should dedicate their lives to his service is perhaps the greatest tribute to the reality of the powers and possibilities inherent in him, and which they understood and accepted intuitively. As they saw it, he was worth serving. They backed him to win. His success their sole reward.

I do not think it ever entered Churchill's thoughts that he should fight any battle but his own. He was emotionally and instinctively a one-man show, incapable of that devotion to causes that involves an immolation of self. If selfishness is a conscious act, then he was never selfish. His duty was to life and to himself. If he served others it was solely as a means to his own advancement, to the realization of the personal power he sought. But this was not a conscious choice. He was not false to any man. His passage through life would provide a number of clear opportunities, a number of hand-holds, and as he climbed the way would doubtless become clear. It was for him to recognize and to grasp opportunities, to recognize who might or might not be useful, to climb ever upwards upon people and events. People who had served their purpose would be as swiftly forgotten as the small ridges and irregularities on the face of the rock, providing hand and foot holds for the mountaineer whose eyes are fixed steadfastly upon the summit. It is not only dangerous, but a waste of time, to look back.

Disciplines, save for those he would learn to impose upon himself and others, were totally rejected. He had no real ties, and it is difficult to imagine a man less trammelled. He could travel his road as free as air. He acknowledged no superiors and few equals, cherishing a sentimental regard for monarchy, and saving his capacity for reverence and awe for the institution of Parliament, his only temple. All men and women were either his servants in varying degrees, all means to whatever ends he might choose, or else as rejected or 'non-existent' to him as the flunkeys at his table.

In the year 1895 Churchill first realized the nature and extent of his privileges and tremendous opportunities, greatly enhanced beyond the natural endowments of his birth by virtue of his father's political attainments and his mother's brilliant qualities as a hostess in her own right. Men like A. J. Balfour, destined, with the enigmatic and enormously influential Lord Esher, to be one of the first great architects of Britain's ability to wage war, and Sir Henry Drummond Wolff were close family friends, as were also Rosebery and Morley, Ripon and Salisbury, and a host of others filling the key positions in all the civil and Service departments of Britain.

Churchill knew instinctively who mattered most, and by the time he had found his feet and his confidence in 1896 he did not hesitate to air his opinions even to the ears of the very great. There was no doubt then that the two or three hundred families revolving round the exclusive social seats of power centred upon the great London houses of Lansdowne, Devonshire and Stafford, were the rulers of Britain. The leading social and political figures of the day were usually synonymous, and when they were not, as in the case of that 'outsider' Joe Chamberlain, Lady Randolph maintained the channels of warm personal contact for her son.

In his mother Churchill had an ally worthy of him, ready to fight his battles at home with the courage and tenacity of a tigress. There was no ear closed to her, no string she dared not pull, for her son's advancement in whatever direction he might choose to go. She would harry Lord Salisbury, the Prime Minister, and the Service chiefs with an unflagging tenacity. Even though her eldest son might often astonish by his boyish brashness, his precocious readiness to advance his own immature position, he had a saving grace of indefinable charm, a kind of personal force and belief in himself which was at once disarming and disconcerting. Great vitality is an irresistible quality, and in spite of his reckless speech and lack of the graces, he seldom offended the elder statesmen of his late father's intimate circle.

But he was also well capable of seeking out and making his own contacts. He was quick to admire the great, and especially the brave men of the past who no longer afforded a challenge to him. Thus he found a welcome at the home of Lord William Beresford, a V.C. of the Zulu war, a brother of the sailor Lord Charles Beresford, and third husband of Lilian, the American widow of the eighth Duke of Marlborough. At the home of Lord William at Deepdene, Churchill made his number with the redoubtable Sir Bindon Blood, through whom he hoped to gain some experience of fighting on the north-west frontier of India. Thus he prepared the way for his adventures with the Malakand Field Force nearly two years in advance.

It was at Deepdene also that Churchill was able to bring himself more closely to the attention of the Prince of Wales, afterwards Edward VII, and an early admirer of his first efforts as a war correspondent.

Few young men can ever have left their country's shores to seek adventure and fortune with their home bases better secured. It was too early yet for him to know himself, or even to seek to define his aims with clarity. His dream of being a soldier did not include the routine of soldiering, but had the nursery quality of the more usual child's dream of being 'an engine driver'. The dream does not entail learning the job, serving the apprenticeship, stoking the furnace, or doing any work. It is simply an end-dream of being, miraculously, it. In such a manner Churchill thought of himself as a general, except that in a fairly clearly defined way he imagined such a rank as his right. Certainly he would wait for it, and even work for it, after his own fashion. It was the one abiding dream, never forgotten, never to be fulfilled.

Towards the end of 1895, before he had properly made his mark in the social hierarchy of Britain, Churchill had the long winter army leave to fill. Where should he go? What should he do? He longed for personal physical danger, for the 'blooding and ordeal of the Indian brave', as passionately and deeply as many men long for the first crisis of love. Fortunately, there was a small war in Cuba, where the Spaniards were having grave trouble with the guerrilla fighters peculiar to that island 'pearl of the Antilles', anxious to throw off the Spanish yoke, or whatever yoke might be upon their necks. A considerable reinforcement was on its way to Cuba. Churchill's Colonel Brabazon was pleased for his young subaltern to seek such an adventure. Churchill's father's friend, Sir Henry Drummond Wolff, was British Ambassador in Madrid.

Nothing could be more simple than that Churchill should proceed to Cuba bearing letters and the highest recommendations to the Spanish Commander-in-Chief, who would be certain to attach him in an honorary and privileged capacity to the Spanish forces. He might even have the luck to be under fire, an essential experience to establish the morale of the young soldier, and for which there is no substitute.

The adventure had Lady Randolph's blessing, for her son would travel by way of New York to make his first contacts with his mother's country, and to meet some of those whose blood and instincts he shared.

In November 1895 Churchill sailed for New York.

# CHAPTER V

※

CHURCHILL lived his whole life in the bold, opportunist spirit of adventure that took him to the Cuban war by way of New York in the winter of 1895. He was twenty-one years old, a subaltern in the 4th Hussars, a scion of one of the most noble and powerful families in Britain, and emerging into the broad sunlight of a world filled with glittering, if undefined, prizes. He was as vividly alive as a dragonfly spreading its wings for the first time. His sense of absolute freedom unique and irresistible.

For fifty years thereafter he lived and walked with destiny, knowing every next moment wrapped in mystery, and that was the spice and essence of life to him. To turn aside from one known or threatened danger might well be to move into the path of another. He never turned aside, living always, as he put it, with 'the sense of hope', and resolved never to take no for an answer. Had that been all, then he might have been another d'Artagnan on the grand scale, his life the very stuff of adventure books for boys. But in his imagination he wore the mantle of Marlborough, and believed that personal power was his right.

Churchill was met on the quayside in New York by Bourke Cockran, a great friend of the Jeromes. He had never met, or seen, or imagined any personage remotely like Bourke Cockran, or dreamed of a wonderland of such remarkable possibilities as New York. In that same year a young man named Bernard Baruch, destined to be Churchill's greatest friend, the man nearest of all to his heart, was rapidly making his first $3,000,000 in the financial jungle that had provided such excitements for Jeromes, Vanderbilts, Fisks and a handful of others thirty years earlier. But times had changed: a man now needed ten million dollars before he was regarded as a 'millionaire'.

Thus, at an immensely impressionable age and at a key moment in his life, Churchill added his mother's country and its people to himself. His delight in all he saw remains infectious over the years. He bubbled over. At home the courtesies and formalities of society, which he had observed meticulously, had irked him. The wildness and easy ways of New York delighted him and rendered him lyrical. It was a place wherein the proprietor of a 'gambling hell' could be also accepted as among the most cultured and worthwhile citizens. Richard Canfield, who never had less than half a million dollars on hand at his premises on 44th Street, was at the same time one of the keenest collectors of paintings and antiques, a man of judgment withal.

Churchill observed an adventurous spirit in all the business of living, in contrast to the formal charade of English manners. Politics and money making were fun.

At that time his uncle, Travers Jerome, the son of Leonard Jerome's brother Lawrence, was District Attorney of New York, and one of the very few to frown upon the 'Canfields' of the city, attacking graft and corruption in Tammany Hall and elsewhere in an uncompromising spirit that brought the angry complaint from Senator Plunkitt that 'nobody thinks of drawing the distinction between honest graft and dishonest graft'.

To Travers Jerome there was no such thing as honest graft. Thirty years earlier the rivals of the Jeromes had complained that they had had 'too much sense of honour, and no sense of sin'. Now the victims of Travers Jerome complained that he had too much sense of sin.

But the name of Jerome was still one to conjure with, and Churchill's grandfather, Leonard, and his brother, Lawrence, had left vivid memories. It was only a year or two since the New York papers had headlined the news of the dying Lawrence, 'The Prince of Good Fellows slowly gives up the Fight'. Leonard had matched his brother in good fellowship and outstripped him in achievement while leaving memories untainted by a trace of bitterness. No one could say half as much for the Vanderbilts, leave alone the Jim Fisks and Jay Goulds who fought for and won and lost fortunes in that jungle.

All this, and much more, Churchill knew from Bourke Cockran. He could take pride, as well as pleasure, in his American family. But he was only half Jerome and part Indian, half Spencer and part Churchill. There was nothing in his American ancestry a tithe as potent as a Marlborough, and thus there was a dark, confused mixture deep in him, that might serve to stoke the fires of his dreams and deny him the reality. The best of both worlds could not be his, or any man's, yet it was certain that, with his nature, he would come to desire all.

It was in New York, too, and in that company, that I believe a doubt was sown in his heart, soon to be nourished by the attitudes he provoked in his companions, that he was not a 'gentleman' by the standards of the army and his class. It is certain that New York, its life, its people and politics gripped his imagination at first sight, and evoked responses in him never to be quenched.

He grew lyrical about Bourke Cockran. 'I have never seen his like, or in some respects his equal,' Churchill wrote years later. Yet one doubts that Cockran was much more than a shadow of Leonard Jerome in his prime.

In 1895 Cockran was middle-aged, a man with an 'enormous head, gleaming eyes and flexible countenance', and showing his young friend round the town with immense gusto. Originally a 'democrat and Tammany Tiger', but ready enough to speak on any platform, or for any cause that took his fancy, Cockran was as politically consistent in his inconsistency as Churchill himself would be, a man absolutely after Churchill's own heart.

In the United States politics was 'all crisp and sharp', Churchill wrote, and with no 'frayed edges, borderlands, compromises, anomalies' as in our affairs. In America, it was clear, a man *had* to be a political acrobat, and possibly a financial acrobat as well, or he would never reach the top.

I think it possible that if the soldier coupled with the Marlborough image had not been so strong in Churchill's mind at that time, or if he had seen a little more of life and adventure, England might have seen him no more. But he did not see himself then as a politician. There can be little doubt that he was 'born' for the part he might have played to perfection on that stage from start to finish, cutting a tremendous figure, all crisp and sharp himself, and with no frayed edges. When he came at last, after fifty years, to address the United States Congress, he sounded a wistful note ... 'If my father had been American and my mother British ... I might have got here on my own.'

'For the moment he was American,' wrote Margaret Coit. 'It was as if he were Prime Minister of the United States, too.' She had put into words the hopelessness and substance of his life-long dream.

Where Britain irked and often inhibited him, America would

have applauded, provided stimulus and outlets for his energies that would have given free rein to his personality. No one would have looked down his nose at such a man, as many were to do in Britain. There Churchill could have displayed the diversity of his talents, political, journalistic and probably financial. He would have been a starter in the same field as Baruch, and many would have backed him to win—except that, like his grandfather Jerome, Churchill always loved life and adventure more than money.

This new nation, bursting with energy, confronting new horizons, and not too fussy about ways and means, would have claimed his undivided loyalties, even to himself, and there, I believe, he would have blossomed into the wildly flamboyant pattern inherent in his nature.

But Churchill was on the eve of his first adventure of war, and nothing, not even New York and Bourke Cockran, could compete in his imagination with such a prospect. In a week or two he sailed for Cuba, bearing with him a dream that would never fade. It was his Achilles heel.

## II

I suspect that Churchill's brief encounter with life and death under the hot Cuban sun was of vital importance in his life, providing him with the kind of personal secret about himself essential to his growth, and the flowering of his personality. For every boy and girl dreams, and some very few challenge the reality, and it is like opening a door into a new world which, otherwise, will be forever closed.

There is then, I hold, a special quality about a man's first adventure that is the cornerstone of all else. Whatever happens afterwards, however rich in dangers and excitements the future may be, this first experience, of danger, of life and death in the sun, remains the key, like a first love to a lover, an essence in the heart, nourishing the spirit and seldom, if ever, to be spoken.

Churchill's output on a thousand and one aspects of his crowded life is voluminous, yet of his short time in Cuba, his first adventure, he has said very little, for it is the one adventure that belongs to him and to nobody else.

After a journey of some discomforts and difficulties he was attached as a very privileged observer to leading Spanish troops whose rôle was to seek out and destroy Cuban guerrillas, masters of ambush and swift disengagement.

In more formal warfare, even as it was to become, soldiers knew themselves reasonably safe and secure in the rear, and in their well defended camps. When they were not going into battle, or involved in battle, they slept soundly, ate well, and forgot about fear. But in operating against guerrillas, death lurks anywhere and everywhere. It cuts men off from life even in the midst of love, polite informal converse, a dinner party, or a swim in a lagoon. It imposes a special strain upon the nerves of regular troops. They are not threatened with defeat, but sudden death to any one of them at any hour of night or day.

Of such a quality was Churchill's first experience of warfare. For many months the Spanish authorities had been harried by the rebels and subjected to many minor disasters and discomforts. They hoped to control the situation effectively. More than sixty years later their American conquerors would still be trying to do the same thing, and with even less success.

Churchill's sympathies at first favoured the guerrillas, but shifted mildly in favour of his hosts, mainly because one feels a natural dislike of rudeness and an equivocal position. Inevitably the possibility of being a 'guerrilla' himself was denied to him, but his support of guerrillas whose cause in any way supported his own was established, and would bear abundant fruit. It irked his Imperial pride to discover that the Spanish regarded their empire with emotions similar to the British outlook on their own. Cuba, in fact, was to them as Ireland was to us. He regarded the Spanish attitude as presumptuous, while recognizing it as reasonable. Politically he remained unaware of the significance of the Cuban unrest, nor did he seek the social significance of his experience. His precocity was not of that order. But he did appreciate the hopelessness of the Spanish position and the nagging power of dedicated guerrillas. Imperial power and guerrillas were corollaries. It was the business of the one to contain the other.

Churchill was attached to the personal entourage of the Spanish general of division, to ride with that gentleman and his staff at some fifty yards behind the forward company, and thus to observe at close range whatever might occur. As a non-combatant he wore a loaded revolver as a means of personal defence if it should be necessary, but he was as vulnerable to a bullet as those whose cause this was.

A few bullets had whistled through the hut in which he had slept. He would have preferred the floor to his hammock, but since his companions showed no inclination to move, he merely observed that the officer in the hammock between his own and the outer wall was of substantial bulk, a bulwark, and slept himself. In the middle day a horse was shot within a yard of him as he relaxed on his feet outside his hut. The bullet could not have missed Churchill's head by more than inches, and was probably meant for him. An air burst from an '88' might easily prove more dangerous in later wars, and frequently did, nevertheless there is nothing personal about it. To be observed by the enemy at close range, and shot at is an experience of a very different nature.

Later, as Churchill sat his horse at the general's side and the forward company engaged a band of guerrillas with brisk fire, the fierce smack of bullets against the trunks of the surrounding palm trees drew a pattern of fire of which the command group was unmistakably the centre. There were, also, the bullets one did not hear, and especially the bullet one would never hear. Churchill was glad to discover that he could sustain a studied nonchalance in keeping with his more experienced companions. No man knows for certain that he will succeed in this until it happens.

The size of an engagement is not of any great personal importance, for no man's range of sense and vision extends beyond a very limited perimeter, and to be caught in a small ambush is usually more dangerous than to be involved in a major battle. Churchill observed these things in a manner that, were it not for achievements of far greater magnitude, would enable him to become one of the greatest war correspondents of his times. His grasp of tactics was swift and sure, his detachment and observation admirable. He subscribed to a saying of Kinglake's that 'a scrutiny so minute as to bring an object under an untrue angle of vision, is a poorer guide to a man's judgment than a sweeping glance which sees things in true proportion'. Churchill assuredly became a master of the sweeping glance.

On his brief Cuban adventure he had by chance acted in the rôle that suited him best, that of a freelance observer without regimental duties. A platoon commander, in any case, is inevitably dedicated to the minute scrutiny. But it is unlikely that Churchill had formed any definite opinion about his future at so early a stage. He was highly susceptible to all the currents of fortune, and feeling his way. His first adventure had been an interlude, a holiday of a kind never to be repeated. When he returned to England he had left boyhood behind him, and was about to embark upon his career, whatever it might be. He would carry his childhood with him always, for that was the spring of his dreams from which all else must flow.

Churchill's experience of being 'under fire' had been of great value. He had noticed, with some surprise, how few were killed even under a fusillade at close range, and he had learned a lesson for which his nature was well adapted: that it is pointless, and often deadly, to attempt to move out of the path of the invisible and unpredictable. One might as well, or better, keep straight on. Death may be a hairsbreadth to one side or the other. No one knows. A shelter may be the scene of total disaster. It may be at least as safe under the sky, and far more pleasant. This was his view.

Churchill did not attempt to exaggerate his experience, least of all to himself, but he found that he was able to move more easily as a man among men, that he had acquired poise, and was able to air some of his immature views without offence.

He had also discovered in Cuba the virtues of the siesta and the dawn, and that it is difficult to enjoy one without the other. He was fortunate in that life seldom denied him the opportunity to take a siesta, and thus he learned very early in life how to conserve his energies and confront the jaded with his fresh and agile mind.

In the autumn of 1896, having made good use of his spell at home, he sailed with his regiment for a tour of duty in India, wrenching his right shoulder severely in his impatience to disembark from a skiff heaving against the wharf at Bombay. The slight disability was permanent. It hampered him at polo, but did not defeat him. Bad luck and good luck were the sides of a coin, and were simply luck, to be turned to advantage. But his shoulder forced him to wield a revolver in place of a sabre when the time came for him to take part in the famous charge at Omdurman, and thus robbed him of the authentic feeling of the charge. The sabre belongs to the charge as a bow and arrow to a Red Indian.

At once in India Churchill set about the task of mending the gaps in his education. Sharing a bungalow with two brother officers, and waited upon hand and foot, there was no lack of opportunity for study. Polo claimed the major portion of his physical activities, and the maintenance of ponies and his way of life provided him with an insoluble financial problem. Almost at once he realized that unless he was to be involved in acute financial embarrassment, long sustained, he would have to do something drastic. The first move was to acquire knowledge. Philosophy, religion, ethics were mysterious. History was little more than an eighteenth century glow of battles, to which had been miserably added *The Student's Hume*, a deadly piece of condensation, as dry as dust.

Lord Randolph's love of Gibbon made of that author's *Decline and Fall* a natural 'bible', and according to many a literary model. Gibbon's eulogy of his old nurse won him also a special place in Churchill's heart: 'If there be any, as I trust there are some, who rejoice that I live, to that dear and excellent woman their gratitude is due.' It should be Mrs Everest's epitaph also.

But beyond that point in his education Churchill felt very keenly a lack of guidance. His mother helped to provide him with books, but there was none to say, 'read this with that' or 'do not take too much notice of this man, unless you have also considered so and so'. Many of Churchill's enemies have scoffed at his reading through the torrid Indian afternoons. 'I suppose he (Churchill) was the youngest man ever to have read Lecky!' wrote Francis Neilson. 'But what shall we say of a poorly educated young man of twenty-two reading Schopenhauer and Darwin?'

Neilson would have had him substitute Hooker, John Locke and Adam Smith for Schopenhauer, Malthus and Darwin. Perhaps Churchill was fortunate rather than otherwise in making his own choices, and finding his own way, for who shall say what is best for any man?

After Gibbon, Churchill consumed Macaulay with an appetite stimulated by his school love of the *'Lays'*. If Lecky on *Rationalism* confused him, he emerged swiftly and reasonably unscathed from that confusion. Christ, like Socrates, was a man of so great merit as to be in a sphere above and apart from other men, but none the less a man, not a God. He lamented with Shaw that neither of these spoke in their own defence.

Plato's *Republic*, together with a book by Welldon, the Headmaster of Harrow who had birched him only a shade less fiercely than the monsters in charge of his preparatory school, introduced him adequately, he hoped, to Socrates. Schopenhauer on

*Pessimism,* Darwin on the *Origin of Species* and Malthus on *Population* do not seem to have done Churchill the smallest harm, and very probably a great deal of good. He found his own way, and many with more guidance were less fortunate. He found time to ponder Winwood Reade's *Martyrdom of Man* and to relax with his much-loved R. L. Stevenson. He would even read that author's *Kidnapped* a year or two later while hiding from his pursuers, and all else forgotten.

His annoyance on discovering that his lack of Latin and Greek were still a bar to a University education was shortlived.

Undoubtedly throughout the first year in India his mind was finding its bearings, and forming some very shrewd opinions. On the voyage out he had struck up a friendship with Colonel Ian Hamilton, and revealed at that early stage his taste for war corresponding. Greece and Turkey were then on the verge of war. Hamilton was on the side of Greece, Churchill for Turkey. In any case, he confided, he would like to be there 'to see the fun'. The phrase recurs whenever battle or adventure loom into sight. It is the phrase of a child, resolved to preserve a special kind of dream about war and glory, and life itself.

In 1897 he grasped an opportunity to take three months' privilege leave in England although he had served so short a term. Already he knew in his heart, if not very clearly in his mind, that he had no intention of pursuing a military career. He needed, and demanded from life, a special kind of freedom and privilege in which to develop. He expected and demanded help on every hand, and pursued his aims with a nagging persistence that would not be denied. The last three years of the nineteenth century were the most important in his early life. In them he found his metier; the framework within which he would pursue his dream in the shadow of Marlborough. The Monarchy would be the mystic symbol of his God; Parliament his authority, and his temple. Thenceforth he would be the architect of great things.

One of those few who served him intimately and loyally for thirty years expressed something of this to me: 'I suppose that self-analysis must always have been impossible to Winston. How could it be? When all his acts were dreams and the dreams seemed to come true? Were they not *his* dreams?'

And again: 'When he was out of power in the thirties, he was exactly like a child whose toy is broken. He ran to anyone for comfort, thus inspiring the same pity (akin to affection) as would the child with its broken toy. If the passer-by happened to help mend his toy, or, better still, give him a new one, he ran off happily to play with it, with no sense or need for gratitude to the kindly stranger.'

And the strangers were kindly; almost always. The same writer exclaims: 'Winston, the brilliant, great imaginative, ever-dreaming child, whom no one ever taught to control his imagination, or to be disciplined or to think of others! But, and here is the great question! Why did not they? Why did not those who said in his boyhood and youth how horrid he was, why did they apparently do nothing about it? *There* is a question which simply *must* be answered.'

It seems to me to pose the problem of power, and I cannot fit Winston Churchill into the 'Round Table'. He is neither an Arthur, a Lancelot, a Galahad or a Merlin, but a kind of potent Puck, a mixture of a mischievous sprite and an emperor without any clothes, and much else besides. Perhaps the answer lies with the strange docility of the human species, and the awful fear of liberty and freedom which holds western man in chains, and disposes him to cling to dreams rather than face reality.

Churchill's development from 1897 onwards was swift and exciting. In close conclave with his mother he made tentative plans, and established contacts for his advancement. Already he had decided to try his hand at writing to pay his way, but he had not quite finished with soldiering. He was well aware of the unpleasant consequences of falling foul of the military machine, even for a young man of his name and social standing. He sailed dangerously close to the wind, but would not be deterred. He perceived that his brother officers in India were less than enchanted by his behaviour, but nothing, not even the icy silences and obvious distaste for him of Kitchener, at that time Sirdar of Egypt, nor the miserable embarrassments soon to be suffered by Lord Roberts in his precocious and unwanted company, could put him out of countenance. With a nonchalance far rarer than his bearing under fire he would ride at the sides of these great soldiers, confident that in time they would get used to him. The remarkable fact is that they did get used to him.

A personal telegram to General Sir Bindon Blood, forming an expedition on the North West Frontier of India in 1897, gained him a place in the Malakand Field Force, and a clear field for his first work as a newspaper correspondent. He had arranged to send his war despatches to the *Pioneer* of India, while his mother had no difficulty in persuading the editor of the *Daily Telegraph* to pay £5 a column for her son's letters. He made an excellent beginning, serving with great dash and initiative in the deadly skirmishes and ruthless reprisals attendant upon such a campaign, and sending a series of remarkable despatches to London. Unfortunately for him, as he thought, the campaign was brought to a somewhat premature close, and no further employment was to be found for him in that quarter.

Churchill had had little difficulty in persuading his Colonel to give him the leave necessary to carry out his first assignment, but upon returning to his regiment at Bangalore he found that the climate had begun to cool.

'My brother officers when I returned to them were extremely civil,' he wrote. 'But I found a very general opinion that I had had enough leave and should now do a steady spell of routine duty.'

Nothing was further from his thoughts or intentions. An expedition under Sir William Lockhart was about to penetrate into the mountainous Tirah region to suppress an uprising of the wild Afridis. The expedition promised unusual excitements and dangers, and would provide a valuable experience and a vivid story. Churchill resolved to force himself into the entourage of the general.

While in England Lady Randolph laid 'vigorous siege' to Lords Wolseley and Roberts, urging these unwilling gentlemen to write to Sir George White, Commander-in-Chief in India, in her son's behalf, and at the same time attempted to pull many other less obvious, but potent, strings behind the scenes, Churchill acted with vigour on the spot.

Bringing himself to the personal attention of Sir George White, who knew perfectly well what he was after, he remarked that gentlemen's 'civility', but swiftly discerned that the subject of himself and the Tirah expedition was 'unmentionable'.

Churchill's one real remaining hope of furthering his career and feeding his ambitions lay with Colonel Ian Hamilton, his friend of the outward bound voyage to India, and commanding a brigade under Sir William Lockhart. But Hamilton was temporarily *hors de combat* following an accident, and unable to help.

Marooned, perforce, at Bangalore with a share of unavoidable regimental duties, Churchill drew some comfort from news of the severe setbacks sustained by the expedition. 'After all,' he wrote, 'they had been very selfish in not letting me come with them.' Meanwhile he bided his time, turning apparent misfortune into fortune, by working hard on the story of the Malakand Field Force, and trying his hand at a novel he called *Savrola*. It was in fact a most important period of a first taking stock, and essential to his development, the first of many pauses imposed by forces beyond his control, and without which the whole pattern of his life might well have been greatly changed. His book *The Malakand Field Force* was a first-class piece of reporting, lucid, intensely readable, precocious, but disarming and personal. Its success was immediate. The Prince of Wales wrote warmly expressing his pleasure in it. Even Lord Salisbury was impressed. It was a very good beginning indeed.

*Savrola* was of a very different order. In middle age, in common with many writers for whom the novel is not the chosen medium, Churchill tended to regard it as an indiscretion. It was published in *Macmillan's Magazine*, as well as in book form, bringing in the satisfactory sum of £700. He hoped his friends would not read it. Probably it caused him some embarrassment. But *Savrola* is a remarkable book on the dreams and ambitions of Winston Churchill. In it he reveals himself with the unguarded innocence—or naïvety—of youth, soon to be controlled by discretion and growing experience. It charts with extraordinary clarity the kind of rôle in which he saw himself as the leading actor, the 'Liberal Statesman', the 'Liberator', the saviour of a people—and ultimately discarded. He saw himself as a politician, not as a soldier. The hero, a democrat (whatever that may mean!), leads a popular revolt, gains control of the army and navy without commanding them, and becomes President of the Council of Public Safety. An interesting point is that the hero does not bear malice even against the corrupt, the 'mean and odious' who survive to flourish. This was ever a characteristic of Churchill.

The people of his imagined country, *Laurania*, fit into a Ruritanian, or better still, a Latin American setting. Cuba may well have inspired the background. The book ends on a note of astounding prophecy, ushered in by a split infinitive too painful to reproduce, and typical of his 'worst writing in his shirtsleeves' until Edward Marsh came along to do his tidying up. For the benefit of those readers who might like to know what happened next in Laurania he recounts that they may 'read how, after the tumults had subsided, the hearts of the people turned again to the illustrious exile who had won them freedom and whom they had deserted in the hour of victory. They may scoff at the fickleness of men, read of the return of Savrola and his beautiful consort to the ancient city he had loved so well. . . . Of the old nurse, indeed, they will read no more, for history does not concern itself with such.'

'But the chronicler, finding few great events . . . to recount, will remember the splendid sentence of Gibbon, that history is "little more than the register of the crimes, follies and misfortunes of mankind", and he will rejoice that after many troubles, peace and prosperity came back to the Republic of Laurania.'

It is all there, even to Mrs Everest, and the early influence of Gibbon. It seems to me a prevision of the rôle and fate in store for him nearly fifty years in the future. He had difficulty with the 'love' interest, and sought the advice of his brother officers, but the result is artificial.

He had also the illusion at this stage, and retained it for many years, that he had modelled his writing upon Gibbon and Macaulay. Doubtless he was greatly influenced by these two powerful and brilliant historians, but I cannot discover a trace of their 'styles' in the work of Churchill. His work and manner are his own, and it is curious that he should have found it flattering when some critics denied him, in effect, his natural and individual talent.

By the time this work was done, and safely in the hands of his magnificent 'agent' and 'Public Relations Officer', Lady Randolph, Colonel Ian Hamilton was recovered and back again in command of his brigade. Churchill had maintained careful contact and pressure by correspondence. It was useless, he knew, to pursue his desires further through the 'usual channels'. He had already received an icy rebuff from the Adjutant General in Calcutta; one which could not be described by any stretch of the imagination as within the bounds of 'civility'. It was a warning of which Churchill had taken heed. He could not afford at this stage of his career to affront his seniors, and he may have been dimly aware that many of those at home who responded so amiably to his mother's appeals on his behalf acted for her sake, and not for his. The day would come when he would need goodwill on his own account.

Meanwhile Colonel Hamilton had approached Captain Haldane, Sir William Lockhart's aide, and a man of unusual influence in the army. Haldane had been non-committal. 'He is not friendly towards you, neither is he hostile,' Hamilton wrote. To Churchill it was a challenge he must accept. Once satisfied that Haldane could achieve the impossible if he would, Churchill embarked for Peshawar without seeking permission from his Colonel. It was a calculated risk, and he took it boldly. With no more than forty-hours remaining of a short leave it would be impossible for him to regain his regiment on time in the event of failure. A severe reprimand, almost certainly prejudicial to his career, would be the result. He still needed the army and the privileged opportunities it afforded to him while establishing himself as a writer and war correspondent. He would burn his boats in his own time.

Nevertheless on the face of it he had less than an even chance of success with Haldane, and his extreme perseverance looks rather like obstinacy. His chances, he knew, must depend mainly on the personal impression he would make, and he was becoming well aware that he often made a very bad impression, and that Haldane was probably aware of his reputation for being self-assertive and pushing. But this could be an advantage.

Haldane's greeting was 'none too cordial', but he was ready to listen to all that Churchill had to say. Together they paced up and down outside Haldane's tent for half an hour while Churchill put his case in a restrained and straightforward way. Haldane was a dedicated soldier. Churchill was not. From all that Haldane said afterwards—and he was always rather reticent on the subject of Churchill—it is almost certain that Churchill ruthlessly pruned his argument of any suggestion that the adventure he desired would be useful to his military career. After half an hour Haldane left Churchill alone on the gravel path with a 'fast beating heart', and went in to the Commander-in-Chief. A few minutes later Churchill was on the personal staff of Sir William Lockhart, his regiment and the government of India informed, and nothing more to worry about. He had few illusions as to the impression his behaviour would make on his brother officers. It was unfortunate, but as he saw it, unavoidable.

The Tirah campaign petered out prematurely, but the exercise in pursuing his own course had been of great value. He learned a great deal. He behaved himself, and cultivated Haldane with extraordinary care against the future. A few months later he was to continue on his chosen course with an audacity and brazen effrontery for which it is hard to find a parallel. Neither Lord Roberts, nor Sir Herbert Kitchener, nor Haldane, nor his brother officers, nor indeed anyone else whom he encountered could put him out of countenance, nor, it seemd, discomfort him in the least degree. There is no doubt at all that his contemporaries regarded him as a poisonous young man, and he was well aware of it.

### III

Churchill's brief attachment to the Tirah expedition on the personal staff of Sir William Lockhart marks an important stage in his career, and in his personal development. Probably the writing of *The Malakand Field Force* had convinced him of his latent ability as a writer and war correspondent, and *Savrola* had cleared his mind. Now it was vital to make the greatest possible use of his birth, his contacts, and his mother's tremendous support in the background, and by these means to gain experience, to seek adventure and material for a stream of articles and books, and to use his 'military career', while it lasted, to these ends. He sailed dangerously close to the wind, but with all his senses alert for the sudden gust that might blow him off course, or even on to the rocks.

When he took train to Peshawar to beard Haldane outside his den, he knew the course he wished to steer, and he seems to have taken heed of the passage in Gibbon's autobiography which reads:

'Wherever the distinction of birth is allowed to form a superior order in the state, education and example should always, and will often, produce among them a dignity of sentiment and propriety of conduct, which is guarded from dishonour by their own and the public esteem.'

Whatever the inspiration, Churchill's conduct and bearing were exemplary, and he made a lasting good impression on the man whose shoulders were to serve him as springboard to success in his escape from the Boers. Yet, in spite of all Churchill's abuses, General Sir Aylmer Haldane commented fifty years later on those distant days without a trace of malice.

'I cannot recall,' he wrote,[1] 'exactly how long he [Churchill] remained with us at a time when the activities of the Tirah Field Force had practically come to an end. The period, however, was quite long enough to allow one to form an opinion of the young cavalry officer who was widely regarded in the army as super precocious, indeed by some as insufferably bumptious, and realize that neither of these epithets was applicable to him. On the contrary, my distinct recollection of him at this time was that he was modest and paid attention to what was said, not attempting to monopolize the conversation or thrust his opinions—and clearcut opinions they were on many subjects—on his listeners. He enjoyed giving vent to his views on matters military and other, but there was nothing that could be called aggressive or selfassertive which could have aroused antagonism among the most sensitive of those with whom he was talking.'

It is clear that Churchill had discovered that blend of his characteristics which made him often a delightful companion. Those few who had the good fortune to meet him in the course of this brief episode had the rare experience of enjoying his very great charm, his boyish enthusiasms, his enormous zest and appetite for life, all in themselves the most infectious and stimulating of traits. It was for them, as well as for him, a pleasing interlude. He was a visitor, a guest rather than a competitor in the military sphere. His ambitions did not concern his companions in the smallest degree, and his behaviour could not throw additional burdens upon them, nor be a source of envy, nor, above all, did he hold a mirror to their eyes into which they would have preferred not to peer.

Churchill, knowing his true course, did not attempt to conceal it from Haldane, who understood quite clearly that 'he had no intention of making the army his profession'.

Shortly after the close of the Tirah campaign, Haldane met Dr Welldon, Churchill's Headmaster at Harrow, at that time taking up his duties as Bishop of Calcutta.

'Talking to me one day,' Haldane recalled, 'he said that he had birched him [Churchill] more frequently than any other boy, but with little effect. This obstreperous, irresponsible pupil had managed to express himself regarding the Head—I imagine in covert terms—in the school magazine; and he added to these

[1] *A Soldier's Saga.*

interesting disclosures, to my amusement, that on one occasion Churchill had even had the audacity to tell him how to perform his duties.'

Haldane would frequently express himself in private in forceful terms about Churchill's subsequent behaviour, but he was never blind to his qualities. Both Welldon and Haldane believed in Churchill's brilliant future, and both predicted a great political career for him even at that early stage. Haldane wrote in his diary that he thought Churchill would be leader of the House of Commons, and probably Secretary of State for India within ten years. The young man must have been very honest during his stay with the Tirah. Undoubtedly his brief exercise in discretion and good manners, so very rarely to be observed, had given him added confidence. Henceforth his behaviour seems to have been most skilfully calculated to achieve his ends, for he would cultivate some of his immediate seniors of comparatively junior rank, while seemingly indifferent to the shocking impression he made upon such giants in the military firmament as Kitchener, Roberts and Redvers Buller. These were old, some of them nearing the end. He was at the beginning.

Immediately following his return to England from his experiences with the Tirah Force, Churchill acted with a ruthlessness and resolution revealing a clear purpose, and a disregard of persons, startling, and even shocking, in a young man not yet twenty-four years old. One wonders at the sources of such an alarming self-confidence, for they are not obvious. He was no longer feeling his way. His mind was made up. He had resolved to help his regiment to win the India inter-regimental Polo Cup in 1899, to resign his commission, to look for an opening into Parliament, and meanwhile to gain all possible experience as a writer and war correspondent.

To carry out this plan he intended, whatever the difficulties in his way, to report the Sudan campaign, about to move into its most important phase under Sir Herbert Kitchener, Sirdar of the Egyptian Army. This would enable him to consolidate his name as a writer with a grasp of strategy and politics. He was already aware of what he calls Kitchener's 'disproportionate opposition', and had already aroused widespread and intense dislike throughout the army.

It was clear that Kitchener disapproved strongly of Churchill, and was frankly hostile to his advancement. He had been adamant even in the face of a personal appeal by letter from Lady Randolph. It may seem strange that anyone in a position as exalted as Kitchener's should have cared one way or the other about the attachment of a very junior officer to his forces. How had Churchill managed so swiftly to achieve so fearful a reputation? Certainly neither his name nor his work could justify such a situation. His name was good, his despatches excellent, his book precocious but masterly, his ambitions in no wise a threat to the careers of his brother officers, nor a probable source of embarrassment to his superiors.

But the Sudan campaign had aroused Churchill's emotions as well as his ambitions, and he would never take no for an answer. Gordon's death at Khartoum at the hands of the Mahdi in 1884 lived in the galleries of his mind along with names like Majuba, crying for vengeance. Nothing should stand in his way. Taking advantage of Lord Salisbury's expressed admiration for his story of the Malakand Force, and the family friendship, he conducted himself with great circumspection in an interview with the most powerful man in England, and at once, through the good offices of Sir Schomberg M'Donnell, the Prime Minister's private secretary, enlisted his personal support

Surely even the proud and obstinate Sirdar would bow gracefully to wishes (of so unimportant a nature) expressed from this most exalted quarter! For, as Churchill wrote, Salisbury was 'The Great Man, Master of the British World, the unchallenged leader of the Conservative Party, a third time Prime Minister and Foreign Secretary at the height of his long career....'

That Kitchener not only maintained but underlined his refusal in a 'sour reply' stating that there were no vacancies, and if there should be any at any time 'the young officer in question' would not be preferred, is a kind of triumph of peculiar distinction for a mere youth, a lieutenant in the 4th Hussars, a failure at school, and crammed into the army at the third attempt.

Churchill was undaunted and undismayed. He approached Lady Jeune, an old family friend, the wife of Sir Francis Jeune, a distinguished judge, and a woman of great influence, especially in military circles through her friendship with Sir Evelyn Wood, the Adjutant-General. Fortunately for Churchill, Kitchener's high-handed methods had irritated the War Office. A word at the right moment, carefully stressing the sympathy of the Prime

Minister, brought success. Sir Evelyn Wood found a loophole. In good time for the campaign, Churchill was outward bound at his own expense as a supernumerary lieutenant with the 21st Lancers. He had also arranged with Algernon Borthwick, of the *Morning Post*, to send despatches at £15 a column in addition to a modest commitment for the *Pioneer* of India. Some financial success was essential if he was to stand for Parliament.

Thus Churchill, a young man with a great name, a poor record and an unpleasant reputation, aided by a beautiful mother of extraordinary diligence and resource, prevailed against the expressed will of a famous commander-in-chief of exceptional power and obstinacy.

# CHAPTER VI

❦

THE Sudan campaign marks the opening of a new phase in Churchill's career. He knew clearly what he intended to do, and why. He would pursue his course with the ruthless, but flexible, determination of a free adventurer who knows no duty greater than to himself. He knew that he was enormously privileged, and would have deemed himself a fool—if such a thought had been possible to him—not to have taken full advantage of his position.

In his preliminary canters he had discovered his strengths, and some of his weaknesses. He had perceived that it might be possible for him to savour the full fruits of freedom without suffering its worst difficulties, sacrificing little more than the good opinions of those of his fellows whose lives were dedicated, unquestioningly, to service, duty and loyalty. Aristocrats and tramps, it has been said, are the last refugees of individualism and freedom. He combined them in himself.

While he would have preferred to be liked, and speculated mildly on the disapproval he aroused in many quarters, he assumed a peculiarity in others, not in himself. His egocentricity was his armour. Nevertheless he was careful to cultivate the good opinions of those who might be useful to him, and his behaviour could be not only impeccable but charming. His boyishness, which had in it both the innocence and barbarity of a child, was appealing and difficult to deny. His tremendous and obvious zest for life was infectious and often irresistible. His boorishness and total lack of consideration for the feelings of others were, he had discovered, equally irresistible. Immune to the iciest of rebuffs and the most deliberate of snubs, he intruded himself without apparent embarrassment into whatever company suited his convenience. If no one offered him a greeting, a place to sit, a drink, he helped himself and waited, not without amusement, for the ice to melt. He was impossible to ignore for long. Yet, it is difficult to believe him utterly insensitive. His childhood had been too solitary. In his very early schooldays he felt his isolation, a very small and lonely boy most bravely preserving his integrity, and refusing to be coerced by the birch most cruelly used against him.

Holidays would one day come, and he would be back with his friend in his nursery. All would be well.

Churchill's determination to witness the final destruction of the Mahdi, and the end of the savage Dervish Empire, was not merely the excessive obstinacy and arrogance of a young man opposing the excessive obstinacy and arrogance of a man of great power, vastly his senior in rank and years. Underlying all his exuberance and desire 'to see the fun', was a most serious purpose. He needed money. He wanted keenly to relieve his mother of the necessity to provide him with £500 a year, and he had good cause to believe that he could make a success of writing as a foundation for a political career. He had resolved to live by the pen and the sword as long as possible, and thereafter to write himself into politics.

In the Sudan he gained the basic material for his history of the River War, and enjoyed every moment of the mental and physical adventure. From a black spur of rock he observed the great mass of the Dervish army advancing over the plain, a black tide shot through with the glint of spears, an immense thunder cloud, turbulent and terrible and made of 100,000 men dedicated to death by the sword.

From the same vantage point he saw the brigades of the British and Egyptian army marching in open columns, the cavalry and the Camel Corps on the distant flank, the guns strung out in long lines, and on the Nile the white gunboats, the dhows and river craft heavily-laden with supplies.

With this picture indelibly in his mind for as long as he might live—and it might be no more than an hour, which is the bittersweet essence of war—he rode with the news to Kitchener's side without a qualm.

Perhaps one of the most remarkable things about this whole adventure is Churchill's attitude to Kitchener. He was entirely without awe of that formidable figure, and not in the least concerned to keep out of the Sirdar's way. He reported the state of the enemy with perfect aplomb, even making allowances for that soldier's dislike.

I have remarked earlier that he was endowed with a kind of *hubris*, and such episodes may be thought to justify my use of the word. On the other hand, one is drawn constantly to the eternal child in Churchill, the child who puts his hand into an adult hand without a thought, not questioning that it will be accepted, the child who, bearing no malice, conceives of none, the rebuke of the night forgotten by morning, an ephemeral thing of yesterday, and of no more consequences. Perhaps that, too, is a kind of *hubris*, common to many children and out of which they normally grow.

It did not occur to Churchill ever to avoid anyone. If they did not like him, it was not only unfortunate for them, but curious. No doubt they would get over it. You, whosoever you were, would best become accustomed to his presence. He would always be there, if he so desired.

There was not to be a battle on the day that Churchill reported in person to the Sirdar, and for tens of thousands of men there would be yet another dawn. In the light of that dawn, with the desert sun behind him, Churchill saw again the Dervish host, and heard a long sustained growl swelling out of the desert as they proclaimed their God of Islam and his prophet. He had taken six men with him on his patrol, nevertheless he was alone ahead of them on a ridge between two spurs. 'This is an hour to live,' he wrote.

A few hours later, with all that dark host of the Mahdi torn to bleeding flesh and naked bone, Churchill charged with the 21st Lancers at Omdurman into one of the last living groups of the enemy, two or three thousand strong. The charge did not frighten men who had withstood the wild and ferocious onslaughts of Abyssinian horsemen. They stood their ground, taking a heavy toll of horses and men, an eye for an eye, a life for a life, the losses severe on either side.

Between them, but for the horses, there had been something near an equality of weapons for the last time in those particular phases of punitive Imperial warfare. When the onslaught was spent the Dervishes withdrew in good order.

Talk of fun! Where will you beat this! These are not the expressions of a boy reading *Treasure Island*, playing with mock weapons, but of a man, a statesman, more than thirty years later, savouring again the thrills of those golden days. 'Twenty to twenty-five, those are the years!' A man who had seen the bleeding bowels of men, the breasts pierced through with spears, the hacked limbs, the shattered heads and faces half shot away, and known all the stench of blood and human offal in his nostrils. He was not a stranger to the butchered bodies of men plucked by the vultures, nor unmindful of the widows and orphans.

Many were shocked by his constant use of the word 'fun' to describe his reaction to war and battle. Some noted that he continued to use the word throughout his life. But it was an honest word, honestly used. Perhaps he was unfortunate in that his imagination did not dwell upon wounds, and tortured bodies ugly in the rigours of death, but he faced these things squarely according to his nature, nor ever sought to minimize the horrors, the cruelties, and the ultimate squalor and hideous face of war.

Fun is the expression of a boy; there's the rub. Arthur uses it in that great tragi-comedy of T. H. White's[1] in his first battles against Lot of Orkney. But Arthur used the word with the thoughtlessness of a boy. He was slow-witted and slow to think, but when he was rebuked by Merlin, reminded of the swollen bellies soon to burst, the legs upthrust in grotesque and hideous symbols from pond, dyke and ditch, reminded, too, of the widows and orphans, Arthur used the word no more. He needed Merlin to stoke the fires of his slow, but honest, wits, to spur his mind to think, to prick the springs of his compassion. Arthur was merely a thoughtless youth and slow in his growing-up.

But for Churchill it was always fun. He did not seek to hide the realities under cloaks of glamour, nor could a Merlin have reminded him of any detail of horror. It was simply that he did not *feel* the weight of sorrow and tragedy. He wrote with passion, but was always a stranger to compassion. As soon blame a man for that as blame a man for being born with one eye, or without his toes.

When the campaign was over Churchill took the trouble to study the background, and had the good sense and fortune to consult Lord Cromer on the content and style of his early chapters. This saved him from some of the errors and ill-considered judgments of youth, and gave his work a certain gravity it might otherwise have lacked. In his exuberance with the magic of words, inspired by the awesome grandeur of the desert and the Blue Nile he almost wrote that great river into the scorching sands, to shimmer, colourless, a mirage. Nevertheless, the book was im-

[1] *The Sword in the Stone.*

pressive, revealing a cool and lucid grasp of essentials, and written with restraint as well as with pleasure.

G. W. Steevens, the brilliant and experienced correspondent of the *Daily Mail*, met Churchill on his journey home, and remarked his joy in the writing. It was his strength and his weakness. He would not chain his mind to tedious labours inseparable from scholarship, for work must always be 'fun' too. That was the irreparable loss to him of his wasted schooldays, for he had failed to learn the one vital lesson, seldom to be learned in later life, of sticking to work one does not like, day after day until, wonderfully, one comes to understand, to appreciate, if not thoroughly to enjoy in the sense of 'fun'.

Churchill felt his lack of scholarship in his first political contacts with highly cultivated minds, and found, somewhat to his dismay, that it was impossible to do late what he had failed to do early. The 'Merlins' of Cambridge were not for him. Yet he was, in fact, far better read than most of his contemporaries, and with his prodigious memory he was under no real handicap with any man.

In that year of 1899 he had not only contrived to lay the foundations of his literary fortunes, to play for his regiment and help to win the India Polo Cup, but also to make a first sortie into politics. In the spring of the year he fought a by-election at Oldham in the Conservative cause, losing narrowly and arousing fears in the minds of his political chiefs that Lord Randolph's spirit might live again in his son. Churchill, like his father, thought for himself, and revealed that brand of *gaminerie* that had stuck in the flabby guts of Tory mediocrity and led to the political destruction of Lord Randolph. Not for nothing had Lord Randolph sparked his 'Fourth Party' to torment his own front bench, and attempted to broaden the base of the party. He had invented 'Tory Democracy', that brand of democracy, as he remarked naïvely, which votes Tory.

Even more than his father, Churchill was his own man in politics as in all else. He would be on the winning side, the only possible side for one who believed that power was his destiny. He had that true joy in living which comes, as Shaw wrote, from 'being used for a purpose, recognized by yourself as a mighty one'. He was also a man of courage, a virtue esteemed above all by Bunyan. Few doubted that he would become a power in politics in the years immediately ahead, but on which side?

Churchill gained valuable experience in this first venture. Had he succeeded it would have been somewhat premature, for his fortunes were not yet sufficiently established, and it was in his nature to burst like a bomb upon the political scene. He perceived at once, but it did not worry him unduly, that he had begun to make enemies in wider spheres. In writing of this many years later, with the utmost frankness he commented, not without a glint in his eye: 'It is melancholy to be forced to record these less amiable aspects of human nature, which by a most curious and indeed unaccountable coincidence have always seemed to present themselves in the wake of my innocent footsteps, and even sometimes across the path on which I wished to proceed.'

He was one of the greatest side-steppers of all time, gathering strength in the quiet pools, always alert, using himself to the full in one way or another, but ready and resolved to leap the cataracts ahead.

Arthur Balfour, he knew, regarded his effort at Oldham more in sorrow than in anger, and had a genuine liking for him. There was nothing to worry about. Later in the year he walked with the 'outsider' Joe Chamberlain on the lawns of Lady Jeune's riverside house, noting the 'bundle of old clothes' that was all that was left (so they said) of Labouchére, the flaming radical, the bearer of many torches. Perhaps, had he walked with any man but Chamberlain, Churchill might have talked with profit to the dweller within the bundle of old clothes, the founder of *Truth*, the onetime diplomat and politician whose experiences embraced the Turkish Empire, and the Balkan States in the mid-nineteenth century, and the Jameson Raid at its end.

But the powerful scent of the Boer War was on the wind, and the enemy of Rosebery and Chamberlain might have given it a bitter tang, for which at that time Churchill was in no mood.

Meanwhile he had corrected the proofs of his *River War*, and soon it would help greatly to consolidate his position as a war correspondent and writer. When the chance came late in 1899 he could command the then magnificent sum of £250 a month from the *Morning Post* for his services in the field. He could afford to fit a false bottom to his travelling waggon, and stuff it with good liquor to the floorboards. And how should men die better! He could not hope to match the experience of G. W. Steevens of the *Mail*, nor the erudition and political integrity of

D

his old senior at school, Leo Amery, but he had a zest and a gift for the vivid phrase that struck sparks from the rusted anvils of mediocre and dull minds, and even informed the scholarly and wise. He was in a happier rôle. He had resigned from the army, and was less likely to make enemies amongst his new companions. They were accustomed to eccentrics, as well as to the self-assertive and pushing. He was not unwelcome in the tents of the war correspondents.

Soon Churchill was forcing himself ruthlessly upon poor old Lord Roberts, and faintly amused by the Field Marshal's embarrassment and discomfort in his presence. Like everyone else, Lord Roberts would doubtless get used to him in time. Churchill was unable to conceive any other remedy. Not for a moment did it occur to him to look into himself for a cause, perhaps a solution. He was as he was. The world could not take him or leave him: it must take him. He was a free man, an adventurer born, a maverick outside the docile herd, a constant menace to the drovers. But it is unlikely that he knew it.

## II

In 1930, in one of his rare periods of reappraisal, Churchill looked back on these early years. He was fifty-six years old. Parliament had rejected him, and his name throughout the country did not bring back a clear and unequivocal echo, his image was blurred; startling, amusing, sinister. Like his father, he had worn the robes of the Chancellor of the Exchequer, and had gone thereafter into the political wilderness. Unlike his father, he was not the victim of a fell and terrible disease and doomed to die, nor did he suffer from any clearly discernible political principles. His health was excellent.

Perhaps, as he looked back, he had his first real doubts of his destiny. Amery, who had observed him from his schooldays, and with a cool objectivity, knew that he had always 'a conscious fitness to lead', but thought that 'even his own confidence in his star must at times have been seriously shaken'. But Amery had not served with him in the army, nor had Churchill's long flirtation with liberalism troubled Amery's staunch and flexible intellectual conservatism.

At that time England was in dire need of a leader to rally the country to meet the acute crises of peace. There was no one in all

Europe to match the stature of Lloyd George. His genius and dynamic energy had brought victory for England in the most devastating and terrible war in history. His great acumen and political foresight might have cleansed away the bitter dregs of the aftermath. His political courage might have steered England through the miserable shoals of the next decade, but Lloyd George 'at that moment,' wrote Amery, 'lay helpless under the surgeon's knife.'

No one, not even Churchill, imagined at that hour that he might be the man. He had not fallen 'like Lucifer, never to hope again'. Simply he had fallen. His voice and his talents might rally a nation to war, but not to peace. He was about to embark upon the most ambitious and scholarly literary work of his career, his life of Marlborough. It would be a labour of love. It might be history. He would also lay the foundations of the future for himself.

But the powerful dislike he had created for himself in his early days still lived and confronted him, not in the frames of little men, wasted and embittered by a loathing and contempt so long sustained, but in men of his age and older, as hearty as himself, alert of eye, brilliant in wit and achievement. It puzzled him. He could not account for it. It would endure to the end, and beyond the end, stoked constantly by his deeds, aggravated, it might be, by some fatal flaw in his character.

The very serious 'resistances' he had encountered in his endeavours to join Kitchener's forces in the Sudan led him to wonder what was the matter with people, but not with himself. At the outset of his army career he had met with nothing but friendship and encouragement. Now, a year or two later, 'The first stage was over,' he wrote. 'I now perceive that there were many ill-informed and ill-disposed people who did not take a favourable view of my activities. On the contrary, they began to develop an adverse and even a hostile attitude.'

Churchill's regiment had been very 'nice' to him when he had finally taken his leave of them. They had drunk his health, but he could have been in little doubt that they were glad to see the back of him.

What the devil could it all mean? He knew that he was self-assertive and threw his weight about, but how else could a subaltern with his ambitions, and lack of funds, hope to succeed! It meant a great deal of leave. It meant the avoidance of routine duties, but how else could he report campaigns in which his regiment was not engaged? It did not seem to occur to him that he was brazenly using the army for his own purposes, and that the army did not like being used in such a fashion, especially by a young man curiously without tact and, as the Spaniards say, *sin verguenza*.

Churchill provoked intense dislike in almost everyone who had the misfortune to serve with him, and it has remained a source of some astonishment to many that his behaviour was tolerated. It was tolerated because it had to be, because there was also a fascination about Churchill, his urgent boyishness, a sense of exhilaration that could endow the lemonade of life with the qualities of champagne, and it was tolerated because he was in a curious way too vulnerable. Yet for ordinary men, subscribing to, or not questioning, conventional principles, prejudices and duties, and unwritten codes of loyalty, Churchill posed an intolerable problem. For ordinary men have no armour with which to defend themselves against the ruthless and unscrupulous adventurer, disguised in their clothing over what appears to be the hide of a rhinoceros.

It is far too simple and misleading simply, as some have done, to brand Churchill as a cad, and his various collections of cronies a 'cadocracy'. The word does not fit him, especially in its late Victorian and Edwardian significance. He was meticulous in his financial affairs, and in his behaviour towards women. Nor had he the hide of a rhinoceros. He was frequently hurt as a child is hurt when adults chide him for rudeness, treat him with a coldness amounting to cruelty, or have no time or patience to indulge his play. Churchill often sulked. But like a child he always came back, yesterday forgotten, sure that he must have chosen a bad moment, that he would be accepted with smiles, not wondering whether you like him or not.

Such behaviour is vastly aggravating in an adult body, and puts the burden of rudeness, even of brutality, upon others, themselves sensitive; or acceptance of the unwanted company. Churchill often made those who did not want his company feel 'beastly'.

If it is accepted that Churchill was an adventurer in his nature, it would have been impossible as well as ridiculous for him to be scrupulous in pursuing his ambitions. A scrupulous adventurer would be as hopelessly disadvantaged as a scrupulous woman in her pursuit of life and fulfilment. Churchill's ruthlessness and lack of scruple were of that feminine order, and an integral part of him. These qualities coupled with his bogus grown-upness (which some have mistaken for bogus male-ness) were lifelong characteristics. Those who saw in him a feminine streak err. He had certain feminine traits allied to an extreme Narcissism, a sign of his lust for power. His close and particular alliance with women from the cradle, and his exclusion from real contact with his father, endowed him with a kind of feminine guile.

Probably the only human being he ever understood was Mrs Everest, and but for his mother, and later on his wife, the loss of Mrs Everest might have been irreparable. He could never, especially at the height of his power, do without such a figure.

But in the early days the dislike of many stemmed also from envy, and the plain fact that Churchill was not a true adventurer and did not play the game according to the rules. The dice were too heavily loaded in his favour. He was an outsider who would not stay outside, scoffing at the rigid conventions and duties which held his companions bound within the herd, himself enjoying all the advantages of freedom, yet demanding the protection of the herd, its warmths, its comforts; not even, in truth, bothering to demand, but merely unquestioningly accepting that these abandoned rights were still his. Thus he was a traitor at once to 'aristocrats and tramps'. Instead of breaking the 'navel string' he sought to strengthen it, maintaining his lines of communication and retreat, and establishing a safe base at home.

Because of these things Churchill's freedom was never total. Had it been so, men might have followed his varied adventures and the fulfilment of his ambitions with pleasure, excitement and admiration. Instead, he expected also the rewards of the duties he ignored, of the patient labours at which he scoffed, of services he would not give. How dared he to hanker after the insignia, the privileges, the rôle of a general officer without undergoing the long routine of soldiering, the usual ordeal of the warrior, of competing with his fellows, of taking his place in the queue!

Even so, a deeper truth may be that Churchill held a mirror to his contemporaries into which they disliked to gaze. His insistence on freedom emphasized their bondage. Constantly by his antics he drew attention to the prisons of convention, duty and discipline—even of fear—in which they lived, and which they preferred to deny. He made nonsense of their pretences to freedom and liberty, and at the same time he did not take the social and conventional risks inseparable from the life of a true adventurer. He had a need for danger, at least as great as hunger and thirst: he courted danger in place of women, his emotions too strong and insistent to be stilled.

It is the Englishman's disease to prefer illusions to reality. The docile herd hates and envies its outlaws, and hates all other forms of slavery than its own. It lives within a cage bounded by its laws and conventions, constantly making new rules to strengthen the bars, terrified even to discover that there is an 'outside', and hating those who not only escape—which is an insult—but even more those very few who by some rare privilege of birth and personality hold pass keys to both worlds.

To paraphrase Shaw, a man instinctively disparages the quality which makes another dangerous to him, and instinctively flatters the fault that renders him harmless. Churchill's behaviour amused dedicated soldiers, not too senior in years, like Haldane and Hamilton. It did not matter to them if he wanted to be a general as well as a politician, a war correspondent and adventurer. They had chosen their way and he his. But such men are rare; seldom to be found in the ranks of the young in the early stages of following their careers. He reminded his brother officers at Bangalore that their freedom was a myth. He did not conceal his contempt for 'plodders'. They did not suffer him gladly.

It is remarkable how widely cads are tolerated in every walk of life. The cad, the pusher, the shameless one, always wins. He is immune to all non-violent measures, and I think it is clear that whether you are Lord Roberts or Kitchener, or Hugo Baring, or Reginald Barnes sharing quarters, the only thing you can do with the Churchills of this world is to resort to violence. But such a course is intolerable in itself, and often hopeless. One may be too old, too young, too small or too big. Most people are certain to dislike brawling. Thus one sees the incorrigible cad continuing on his chosen road, untroubled, often sublimely unaware, callous of the corns upon which he treads, unmindful of the nerves he lacerates.

It was a great, if temporary, relief to many when Churchill resigned his commission in the army and catapulted himself into the Boer War and politics.

## III

In the Boer War Churchill found his feet, found his seat in the House of Commons, found his audience and laid the foundations of his legend. Whether on or off the stage, whether hissed or applauded, he would hold his audience for half a century. They would never cease to be aware of him, to be aroused by his name, delighted or distracted by his antics, to be angered and dismayed by his irresponsibility, his unpredictability, to be stimulated often against their judgment by his words and deeds. Such a figure, it may be, was necessary to the times he lived in, a child of the century, as adaptable as a chameleon.

Yet never throughout all the years of his virtuoso performance would he arouse unstinted admiration, or still the doubts of his reliability, to bring the whole audience to its feet in acclaim devoid of reservation, until forty years on, in that hour when his audience would become one with him, identified with him, no longer as audience but as a great supporting cast, a 'Greek Chorus'. In that hour he had ceased to be an actor, for all were actors in the living drama of a fight for survival. It was a triumph, when it came, of a man become miraculously whole, at one with his destiny, integral with life and death, a triumph surpassing, it may be, in its total quality all that had gone before, not only in the history of England, but in the story of the world. Not even Shakespeare had written or imagined such a part, and only a Shakespeare might have done for him what, had he been a dramatist, he might almost have done for himself. For a time his fellow countrymen, stirred by his vocal images kindling real deeds, became all Shakespeares, their realities suddenly become manifest in the thrilling words of Henry V, or the pungent deadly gloatings of Richard III.

But the Boer War through which Churchill burst upon a wider scene was itself a play within a play, a prologue, a foretaste of things to come, a dress rehearsal of the first importance which would reveal the inadequacy of the performers and all the 'props' of war and diplomacy, and which would pitchfork Britain into the twentieth century with better hopes of survival. It was played out before a tremendous and variously fascinated audience, almost a world audience, roused to a startling and sustained hysteria in England itself, revealing long pent-up emotions difficult to assess, perhaps a manifestation of a deep hunger for violence in one of the most inhibited races on earth, obedient, hypocritical, strangers to revolution for centuries.

Abroad, in the United States of America, in all Western Europe, in Germany in particular, it aroused anger, bitterness and hate, no less revealing of long suppressed attitudes of envy of a British supremacy so long sustained, infuriating in its growing pomposity and benevolence. While old Redvers Buller, the general who had 'plodded on from blunder to blunder' and thus had won a revered place in British affections, showed himself virtually incapable in the field, supported by a War Office asleep, or dozing, since Waterloo, half the world licked its lips in anticipation of witnessing the pricking of the British bubble of power by a bunch of Boer sharpshooters, thumping Bibles and intoning terrible passages of the Old Testament as an accompaniment to the most accurate shooting any troops had ever faced.

Many were waiting to tear at the flanks of a moth-eaten British lion, an exhausted old bogus man-eater, pathetic and ridiculous, gravely harassed and peering myopically at its hard riding, marvellously mobile and deadly enemies. But the great empires of the world do not fall in such a fashion; their ends are neither farce nor comic opera, but tragedy. While the world observed, contributing its jeers, but wary of open threats, many of the subtleties of the performance were missed. Britain was slowly learning, painfully but surely, the new techniques of warfare, which she would soon have to put into effect. She learned sluggishly at the cost of many lives, but at first hand, and marginally better than others.

Buller and Roberts were in leading rôles in the field for their farewell appearances, complete with all the elaborate and sumptuous paraphernalia and trappings of the past, like the potentates they were. Kitchener, ruthless and humourless behind his luxurious moustache, was ready to take over their rôles, supported by good men whose names have mostly disappeared entirely from the public mind.

These were confronted by the sombre bearded figures of Botha and Piet Joubert, Cronje and Christian de Wet, Paul Kruger and Koos de la Rey, all of them 'improperly dressed'. And in the ranks of the Boers was young Jan Smuts, who would have been astonished to know that a British Field Marshal's baton was 'in his knapsack'.

Ian Hamilton was there, become a general, and so was Captain

Haldane. French, Haig and Allenby were among those in junior rôles, having the first glimpses of the 'lines' they would need to inscribe on their hearts and souls as well as on their minds before they were done.

Milner was High Commissioner in the Cape, and Cecil Rhodes would be ready to welcome French at last into Kimberley, while Baden Powell, a showman to rival Churchill himself, would print his image on postage stamps in Mafeking, and link his name not only with Boy Scouts, but with a new word to describe outbreaks of hysteria, usually associated with victory in war or battle.

At home in England, Joe Chamberlain pulled most of the strings, while Lloyd George, and that animated 'bundle of old clothes', Labouchére, cried 'Go for Joe!' and suffered the brickbats and assaults of war-mad mobs, until they prevailed.

Such was the cast of players to usher out the old century and usher in the new, and Churchill would outlive them all, outplay them all, doomed to live beyond his hour, denied the hero's death that must have started half a world in tears to his obsequies.

For Churchill the Boer War became a series of *tours des forces*. He rode upon successive waves of adventure with unfailing èlan, and a flair for being in the right places at the right time. Even when he appeared to make an unfortunate choice it turned out to his special advantage. He rode with fortune, always in the main stream of colourful events, a sombre and careful observer of disaster, a jubilant partaker of victory. He rode with despatches from Hamilton's column to Lord Roberts's tent; with his cousin, the Duke of Marlborough, galloping at his side he brought the news of the surrender of Pretoria. In between he had seen much action. He had been captured, and escaped. He had observed at first hand the tragedy of Spion Kop while 'the greater part of Buller's army of 30,000 men stood idly by',[1] and Buller himself, 'blinded by fury', recalled the one battalion that might have averted the final disaster.

Churchill had arrived in South Africa heralded by a letter from Chamberlain to Milner, recommending 'a very clever young fellow with many of his father's qualifications. He has the reputation of being bumptious, but I have not myself found him so. ... He wants to be in Parliament, but want of means stands in his way.'

The means were not wanting for long. Churchill's personal

[1] Rayne Kruger, *Goodbye, Dollie Gray*.

stage was filled with a galaxy of part players. His brother Jack was there, as well as the Duke of Marlborough. His mother, Lady Randolph Churchill, had been the inspiration behind the organization of an American hospital ship, and sailed with the ship to South Africa, herself touring some of the battlefields and becoming, perhaps, the first of the 'Stars' to write her name on a piece of high explosive to be hurled at the enemy. A 4.7 inch gun mounted in a railway truck was christened the 'Lady Randolph Churchill', and first opened fire on a low kopje at 5,300 yards. The cartridge case was sent to Lady Randolph as a memento.

The financing and equipping of the hospital ship *Maine* was a fine piece of organization. Lady Randolph was chairman of the committee, supported by Churchills and Jeromes, the Duchess of Marlborough, Lily, Duchess of Marlborough, Mrs Moreton Frewen and Mrs Jack Leslie, and others, including Mrs Joseph Chamberlain and the Countess of Essex. The ship did good service and helped to keep the Churchill name in the public eye. But the spotlight never moved for long from the dashing figure of Churchill himself, the war correspondent carrying all the 'guns' of privilege, and the immense advantage of having been so recently a soldier himself, and only too willing to act in a dual rôle whenever the chance occurred.

Nevertheless his fellows did not regard him with malice or envy, for many of them were men of stature, including Leo Amery, Rudyard Kipling, Edgar Wallace and H. A. Gwynne, later editor of the *Morning Post*, in the British contingent. It was the first war to grip the imagination of almost a world public. It saw the advent of the cinematograph camera, and brought some of the actual scenes of war before the eyes of civilians.

## IV

Little purpose could be served by following in any detail Churchill's brilliant course through the long-drawn-out war, but it may be of value to examine briefly, in the light of General Sir Aylmer Haldane's belated testimony, the two major episodes which led directly to his first real financial success and his entry into politics. It was Churchill's courage and resource in the famous Boer ambush of the armoured train, followed a few weeks later by his escape from his captors, which lit the popular admiration and acclaim which carried him on its crest to Parliament.

Churchill's detractors, questioning the accuracy of his personal accounts of his adventures, incensed perhaps by a lack of modesty in the hero, were swiftly silenced by the issue of a sheaf of writs. Fifty years went by before Haldane, an intimate observer and principal actor in the same scenes, contributed his own account. No two accounts of exactly the same events ever match, however accurate the observation of those involved, and especially is this true of dangerous events in which the observers are personally involved. Certain events, even of a minor nature, imprint themselves upon the mind, while others of great portent are missed. A man lives his own life, and not another's.

Haldane, having befriended Churchill in the Tirah expedition, was ready to help his young friend again in South Africa. The two men met in South Africa as Haldane emerged 'feeling rather lugubrious', having received his orders to take the armoured train through to Chievely. Many of those in the know thought that 'the occupants were being sent to their death'.

'I told him what I had been ordered to do,' wrote Haldane, 'and aware that he had been out in the train and knew something of the country through which it was wont to travel, suggested that he might care to accompany me next day. Although he was not at all keen he consented to do so, and arranged to be at the station in time for the start.'

Haldane makes it clear that he wanted Churchill with him because he was a soldier, and not as a war correspondent. His offer was not open to others. It was almost certain to be a dangerous business and he didn't want onlookers. Thus, it seems evident, Churchill had not stolen a march upon Amery and his brother war correspondents. Churchill, always impishly quick to support his contention that bad luck could be turned to advantage, boasted to Amery some years later:

'If I had not been early, I should not have been caught. But if I had not been caught, I should not have escaped, and my imprisonment and my escape provided me with materials for lectures and a book which brought me in enough money to get into Parliament in 1900—ten years before you.'

The armoured train left Estcourt at 5 a.m., stopping at Frere before going on to Chievely, and Churchill had left his companions still sleeping in their tent when he ran down to the station to catch it. Shortly after leaving Frere, Haldane spotted some Boer waggons, stopped the train and sent Churchill to a vantage point to have a closer look through binoculars. Almost at once Haldane, detecting a movement nearer at hand, whistled his scout back. Churchill regained the train almost in a dead heat with a Boer shell which derailed an armoured waggon and a truck.

'Churchill, quick witted and cool, was speedily on his feet,' wrote Haldane.

Meanwhile, the Boers had blocked the line in the rear of the train, and while Haldane stayed forward to confront the main body of the ambushers, Churchill went back on his own initiative to save the train from complete disaster. On this Haldane reported:

'His self-selected task, into which he threw all his energy, was carried out with pluck and perseverance, and his example inspired the platelayers, the driver of the locomotive and others to work under the fire which the Boers were directing on the train.'

After more than an hour of struggling with the engine, hissing steam and with flames bursting from the fire-box, it finally got away laden with wounded. Churchill then began to make his way back to rejoin Haldane and 'see the fun'. According to his own account, he walked straight into the arms of Louis Botha, managed to rid himself of the ammunition which he had no right to be carrying (he had left his Mauser in the engine cab) and was soon herded with Haldane and the rest of the prisoners.

Churchill seems to have realized at once that his adventure might be a stroke of fortune.

'At the time we were all feeling, not unnaturally, very disconsolate,' Haldane wrote. 'But Churchill must have been cheered by the thought, which he communicated to me, that what had taken place, though it had caused the temporary loss of his post as war correspondent, would help considerably in opening the door for him to enter the House of Commons. As we trudged along wearily over the damp veldt he remarked to me that in allotting him what I might call the "star turn", I had effaced myself, while his work of clearing the line had brought him into prominence and in full view of the Durban Light Infantry and the railway personnel, and that those of them who had escaped on the engine would not fail to make the most of what they had seen when they got back to Estcourt.'

It had been a great piece of luck for Churchill to play his brave and resolute part before an audience, and Haldane, amused rather than offended by Churchill's frank delight in the probable 'headlines' that would greet his adventure, nonetheless lamented the impulse that had induced him to offer his 'impetuous young friend' a ride on the train. He would, perhaps, have proceeded with more caution left to himself, but Churchill, he observes, was prompted always by Danton's motto, *de l'audace, et encore l'audace, et toujours de l'audace*.

The remarkable feature of Haldane's account of the adventure is that it agrees so well with Churchill's, but it should not be a matter for undue surprise that the accounts of the escape in the Haldane and Churchill versions differ widely. Enemies of Churchill swear by the Haldane version; friends of Churchill feel that Haldane (not without reason) must have taken a somewhat jaundiced view. Fortunately, I have an intimate friend of long standing who was also an intimate friend of the two characters most closely involved. He has heard the story on various occasions from the lips of both men, as well as having read their accounts. Himself an admirer of Haldane, and with few illusions about Churchill, he none the less accepts Churchill's account of his escape from the Model Schools as 'the truth', knowing well the many-sided nature of these kinds of truth. Whatever Churchill's faults, I have little doubt in my own mind that he was a 'born' reporter. In reporting himself and his own deeds, as he did with sustained exuberance throughout his life, he is at times guilty of embroideries and suppressions, but he was a genuinely brave man, and as such he could be satisfied to write the truth as he saw and experienced it. In other fields, in his relationships with others, he is less reliable.

But there can be little doubt that when he insisted on becoming part of the escape plans of Haldane and Sergeant-Major Brockie, his presence did prejudice greatly the chances of his companions. In the first place, Churchill was very much in the Boer eye, and would certainly be missed almost at once.

'With Brockie only as an associate there was nothing to fear, but with another accomplice, and he the impulsive and talkative Churchill, the matter wore a very different aspect,' Haldane wrote.

Again, Lieutenant Frankland's[1] diary, under date December 15th, records:

'First, and most important of all, Churchill has escaped. Whether he has made it good or not is still uncertain; but he has now gone two days, and I have great hopes. Besides the excitement there has been a very amusing side to the affair. Of course, Churchill was the very last person who ought to have gone. He was always talking and arguing with officials, and was therefore well known and, indeed, scarcely a day passed without Dr Gunning or Mr de Souza inquiring for him.'

De Souza was the Boer Secretary of War, and Churchill involved him constantly in 'animated discussion about the causes and justice of the war'.

But the aspect of the affair that was above all an irritant to Haldane and Brockie was that Churchill as a war correspondent was almost certain to be released anyway within a day or two. Many stated that General Joubert had dubiously accepted Churchill's non-combatant status, and had the order to release him a day or two after his escape. Joubert may well have found it difficult to equate the varied accounts of Churchill's bravery, then appearing in the Natal papers, and that the armoured train owed its escape to his exertions, with a non-combatant. On the other hand, the Boers were great 'face savers'.

Frankland, the onlooker, whose good will and intergrity may scarcely be doubted, is perhaps the most reliable of the commentators. His diary reads:

'... Curiously enough, the day after Churchill had escaped an order is said to have come from General Joubert for his release. However, I have no doubt that this was all made up to excuse themselves for not being able to catch him. I do hope he gets away....'

[1] Colonel Frankland, killed Gallipoli, April 1915.

Back in the Model Schools, Haldane and Brockie had stifled whatever anger they may have felt and had done their uttermost to disguise Churchill's disappearance. Haldane's account reads:

'The war correspondent of the *Morning Post*, having successfully evaded the vigilance of the guard and, so far as we know, got clear of the Boer capital, the next thing, no matter our feelings of annoyance, was to conceal that fact for as long a time as possible, so as to give him a good start on his journey to the frontier. To effect this a dummy figure was contrived and placed in his bed, and this had so natural an appearance that when, on the morning of the 13th, a soldier servant arrived with a cup of coffee for the now absent one, he placed it on a chair beside where he supposed he lay, but failed to notice that the person for whom it was intended was inanimate.'

This report may be for many, experienced in the prison camps of later wars, the most remarkable of all, but in Churchill's own account, the earliest of all and written while the memory was green, he states that he left a letter to be delivered to his ex-hosts on the morning after his escape. So much, in any case, for what are known facts. Time and memory, as well as a writer's sense of drama and design, may play curious tricks with the sequences of events, but often distortions of facts reveal more of the essential truth than truth. Indeed, the 'facts' must as often obscure truth as reveal it. But whatever a man writes he provides a window to himself, and for me Churchill's dispatch, dated Pretoria, November 30, 1899, is more revealing of his character than all the rest. In it he describes a dream. He had just become a prisoner of war. He wrote:

'The bitter wind of disappointment pierces even the cloak of sleep. Moreover, the night was cold and the wet clothes chilled and stiffened my limbs, provoking restless and satisfactory dreams. I was breakfasting with President Kruger and General Joubert. "Have some jam," said the President. "Thanks," I replied, "I would rather have marmalade." But there was none. Their evident embarrassment communicated itself to me. "Never mind," I said, "I'd just as soon have jam." But the President was deeply moved. "No, no," he cried, "we are not barbarians. Whatever you are entitled to you shall have, if I have to send to

Johannesburg for it." So he got up to ring the bell, and with the clang I woke.'

The one certainty is that Churchill had the best of all possible worlds, for his escape rounded off his whole adventure and gained him his ten-year lead over Leo Amery. If it is true that had he waited even another day in the Model Schools he would have been released, then he had a tremendous piece of luck, gaining fame and fortune by a matter of hours!

These events brought down the curtain on the first act. He was soon back in the field, and this time not only as a war correspondent, but with an honorary commission in the South African Light Horse. In spite of the absolute ban on soldier-war correspondents which his own exploits had done much to provoke, he had wheedled his appointment out of General Buller.

Churchill once said of David Lloyd George that he could 'talk a bird out of a tree'. His own performance in talking old Redvers Buller into granting him the dual rôle in the field was scarcely less of a miracle. As Assistant Adjutant of his new regiment, able to go wherever he listed when not directly involved in his military duties, he enjoyed again the best of both worlds.

V

The last long-drawn-out acts in South Africa began to mature Churchill, not only as an observer of warfare, but as a man resolved to play a part in the government of his country. He was the spectator of the constant dilemmas and disasters overtaking a ramshackle war machine manoeuvring an archaic army, at times as helpless against Boer rifles as Tshaka's Zulus with their assegais had been against British fire. Indulging a constant flirtation with death and danger, his imagination stimulated to the full, he had climbed to the ridge of Spion Kop to look down upon the British dead heaped in the shallow trenches. He had observed with clear head and eye the unbelievable blunders of generals pickled in a dead past. He knew at first hand the devastating effects of 'modern' rifle fire directed by marksmen upon slow-moving, bunched infantry. He was not slow to make his voice heard, and thereby to court honourable unpopularity, and the anger of military ancients. His statement that a well-mounted Boer was worth three to five regular British soldiers was calculated to infuriate, and did. But it was not a criticism of British troops, whose individual heroism often moved him deeply. Churchill had at least perceived that old ideas must be swept away, even if he did not know with what to replace them. Slowly the experiences of the Boer War were stirring the moribund British military mind just in time to save her from almost certain disaster in the world war so short a time ahead. Even if it is not quite true that 'The Boer War saved the British Empire',[1] as Rayne Kruger wrote, it certainly pitchforked Britain into the twentieth century with her dreadful complacency severely shaken.

Perhaps of at least equal importance was the clear indication of the hatreds almost the whole world nursed against Britain. In the United States few sympathized with the British cause, and the books soon coming from the pens of her reporters, and partisans serving with the Boers, told stories which would have been regarded as shocking and shameful lies in Britain, instead of merely revealing the other side of the coin.

In all Europe it would have been difficult to find a supporter. Even in Norway Ibsen's voice, at last heard wondering whether Norwegians (and the world) really supported 'Kruger and his Old Testament', failed to move the sympathies of his countrymen. From Holland, an irate Queen exhorted the German Kaiser to take the lead in organizing united action against the British, but that vain and ambitious despot bided his time, content to observe the discomfiture of Britain without permitting his hatred to blind him to the realities of British power, especially at sea. The iron was not yet hot.

When Churchill returned at last in triumph from the war to receive, among others, the plaudits of the people of Oldham, to give an account of his adventures, and soon to win the seat for the Conservative Party in the 'Khaki Election', he had begun to learn his new part, aware of the many serious political problems, domestic and foreign, demanding urgent attention and of his need for serious study. He was still brash and bumptious, especially in the eyes of his own class, but he was also a brilliant and resourceful young man watching with shrewd eyes the setting of the stage, the changes in the scenery, and weighing up the parts and performances of the leading players. It is unlikely that it escaped his notice that men like Chamberlain, and others climbing to wealth and power out of the middle classes, did not

[1] *Goodbye, Dollie Gray.*

find his manners distasteful. They, too, had found the need to push or be left behind.

He realized that he had many disabilities to overcome as a politician which had not handicapped him as a soldier or writer. He found that he had to organize his thoughts most carefully, to write out and memorize speeches, to curb the looseness of his tongue, for even indiscretions had to be carefully calculated. There were also physical handicaps. His tongue involved him in 'an unpleasing lisp'; his voice was harsh and unmusical, grating on the ear. His words came fluently—too fluently, for he found difficulty in changing the direction of his thoughts while on his feet, slow to counter repartee, and unexpected argument.

Nevertheless that he was a man to watch, and probably destined for high position in the State, few doubted, and least of all himself.

PART TWO

WRITER AND POLITICIAN

# CHAPTER VII

It was swiftly evident that in politics Churchill had found the medium for the full display and development of his talents. His success as a politician was rapid and unorthodox, yet lacking a foundation of strength. He failed to create confidence in his colleagues and in the public. He had sailed close hauled into these new and turbulent seas, ready to tack to any quarter, susceptible not only to the prevailing winds (as soon as he should discover them), but to all the nuances and vagaries of the cross currents beneath the surface. His guns were masked, their range and fire power a matter for speculation.

Churchill would have agreed with Montaigne that good and bad fortune are 'two sovereign powers', and that 'it is unwise to think that human wisdom can fill fortune's rôle'. His will and reasoning, and certainly his course, would be moved 'sometimes by one breeze, sometimes by another'. His views were profoundly simple, for he believed in himself and his destiny. His weakness was in his inheritance of a vision that was already fading fast in reality, but not in his imagination. He believed in Britain as the heart of a mighty Empire, mistress of the seas and of a quarter of the peoples of the earth. Europe remained for him the Europe of the great Marlborough. When at last he was compelled to relinquish these brilliant dreams he exchanged them for others equally unreal. Thus, in Havelock Ellis's phrase, he was 'suspended from a hook which had ceased to exist'. But he was not alone. Two world wars of appalling barbarity, inflicting dreadful sufferings upon millions of men, women and children, would fail to banish such visions from the minds of sentimental men. The legend of Britain, of which Churchill was to become an expression, a legend in himself, was more powerful even than the legend of ancient Rome.

From the first the aura of the House of Commons appealed to him deeply. The House was to become his spiritual home. It was in itself the perfect setting for drama, its very air, its walls, its richly upholstered benches, held by the focus of the great table, the mace, the canopied Speaker's Chair, alive with its own story. You could sit silent on its benches, or in its deserted galleries, and let it flow into you and out of you, like prayer, the accumulated prayer of centuries, of a nation in its long growing. For half a century this House would be Churchill's stage and much more besides, for it filled a need in him greater than self expression. In the end it demanded and received his respect, affection and reverence, and because this was, in a sense, his true 'God' he could play pranks, even blaspheme, and be sly, and be forgiven. No man in England's history has belonged more truly to the House of Commons than Churchill.

In five years, by the time he was thirty-one, he had become a Minister, Under-Secretary of State for the Colonies in Campbell Bannerman's government. In seven, a Privy Councillor. In ten, he was Home Secretary under Asquith, and about to marry and to embark upon a new phase of his life. Not for an instant had it ceased to be 'fun', and both Churchill's friends and enemies recall the brief exchange with his under-secretary, Charles Masterman, after Churchill's flamboyant behaviour at Sidney Street. 'What the hell have you been doing now, Winston?' Masterman burst out. 'Now, Charlie, don't be cross. It was such fun,' Churchill answered. He had been disarming his friends in such fashion from the nursery, and would so continue almost to the end of his days. Nearly forty years on he would placate the grave and anxious Alan Brooke in almost the same words.

In those years Churchill had made few real friends, but he had inspired a remarkable devotion in one man, his direct opposite, who for more than thirty years would be his faithful amanuensis, his 'prompter', the jealous guardian of his written and spoken words, and thereby, in a measure, a sharer in his successes and disasters. This was Edward Marsh, and when a visitor asked Marsh what were his politics, Churchill answered for him, that he was a good 'Winstonian', of course. In a word those were Churchill's politics, and perhaps that explains the virulence of his enemies, nearly all Radical Liberals of the old school, or the Tory mediocrities who had destroyed his father.

But the skeins of politics were curiously tangled and devious as England emerged into the twentieth century with the labour pains of the Boer War, and all the 'after-birth' of Victorianism slow to fall off. Churchill was blamed because he was not a true

'Cobdenite', because he made brilliant speeches on land values, and did not press that cause home, because he saw the German menace and was sympathetic to the French, because above all he was a dangerous ally as well as a dangerous enemy, and not to be trusted as a good 'Party man'. Yet it remains difficult to discover the inspiration behind the virulent hatreds that endured for fifty years, becoming obsessions. One of his old liberal colleagues was still at the age of 94 going through his great speeches for phrases borrowed from others. Thus Clemenceau had inspired 'We shall fight on the beaches', and Byron 'Blood, sweat and tears'.[1] No man better remembered or better stored the telling phrase against the day when he might adapt it to the demands of the hour. And why not? It our mouths our words become our own, and it does not detract from Philippe de Commines that when he said 'that a man must take care not to do his master so great a service that he will not be able to find a proper reward for it', that Tacitus had said it before him, as also had Seneca, and doubtless many others.

That phrase of de Commines illustrates a characteristic of Churchill worth emphasizing, for he could not bear to be in debt to any man, and those who were content to serve him far beyond repayment understood it well. It did not matter. The gain was in the service, in the close association with an exciting man whose performance was well worth aiding. Actors and actresses have had such service from their faithful dressers, the hearers of their lines, their producers, and the reward for all these behind the scenes is in the success of the star each has helped to build. Thus Lady Randolph, and from 1910 onwards Clementine Hozier, nourished this man with all his great potentiality. It was enough.

Men like Edward Marsh and Desmond Morton knew very well what they were doing. They knew their charge very well, and their rewards lay in being privileged and intimate observers of his tremendous performance. They met him as he came off the stage borne on the curses or the applause of his audience. They knew the worth of his tears, and delighted in his puckish humour, his courage, his immense energy and resilience. The tears streaming down his cheeks, as he left the Chamber after a magnificent speech, he remarked to his Private Secretary, installed behind the Speaker's chair, 'that got the sods!'

Churchill exerted a powerful fascination for almost all men,

[1] *The Age of Bronze*, Canto xiv.

amusing his intimates and elders, his brother actors on the stage of politics, as often as he angered them. His intellectual and political superiors recognized his great potentialities for triumph or disaster, perceived him clearly warts 'n' all, and spoke of him with brilliant insight, yet without malice or venom. Arthur Balfour was almost certainly fond of him, and so was Herbert Asquith. Rosebery, whose world was coming to an end, watched him with affection and grim foreboding. Even old John Morley, of a vastly different school, finding him devoid of principles, and a dangerous man, could not resist his personal appeal.

Churchill's execrable manners with those he considered his social inferiors did not affect his relationships with men who had risen out of the rough and tumble of life, and were most nearly his friends and companions. He was at ease with Joseph Chamberlain, in awe of David Lloyd George, uneasy with Birkenhead, and relaxed with Baruch and Beaverbrook, and they with him.

All these in their fashions were stirred by similar impulses, and drew their strength and their weakness, their good and their evil, from the same deep spring. They sought power. With the exception of Chamberlain, and Lloyd George, they believed that the ends they sought justified the means, and said so, believing wrongly that they shared this dangerous faith with Ignatius Loyola who had brilliantly argued the complete reverse.

Churchill's pursuit of his own destiny could not offend others involved in the same kind of race, especially when their ends were not in conflict and might even prove complementary. Besides, his case was vastly different from theirs. He did not so much seek power as prepare for it, yet without consciously defining for what it was that he prepared. Joe Chamberlain sought political power for political reasons, and so did Lloyd George, the dedicated social reformer. Beaverbrook sought to manipulate political power behind the scenes through wealth and the influence of newspapers. Churchill's destiny was mystical. He was 'the sword in the stone' awaiting the hand to pluck him free, invincible, Excalibur! It would be a Nation's hand; its strength, and the virtue of the sword, residing in the purity of its intention. The truth of the legend would be proven.

The early years on the political stage steadily revealed these attitudes.

## II

In Churchill the writer and the man of action were marvellously blended in a partnership that is inseparable. He lived life with tremendous gusto and matched his deeds with words. Through those periods when he was, perforce, off the stage he indulged his love of intrigue, surrounded himself with willing aides and sharpened his weapons. At the peak of his life he achieved the dream—or the nightmare—of the war correspondent and produced the action his nature demanded. If there were no battles he made them.

But writing could never have been for him an alternative career. Overwhelmingly he was an actor, not an observer or chronicler of the deeds of others, save only as their parts were complementary to his own, or were his inheritance, which was his to explore in the cause of his own growth and development. In his careful studies of Lord Randolph Churchill and the great Marlborough he came as near as it was possible in his nature to the scholarship he never derided in others, but did not attain. Through these studies he gained valuable insight into the political and military background of Britain and Europe, but it was his weakness that his inherited attitudes became the rock upon which he built his career. He was not an intellectual, but always a romantic inseparable from his emotions, and unable to shed his obsessions. He would tackle any kind of hard work, except hard thinking, which is the hardest work of all. Thus, as Amery pointed out, he remained a mid-Victorian, unable in his heart ever to accept the idea of Empire into Commonwealth, or to understand the political and economic creed of socialism. To Churchill, but not to Amery, the 'High Tory', there was always an 'impassable gulf' between his ideas and these vital issues of his time. He used all his eloquence to fight Imperial Preference, and to hinder the admittance of the Colonies and Dominions as free voices in the councils. As Colonial Secretary he refused to consult the Colonies on foreign affairs, and was a bitter opponent of Dominion status, fighting against Indian freedom to the bitter end.

In these attitudes, which were a part of him, it may be possible to detect his Americanism, for he shared the American desire to dominate the world on the British nineteenth century model. No man was a greater fighter for England, yet in a real sense he fought for a dream of an England and Empire that had perished with the nineteenth century, and could never be revived. He fought a lost cause, and that he seemed, at times, almost to be achieving the impossible must be written on his monument, a mark of his greatness. No man ever came nearer to making dreams come true, and not for himself alone.

In studying Churchill's life his stupendous energy becomes a rebuke even to the normally industrious. He appears to be going full blast for twenty-four hours a day. He was, in fact, a master of the 'cat-nap' and a believer, since his brief sortie into Cuba, in the virtues of the siesta.

For relaxation he learned to paint seeking at various times the advice and help of the Sickerts and Laverys. Walter Sickert did a portrait of Churchill that made him look like 'Horatio Bottomley in a pub', according to Marsh whose judgment on pictures and on Churchill could be trusted. In fact, Bottomley, the outrageous demagogue, the shameless rogue, was a coarse and vulgar proletarian version of a lesser Churchill, a Churchill of the gutter, bereft of an inheritance.

With such men as Bottomley, as with Beaverbrook, Birkenhead and Baruch, Churchill shared the common denominator of energy, the greatest single factor in success. He was never idle and never bored. If physical relaxation in excitement eluded him he might lay bricks and build a wall. His leisure was filled with good talk and good, but often random, reading. His agile mind grappled eagerly with many complex problems, but because he shunned the hard labour of deep thinking, his apparent mastery of a subject often led him to over-simplification. He culled telling thoughts, ideas and phrases from a multitude of sources, and stored them all in his prodigious memory against the day.

With these assets and many more Churchill was endowed, when like a salmon stirring to the thrilling currents of the open sea he embarked upon the ocean of his political life. He was unafraid and full of confidence, but aware of many of the handicaps and hazards he must overcome. He had won his seat in Parliament by a narrow margin and on a tide of emotion. Such a tide could not be relied upon to carry him far, and he was swiftly aware of undercurrents in the Tory camp not flowing in his favour. Name and privilege were still great assets, but were no longer certain passports to power.

In 1901 Churchill began to set his house in order. He needed money and he needed to overcome his physical difficulties, particularly of speech. He killed these two birds with one stone by lecturing and constant careful rehearsing. His speeches and lectures demanded the most careful preparation and learning by heart. He found it extremely difficult to deviate from his text, and could not change the direction of his fire if debates in the House, or out of it, did not go in the way he had anticipated.

But this was not enough. In the company of Tory and Liberal intellectuals he felt that his knowledge lacked a solid foundation, and that he was at a disadvantage. If he were to hold his own in debate, and put forward ideas of real validity, he knew that he must master the basic strategies governing European nations, the Balkans, Russia and the Middle East, that he must understand the military and economic importance of India to British power, and the nature of the rapidly expanding trade rivalries, the ambitions not only of Germany, but of the United States of America and Japan, and even some of the probabilities governing the future of China, and the march of subject peoples everywhere towards independence.

In the light of these factors, and many more constantly changing or shifting emphasis, he had to attempt to grasp the nature and reality of British power, and how it might be maintained in a dangerous, threatening and changing world. This above all was his field of political activity arising out of his inheritance and fitting his nature.

Nevertheless if he were to achieve support and the power which might presently flow from it he must explore the moods and aspirations of the British electorate whose votes hinged on very different things, who were deeply concerned with domestic affairs, with Ireland, with factory acts and wages, with the taxation of land values, with education, free trade and Imperial preference, and even with hosts of problems, many of which seemed trivial. He was astonished and amused, as well as exasperated, to find Lord Hugh Cecil passionately concerned to resist a Bill allowing a man to marry his deceased wife's sister. Debates upon such issues roused strong emotions and occupied a great deal of parliamentary time. It seemed to him in the light of the tremendous undercurrents stirring beneath the smooth surfaces of diplomacy that the mother of parliaments fiddled while the world was incubating for a spontaneous combustion.

Foreign affairs, Churchill swiftly discovered, were the preoccupation of the very few, and would be unlikely to influence a vote in 'normal' times. But he observed with pleasure that fierce passions often ruffled the surface of political life, that courage was demanded of those who supported minority views, and that there were many subtle parliamentary techniques to be understood and mastered. But in the constituencies different techniques were necessary. In the still 'feudal' agricultural areas, as well as in the industrial towns with their rapidly expanding parvenu middle classes sitting on top of a mass of workers, a bitter hatred of 'liberalism' animated the new class supporters of the Tory Party. Even as late as 1906 a liberal was 'a Red' to the newly rich in the new suburbias.

Pacifism, like liberalism with which it was associated, was a dirty word, and at the same time the deep underlying mood of England. A better name for it might be neutralism. But Churchill observed that Lloyd George, Labouchére and the 'pro-Boers'—the 'peace-mongers'—were no longer slipping out by the back ways under police protection to escape the violence of the mob. Rotten eggs were giving way to nosegays, swords to ploughshares. Lord Randolph's old slogan 'Peace, Retrenchment, Reform' might be the platform to success.

At least it was apparent that the best formal education Britain afforded would be inadequate to prepare a man for a political rôle. Churchill perceived that he could be at least as well equipped as the next man, if not better. One book thoroughly understood and digested was more useful than a hundred skipped, he commented. He had certainly digested Gibbon and Macaulay, even though he had found Mill's *Essay on Liberty* and Carlyle's *History of Frederick the Great* unsympathetic reading during his confinement at Pretoria.[1]

The exciting thing was the challenge of the twentieth century: it was vast, and it would grow. The complexities of today would be the simplicities of tomorrow, and upon such seas a man must steer by his instincts while fixing his gaze upon some vital star in a firmament of growing confusion. Churchill recognized the nature of the challenge, and faced it with a self confidence and courage which would be his greatest assets. There was no blue print for political or national survival, no true guide to the arts of statesmanship. 'Of course, I am a man of peace!' he often said, but his voice was the voice of a man of war.

[1] *London to Ladysmith.*

Churchill made all haste to get into the political arena. Within a year he had turned the £4,000 of capital with which he had emerged from his military and journalistic adventures into £10,000 which he had given into the competent hands of Sir Ernest Cassell for safe investment. It was little enough, but it was a good beginning giving him a measure of independence. In earning the money he had also begun to overcome his awkwardness of speech, and had made contact with a wide variety of audiences. He had embarked upon a lecture tour of the United States under the wings of the two shrewd 'politicos', Bourke Cockran and Chauncey Depew, friends of his Jerome family, and had faced and disarmed hostile audiences in Chicago, learning the elements of the 'ju-jitsu' technique in debate. He had had the honour of speaking under the chairmanship of Mark Twain, who did not share his views. He had also delighted the pro-British audiences he met in Boston. The Boer War had aroused passions in America at least as violent as those at home. It was worth pondering. In gaining as much as £100 for a single lecture he had learned to trim his sails to the prevailing winds without losing sight of his star.

With this experience behind him he took his seat in Parliament, studying his ground with the utmost care. He did not hesitate to attack his own front bench, especially in the person of St John Brodrick, the Minister of War, and observed a year or two later in his life of his father: 'Even in a period of political activity there is small scope for the supporter of a Government. The Whips do not want speeches, but votes. The Ministers regard an oration in their praise or defence as only one degree less tiresome than an attack. The earnest party man becomes a silent drudge, tramping at intervals through lobbies to record his vote and wondering why he came to Westminster at all.'

Churchill was never in the slightest danger of becoming a party drudge, or of wondering why he had come to Westminster. He observed the manners and matter of men like Lord Hugh Cecil, and sensed that the electoral tide was moving against the Tories. Perhaps his American tour had helped him to understand the attitudes of the pro-Boers. For his part, he had always respected the Boers as fighters, and was not without sympathy for their ambitions, especially if these ambitions could be compromised within the framework of the British Empire. In his discussions with Boer leaders during the brief period of his captivity he had begun to realize that compromise was the basis of politics. In Parliament Churchill learned to shift his tactical positions while clinging fast to his strategy, which was neither Tory nor Liberal, but purely Winstonian. But he was committed in two major ways, and in these he would never change, nor consider compromise; he believed in the absolute authority of the British Empire, and he hated the doctrines of socialism. In these two vital issues of his lifetime he was in fixed positions, unable to advance, refusing to retreat, condemned therefore to be overwhelmed as the tides of inevitable change flooded over him.

In 1902 Churchill was given complete access to his father's papers for the purpose of writing a life of Lord Randolph, and in the course of this task it is reasonable to suppose that he discovered a basis for his own political attitudes. He did more, he escaped for a little while from the strait-jacket of his egocentricity, and strove to enter his father's mind through all its phases. In contemplating the tragedy of his father he found the best in himself, and was a brilliant advocate for the defence of an individual, however close, other than himself. The dreadful disease from which his father had suffered and died, and which had reduced his agile mind at last to a pitiful impotence, aroused compassion in the son. It may be—indeed, it is probable—that the disease, long submerged, had undermined the stability of Lord Randolph's mental attitudes long before its presence had become unescapable to his intimates, and at last clear to all. But for this Churchill might well have achieved and enjoyed his father's company and confidence during his lifetime, and known the paternal intimacy he so sorely lacked.

As it was he defended his father's memory nobly, and with great skill and dignity. He was able to solicit the advice of Lord Rosebery, and others of his father's friends, and to enjoy the benefits of their libraries, their personal memories, and their matured views. Perhaps, most important of all politically he could gain an insight into the Tory attitudes that had so alienated his father. The Tories of the day regarded themselves as rulers almost by divine right. With the exceptions of a few Whig aristocratic families they alone were 'gentlemen'. Thus any 'gentleman', not a Whig by his heritage, was a 'traitor to his class' if he left the Tory ranks. But, as Churchill saw it, his class had been traitor to his father so that 'a nature originally genial and gay contracted a stern and bitter quality, a harsh contempt for what is called

"Society", and an abiding antagonism to rank and authority'.¹

If Churchill did not share this view, at least he sympathized with it, although he does not appear to have considered that the change in Lord Randolph's nature might have been due, at least in equal measure, to the slow workings of the poisons within him. However that may be, his book is brave, humane and civilized, a work of distinction most warmly and vividly written, filially partisan, and an outstanding landmark in Churchill's own life.

In the years 1901 to 1905 covering the period of his study of his father Churchill was developing both as a writer and a politician in harmony. It was his political apprenticeship. He could listen to the private views of Salisbury on the one hand, of Balfour or of Chamberlain, and to Rosebery and Morley on the other. It was at a time when the major issues in politics were embodied in the problems of Free Trade or Protection. Chamberlain was introducing his ideas of Imperial Preference while, to the Liberals, in the words of Campbell Bannerman, to question the virtues of Free Trade was 'like disputing the law of gravitation'.

It would have been difficult to imagine in 1902 that Campbell Bannerman would ever lead a united Liberal Party, that men like Rosebery, Asquith, Haldane—and Churchill—would ever be reconciled to such leadership. But they were. There was a great deal of 'reconciling' to be done, for there were tremendous issues beneath the surface, manifest in the profoundly opposed underlying attitudes of the great figures of the day to the rising challenge of Germany. The problem was deeply emotional, arising out of fixed attitudes of mind on the 'rights' of the individual, on 'democracy', on 'authoritarianism', on racial prejudices.

To Rosebery the meddling of Edward VII, and the *Entente Cordiale* with France in 1904, was a signpost on the road to tragedy. He remarked to David Lloyd George at Dalmeny: 'Well, I suppose you are just as pleased as the rest of them with this French agreement?'

And on being assured that Lloyd George was 'delighted', Rosebery went on: 'You are all wrong. It means war with Germany in the end!'²

But that Rosebery was right did not make 'the rest of them' all wrong. Churchill, enjoying Rosebery's friendship and respect-

¹ *Lord Randolph Churchill.*
² David Lloyd George, *War Memoirs*, Vol. I.

ing his views, welcomed the entente with France and knew with all his instincts that Germany was the enemy, the only nation capable of offering a major threat to the British Empire. He was very early in the midst of intrigue, sharing with a select few the knowledge of Fisher's plan to 'Copenhagen'[1] the German Fleet at Kiel, and thus to scotch the danger in the bud. The threat of war, so real to Fisher that he even predicted accurately the date of its final outbreak, was the spectre always in the wings, and never far from the forefront of Churchill's mind. Nevertheless, as a politician he immediately concerned himself with all the many facets of political life. Political attitudes were in a state of flux, and the long reign of the Tories, perpetuated by the deep cleavages over Home Rule, must soon come to an end. Domestic issues of many kinds divided the parties and the nation. New problems had arisen demanding urgent attention. Even Balfour's Education Bill aroused fury.

Churchill's speeches, carefully prepared and learned by heart, left him very little room to manoeuvre, but revealed the tenor of his thoughts. His sympathies with the Boers pleased the Liberals, and mildly disturbed his own front bench. He showed that he could think of simple Boer farmers as 'country squires'. Later he was to utter one of his finest and most eloquent phrases in dealing with the problem of the Transvaal. He wanted Boer and Briton to live together in peace, sharing the responsibilities of Government under the Crown.

'With all our majority,' he said to the Tory opposition, 'we can only make it the gift of a party. You can make it the gift of England.'

By that time he had moved to the Liberals and was Under Secretary of State for the Colonies. He had split with the Tories on the burning issue of Imperial Preference or Free Trade. Inevitably he was under his father's influence, inheriting his belief in 'cheap food' and accepting Free Trade as a natural state. The Tories, with Balfour's attitude ambivalent, with the Chamberlains passionately for Tariff Reform, with powerful men like Derby gravely uneasy, were hopelessly split on this issue, and when Churchill called upon all Free Traders to stand together and cried 'Thank God for the Liberal Party', it was too much. In

---

[1] This was never British naval policy. Fisher had horrified the King when he spoke of his plan—or idea—in 1904 and 1905. *Fear God and Dread Naught,* Vol. II.

March 1904 Balfour led the Tory Party out of the Chamber in the course of a Churchill speech, and provided Churchill with a physical basis for his conviction that the Tory Party left him and not he the Tory Party.

In fact, it should not have surprised anyone when Churchill crossed the floor of the House to sit beside David Lloyd George, the man who was to be his mentor, almost one might say his 'Merlin', for twenty years. His father might have done the same thing, for he had tried to form a 'cave of Adullam' against the Tory element of his time, and Churchill was brooding upon his father's wounds. Lord Randolph had been destroyed not only by the Party leaders, but by a Tory mediocrity, implacable in its backwoods stupidity. Thus Churchill supported his father's political faith, and had begun to state his own. He believed that he was more Liberal in his views than Tory. But Churchill was a child, if not of the twentieth century, at least of a newer age than his father's. Above all, as I have reiterated, he was his own man.

If one accepts that Churchill was always guided by a 'personal dream' allied to a powerful sense of a high destiny, and what Amery called 'a conscious fitness to lead', it is not difficult to understand his political course. He was bound to form his own opinions upon a wide variety of issues, and was never the man to keep his thoughts to himself. His loyalty was not to Party, nor to any man or collection of men, but to his conception of England, and to the monarch.

But his England was an England that had already ceased to exist, and in this simple fact lies Churchill's tragedy and our own. He was an Elizabethan, and as Amery expressed it: '. . . his patriotism has always been for England; the England that fought Philip of Spain, Louis XIV, and Napoleon in the past; the England that in his own lifetime overcame Kaiser Wilhelm and Hitler.'

The other England, the England making the magnificent transition from Empire to Commonwealth, was not for him. He denied it, and he fought it, that Commonwealth which, as Amery wrote, was 'still in the making, but already the only practical framework and foundation for the planning of our economic and defensive policy in the new era of great world units—that conception has never seriously influenced his thinking, his eloquence or his actions'.

Churchill's limited and archaic vision was his basic weakness as a statesman. As a politician he suffered from wearing his heart on his sleeve. He was easily and honestly deeply moved by much that he saw in England, by the extreme poverty of the millions who dwelt in slums, by the conditions of the working class. A politician cannot afford to speak his mind. If he is horrified he must conceal his horror; if he is delighted he must conceal his delight. His political attitudes must be the product of hard thinking, consistent with the 'possible'. It never occurred to Churchill to be other than himself. He too often said exactly what he thought, and swiftly acquired a reputation for being as dangerous to his friends as to his enemies.

Yet Churchill could not be denied. Almost at a bound he became a figure of importance in the House and in the country, a powerful and disturbing enigma, breeding distrust in the hacks and dedicated workers in all parties, yet as fascinating as fire, and as dangerous to all those who wanted of him much more than he had to give. He had been born with his private and personal faith in Empire and Monarchy, nurtured on his nursery flood, and in India, the Sudan and South Africa. Now he had discovered Parliament as his 'Temple'. It would have been blasphemy to question his faith, and only a 'religion' of an equivalent grandeur and with a deep emotional personal appeal would ever challenge or replace it in his heart and mind.

But Churchill was never more attractive as a human being, nor more wholly English, than in his Edwardian days. He was progressively called unprincipled, irresponsible, unpredictable and dangerous, and finally the greatest political acrobat of his times, by all those who failed to recognize the sources of his drive and dreams and thought he should have been 'somebody else'. He might have echoed his father, and cried that to be dependable meant to be dependent, and that he was irrevocably independent. He aroused bitter hatreds in old-fashioned Tories and in Liberal Radicals, and these have never been quenched, feeding themselves through the long years on their frustrations and gleaning the masses of derogatory, and often witty and deeply perceptive remarks of his great and not so great contemporaries. It is simple to find in all the mass of writings, in parliamentary reports, in innumerable political pamphlets and biographies, in his own massive work of self defence, support for almost any 'version' of Churchill one fancies. But the true man is no 'version'; he is himself.

In the Edwardian years and up to and into the Great War he was a questing mind and spirit, irrepressible and irresistible, admiring the intellectual qualities of men like Asquith, Grey, Haldane and Morley, and studying the political techniques and manoeuvres of Balfour and Joseph Chamberlain. He recognized quite clearly his own educational gaps. Greek had denied him the University apprenticeship so useful in politics, especially in debate. But he had had his own 'university' in his early experiences, and he was not alone. Lloyd George was self educated, and more than a match for any man. Max Aitken, afterwards Lord Beaverbrook, was already making his presence felt behind the political scenes. F. E. Smith, afterwards Lord Birkenhead, had come up the hard way. These were his natural associates.

Churchill's enemies like to recall that Morley called him 'unprincipled'; that old Sir William Harcourt never had any faith in him; that Harold Begbie thought him ponderous in debate; that Asquith, who had a genuine affection for him, did not think that he would 'ever get to the top in English politics, with all his wonderful gifts'. Even Lloyd George, who must have known him best of all as a politician, thought that he was as dangerous inside the Cabinet as he was dangerous outside, and that he would always need a powerful guiding hand.

For Churchill there was only one way up, and either it would be his destiny, or it would not. He could not be judged by normal political standards, but inevitably he was. In a bitter rage surviving over fifty years old Francis Neilson, then in his nineties, wrote:

'Morley was not the only cabinet member who had been associated with him, who found him destitute of political morality. To scoff at the principles laid down by Richard Cobden and Henry George was a despicable act of ingratitude.'

It is remarkable that Churchill's comments on Philip Snowden[1] should have aroused such a response so many years later. It reveals something of the extent of the distrust he sowed in those early years, and which he never outlived. Yet Morley always treated Churchill with kindness and consideration, read the proofs of his life of his father with scholarly care, and wrote many valuable private criticisms and suggestions. So also did the

[1] *Great Contemporaries.*

exquisitely sensitive Rosebery, whose friendship survived Churchill's refusal to use Rosebery's beautifully phrased introduction to his life of his father.

In the political arena Joseph Chamberlain remained on the friendliest personal terms, urging Churchill to stick to his guns when he supported Free Trade in direct opposition to the Tory Party, and joined the Liberals. Balfour liked him, and so did Lloyd George.

Yet whatever else one may deny Winston Spencer Churchill in those days one cannot deny him great charm. There was something 'Puckish', boyish, fresh about him, immensely attractive and promising excitement. He liked to hold the stage, but did not deny it to others. It was difficult to be dull in his company. His appearance matched his 'unpleasing voice', yet in a curious way neither his appearance nor his voice counted against him. Guedalla quotes one of Churchill's contemporaries in 1903 who described him as 'a little square headed fellow of no very striking appearance, but of wit, intelligence and originality'.[1]

Others were less kind. He was a sturdy, sandy-haired figure with a pugnacious jaw on occasion, giving an impression both 'powerful' and 'ugly'. There was an amusing exchange in the House between Churchill and Lloyd George soon after the birth of Churchill's son. He was a pretty baby, Churchill said. 'He must take after his mother,' Lloyd George commented. 'No, after me,' replied Churchill.

It would be as misleading to give too much weight to the help he received on all sides, as it would to the mass of criticisms. There are few who will deny their help if it is sought, and many shy men and women worry out problems in isolation and solitude when willing help is all about them. Whatever else he may have been, Churchill was not shy. It would not have occurred to him at any time in his life that he might not be wanted, or that services he desired and sought with a total lack of inhibition would be denied. For this reason, if for no others, such services will seldom, if ever, be denied.

---

[1] *Mr Churchill.*

# CHAPTER VIII

❧❀❧

December 1905 is an important landmark in Churchill's progress as a writer, a politician, and as a personality. He was just thirty-one years old, and already he emanated an aura of authority, irresistible to the overwhelming number of his fellows, and one of the essential characteristics of all men destined for power, if not for greatness. No man may find himself in possession of a more dangerous, or more potent weapon.

The authority of those who leave their marks indelibly upon the story of mankind appears to derive from some inner source, and is difficult to define in physical terms. Those who possess it may be undersized, ugly, uncouth, physically weak, even cowardly, and bear no outward signs of their peculiar power, yet at a word or look those, seemingly of far greater physical and intellectual stature, obey or quail. Thus those beyond the aura marvel at the power of puny and evil tyrants to impose their wills upon whole races of men.

In its loftiest manifestation Christ could say 'leave your nets and follow me'. And at his simple bidding men would leave their business, and accept his authority without question. Doubtless authority of that order arose from a mystical source, yet it must also have arisen out of an inner certainty that all the possessors of authority share.

Were a man to question such power in himself it would cease to exist. It works like a spell, independent of words and deeds. A man may be invested with authority, assume it, wear it like a close-fitting garment, but it is not his. Those, for example, who have closely served Prime Ministers of Britain, enjoying their friendship over many years, have remarked how strange it is that a man who yesterday was David, or Neville, Winston or Clem to them in long accustomed ease of manner, on the morrow becomes, mysteriously, 'Prime Minister'. The value of such authority lies in the values others put upon the sources of the investing power, a nation, a monarch, the head of a State. Such wearers of authority at their highest are merely proconsuls, and in a sense Winston Churchill was one of these, yet possessing an aura of authority in his own right. Power is so terrible, and so totally corrupting, so much at the very core of the problem confronting the human race that no man is immune. In possession of unbridled power Churchill might well have been a veritable Caligula.[1] This is not a criticism, but a measure of power in the hands of men of authority, for the world has many little Caligulas, and has suffered from too many big ones.

Churchill's particular and personal authority arose out of his birth and breeding, the conditions of his childhood, and above all from the strength of his imagination. He was always consciously an individual, unique, stubborn, resolute in his own judgment against all men even as a boy. In his young manhood his authority was valid among his contemporaries. He did not so much demand privilege as accept and assume privilege without question. He had his own unwritten rules, as vague and powerful as the 'Constitution'. By the time he was thirty-one years old his personal aura of authority had become evident in a wider field, gaining for him not only political recognition, but also a loyal servant and faithful friend of distinction and quality in the person of Edward Marsh.

Churchill was born to trouble 'as the sparks fly upwards', his course promising danger, excitement, achievement. The essence lies in that in serving such a man, men know that they serve some force greater than any they might hope to generate, that in serving they are more likely to fulfil themselves, even to scale peaks previously unimaginable, than if they were quietly to pilot their own little craft alone. Thus they hitch their waggons to a star, ready to rise with it, or to fall.

Yet had Churchill been merely a young politician, however great his potential in that field, it is unlikely that he would have gained the services of Edward Marsh. But he was also a writer, and above all he cast a spell.

In that December of 1905 Arthur Balfour, whose services to his country were barely to be acknowledged or understood for more than half a century, had resigned the Premiership, making way for Campbell Bannerman to form a Liberal administration. In that administration, to the surprise and chagrin of many,

[1] Beaverbrook recognized the tyrant in Churchill.

Churchill was appointed Under Secretary of State for the Colonies.

From the point of view of those Tories, Chamberlain, Amery and Max Aitken among them, dedicated in various ways to the inevitable transition of Empire into Commonwealth, a galaxy of self-governing Dominions and Colonies, and whose immediate policy was 'Imperial Preference', few appointments could have been worse than that of a 'mid-Victorian' struggling intellectually with the works of Cobden and Henry George, and a declared champion of Free Trade and 'cheap food'.

From the point of view of those who hoped for liberal and generous settlements in South Africa perhaps few could have been better. As a student of war Churchill knew, but too easily forgot under emotional stress, that only the generosity of the victor might ensure 'peace'. He knew that Castlereagh, rather than have the beaten enemy, France, torn apart would have gone to war with his allies. He had been deeply impressed by Grant's noble gesture after Appomattox when he sent the rations of his own lean and hungry troops to the beaten Confederates, and gave Lee back his surrendered horses to speed the plough. But he also knew, and a little later wrote: '. . . how rarely in history have victors been capable of turning in a flash to all those absolutely different processes of action, to that utterly different mood, which alone can secure them forever by generosity what they have gained by force.'

Churchill in his first important appointment hampered the growth of the Commonwealth, and denied to the members of the Empire the knowledge and consultation rapidly becoming their absolute right, and Britain's own urgent necessity. The 'Mother Country' must, in his vision, remain supreme, the arbiter over her children. But he helped in procuring a generous peace in South Africa. His friendship with Botha, his life-long friendship with Smuts, his genuine respect for the dignity and aspirations of the Boers, coupled with his grave and honourable misgivings about their treatment of the native African, adorn his long and turbulent record.

Even in that early stage of his progress his inner thoughts were inspired by the processes of war. He was exceptionally well-informed at a time when foreign policy and problems of strategy were not even known to all the members of the Cabinet. Churchill knew of the steady reappraisals of British power and strategy which had been given new impetus by the South African War. In 1904 Balfour had founded the Committee of Imperial Defence, and in January of that year a committee considering military problems under the chairmanship of Lord Esher had produced a strategic document of immense importance. All the means of assessing and co-ordinating British power were then under way, and Maurice Hankey would become the Secretary of the Committee of Imperial Defence to keep his fingers on the pulse of Britain for thirty-seven years.

Meanwhile Lord Fisher, having begun to reorganize the Navy in the Mediterranean in 1898, had now embarked upon the task of blowing the cobwebs out of the Admiralty. There were few outward signs of these activities, but the reorganization of British power had begun at the heart to ensure that the life blood would pump steadily to the furthermost limbs.

In 1905 the Russo-Japanese war startled the Western world, forcing it to face a new challenge, for a major power had arisen in the Far East, and henceforth the confines of war must be extended, perhaps to embrace the world. The cockpit of Europe remained, a powder barrel among many. It was no longer enough to worry about the anachronism of the Austro-Hungarian Empire, the shocking barbarities of the Turks, the ambitions of Germany, and the machinations of Russia and Germany in the Balkans, the Near and Middle East. Now there was a major disturbance in the balances of power, and with a deep emotional significance, the defeat of a great European power by a Far Eastern Yellow race whose growing power and significance in world affairs had not been realized or understood.

Such facts were feeding steadily into the mind of Churchill. He understood well that Britain was at once a great maritime power whose naval strategy should dovetail with that of France in the West, and a great Indian military power. The Far East was second only in importance to the defence of Britain herself, while in the middle lay the Middle East. This was the broad framework of British defensive strategy in which the new Committee of Imperial Defence was working against time to fill in and strengthen the detail. The priorities, once they were seen and understood, were not debatable. Britain must never permit herself to come to grips with a great military land power in the West. She was the great amphibian. Thus she was concerned to support Turkey, whatever the horrors of her regime or the nature of her internal disturbances, against the expansion of Russia, while at the same time she must support a Franco-Russian alliance against the ambitions of Germany and the dangerous possibilities inherent in the decaying Austro-Hungarian Empire and the restlessness of the Balkan States.

Yet Britain must beware of hard entanglements, keeping herself free to manoeuvre. Her defence and all that it meant in a world dominated by creeds of force, and ruled in the main by 'juvenile delinquents' grown to man's estate,[1] nurtured on illusions, and sustained by the mystiques of authority vested in ritual, must be maintained by the Royal Navy, the world's self-appointed policeman enforcing the Pax Britannica. Not one of the world's gangsters would be likely to acquiesce indefinitely in such a maintenance of peace and power, nor would any nation concede a monopoly of political morality to the greatest edifice of conquest the world had seen, and one whose weaknesses had been revealed so recently in South Africa.

In his capacity of Colonial Secretary Churchill would have an opportunity to gain a wider perspective on the strategic problems already facing the Empire on the seven seas. Above all, the Russo-Japanese war should have caused him to focus his gaze upon the Indian Ocean, and upon the military power and potential of British India. In his nature, in his blood and bones, he was endowed with a kind of 'card sense', and a gambler's instincts, in the heady and dangerous game of power, nor was there any real danger that reason would prevail over his fundamental illusions. The star of his destiny glowed steadily.

In December 1905 when Churchill stood at this new threshold he attended a party given by Lady Granby, and there met Edward Marsh, a civil servant in the employ of the Colonial Office. The two men had met briefly at a country house, and the gentle Marsh had been startled, rather than repelled by Churchill's truculence on that occasion. 'The first time you meet Winston you see all his faults,' Constance Lytton remarked reassuringly, 'and the rest of your life you spend in discovering his virtues.'[2]

Since the rest of their lives lay ahead of all these young people the statement was rather wild, but Churchill certainly 'grew' on all those who were sympathetic to his nature. The Lyttons,

[1] Phrase inspired by James Gould Cozzens, *Guard of Honour*.
[2] Christopher Hassall, *Edward Marsh*.

Marsh's dearest friends, had been quick to see the possibilities inherent in a partnership of opposites, and Pamela Lytton had suggested to Churchill that in Marsh he would find the ideal secretary, and, she might have added, confidante and friend. The meeting at Lady Granby's had been contrived to bring the two men together in a congenial atmosphere. It was at once a success, and Churchill was observed to be deep in consultation with his Aunt Leonie, Mrs Jack Leslie. Her opinion clinched the matter so far as Churchill was concerned, and he offered the job at once to Marsh. But Marsh, immensely attracted, doubted his ability to serve and stand up to a man of such dynamic energies and enthusiasms. He sensed that he was at a turning point in his life, and that to work for Churchill might constitute a challenge too harsh for his spirit, while at the same time offering him a chance of fulfilment beyond any normal expectation. There was in Marsh nothing of the sycophant, and he had no conception of how much he had to offer.

Two days after the meeting at Lady Granby's the two men dined alone together at Mount Street, and the long partnership was sealed. Marsh knew that he had found his man, but remained fearful of the prospect. Constance Lytton again reassured him: 'You say he will expect much, but so will you, and when you both live up to each other's standards, as I expect you will, you'll be a quite splendid, taut combination of forces.'

It was, as the Lyttons saw it, a perfect marriage of opposites, and for the next twenty-five years it is difficult to measure Churchill's achievements without considering the contribution of Marsh. Indeed, the contribution continued for fully fifty years, long after Marsh had retired from public life. It was a remarkable stroke of luck for Churchill, for in common with most total egocentrics he was a bad picker of men, and was virtually incapable of being a part of a team, even as the chief.

Both men were joined in harmony at the outset of their careers. Marsh was gentle, scholarly, a man of wit and humour, gregarious, cultured, at ease as much with women as with men, a rising connoisseur of the arts, a man of impeccable taste, above all a man born to be a hero-worshipper, given the right hero. Debarred by grave illness in youth from the great challenge and contest that may only be met and resolved in the depths of physical love, wherein, it may be, lies man's ultimate salvation, such men must live life in other ways.

Churchill's nature deeply needed such a man, for he too would not meet the challenge and would retain through all his days an adolescent boyhood 'dream of Fair Women', and preserve intact the armour of his egocentricity. He needed a man who would be a foil, one with no love of physical or political adventures, a man of innate loyalties, and of moral courage within the confines of his interests. Neither man was prepared to probe life to the depths, preferring to live brilliantly on the surface. Churchill was quick to recognize the value of Marsh's character, and the honesty of his literary criticism. Moreover Marsh's nature would call forth the best of which such a man as Churchill would be capable, permitting him to perform the rôle of protector and patron, at times pupil. No two men could have been more complementary to each other, and of all those who served Churchill behind the scenes no other had so great an influence upon the quality, but not the content, of his writing and speech-making. Marsh did not mind what Churchill said, but he cared very much about the way he said it. But even Marsh could not marry the spoken and written word in perfect harmony, and Churchill's work was always to suffer from the literary flaws of rhetoric. Churchill recognized this himself. He was overwhelmingly a political animal, and he remarked to P. J. Grigg (among others) when correcting the proofs of his *The World Crisis*, 'Of course, what I ought to do now is to start all over again and write the book in my own hand.' As Grigg commented, 'he never eliminated altogether the traces of their oratorical origin.'

Nevertheless Churchill's literary debt to Marsh was very great, for while Marsh's political interests and influence were negligible, his love of poets and poetry stirred Churchill's humanity and involved him in a wider social world than he might have known otherwise. Marsh was deeply interested in the small change of life, Churchill almost solely with the limitless credits, the wide horizons, the 'big business' on the world's stage. Marsh was scarcely a player in his own story, Churchill was seldom off the stage. They loved the glitter and the gold, and preferred to ignore the squalid machinery. Neither was prepared to open or to enter any of the doors lining the shining corridor, each one marked 'Danger, Keep Out!' for behind each door lie harsh realities that demand the involvement of the human personality, discovering thereby the springs of compassion. No actor on the open stage of life can afford to open such a door, for the audience is waiting, and all such doors must remain forever closed to those whose aim is power.

Whatever might lay embryonic within the shell of a Churchill would never be known, for the life within would never dare break out and destroy the shell. Such men may not be judged as saints or sinners, nor measured against them, but as superb performers seeking and gaining the applause of multitudes. Thus it would be as absurd to seek true magnanimity or compassion in a Churchill as it would be to seek a living adult cockerel in an egg.

It does not detract from a man's performance to attempt to observe it within its limitations. Churchill, the rapidly developing actor, the superb journalist, the born politician, the man of destiny rushing to grasp his star, is the man I am attempting to discover. God is not his vision, for he is his own vision. A rocket cannot pause in flight. Such is the framework, and within it Churchill and Marsh together as a team were at their romantic best in public and private, and to the extent of the possible Marsh was his master's tutor in the humanities. Undoubtedly he was Churchill's highly critical and appreciative literary editor, his producer, his tireless rehearser and 'prompt' in the wings, his unfailing and faithful audience.

Together this strangely assorted pair, the bulldog and the sparrow, plunged into the turmoil of politics without a moment's delay. Before 1905 was out they were in Manchester, walking the drab streets in a grey drizzle, shocked at the narrowness and poverty of the lives such scenes evoked, but did not reveal. 'Fancy living in one of these streets,' said Churchill, 'never seeing anything beautiful, never eating anything savoury, never saying anything clever.'

To Churchill such lives and the people who lived them were never 'real', but he had a greater instinct for their 'feelings' than his friend Lord Clonmel who antagonized a working-class audience at Leamington, much to Churchill's amusement, with the words, 'the working classes must no longer lie and rot like sheep in their pens, as they have done for the last 100 years'.

Marsh, knowing no more about the real working class and their condition than his chief, was well acquainted with the threadbare poverty of poets, painters and musicians, and was able to save Churchill from such gaffes. All Churchill's speeches were carefully written and rehearsed in remarkable contrast to the fluency of his conversation. But Churchill's mind was too dangerous an instrument to be used spontaneously in public.

Marsh's ear was not at once attuned to audience reaction, but he quickly discovered that passages sounding well in the privacy of their rooms, did not always produce the hoped-for result either in the House or on the hustings. Different techniques were needed for different audiences. The two men learned together. But Churchill was an actor in the tradition of Irving, Martin Harvey and Tree (perhaps with a dash of Tod Slaughter!), and those giants of the boards who, whatever parts they played, were always themselves.

Churchill was at his best in the real theatre, and a speech given from the stage at Drury Lane, the stage set in a rural scene, with C. G. Masterman 'under a thatch roof sniffing a bunch of jonquils', was memorable among many. It is one of those speeches that has been preserved and quoted by his old radical enemies who read into his Edwardian speeches all the proofs of his perfidy, denying him even the transient honesty of thought that is his due, or allowing for his growth.

'There are only two ways in which people can acquire wealth,' Churchill said. 'There is production and there is plunder. Production is always beneficial. Plunder is always pernicious, and its proceeds are either monopolized by a few or consumed in the mere struggle for possession. We are here to range definitely on the side of production and to eliminate plunder as an element in our social system. The present land system hampers, hobbles and restricts industry.'

Again, speaking at the King's Theatre, Edinburgh, in 1910:

'In this country we have long enjoyed the blessings of Free Trade and of untaxed bread and meat, but against these inestimable benefits we have the evils of an unreformed and vicious land system. In no great country in the new world or the old have the working people yet secured the double advantage of Free Trade and Free Land together, by which I mean a commercial system and a land system from which, so far as possible, all forms of monopoly have been rigorously excluded.

'Sixty years ago our system of national taxation was effectively reformed, and immense and undisputed advantages accrued therefrom to all classes, the richest as well as the poorest. The system of local taxation today is just as vicious and wasteful, just as great an impediment to enterprise and progress, just as harsh a burden upon the poor, as the thousand taxes and Corn Law sliding scales of the "hungry forties".

'We are met in an hour of tremendous opportunity. "You who shall liberate the land," said Mr Cobden, "will do more for your country than we have done in the liberation of its commerce." '

No wonder the Radicals dared to hope that they had at last found a champion worthy of their cause, and when he failed to follow his words with deeds they nursed their bitter anger and disillusion against the 'turncoat'. But they were wrong in thinking that Churchill did not mean what he said. It was superficial and unthought out. He was newly aroused in the battlefields of peace, charging whatever windmills came within range of his lance, outwardly valiant and with tremendous gusto.

'The bearing of Free Trade on international relations is peace,' he thundered in 1908. 'Who can possibly suppose that the Free Trade policy is not the surest, perhaps in the end the only really sure road to international peace?'

So the Liberals never forgave him, and Marsh, listening in the front row at every performance, his ear tuned to his chief, awaiting the peroration, the extempore phrase which might make or mar the whole—like Lord C's sheep at Leamington—wished he had some needlework to help while away the time.[1]

II

Those years until the outbreak of the First World War have left an impression of incessant activity, of a man living life at a great pace, determined to drain every cup within reach, to savour every moment. Churchill was like a young actor trying his luck on the 'halls', playing in repertory in the provinces, stumping the country from end to end, insatiable, but without a moment to lose. He did not expect to live long, and said so gaily. The middle forties had accounted for his father and uncle, but the fact did not depress him. He did not fear death. He would

[1] Christopher Hassall, *Edward Marsh*.

cram at least as much into his short span as most men would experience in a century. Politics and the beginnings of intrigue, the glimpses of 'inner councils', the small pieces of knowledge known only to the very few, were nectar on the tongue, suffusing the whole body with a glow of expectancy. He delighted in travel, in Europe, the Near East, in Africa, no longer the soldier-war correspondent at times uncertain of his reception, but already a 'Very Important Person', a Minister of the Crown. He delighted also in intimate social occasions, relaxing in light conversation, still capable of sharing the limelight with others, even of listening.

His boyish romanticism often made him a delightful and amusing companion, wearing his lady's glove on his shining helm, his lance ever at the service of the 'good and the beautiful'. Stoutly he affirmed that his love would defy even the loss of his lady's nose! He would not argue as to whether the man or woman in marriage should love the other, for clearly both should love equally. The rest of the company—it was at the Duchess of Rutland's—did not consider such a total possibility. He was a charming guest. Had he been Launcelot he would have been content with a smile from Guinevere's eyes, to kiss the hem of her garment. As he had seen the vision of his mother, remote, shining for him like the evening star, so he saw all elegant and beautiful women. The fires of Marlborough did not burn in him, rather he dwelt in a world of romance and chivalry, and lived with zest on the surface of life with its myriad interests. Whatever might be hidden in the deep well within him would remain forever undiscovered, the dark sin, the shining virtue, the struggle of Lucifer with God that lies somewhere at the core of every man.

Early in 1906 he was already showing signs of mild Francophilia, inherited in part from his mother. In Paris he purchased the complete works of Maupassant, Balzac, Musset, Voltaire, a total of 267 volumes including Manon Lescaut, Chateaubriand, and the correspondence of Louis XIV and Marie Antoinette. To these, two years later, Marsh added the complete works of St Beuve as a wedding present to the man who was living up to every inch of Marsh's conception of a hero.

Acknowledging the gift, Churchill wrote:

'Few people have been so lucky as me to find in the dull and grimy recesses of the Colonial Office a friend whom I shall cherish and hold to all my life. Yours always, W.'

But he had found also another friend, and more than a friend, to cherish and to preserve intact his dream of fair women. In 1908 he married Clementine Hozier, and at last had his own lady in his house, and to live, as he said, 'happy ever after', like a fairy tale. Lady Randolph, who had never faltered in the service of her son, adorning his entourage in his political combats as gracefully as she had adorned his father's, could retire from the lists. She was still beautiful. She had married George Cornwallis West in 1900. She deserved her rest.

In retrospect Churchill now looks among the luckiest of men. With Clementine Hozier and Edward Marsh both in their different ways devoted to him with a selflessness seldom if ever surpassed, he was magnificently endowed with all to play for, his whole mind and energy free to pursue whatever course he fancied to gain his destiny. All the niggling grind and detail of living that too often saps the mental and physical energies of the less fortunate was out of his hands, and soon out of his mind.

In 1907, following a brief Mediterranean tour which had included visits to Greece and Turkey, two countries that tugged at his emotions like the sign of *pisces*, he took Marsh with him on an expedition through Uganda to the head waters of the White Nile, and thence back to the coast and by ship and rail to his old hunting grounds of Egypt and the Sudan. Marsh, suffering the minor tortures of such a journey with remarkable good humour and equanimity, delighted Churchill. He had begged Marsh not to carry a gun on *safari*, for the weapon would almost certainly prove more dangerous in Marsh's hands to his friends than to his 'enemies'. Thus Marsh met and stood his ground before a rhinoceros charging like 'a railway engine which had come off the line' with nothing more effective than a pink umbrella. Fortunately the animal, mortally wounded, sank suddenly to its knees and expired before Marsh could carry out his plan of leaping to one side at the last moment.

The purpose of the expedition was to follow the course of a proposed railway to link Lake Victoria with lakes Chioga and Albert, and the friendship of the two men was cemented by the mutual experience. Marsh's faith in Churchill as a man of action was confirmed, while Churchill was impressed with Marsh's remarkable *sang froid,* and an unemotional poise that had induced certain tribes to mistake him for the 'head man' of the expedition. To Churchill this was as though a king's jester had been mistaken for a king, and very funny. Had Marsh possessed a different stature, and constituted in any way a rival, the offence would have been unforgivable, crystallizing in that cold chamber of Churchill's mind where such incidents were stored, never to be forgotten.

Back in England in 1907 the death of Campbell Bannerman and the formation of a new administration by Herbert Asquith advanced Churchill to Cabinet rank as President of the Board of Trade. This meant a by-election in North-west Manchester, and when Churchill lost by a narrow margin the Tories were able to yell their schoolboy jibe at him—'What's the use of a W.C. without a seat!'

Churchill could afford to smile. Within minutes of losing Manchester he was offered a safe seat at Dundee, and at once journeyed north to be met with the slogan 'Your Winston will cost you more.'

It was a 'dog's life', according to Marsh, but with lighter moments. Dundee was an easy Liberal victory, relieving Churchill of an electoral struggle for many years. His course seemed clear to the top. By 1910 he was Home Secretary, flexing his muscles, exhilarated by the aroma of the forbidden fruit in the enchanted garden wherein coiled the serpent of power. He was at last within the walls.

1910 was a turning point in many ways. In May the death of Edward VII marked the end of an age, a small span of years to which men and women would come to look back with an almost unbearable nostalgia. In a sense the very last dregs of the seventeenth and eighteenth centuries had at last drained away, the last dregs of a world with aspirations towards culture, and away from barbarism, an age in which war, diplomacy, politics were conducted with a certain finesse and decorum disguising the mailed fists of power. Even slaves had clung to vestiges of dignity.

Undoubtedly the flowers of culture had blossomed upon a dung heap, but the stench had seldom been so offensive, even in the worst times, as to overwhelm the heady scents of the blooms in the exclusive gardens. Now, all at once, the blooms were overblown, the game was over. The stench of war had been growing in the still air, harsh, acrid, frightening; a new kind of war. The world was about to plunge back into barbarism.

Churchill had walked Marsh over the battlefields of the Franco-Prussian war. It would not be like that again. On the coast of England he had built sand forts in the manner of Vauban for the amusement of his firstborn son, as though recognizing that war even in miniature would need a playground more spacious than a nursery floor. The 'Battle of Sidney Street' was perhaps symbolic of the end of a particular kind of 'fun'. Marsh had shared his chief's enjoyment in that much publicized outing, and lamented the 'booing' with which audiences greeted the showing of the 'battle' and its principal actor on the bioscope.

'Why are London music-hall audiences so uniformly and so bigotedly Tory? You would have thought a stray Liberal must occasionally find his way in by accident—but it seems not,' Marsh wrote.

But the boos and the cries of 'Shoot him' were signs of public recognition of Winston Churchill. He was a symbol of something new, of something beginning to frighten them, both fascinating and dangerous. It was difficult to imagine a Home Secretary behaving in such a manner, but there it was before their eyes, disturbing.

Churchill never forgot Marsh's observations about the audiences. Power must lie either with Tory or Labour. Liberalism was a state of mind rather than a growing political force. He would remember when the time was ripe. Meanwhile as Home Secretary, new doors were opened to him. He was a member of the inner circle of the Cabinet, his prestige and influence widely recognized. The enigmatic Esher sought his support for the appointment of Maurice Hankey to the secretaryship of the Committee of Imperial Defence, an appointment heaven-sent in its remarkable aptitude.

But Churchill's influence had outstripped his outward position even then for some years. It did not stem, as did Esher's and Fisher's, from friendship with the Monarch. Many men had enjoyed an easy relationship with Edward VII that would be unlikely to recur in quite that vein. Viscount Esher, an impressive but vague figure behind the scenes of diplomacy for many years, owed much to the King's friendship. He had been a key figure in the first foundation of the Committee of Imperial Defence, and described by Hankey in Barthelot's words: 'I shall be everywhere and I shall be nowhere'; 'he had no official position or status, and yet he had a finger in every pie,' wrote Hankey.

After the year 1910 Churchill's fingers had begun to stir the pies. As Home Secretary he had begun to reveal his calibre. 'We were still a long way from the rich mellow voice,' Amery wrote. But the signs were there, and the telling phrase, even though Balfour could aim darts to penetrate the chinks in Churchill's armour.

'The Right Honourable Member's artillery is very powerful. But it is not very mobile. It has continued firing away at a position we have never occupied.'

Balfour expressed the dislike and fear of the Tories, for the use of power in Churchill's hands was manifest at the time of the Curragh mutiny, and the Tories were to pursue him with bitterness, fearful of his ruthlessness of action. But he was also a man of words, and in his speech in the Home Rule debate he used a phrase that would recur in a different context. He thought that the Irish demands should be granted. 'Never before had so little been asked, and never before have so many people asked for it,' he said.

1910 not only marked a vital point in Churchill's career, but also in his association with Edward Marsh. Herbert Gladstone, newly created first Viscount Gladstone, had been appointed Governor-General of South Africa. He wanted Marsh as confidential secretary and master of ceremonies. It was a very good job, opening new vistas of promotion for Marsh, but he preferred to remain with his hero who had been 'niceness itself about not standing in my way'.

'It would mean chucking Winston for good, and that would simply be too great a wrench.'

His loyalty never faltered in good times or bad. Together in 1911 they entered the lists of war when Churchill became First Lord in succession to McKenna. The new broom swept hard and mightily, and soon, Marsh commented, there was a new commandment: 'The seventh day is the Sabbath of the First Lord, on it thou shalt do all manner of work.'

The warrior had crossed the frontiers of his kingdom, appointed by Herbert Asquith, one of the finest political intellects of his times, a man, moreover, fully awake to Churchill's strengths and weaknesses. The event may be a small measure of the urgencies making their impacts upon the minds of those in high places. It may be almost a recognition that an age was coming to an end, and that new men and methods would be needed. David Lloyd George had become Chancellor of the Exchequer, a man of peace about to make a memorable speech at the Mansion House that would cause the war lords of Europe to pause.

Thus in 1911 the two men who were to grasp the helm, and pilot the ship of State through the first two phases of unparalleled storm and disaster, were already on the 'bridge'.

# CHAPTER IX

'MR MCKENNA and I changed guard with strict punctilio,' Churchill wrote of the exchange of jobs that put him in the seat of the First Lord of the Admiralty for 'four of the happiest years of his life', and Mr McKenna in the chair of the Home Secretary, an office he adorned with exceptional humanity and tolerance throughout a period of inhumanity and violent intolerance.

The punctilio thinly concealed the exhilaration of Churchill in the prospect before him, and the bitter disappointment of McKenna at being removed from a task he had performed with energy, skill and foresight. But in that hour Churchill was the man. He had sat at the feet of the ebullient Admiral Fisher for nearly five years. He had absorbed a great store of naval knowledge, most of it sound, from the lips of the violent, ruthless and dedicated old sailor who had refashioned the British Navy, hauled its ships and men out of the doldrums of half a century of 'spit and polish' and little else, and ruffled so many feathers that he had split the Service in a conflict of loyalties from top to bottom. But even that was doing more good than harm, for in Admiral Lord Charles Beresford, his implacable foe, no less a patriot, he had made an enemy worthy of his steel.

Fisher had steadily prepared to meet the German challenge he believed would come, and longed to strike a pre-emptive blow before the Kiel Canal could be made ready to bear von Tirpitz's new warships to the open sea. He had no fear of the challenge, but it seemed to him reasonable (and humane) to nip it in the bud. Germany might dominate Europe if she could, tragic as that might be, but the sea belonged to Britain. It was neither second sight nor warmongering that led the old admiral to predict the month and the year of the First World War years before it came. His was a single vision, unblurred by the complex of factors and events in the minds of others, and fixed simply upon the extensive programme of works preparing the Kiel Canal for the passage of large warships. A simple calculation gave him his simple answer.

There had been good and bad First Lords of the Admiralty. McKenna had been very good, working closely with Haldane at the War Office, who was refashioning the army to provide the kind of troops necessary to support a great sea power. No one foresaw then the possibility that Britain might provide a continental army beyond the limits of a well-trained expeditionary force.

Churchill took over a finely tempered weapon, ready for immediate action, and growing rapidly in answer to German naval building and the challenge of the New German Navy Bill about to provoke the furious spurt over the last lap of the race. Behind Churchill's chair a great chart flagged daily the multitude of British naval vessels on the seas of the world. They were his eyes and ears, and he was the heart and brain, controlling, in constant contact with his admirals. The sensation, the reality of power, tingled in his blood. He sat at the hub, his hand on the helm. Henceforth the Admiralty would live constantly at the alert, prepared for battle.

At the very moment when Asquith, the Prime Minister, had held out to him this task that struck all the chords in his nature, he had seen the silhouettes of two battleships sailing out of the Firth of Forth. It was a most potent omen. In his mind's eye he saw the cruiser squadrons, the destroyer flotillas, pounding the grey seas, and there a part of his heart was also, craving physical adventure and the thrill of action. Crisis had followed crisis, and for the third time in less than six years Europe had trembled on the brink of war as Germany, boasting her invincible power and bursting with martial pride, had imposed her will, twice upon France and once upon Russia, by the naked threat of war. Thus she had sown the wind.

'All the alarm bells throughout Europe began immediately to quiver,' wrote Churchill of the last crisis that had brought him to the Admiralty. They had never ceased to quiver since the turn of the century, and he had watched with a growing fascination from which few men would have been immune, for had not Tolstoi written of the imminence of battle that 'gives a peculiar brilliance and delightful keenness to one's impressions...'?

Churchill was at instant readiness, restless, invading everybody's business, already harassing Ministers and Heads of Departments with memoranda couched in a manner that would become memorable. Even as Home Secretary he had taken it upon himself to set guards to safeguard the security of the naval magazines. It had not been his 'pigeon'.

It is a curious experience to study the official histories, the political and military biographies and autobiographies covering the years of Edwardian England. In Churchill's works, the most voluminous autobiographer of them all, the years 1902-11 scarcely exist. It is almost as if he had gone into hibernation in the aftermath of the Boer War, to awaken in October 1911 in the seat of the First Lord. In one of his essays there is a brief glimpse of the 'German splendour', and that is almost all.

Yet in those years Europe and Asia were rumbling in the preliminary minor eruptions that would lead, almost inevitably, to disaster, while 'domestic fury and fierce civil strife' not only cumbered all the parts of the British Isles, but also of France, as autonomy reacted to the challenge of reform. Even in Russia the voice of the people could be faintly heard, and the whole world was stirring to new ideas. It was not surprising that the majority of European statesmen and politicians were overwhelmingly concerned with home affairs. In Britain the co-ordination of knowledge had begun through the Committee of Imperial Defence, and the committees sprouting from that stem, but these things were in their infancy. The Chiefs of Staff of Britain and France discussed problems that would almost surely prove mutual; but how mutual? What alliances, what commitments had been made? It seemed that no one knew.

In Britain the ignorance of foreign affairs even on a Cabinet level was profound. Edward Grey, the Foreign Secretary, with the reputation of 'a strong, silent man', was certainly silent, keeping his own counsel. He knew a great deal, but what did he feel? His life revolved between Whitehall, his house in Northumberland, and his fishing lodge in Hampshire. He seldom travelled.

Asquith, the Prime Minister, was gravely concerned with the march of events in Europe, but was fully occupied with home affairs. David Lloyd George, destined to pilot Britain and its Empire through the First World War (with Churchill under his wing), was totally involved 'with great schemes of social reform, old age pensions, health insurance, etc."[1] I quote Lord Hankey because old men forget, and Hankey remembers.

Balfour was a Tory of an old school, a link—if link there could be in such a chain—between the Toryism of Disraeli and the political junketeers led by Bonar Law. Such men as Balfour, and young Tories like Amery, were poles apart from the Tory reactionaries erupting out of the challenge of reform. In 1912 a great Tory rally at Blenheim Palace was the scene of lavish excitements. The Duke of Norfolk presented Curzon with a sword of gold. Home Rule for Ireland would be opposed by Ulster with civil war and the sword, and Bonar Law's 'reckless rhodomontade', as Asquith called it, the set-piece of the gathering, even startled the King. Every *parvenu* and man-on-the-make in Britain rallied to the new Tory banner, and Max Aitken had marked down Bonar Law as a political tool to serve him in manipulating the kind of behind-the-scenes power he longed for. Education, the Parliament Bill, and above all Home Rule, created bitter animosities that could be felt in almost every home throughout the country. The insularity of the island was almost total, and this state of affairs is reflected in most of the works covering the period. Affairs that absorb one thousand pages of official history seldom consume a paragraph in the recorded memories of men in high places who lived through those years. Tangier, Agadir, Fez are merely the names of places in the indexes.

Even the members of the Cabinet, and the heads of the Services, were ignorant of entanglements and the significance of alliances that might plunge the world into war, or save it. But for Balfour's foresight, and Esher's toil, Britain might well have toppled blindfold into the abyss.

With the death of Edward VII the Emperor of Germany had secretly rejoiced, for he had feared his uncle's influence and mistakenly imagined his successor to be a nonentity. He was sublimely unaware that the affairs of men were already moving fast out of the hands of princes, and that King George V of England was rapidly learning more about the nature of what was loosely called democracy than all his ancestors, and his multitude of cousins, put together.

It is curious, but probable, that King George V was more vividly aware of the dangers threatening Europe and his country and Empire than perhaps anyone else in Britain. Gloomily assess-

[1] *The Supreme Command*, Vol. I. 1914-18. Lord Hankey.

ing his inheritance, conferring with Asquith and Grey, listening to the shrewd Bonar Law who boasted that he had given the King the worst five minutes of his life, deeply troubled about the Navy he loved, and not sharing his father's confidence in Fisher,[1] disturbed by the tragic probability of civil war in Ireland, upset about the challenge of and to the House of Lords, yet sympathetic to the demands of the times, he found little comfort at home. Abroad, things were much worse. The peculiar mixed bag of relations his grandmother had spawned to occupy almost every throne in Europe, made the King acutely aware of the dangers from without. He was a far, far better man than his feeble and timid cousin Nicky, Nicholas II, Tsar of all the Russias, and an incomparably more honest and stable man than the vain, neurotic, boastful misfit trumpeting the German splendour, and backed by the most powerful military machine in the world.

There was little comfort in the visits of Prince Henry of Prussia, whose anxiety not to offend anyone resulted in conveying wrong impressions wherever he went.

At the time of the Tory rally at Blenheim Palace, Sasonoff, the Russian Foreign Minister, was a guest of the King at Balmoral, politely discussing the vexed question of the combined railway project between Russia and Germany. The King feared that German efficiency would soon enable them to dominate a railway through the Near East to the frontiers of India. Meanwhile, Russian desires for a stable Persia did not fit in with the British resolve to prevent the return of the Shah. Stability at the price of tyranny seemed too steep.

The Americans were also appearing upon the horizons of that exotic, dangerous piece of earth, its subterranean passages rumbling with the liquid gold of oil. As yet they were as a cloud no bigger than a man's hand.

The King was not alone in his anxieties. The Committee of Imperial Defence had begun to open the doors of a balanced knowledge to a select few. The Service chiefs, from their particular viewpoints, began to know, and better understand, the trends in the world, and were no longer as isolated from each other as formerly. Esher, with 'a finger in every pie', as Hankey commented, seldom missed a meeting of the Committee in the last decade of the old world, and was well briefed on the complex

[1] I do not imply that the King was on the side of Lord Charles Beresford.

politics of France. And Esher was a confidante of the King, able to advise and inform.

Kitchener, whose face and pointing finger were destined to hypnotize a nation's manhood to the slaughter, was as immutable as the Sphinx behind his huge moustaches. Perhaps he had served too long in Egypt. It was difficult, if not impossible, to know what he thought, or if he thought.

The old school still sat in the seats of power, but Lloyd George and Churchill were the coming men, about to be brought together in closer partnership by the turn of events, recognizable then as the force they might become. Lloyd George, in his rôle of Chancellor of the Exchequer, with his hands on the nation's purse strings, and deeply concerned with the Navy estimates, was having his vision extended. Churchill, a man his elders were finding it increasingly difficult to keep out of the innermost counsels, contrived to be in, at least on the sidelines. He had played his parts well on the political stage, putting his mind and energy to every task, refusing to be hemmed into the narrow orbits of his departments, whether the Colonial Office, the Board of Trade or the Home Office. He had begun to do well as Home Secretary, formulating sound plans for prison reform among other things.

But Churchill's imagination had been gripped by the terrible promise of the trends in Europe. Perhaps more than most men he sensed the horrors of things to come. His weakness would be that he could not escape from the 'glorious past', from the formal patterns of Blenheim, Ramilles, Oudenarde and Malplaquet—nor from Omdurman—nor from the music of words. Yet at the same time he knew that such set-pieces of violence, calculated skilfully to political ends, and seldom encompassing the ruin of opponents, were mere charades dictated by reasonable ambitions, directed by diplomatists, conducted by generals, performed by skilled professional players, supported by—in the main—willing extras, or those with little choice.

Few who have played active parts in the two world wars in which this country has been involved, or in any of the lesser wars, from Spain to Korea, will be likely to scoff at Churchill, or misjudge him, because his imagination was stirred, and his blood quickened more by conflict and the imminence of conflict, than by the forms of peace. It is a malady shared by an overwhelming majority of the human race.

In 1906 Churchill had been the guest of Germany, a close

observer of the elaborate and archaic military manoeuvres in Silesia to mark the centenary of Jena. Three years later at Wurzburg he noted great improvements in infantry tactics, and took part 'with glee' in a cavalry charge of musical comedy absurdity against the guns. But the charge was a personal expression for the Kaiser, and not a guide to the tactics likely to be employed by German military leaders.

At Wurzburg Churchill encountered Enver Bey, one of the intrepid leaders of the Young Turks, a man 'who had become in one leopard-spring the hero of the Turkish nation', a man after his own heart.[1] Riding their horses side by side, discussing the Baghdad railway, aware of the anxiety of their German escort to overhear their conversation, they had weighed each other up, impressed with all they saw. Enver Bey was outwardly very different from Churchill, slimly built, an exquisite, a lover of women and luxury, immensely popular in Germany with his waxed 'Kaiser' moustaches. But underneath he was all steel and courage, and an amazing contrast with his huge partner, Talaat, 'The Terrible Turk', a man whose huge hairy wrists and hands and sense of latent physical strength so deeply impressed the American Ambassador.[2] Few more curiously assorted partners could be imagined than these two, the one occupying a tumbledown hovel, the other living in exotic luxury.

To Enver Bey all this display of German military might was neither distasteful nor ominous. His nation, methodically wooed by Germany in the person of the indefatigable von Wangenheim, yet with her ears open to the approaches of France and Britain, would soon have Liman von Sanders and a picked German military staff to train her new armies. Turkey was vital to Germany's dreams of Empire, while also standing at the southern gateway to Russia, guarding the Dardanelles and the Bosphorus.

Yet Turkey, with a basic contempt for all other races, and counting Christians as less than pariah dogs, was not committed. It was too soon for that. Turkey was near chaos, the condition of her people shocking, the lot of Greeks, Armenians, Jews, terrible to contemplate.

Morgenthau, the American Ambassador in Constantinople, was watching it all, not fearing to take a hand in the game, and

[1] *Thoughts and Adventures.*
[2] Morgenthau, *Secrets of the Bosphorus.*

writing it all down. It read like a thriller few would dare to imagine. These things had not escaped Churchill. He had established an easy relationship with Enver Bey. It might prove fruitful.

All knew that the defeat of Russia by Japan had undermined the stability of Europe at least for a decade, and a thousand new dreams were spawning, not alone in Europe, as a result of the Russian tragedy. Into that power vacuum Germany rushed like a blustering wind. The Kaiser cajoled and threatened his timid cousin, Nicholas, the Tsar. He had more than half persuaded him into the struggle with Japan, a struggle in which the Russians had had little heart. None had foreseen Russia's defeat, but in this unexpected aftermath the Kaiser thought he saw his great chance to lever Russia away from France and smash the Dual Alliance. With France in a military doldrums, her army demanding complete reorganization, Germany could divide and threaten, and no nation would dare to oppose her.

France, piloted by her bold and imaginative Foreign Minister, Delcassé, deeply involved in Morocco and with her interests in the old Shereefian Empire, was suddenly warned off these pastures by a Germany feeling all powerful and glorying in the mailed fist. Ignoring the threat, Delcassé stood firm, and provoked the Kaiser to descend in person upon Tangier to voice an ultimatum couched in a manner, and in terms, that shocked Europe. The menace to France was clear, the insult unforgivable. France, unable to fight, climbed down, and began urgently to prepare her armies for the future. Delcassé resigned.

In the midsummer of 1905 Europe had been on the brink of war, and had the matter been left to the judgment of Germany's military leaders her hour would have struck.[1] The Kaiser, drunk with his own glamour and power, was providing all the words, and denying his armies the music of war. It was a time when little or nothing could have barred Germany from total domination of Western and Central Europe, a domination which would have opened a way through the Near East for the realization of her dreams of grandeur.

The Kaiser's personal letters to the Tsar at this time are remarkable. On July 24, 1905, he had persuaded the Tsar to sign

---

[1] Count Reventlow revealed that in the opinion of many German military experts Germany ought to have forced war. The Russian Fleet had been annihilated in the Far East. France was weak. See *These Eventful Years*.

a 'clandestine' Treaty at Björkö of an alliance against Britain, a treaty of which France knew nothing. At once the Kaiser wrote exuberantly to 'Nicky' in a letter dated July 27, 1905. He felt that he had at last devised an instrument to 'cool down English self-assertion and impertinence'.

'Dearest Nicky . . . the 24th July, 1905, is a cornerstone in European politics and turns over a new leaf in the history of the world. . . . Holland, Belgium, Denmark, Sweden will all be attracted to this new great centre of gravity. . . . They will revolve in the orbit of the great block of Powers . . . and feel confidence in leaning on and revolving around this mass.'

The Kaiser continued with a prophetic vision, tragically fulfilled, yet not in the kind of context the Kaiser, or anyone else at that time, could have imagined:

'America will stand on the side of this combination,' he wrote. 'The Continental Combine flanked by America is the sole and only manner effectively to block the way to the whole world becoming John Bull's private property, which he exploits to his heart's content, after having by his intrigues without end, set the rest of the civilized nations by each other's ears for his own personal benefit.'

The Kaiser's effort misfired badly. Britain rallied to the support of France, and at the Algeciras Conference of 1906 Italy joined in an international verdict overwhelmingly confirming France's interests in Morocco. The immediate danger of war had been averted, but all Europe was alerted while the Kaiser soon continued to stir diligently the dangerous brew. The pretensions of the rickety Austro-Hungarian Empire added to the decay of the Ottoman Turks, enormously increased the dangers. The Balkans were a pot needing no outside stirring.

In July 1908 the revolt of the Young Turks overthrew Abdul the Damned, and set off a reaction of desperate hopes and dreams. The Bulgar Tsar proclaimed the independent sovereignty of his country. Austria pompously annexed Bosnia and Herzogovina. The lion-hearted and individualistic peoples of Yugoslavia seeethed with fury and long frustrated passions. For centuries the Yugoslavs had been cut up and parcelled out as appendages of Austro-Hungary and Turkey, their lands laid waste, their men, women and children put to the sword, until their scarred earth was fertilized with their blood.

The Serbs barred Austria's path to Salonika and demanded a narrow strip of territory to join them with their Montenegrin brothers. Austria reacted with a contemptuous refusal. Russia, uneasy, slighted, her people beginning to find a faint voice through the Duma, revealed an upsurge of Pan-Slav fervour. Serbia, knowing that Russia would not stand aside if Austria attacked, prepared for war.

This was the kind of moment the Kaiser longed for, as the arbiter of Europe. 'Standing in shining armour' at Austria's side, in his own phrase, he issued a blunt ultimatum to Russia: Abandon Serbia or you will be at war with Germany. Unless, in short, Russia accepted Austro-Hungarian claims, annexations and pretensions, and Serbia again accepted humiliation, she would be at war with Germany and the Dual Monarchy, and Europe would be ablaze. It was a hopeless position at a hopeless moment. Russia, Serbia, Montenegro were forced to yield.

But by these means the Kaiser was rapidly strengthening the very alliances and combinations of peoples he had sought to destroy. The military weakness of Russia added to the feeble mindedness of the Tsar had precipitated these recurrent crises. Nicholas had been easily lured into the Kaiser's web. He had not the strength of mind to reject his cousin's demands at Björkö. He had set his hand to an agreement at Potsdam in support of German plans for the Baghdad railway. He had committed himself to the maintenance of the *status quo* in the Balkans. He was acutely miserable, vaguely aware of his double-dealing towards France, a prey to haemophilia, and a child in the hands of the monk, Rasputin.

Convinced that he had nothing to fear from any quarter, that Britain was in the depths of crises at home, and almost in the conditions of a rudderless ship following the death of Edward VII, the Kaiser acted a second time against France.

In the spring of 1911 the French had occupied Fez to protect their nominee, the Sultan Mulai Hafid, against an uprising of the tribes. Germany decided that this action constituted a threat to her financial interests in Morocco, mainly in the form of mining concessions to the brothers Mannesheim.

Whatever rights there were on the German side were totally

obliterated by the Kaiser's impulsive act in sending the gunboat *Panther* to Agadir. Again Germany confronted France with the choice of war or humiliation, and for a few weeks war was an hourly expectation. Grey, Britain's Foreign Minister, expected that 'the Fleet might be attacked at any moment'. The urgent notes despatched to Germany from France and Britain remained unanswered.

Impossible here to attempt to chart the underground 'diplomacy' of those curious days of the twilight of a world when the Prime Minister of France, unknown to Britain, and even to his own Cabinet, was striving to negotiate in secret with Berlin through a diplomatic underling, Baron von Lancken. It remained for David Lloyd George, the British Chancellor of the Exchequer, to warn the Germans that they had gone too far.

And at this, as Garvin wrote, 'the world held its breath'.

Lloyd George made his startling speech on the night of July 21st to a gathering of City men at the Mansion House, and it is doubtful if any of those who actually heard him speak took any particular note, but 'the Chancelleries of Europe bounded together,' wrote Churchill, and to Germany, regarding Lloyd George as a pacifist, and almost an ally, it came as a 'thunderclap'.

Churchill and Lloyd George had discussed the situation briefly on the morning of July 21st, and the Chancellor had revealed that he had made up his mind. Germany had made no answer to British protests, and Britain could not be treated with contempt, as if she did not count. Lloyd George was resolved to make it clear that Britain did count, and was resolved to 'maintain her place and prestige amongst the Great Powers of the world'. Europe had been on tenterhooks, dithering and fearful for weeks.

'I would make great sacrifices to preserve peace,' he said to his Mansion House audience, and to the world. 'I conceive that nothing would justify a disturbance of international goodwill except questions of the gravest national moment. But if a situation were to be forced upon us in which peace could only be preserved by the surrender of the great and beneficent position Britain has won ... to be treated when her interests were vitally affected as if she were of no account in the Cabinet of nations, then I say emphatically that peace at that price would be a humiliation intolerable for a great country like ours to endure.'

By that speech Lloyd George and Churchill came together as 'brothers in arms', a relationship neither one of them had expected to enjoy. Opposition to the naval estimates was swept away, and a new impetus had been given to the urgent preparations for war.

This is a bare outline of some of the main events that put Churchill in the Admiralty, and to press ahead with all his energy to make the Navy ready for whatever might be in store. At the same time Haldane in the War Office prepared to put up to six divisions of infantry with supporting cavalry into France within three weeks of mobilization. This would demand naval co-operation and joint planning on a level never before visualized.

But at this stage in the aftermath of Agadir it fell to an Italy, desperate and deprived, to help the avalanche on its way. Since the *Risorgimento* Italy had had, she believed, the worst end of every stick. Her rapidly growing population was emigrating in droves not only to the United States and the Argentine, but even to Germany, France and Tunis in search of work and a decent standard of living. Delcassé's dream of an 'Empire of Atlas' for France had denied Italy her chance in North Africa. Now the break-up of the Ottoman Empire, and the intense preoccupation of the Young Turks at home, tempted Italy to chance her arm and seize Tripoli. Nothing else remained for her between British and French North Africa, and the Germans might find it difficult after Agadir to oppose Italian ambitions.

On September 28, 1911, Italy demanded the Turkish surrender of Tripoli. Her navy allowed Italy to land her troops in Tripoli at will, and sufficed to cut off Turkish hopes of reinforcing her garrisons. These operations were carried out in a leisurely, even a half-hearted manner. Enver Bey, managing to make his way inland, boldly rallied the tribes to harry the invader, and the campaign went into a state of suspended animation for four months while Italian politicians made up their minds to untie the hands of their soldiers. In October 1912 Italy had won her 'Empire' and Libya and Cyrenaica were hers.

By these deeds Italy had brought the Balkan cauldron to the boil, and much more besides. The closing of the Dardanelles had hampered Russian trade. Austria had teetered on the verge of invading Italy. The Triple Alliance had hesitated to follow threats with deeds. But the Balkans were aflame.

Largely thanks to J. D. Bourchier, *The Times* correspondent, one of that small brave band of English men and women who have dedicated themselves to the Balkan peoples in the last century, secret treaties between Greece, Serbia and Bulgaria inspired these small nations to defy Turkey, and to throw off the tyranny that had held them in fearful misery and horror for centuries.

Until this time it had seemed to the Great Powers as impossible to achieve Balkan unity as 'to square a circle'. J. D. Bourchier had achieved the miracle! Albania rose against Turkey; Montenegro did herself the honour of declaring war. In mid-October 1912 Bulgaria, Serbia and Greece delivered identical *ultimata* in Constantinople demanding complete freedom from Ottoman rule, and the immediate demobilization of the Turkish armies. The Great Powers waffled and threatened, and asserted that whatever happened they would restore the *status quo*. Austria shuddered, as it is said that men do when someone walks over their graves. It was all in vain. In any case none doubted that Turkey would swiftly reimpose her will and bring the Balkans once more to subjection. All would be well.

The Turks ignored the Balkan ultimatum, and mobilized to punish their vassals.

But the Turk who had 'swept out of Asia, all conquering and founded the mighty Ottoman Empire' had almost expired in the twentieth century, as so much else was doomed to expire. The promise of the Young Turks, that 'rainbow bent over the world's worst cockpit of inveterate hatreds', was a mere illusion. The Turkish contempt for the rest of mankind was total, as Morgenthau observed.

With an army of 600,000 men, half of them Bulgars, the Balkan peoples fell upon the Turks in Thrace with a fury seldom if ever surpassed, while the Greek Navy barred the way to Turkish transports. Three hundred and fifty thousand men locked together in mortal combat smashed the Turks to ruin at Kirk Kilisse and Lule Burgas, and the remnants of the Turkish army retreated, almost a rabble, behind the Chatalja lines covering Constantinople.

'As the Balkan Christians went down before the Turks in the fourteenth and fifteenth centuries the Turks went down before the Balkan Christians in the twentieth,' wrote Garvin.

In a brief but terrific struggle 600 years of tyranny had ended. When the Crown Prince of Serbia rode at the head of his troops into Uskub, the legendary city of his race, the lion hearts of the bravest people in Europe swelled with a pride that had lain dormant and submerged for far too long.

Nothing startled the Austrians more than these exultant and resurgent Serbs. All Europe, as well as defeated Turkey, had been amazed at the prowess in battle of Bulgars and Greeks. Salonika was cleared. It is one of the most brave and stirring themes in the history of war.

The Great Powers were powerless to restore the *status quo*, as they had threatened. There is no such possibility as the restoration of a *status quo*. It is an illusion, difficult to kill. By the Treaty of London in May 1913 European Turkey ceased to exist and the whole map of Europe would soon be re-drawn.

In Austria, Aerenthals had been succeeded as Foreign Minister by Count Leopold von Berchtold, described by Churchill as 'a fop and a dandy, allured by the glamour and force of the military men, and fascinated by the rattle and glitter of their terrible madness'. It was a malady from which Churchill himself also suffered. But by the appointment of von Berchtold in place of Aerenthals one more strut of moderation and sanity had been weakened in a rickety structure. It would be von Berchtold's lot to light the final fuse of war. There was not long to wait for the first instalment of Armageddon.

## CHAPTER X

※❀※

From the moment of his translation to the Admiralty Churchill's vision was inevitably concentrated upon his main task. It was his responsibility to prepare the Navy to meet the German challenge and to secure beyond a doubt Britain's defences on the seas. He was aware, and said so clearly, that the threat to Britain was starvation rather than invasion. He prepared to prevent both disasters.

Admiral Fisher had prepared the ground, ruthlessly cutting out obsolete vessels, obsolete men and obsolete ideas. It was his dream to build an invincible navy equipped with the largest ships and most powerful guns and he planned to begin the recruitment of officers from the lower deck. He had held it to be an anachronism in a democracy that the officers in command of the defences of the country should be drawn exclusively from a very limited upper class. Similarly the old Admiral had loathed the Tory dominance of the House of Lords, a situation that had finally forced Asquith to threaten the King with the creation of a whole host of Liberal peers unless the Parliament Act became law. Churchill shared these views, and Fisher watched the words and deeds of the new First Lord from afar.

In a speech that delighted the old admiral, Churchill stated that 'we must always be ready to meet at our average moment anything that any possible enemy might hurl against us at his selected moment'. Such words were the essence of wisdom.

At the same time Churchill had devised a scheme whereby up to one hundred young warrant officers each year would be selected as suitable for promotion to commissioned rank, and he announced in the House: 'These are days when the Navy, which is the great national service, should be opened more broadly to the nation as a whole.'

In a famous speech at Glasgow he referred to German naval ambitions as a luxury, whereas for Britain a great fleet was an absolute necessity. The word luxury stuck in the gullets of the Germans at a time when Haldane was on a special mission seeking to open discussions in an attempt to halt the naval arms race. The speech caused irritation and criticism as well as praise at home, but it appealed greatly to Fisher. 'About the very best national and thoroughly reasonable public and patriotic act ever performed was your speech at Glasgow,' he wrote to 'my beloved Winston'.[1]

Churchill, now with the aid of Lloyd George, Chancellor of the Exchequer, laid down two keels to one in competition with the Germans. It was not only a question of ships, but of types of ships, of propulsion and fuel, of armament, of the development of submarines and a naval air arm. Rudolf Diesel had probably revolutionised propulsion, and with that coal, and even oil, might become obsolete. The internal combustion engine might rule the world, and the old 'steam' empires were in a new race which might be dominated by science and technology. It was an unpleasant thought. A constant stream of new and unknown factors, and problems of obsolescence, were constantly hampering the planners of weapons and strategy in a manner previously unknown, and undreamt of.

Churchill tackled all these tasks with immense energy and enthusiasm. Not yet forty years old he appeared to be in his natural element. If war proved once again to be the ultimate instrument of politics and diplomacy he was resolved to be its strong arm. It was straightforward. He had equipped the Admiralty yacht, *Enchantress,* as an office afloat and was able to spend more than two months in each year visiting the naval bases and stations of the British Fleet, while maintaining close contact with his admirals and the Admiralty. It was the combination of physical and mental activity, of everlastingly doing, and with a clear-cut unequivocal aim, that fed his restless mind and spirit.

In spite of these tremendous and urgent preoccupations he was vividly aware of the stirring and ominous events changing the patterns of Central Europe and the Near East. He was probably one of the half dozen best informed men in Britain on foreign affairs and British commitments. In the years 1911-14, while the last dregs of the old world were running out, and the condition known as peace was soon to cease to exist, he cruised

[1] *The World Crisis,* 1911-14.

in the Mediterranean on the Admiralty yacht for three or four weeks in the year, relaxing, often with the Prime Minister, Herbert Asquith, as his guest. He was able, therefore, not only to sail the coasts of war, but to maintain an intimate and fruitful contact with his political chief, and one of the finest intellects in Europe.

Asquith's quietness, his imperturbability, his scholarship, have been mistaken almost for weakness, at least for mildness. Churchill knew well that such an impression was wide of the mark. No man reaches the pinnacle of political power in Britain without qualities of ruthlessness, and if such a one should do so it is only swiftly to be cast down. Asquith was perhaps the greatest peace-time Prime Minister England ever had. The quality of his velvet glove was of the finest; the hand within was of iron.

Together with their wives and personal secretaries these two curiously assorted men of power cruised in the Adriatic, visiting Venice, and sailing the lovely Dalmatian coast, putting in without fuss at Split and Dubrovnik, observing Durazzo and the harbour of Valona. Such names made chords that would echo in Churchill's mind through the long years ahead. They knew well the gulfs of Patras and Corinth, and all the ramifications of the Aegean and the Isles of Greece. They visited the group of islands about to be renamed the Dodecanese by the Italians, and of which Rhodes was the southern anchor. Few men knew better than Churchill the strategic importance of the Dardanelles and Bosphorus. He understood also Russian, Turkish and Balkan ambitions involving these seas and outlets.

As a result of the Balkan wars Serbia had at last won through to the Adriatic, only to be bitterly challenged by Austria. The growing danger signals were clear for all to see. In November 1912 Asquith stated that, 'The map of Eastern Europe has to be recast, and the victors are not to be robbed of the fruits which have cost them so dear.' But less than a year later Bulgaria had turned ferociously upon her brothers in arms, jealous of their occupation of Macedonia, and had gone down to ruinous defeat at the hands of the Greeks and Serbs, closely linked in harmony. Enver Bey, swift to grasp this wonderful opportunity, quietly marched a Turkish army back over the battlefield of Lule Burgas to regain Adrianople. One hundred and fifty thousand Bulgarians had died valiantly, but in vain, stripped by their country's greed of all their gains. Terror and outrage again afflicted or menaced the desperate peoples of Thrace, and the exploding powder keg of the Balkans had generated the means of an even greater explosion.

In May 1913 it had seemed to many that a new and more hopeful future lay ahead, not only for the Balkan peoples, but for all Europe. 'From this pinnacle of chance,' wrote Garvin, 'the hopes of the world fell in a moment and were dashed to pieces.'

Of the important conversations and discussions on the Admiralty yacht, if there were any, I know nothing. Asquith doodled, invented quiz games, polished Greek hexameters, brushed up his Thucydides, and discoursed brilliantly on the Peloponnesian wars. Asquith's learning was as valuable to Churchill in his prime as Amery's help with Latin and Greek had been in his schooldays. But there are some lessons a man may neither teach, nor another learn. Asquith had no need of the lesson the Greeks had learned from Homer, that it is necessary to examine not only a man's deeds, but the image of a mind created by his words. It is doubtful whether Churchill could have learned it.

Edward Marsh wrote in his letters that they were all 'a happy family' on these cruises, and with a great capacity for fun. Asquith's brilliant wife, the volatile Margot, was a tremendous and fearless talker, a match for Churchill, which was not too much to his taste. Clementine Churchill remained, as always, the delightful and impeccable hostess, the soul of discretion, the unfailing friend and companion in the background of Churchill's life. They all played execrable bridge. They went ashore incognito like tourists when the fancy took them. While Marsh declaimed amidst the ruin of the Parthenon, Churchill was restrained from having the place tidied up by a party of bluejackets.

These sailings round the perimeter of war did not represent the full extent of Churchill's journeyings for pleasure in these years. He had visited Spain, and sensed with sensuous pleasure the latent violence beneath the surface of one of the most enigmatic and supremely dignified races in the world. He had found time to stand in a long silence beside Napoeon's death-bed, imposing a pregnant hush upon that chamber of bitter memories in which the Emperor in contemplating the debris of an empire might have achieved personal peace. Churchill had had his Napoleonic dreams from an early age. He had them then; and they would recur, strengthened perhaps by this experience, and by his own reaction to the catalyst of power that transmutes the gold of men to dross.

Yet vividly aware as men like Asquith and Churchill must have been of the storms gathering, and of the storms that had beset these seas and all the lands of Europe for centuries, it is impossible to know the extent or quality of their awareness, or of any man's. The present is a constantly moving point on the conveyer belt of time, consuming the future; a conveyer belt, moreover, not moving upon an even keel, but upwards as a rack and pinion scaling an unknown and awesome mountain range, so that all the scene now and past is forever and with every moment resolving into new perspectives. A skein of events is unravelling without pause, yet born out of past and present. There is no constant, and it may be that to look back too soon is to become 'a pillar of salt'.

At times it may be possible, a split second after disaster, to see, or to think one sees, how it might have been avoided, or turned into victory. Ten minutes later the view has changed again. Ten years later victory or disaster may be seen to be irrelevant.

But it was possible to know in those quiet years before the outbreak of the First World War something of the major happenings in the world, and for men of first-class ability to assess and digest the importance of such happenings. Hate, fear and distortion as we now know them were almost absent. The nature of ambitions was known. Now it has become impossible for any man to know what is happening, or why, or what is the actual result of any small piece of human conflict or negotiation. The alarming growth and speed of communications produces an incessant avalanche of fragments, as meaningless as confetti, and each fragment distorted by men and nations riven with hate and fear, is fed piecemeal into minds similarly riven.

Yet the mind and nature of man remains the hope and raft. 'It still remains true,' said Richard Crossman, 'that the final decisions must be taken by human beings, and the humble study of human nature still remains the criterion of wisdom, whether in a general or a politician.'[1]

[1] Lecture to RUSI. March 1961.

The view forward, and the way chosen, may only be based upon the knowledge of what has happened seen in the light of the ambitions, national, international and personal, of the principal players. We cannot with certainty reach back into any moment of time and say this much this man knew in that hour. And even if it were possible we should need to know what manner of man, what qualities of mind, what pressures and emotions, he suffered or enjoyed, what personal ambitions obscured or clarified his vision, and what were the bases of his unwisdom as well as of his wisdom. Above all we need to know the nature of his dreams, and his conceptions of power.

## II

These travels round the perimeters of war may give an impression that these exalted travellers were in a special position to appreciate many of the dangers threatening Europe and the world. That they were in highly privileged position there can be no doubt, but it seems to me that this position effectively divorced them from an appreciation of the realities of the European situation.

Lloyd George has put on record that in the month of July 1914, a lady, whose name he had forgotten, told him that there was a storm of feeling sweeping Austria and the Balkans 'such as she had never witnessed', and that it meant almost certain war unless 'something was done'. There was not, she thought, a moment to lose. All that we know about the lady is that she was a Hungarian. She had no access to secret papers, nor to chancelleries, nor did she travel with special privileges. She was an ordinary traveller. Her experiences were shared by many other ordinary travellers, buying tickets on trains, being held up at frontiers, finding hotel accommodation, and rubbing shoulders with their fellow ordinary citizens in the cafés and on the boulevards of Europe. Their commonplace knowledge had not percolated through to the chancelleries of the Great Powers. Official reports did not justify the lady's views, Lloyd George noted.

Thus it is clear, I believe, that the privileges which should have enabled statesmen the better to perform their duties were already a serious barrier between them and an understanding of the world they atttempted to rule. They moved in a world of their own. In spite of their extensive journeys, their easy access to foreign ministries, and to confidential reports, leading statesmen were isolated from all the stresses and strains clearly to be felt at lower levels. On the eve of war they expected and received courtesy from their opposite numbers, and crossed closed frontiers in luxurious ease, knowing nothing of those 'lets and hindrances' from which foreign ministers, naïvely or ironically, request and require that the least of their citizens shall be exempt.

In June 1914 powerful units of the British Fleet lay at their moorings alongside the great ships of the German navy. Officers and men shared the hospitality of each other's wardrooms and mess decks, and strolled arm in arm through the streets of Kiel and Kronstadt. Together they stood to pay tribute at the grave of a German officer killed while trying out a new British naval aircraft. The Kaiser was in great form, and about to set off for a cruise on the Imperial yacht. Churchill, while not relaxing his vigilance in the smallest degree, enjoyed himself greatly. He had fulfilled his task of maintaining the strength and readiness of the British Navy to meet any challenge from any quarter, but specifically to meet the challenge of the powerful fleet now released to the open sea by the opening of the Kiel canal. In the previous October he had already prepared for the review of the Grand Fleet in the Solent, the greatest array of warships ever gathered together. His powerful imagination, sharpened by the possibilities of conflict, gave him confidence that not only the Navy, but the people of Britain would rise to meet any challenge. In April in a speech at Bradford, challenging Edward Carson's belligerent posturings in Ireland, he had warned that it would be dangerous for foreign countries to misconstrue the British attitude. 'They do not know what we know,' he said, 'that at a touch of external difficulties or menace all these fierce internal controversies would disappear for the time being, and we should be brought into line and into tune. But why is it that men are so constituted that they can only lay aside their own domestic quarrels under the impulse of what I will call a higher principle of hatred?'

Yet Churchill shared the ignorance of the Service Chiefs and most of his fellow-members of the British Cabinet of British foreign policy. He knew all the details of the military and naval plans, of the staff talks with the French, but he did not know what series of events would set these plans in motion. A German emissary, Herr Ballin, had tried to sound out British intentions on the eve of war. 'If Russia marches against Austria, we must march; and if we march, France must march, and what would England do?' He asked Churchill point-blank. But Churchill did not know. No one knew; not Asquith, not Grey. None could predict the reactions of a British Cabinet to ultimatums of which, an hour before, they had been in almost total ignorance. Thus on August 2, 1914, with the armies of the Great European powers within a few hours of collision, Cambon, the usually meek and mild French Ambassador, was driven to his passionate outburst to the British Foreign Minister:

'There is not a scrap of paper. But there is something more. Every act of yours over the last few years gave us the assurance of your support . . . *est-ce-que l'Angleterre comprend ce que c'est que l'honneur?* If you stand out and we survive we shall not move a finger to save you from being crushed by Germany later; if we lose you will share our fate anyhow.'

It is a story many times told of appalling muddle and confusion, the last days of the known about to be precipitated into the unknown. What would Britain do was the question mark over Europe. Following the murder of the Grand Duke Ferdinand at Sarajevo, Sir Edward Grey had assured the Cabinet that Britain was uncommitted in the event of war. The situation was grave, but war seemed a remote possibility to those who, like Sir Edward Grey, appeared to consider themselves as 'High Priests', aloof from the torments and stresses of lesser mortals.

Lloyd George has borne ample testimony to the mysteries shrouding foreign affairs from all but the most senior members of the British Cabinet in the years before the First World War. 'There was a reticence and secrecy,' he wrote, 'which practically ruled out three-fourths of the Cabinet from the chance of making any genuine contribution to the momentous questions then fermenting on the Continent of Europe, which ultimately ended in an explosion that almost shattered the civilization of the world.'

Sir Edward Grey appeared to regard foreign affairs as a purely personal matter between himself, the Prime Minister, and God, with the Monarch on the sidelines.

'We were made to feel that, in these matters, we were reaching our hands towards the mysteries, and that we were too young in the priesthood to presume to enter into the sanctuary reserved for the elect.'[1]

At a dinner party at Lord Birkenhead's, Lord Northcliffe taunted the distinguished company with knowing a good deal less about what was going on than the editor of a first-class newspaper. The taunt was fully justified.

Thus the world drifted to war, and it is improbable that any act of man could have prevented it. But its course and pattern might well have been changed had Britain stated her position unequivocally at an early stage. King George V had spoken frankly to the Russian Foreign Minister, and even more frankly to Prince Henry of Prussia. The King wrote to Grey in December 1912 informing him of his clear statement to Prince Henry that Britain would go to the aid of Russia and France. Later he had repeated his conversation to Count Mensdorff.

'Do you believe that we have less sense of honour than you?' he had said to Prince Henry. 'You possess signed Alliances: we unsigned Ententes. We cannot allow either France or Russia to be overthrown.'[2]

Prince Henry had been 'horrified', so horrified that he had not dared to give the Kaiser a clear report of his cousin's statement.

Towards the end of July the puppets who thought they controlled events were suddenly confronted with the forces of war moving of their own volition. They had pressed the buttons without knowing, and perhaps only the foppish and vain von Berchtold, Foreign Minister of Austria, knew exactly what he was doing when he demanded the abject humiliation of Serbia. He expressed himself as resolved to 'burn out that wasps' nest' of Serbia even at the cost of a European war. Deliberately he lit the fuse.

The world such men and their monarchs lived in was crumbling while they danced and played on their yachts, in their palaces, at their balls and banquets, and strutted at their glittering parades. The power game had been wonderful and

[1] David Lloyd George, *War Memoirs*, Vol. I.
[2] Harold Nicolson, *King George V*.

exhilarating, the sabre rattling, the displays of might, the chastisement of lesser peoples. The game was up. Austria mobilized to punish Serbia. Russia mobilized to aid Serbia and to protect herself against Austria. Germany mobilized to aid Austria.

Desperately the Kaiser telegraphed to the Tsar to halt his armies, but it was too late. The Russian armies were mobilizing and on the march. The machinery wouldn't go into reverse. The Kaiser then appealed to von Moltke to change his plans, fearful that to march through Belgium would bring in Britain against him. But it was too late. Von Moltke was adamant. The puerile 'Willy-Nicky' letters were finished; and the days of their writers were numbered.

### III

When Churchill walked into the Admiralty on the evening of the 24th July to greet his secretaries, Marsh and Masterton Smith, with the sombre news of almost certain war, he was like a man living in the baleful silence that presages a hurricane, and giving an impression of immense vitality and suppressed excitement. He had returned from a long and dreary Cabinet meeting, discussing the dismal and terrible problems of Ireland, when suddenly he had heard the quiet, unruffled voice of Edward Grey reading the Austrian ultimatum to Serbia. It was an ultimatum 'such as had never been penned in modern times'. It demanded the abject submission and humiliation of a proud and violent people.

Churchill had awakened as from a dream, suddenly roused to confront a vivid and deadly dangerous world, a world to which he was attuned in every fibre of his being. The scenery was rolling back, the stage revolving, making way for hosts of new players.

'The parishes of Fermanagh and Tyrone faded back into the mists and squalls of Ireland, and a strange light began immediately, but by perceptible gradations, to fall and grow upon the map of Europe.'[1]

Now there would be gigantic parts to play, the stage filling up with bold, adventurous actors seizing and demanding romantic acclamation. Had he then come too fast and far for such a rôle?

[1] *The World Crisis, 1911-14.*

On that evening a phase of Churchill's life was moving swiftly to a close, and he was about to recognize the most powerful urges in his nature. Never would he be more true to himself, nor try to understand and to state more clearly what it was that he most longed for, and what he might do best. He was about to suffer the fate of all adventurer-jacks-of-all-trades when the delectable opportunities of which they have dreamed, but for which they have failed to prepare, are snatched from their grasp. Thus it would be with Churchill.

He could look back with satisfaction on all that he had achieved in the years since he had returned in his youthful triumph from the wars. That he had done well few objective observers, I think, would deny. An examination of his speeches from the date of his entry into Parliament reveals a steady grasp of the mechanics of what it is fair to call statesmanship. His crossing of the floor of the House must fail to shock biographers, for never was a man more independent of all groups of men, and since there was no future for independents, the Liberals offered more than the Tories to such a man at such a time. He was an opportunist and must seize every opportunity; moreover, the personality of Lloyd George attracted him deeply, and was essential to his own development. No other man but Churchill ever called Lloyd George 'David', no other man more truly recognized Lloyd George's giant stature. It was almost as if Churchill recognized his 'guru' and went simply to sit at his feet.

But Churchill had failed to find a true political haven. He had travelled the political road with great skill, but had not discovered his own rôle, impatient with the endless spinning and interminable grinding. He had arrived at a time when the preservation and defence of his country's great wealth and heritage was paramount, and its Elizabethan adventures very far in the past. Patience and all the arts of compromise were alien to him. There was much to strive for in the way of social change, but to such endeavours neither his nature nor his spirit were truly attuned. He was a man of action, of physical and mental action combined. He demanded the full adventure of living, the knowledge of endless doing, of travelling hopefully. As First Lord of the Admiralty it was almost as if he had arrived. But in his heart would be forever the boy and the child dreaming dreams that the man must strive to live.

His years at the Admiralty had seemed to provide many of

those things his nature demanded, and perhaps all that a peaceful condition might ever provide. He had fulfilled his naval task admirably, building up the firm foundations laid by his predecessors. But he was also an innovator, constantly exploring possibilities. He had at his right hand a dedicated sailor in the person of Prince Louis of Battenberg, First Sea Lord, more English than the English, and as single-heartedly loyal as perhaps only such a man may be. Moreover, Prince Louis was a man of great moral and physical courage, allied to wisdom, born to responsibility. Together, Churchill and Battenberg had fashioned the Navy into a magnificent instrument of sea power, and together they were to launch it into war. They knew that war was entering upon a new and unknown phase. They were aware that the development of submarines, of mines and naval aircraft, would certainly call for strategic and tactical manoeuvres beyond any man's experience to predict. The twin giants of science and technology were beginning to stir, and had already put all the great and small ships of war under the hand and control of the First Lord, immediately receptive to his will and command.

Politically, Churchill had shown great foresight. He had helped to conceive and evolve war risks insurance to enable owners and shippers to put their ships and cargoes to sea without fear of crippling personal loss. He had prepared cargo vessels to meet some of the new perils they might have to face, and begun to arm them against attack. He had thought out many of the complex problems of blockade, realizing its great potency as a weapon, and resisting the terms of the Declaration of London which would have crippled Britain's ability to use her sea power to full effect.

'You can no more tame war than you can tame hell!' Lord Fisher had said. Rules that cannot be enforced are valueless, and nations fighting for their lives will break any rules to save themselves from disaster. Britain anticipated trouble with the neutrals, and especially with the United States of America, in the event of war and the effective maintenance of a blockade of the enemy. Maurice Hankey, the indefatigable Secretary to the Committee of Imperial Defence, had thought it all out. Britain would stand firm against all pressures from all quarters.

Churchill's immediate actions on the eve of war had been masterly. His conception of holding a review of the Grand Fleet in mid-July 1914 in place of the usual manoeuvres, was a stroke of genius, and resulted in a display of sea power on a scale never before realized. On July 15th the test mobilization had begun, and on the 16th and 17th of the month almost the entire naval power of Britain was displayed in the Solent in brilliant sunshine. Those two days and nights impressed themselves unforgettably on all who saw, and by night the cadets and pupils of the naval schools on the shores of the Solent, having steamed in the shadows of the great ships in pinnaces by day, watched ten thousand searchlights weave in the night sky. Then on the 19th the ships, decked with flags and with bands playing, steamed at 15 knots for their stations.

As the European situation steadily darkened, Churchill and Battenberg held the Fleet together and delayed its planned dispersal. 'The whole of the First and Second Fleets were complete in every way for battle and were concentrated at Portland.' There they would remain until 7 a.m. on the morning of July 27th.

On Sunday, 26th, Churchill was with his family at Cromer, looking over the sea that would almost surely be the battleground of the coming war, perhaps the decisive theatre and the burial place of German naval ambitions. As he looked, Churchill saw in his mind's eye all the ships of the Navy, 'All along the East Coast, from Cromarty to Dover, in their various sally-ports, lay our patrol flotillas of destroyers and submarines. In the Channel, behind the torpedo-proof moles of Portland Harbour, waited all the great ships of the British Navy.' He had maintained contact all through Sunday with the First Sea Lord, and when he reached the Admiralty on Monday morning Prince Louis had given the order to the Fleet not to disperse. The news from the European capitals was worsening fast.

On the next morning Churchill and the First Sea Lord again acted in concert and in wholehearted agreement. On his own initiative, fearful that an overwhelmingly pacific Cabinet might demur, Churchill gave orders for the Fleet to proceed to its war stations. Only the Prime Minister had been told of this bold precaution, and had given his consent without a word, answering Churchill swiftly with a long, hard stare and a deep grunt which the younger man knew how to translate.

These last days were irresistible to Churchill as he conjured up visions 'of gigantic castles of steel wending their way across the misty, shining sea, like giants bowed in anxious thought ... as darkness fell, eighteen miles of warships running at high speed in absolute blackness. . . .' The whole Battle Fleet had run the Straits of Dover without showing a light in the early hours of July 29th. Long before first light they were gone. Nothing in Stevenson or Haggard, or even Dumas, could surpass that and it was a story Churchill was creating, living, writing himself, while making history at the helm of 'considerable affairs'.

On that morning Admiral Fisher called upon his 'beloved Winston' at the Admiralty, knowing all his vision fulfilled. 'The King's ships were at sea.'

Since this bold move was unknown to the potential enemy it could not be construed as provocative or offensive. It was an essential act of foresight, as was also the shadowing of the German battle cruiser *Goeben* and the light cruiser *Breslau*, sighted west of Sicily and steaming fast for the Dardanelles. At the same time precautions were taken to prevent Turkish crews from seizing the two Turkish battleships building on Tyneside and almost complete.

As the last hours of peace ran out the *Goeben* and *Breslau* were within 10,000 yards of the 12 inch guns of the British battle cruisers. The opportunity would not recur: it could not be taken. The British Cabinet had not made up its mind and, but for the violation of Belgian neutrality, might not have done so. Even that was not a clear and simple issue, for it seemed inconceivable that Germany, having built up her massive system of military communications on the Belgian frontier, could have failed to reach some secret agreement for the passage of her armies. And there were profound heart-searchings over Belgian behaviour in the Congo.

Nevertheless, at last the British ultimatum had been delivered to Germany to stop the invasion of Belgium. At midnight on August 4, 1914, the ultimatum expired and Britain was at war. In London and in all the capitals of the warring powers the people were jubilant, welcoming war with an enthusiasm that excited and chilled their rulers. Peace, it seemed, had not been a happy condition of mankind. It was at an end.

While the Prime Minister and his family were in tears, Mrs Asquith noted that Churchill was 'all smiles', and her husband wrote in his diary: 'Winston, who has got on all his war paint, is longing for a sea fight in the early hours of the morning to result in the sinking of the *Goeben*. The whole thing fills me with sadness.'

But the *Goeben*, putting on an unlooked-for turn of speed, had eluded her pursuers, as so much else was to elude the First Lord. The early naval disasters, nearly all of which were well redeemed by the end of the year, added to the grave threat swiftly developing against the Channel ports, pitched Churchill from his high place at the helm into the heart of the struggle. It was vital to hold the Channel ports, but not a task for the First Lord of the Admiralty in person. He could not sit still. His energy was prodigious and immensely stimulated. The compulsion to be physically involved was too much for him, and he was prepared to stake his whole career and political future in exchange for the excitements of the hour. As a soldier-war correspondent he had once found himself, or as much of himself as could be contained in one basket. There was no room or place for all of him, and he would never—save for an imperishable hour—fuse entire. That hour was still a long way off. He was within a few weeks of his fortieth birthday, in the prime of his manhood, and ready to confront his destiny. Nothing could hold him at his post at the Admiralty. He played truant.

The hurricane of the enemy advance on the Western Front was soon to settle down into the dreadful years of attrition which were to deprive Britain, France, Germany and Russia of their finest manhood, and leave the future irrevocably impoverished. The orderly retreat from Mons had misled the enemy as much as it had alarmed the allies, but out of that brave retreat the victory of the Marne was born. Meanwhile the French general, Joffre, was anxious for British support to threaten the enemy communications from the north coast of France. Churchill reacted with speed and enthusiasm, infecting and inspiring the British general, French, and all with whom he came in contact. He had organized a naval division, and established a new flying base at Dunkirk. He landed his marine brigade, 3,000 strong and supported by a fleet of 'armed motor cars', at Zeebrugge. Promptly he landed himself, and whipped up his 'Dunkirk Circus' to bold and valuable deeds, severely harrying the enemy.

At home, he begged Lord Kitchener to supply troops to aid in the defence of Antwerp, but Kitchener was unwilling to commit his raw territorials to such a task. Churchill embarked his own even less trained naval division, and himself rushed to stiffen the Belgian will to hold the Antwerp forts against the enemy tide. 'Of course it would be idle butchery to send a force like

Winston's little army there . . .,' Asquith wrote in his diary, and two days later: 'The intrepid Winston set off at midnight and ought to have reached Antwerp at about nine this morning. . . . I do not know how fluent he is in French but, if he was able to do himself justice in a foreign tongue, the Belges will have listened to a discourse the like of which they have never heard before. I cannot but think that he will stiffen them up.'

Kitchener almost alone in those days struck a note of harsh reality. He knew that it would be a long war, and already visualized and planned the raising of a vast army to fight on the continent of Europe and to change for all time the balance of British manhood and British power.

On September 9th the Kaiser had given the order to take Antwerp, and its fall, as Asquith said, 'would be a great moral blow to the Allies, for it would leave the whole of Belgium at the mercy of the Germans.' But such a blow would be grave physically as well as morally, and Churchill strove valiantly to ward it off in person.

But long before the threat developed Churchill was off like a whirlwind, visiting his own little army. 'The adventurous Winston is just off to Dunkirk to superintend his new flying base. He will be back by lunch-time tomorrow,' the Prime Minister noted hopefully. Within a week or two no one knew when he would be back. He was 'ravening like a tiger' for battle, to win the war single-handed, and telegraphing the Prime Minister to permit him to resign as First Lord. 'Winston persists in remaining there (Antwerp), which leaves the Admiralty without a head, and I have to tell them to submit all decisions to me,' Asquith wrote.

So great was Churchill's energy, so infectious his schemes and dreams, that he made, for a little while, the impossible seem almost possible. His naval brigades, mainly raw recruits, most of whom had never fired a rifle, could not hold at Antwerp, and should never have been committed. Yet Churchill's action at Antwerp 'gained the priceless days needed to save the Western Front as a whole,' wrote Amery in a considered judgment few would question. For two or three days, while the Admiralty lacked its head, Churchill became virtually Belgium, taking the army, navy and civil government into his own hands, and it was not in vain.

When he returned to his post at home he knew quite clearly

what he wanted to do, and what he wanted to be. He had 'tasted blood'. He wanted, above all else, the military command which would have assuredly been his had he not succumbed to his restless longings to write and report war, to become a politician. He was, as Asquith pointed out, 'an ex-lieutenant of Hussars seeking command over distinguished generals, not to mention brigadiers and colonels. . . .'

Churchill pleaded in vain.

'For about a quarter of an hour he poured forth a ceaseless cataract of invective and appeal, and I much regretted that there was no shorthand writer within hearing, as some of his unpremeditated phrases were quite priceless.' Asquith, however, managed to preserve some of it. Churchill's mouth waters at the sight and thought of K's new armies. 'Are these glittering commands,' he pleaded, to be entrusted 'to dug-out trash' bred on the obsolete tactics of twenty-five years ago, 'mediocrities who have led a sheltered life mouldering in a military routine?' etc, etc.

Finally Churchill stated flatly that 'a political career was nothing to him in comparison with military glory'.

Thus, desperately, he strove to jump the queue, to go back to the turning he had passed forever, and walk another road. It remained his dream, never to be fulfilled. He might be showered with honorary degrees by the great universities whose examinations and conditions of entry he had failed to fulfil. He might similarly be honoured with high ranks, and politically wield supreme command, but he had renounced forever his right to 'the glittering commands' earned by those who had stuck it out through the long 'military routine'.

Yet in these first months of the First World War Churchill is a magnificent figure in the manner of Dumas, his complexities merged, his spirit fused, as undefeatable as d'Artagnan. Less than a year later the tragedy of the Dardanelles, and the hatred of the Tory Party, lost him the Admiralty, heaped the bitter rage of multitudes upon his head, and would have condemned any other man to total obscurity. 'You can imagine what a horrible wound and mutilation it is for him,' Edward Marsh wrote to Violet Asquith. '. . . it's like Beethoven deaf. . . .'

Churchill had written to Bonar Law with dignity and restraint, asking to be judged by the true facts. He would wait long for such a consummation in such a quarter, and was without illusions. He had little respect for Bonar Law, 'The raw and rowdy Under-Secretary, whom the nakedness of the land, and the jealousies of his betters, have promoted to the leadership of the Tory Party.' It was one of the phrases he had thought and written down, but had not spoken.

Above all Churchill was too much an egocentric to blame the world or others for his misfortunes. The world did not use him; he used the world; he would use it again.

Meanwhile in May 1915, immediately after his loss of the Admiralty, Churchill was on a farm near Godalming with his wife, the faithful Marsh, and Lady Gwendoline Churchill. Together in that quiet place they mourned the death of Rupert Brooke, and wept for the youth and promise buried in that six feet of foreign soil that would be 'forever England'.

PART THREE

THE APPRENTICESHIP TO POWER

# CHAPTER XI

IT WAS one of Churchill's misfortunes that his deeds were seldom seen in proportion, and attracted extravagant praise or blame. It is necessary always to clear away masses of the sludge of adulation or hate before any kind of balanced judgment is possible. In his early days the episode of Sydney Street, in itself trivial, is remembered while his good work at the Home Office is scarcely noted. The scar left on the public mind by that indiscretion was slow to heal. He was labelled irresponsible and a swashbuckler, at best a man of high spirits, and lacking in the dignity and stability demanded of a man who might be called to high office in the service of the nation.

Five years later, in the spring of 1915, the failure of the British Navy to force the passage of the Dardanelles brought a torrent of blame upon his shoulders, made him also the scapegoat for the tragedy of Gallipoli, and consigned him to the political wilderness. Admiral Wemyss commented that the name of Churchill 'will be handed down to posterity as that of a man who undertook an operation of whose requirements he was entirely ignorant.' In Gallipoli a senior soldier remarked that 'If Winston were to put his foot near the peninsula he would be scragged alive.'

The rights and wrongs of the affair may be argued to the end of time, but it should be possible to establish beyond a doubt Churchill's personal responsibility. He said himself that the Dardanelles was the 'scene of a failure in leadership which would seem incredible if it were not true'. And it is true that Admiral de Robeck broke off the bombardment of the Turkish forts at the moment of victory. The Turks were out of ammunition and were already discussing surrender with Morgenthau, the US Ambassador. It was one of the most costly failures in history, for the results of successfully forcing the Dardanelles might have changed the whole course of affairs for the better.

Pondering on these things, Ashmead-Bartlett wrote: 'One of the proudest thoughts in Mr Churchill's mind must be the fact that the public has refused to acknowledge any other than himself as the author or originator of this attempt to take Constantinople.'

The Gallipoli landings followed immediately upon the naval failure, and Hankey records Churchill's reaction to his clearly expressed fears for the venture. 'Saw Churchill, who jeered at me because I said landing would be difficult; I replied that I had committed my views to writing and that so far they were closely borne out. . . .' That entry was under date April 27, 1915.

Churchill, in fact, deserves the credit for the attempt to force the Dardanelles, but neither the blame for Gallipoli, nor the praise for the strategic conception that *should* have been behind it, is rightfully his. At his best he was a furious tactician with brilliant ideas; at his worst, a frustrated grasshopper, restlessly attempting to exploit too many tactical possibilities at once, and without a clear framework of strategy.

Had the assault on Gallipoli succeeded there might not have been a Russian Revolution, and the effect upon the whole Mohammedan world would have been immense. Turkey would have been out of the war, the Black Sea clear, and the southern supply routes to Russia open. Serbia would not have been invaded, and Bulgaria would have remained uncommitted or on the Allied side. 'How many evils would unhappy, bankrupt Europe have been spared, could the army have but seized that narrow peninsula of Gallipoli?' wrote Ashmead-Bartlett. 'How few realized at the time, when we were dissipating our enormous resources in men, money and material—smearing the whole habitable surface of the globe with British blood—that the key to success and to an earlier termination of the war lay in the forcing of the Dardanelles and capture of Constantinople?'

How few realized at the time? Almost certainly Churchill was not one of them. It was the great turning point in British power, the point at which Britain could have, and should have, reverted to her only proper strategy, disentangling her armies from the Western Front—or strictly limiting that outrageous commitment—and throwing her entire weight against 'the weak under-belly', as Amery expressed it, in an all-out combined operation. For the assault on the Dardanelles and Gallipoli was an operation of the greatest magnitude seen in the true context of British strategy, or it was doomed to disaster.

The great strategic vision was never Churchill's. The importance of these years in the context of Churchill's life is that it becomes clear that the Churchill of World War I is the father of the Churchill of World War II. Turkey, Greece, the Balkans, the 'soft under-belly', even such names as Valona and Pantelleria and, of course, Rhodes, will outcrop in profusion nearly thirty years on. Scores of ideas inspired by the threatened deadlock on the Western Front, burgeoned in the winter of 1914, and in these highly impressionable years from 1911 to 1915 Churchill discovered and explored the geographical framework for his military dreams. The Mediterranean was a magnificent battlefield for combined operations, for the exploitation of land, sea and air power in close harmony. Thus the Mediterranean became his 'nursery floor', his strait-jacket. He forgot that British military power was based upon India. In a sense he forgot the British Empire, for it had been always a dream, and when at last he awoke it was gone.

## II

By December 1914 many were striving to think a way out of the Western stalemate, with its already dreadful possibilities. Kitchener's appeals for men were stripping essential industries of their skilled workmen. Shells and ammunition of all kinds were in desperately short supply and were being fired off at a rate never before remotely imagined. Britain had been well prepared in terms of the known facts of war, but she had not been prepared for this. Nor had the French. The ultimate result might well depend on new factors not yet dimly conceived.

Throughout his whole tenure of office at the Admiralty Churchill had been receptive to new ideas from any quarter, and ready to back any reasonable project with all his energy and enthusiasm. Hankey was already experimenting in his back yard with primitive flame-throwers and smoke-laying devices, while discussing with E. G. Tulloch, a retired gunner, and General Swinton the development of a tracked fighting vehicle from which, finally, the 'tank' would emerge. The impregnability of the Turkish lines before Chatalja in the Balkan War had claimed his close study and attention, giving him a picture of the probable shape of things to come. That was his inspiration. Churchill, meanwhile, had had a vision of a kind of 'land battleship', and 'without waiting for the considered opinion of the War Office', had established a committee to go ahead with plans inspired by Major Hetherington, an armoured car officer in the Duke of Westminster's Yeomanry. Before Churchill left the Admiralty his authority was behind the production of the first tank.

Yet even this development reveals the difficulty of crediting any one man with all praise, or blame. With such a project as the Dardanelles expedition the difficulties are far greater. Similar ideas came from many quarters. In December 1914, Leo Amery wrote a long memorandum advising an advance into Hungary through Serbia. Greece, Bulgaria and Roumania 'could be relied upon to rally to the winning side for the sake of the territorial loot to be secured at the expense of Austria-Hungary and Turkey'.

The French general Gallieni was also convinced that the 'weak under-belly' should be attacked, and that Salonika offered the best approach. Hankey, of course, was thinking and writing on the same lines.

On January 1, 1915, David Lloyd George, arriving at similar conclusions, advocated them with all his eloquence, but in vain. Asquith and Grey lacked the dynamism and drive, as well as the fully developed organization of Supreme Command, to bring such plans to speedy fulfilment. As for Grey, his world was toppling about his ears, and he sought solace in his Hampshire fishing when he might have been studying the Balkan situation on the ground. Italy, in any case, held his thoughts and absorbed his energies, but his cold and austere approach was alienating her. It was difficult to persuade men of an older school that the whole pattern of Europe, and of society as they had known it, was changing. They lived truly in another world. The diplomacy in which they were highly skilled was already a blunt tool. Bold and decisive actions of an entirely new pattern were called for. Opportunities had to be grasped. All that was true of yesterday could be false of today.

Hankey had produced a sound plan for an attack on Turkey, and on January 3rd Admiral Fisher, First Sea Lord and working with Churchill in spite of the King's grave misgivings, wrote: 'I consider the attack on Turkey holds the field.' He wanted 75,000 of French's troops withdrawn from the Western Front

THE APPRENTICESHIP TO POWER        187

and replaced by Territorials, 'and to land them at Besika Bay to the South of the Dardanelles after previous feints at Haifa and Alexandretta by troops drawn from Egypt. Simultaneously the Greeks were to be induced to attack Gallipoli, the Bulgarians Constantinople, while the Russians, Serbians and Roumanians were to concentrate on Austria-Hungary.'

In such plans as these lay the hopes of victory, and of a Britain emerging strengthened, belonging to the present and to the future. In the event Britain was to die on the Western Front, and only a Supreme Commander of immense vision and courage might have hoped to change that before it was too late in the first months of 1915.

'In the history of the world a Junta has never won. You want one man,' Fisher wrote on his memorandum, and quoted Napoleon for good measure: 'Celerity; without it, failure.'

Through the first two weeks of January 1915 the Cabinet wrestled in torment with a score of possibilities of action, and innumerable problems that seemed almost insoluble. A few saw clearly the deadlock and the need to break it. A few favoured —even Kitchener, and French, provided he was not stripped of men in the process—some form of action against the 'weak under-belly'. But no man, I think, save perhaps Hankey, saw the whole strategic problem, or visualized the gigantic possibility soon in the mind of Ashmead-Bartlett. No man grasped that here was the chance that might never recur; the last chance. The saving in blood and hate would have been incalculable.

But problems were multiplying daily. The whole industrial balance of the nation was threatened. Any decision for action, especially for major action, at once appeared hopeless in terms of what are now called logistics. At a Cabinet meeting on January 15th almost all possibilities were argued indecisively. French and Joffre wanted to make an attempt to break the deadlock on the Western Front. Kitchener was ambivalent. Grey was preoccupied with his hopes of Italy. French and Joffre, therefore, would try again. That was the simplest decision, and yet in a sense no decision at all.

'The meeting now seemed to be drawing to an end. The War Council had been sitting all day. The blinds had been drawn to shut out the winter evening. The air was heavy and the table presented that rather dishevelled appearance that results from a long session.... I suppose the councillors were as weary as I was. At this point events took a dramatic turn...."[1]

Suddenly Churchill produced his plan for a naval attack on the Dardanelles. His timing was superb, his presentation masterly. 'The whole atmosphere changed. Fatigue was forgotten.' Whatever may be true or false of Churchill, he proved himself at that moment a master of theatre, and an incomparable natural actor, which is not to impugn his integrity, nor to challenge the quality of his plan. The Navy would shell the Turkish forts, clear the minefields, sail to Constantinople, destroy the *Goeben*.

Churchill's great fault was that he talked too well and thought too superficially. He did not think right through the problems, and it must be said that had he done so the Cabinet would have been unlikely to clutch at his plan with tremendous eagerness. This was just what they wanted; something that could be done. Above all, it was action. It never looked like being the action that would change the course of history. Fisher grew sullen and silent, and finally resigned. The plan went ahead after too many delays. It was never fully backed, and finally it was followed by piecemeal, half-hearted efforts doomed to failure.

Even so, but for the extreme caution of Admiral de Robeck, the Dardanelles would have been forced, Constantinople won, and Turkish neutrality secured. Churchill cannot be held responsible for de Robeck's failure. In his plan for the Dardanelles, Churchill revealed his great virtue as a 'lieutenant' in war. Under the right Supreme Command he might have been magnificent. It was not to be—ever.

### III

By the spring of 1915 the exuberance and optimism with which the British people had launched themselves into the war had given way to a growing unease and impatience, characteristic of a people who dislike facing the facts of any situation at any time. It was still considered in bad taste to state bluntly that the war would almost certainly continue for a very long time, but it was increasingly difficult not to think it.

The awareness of the appalling shortages of the sinews of

[1] Hankey, *op cit.*

war, and the seemingly lethargic thinking that had involved the British people in a deadly embrace with a powerful continental army, coupled with the ill-starred Dardanelles adventure, evoked a demand for major scapegoats. Tory elements in the community, distrustful of themselves, became furious at the leniency with which the Home Office treated aliens. A flood of paper money had suddenly ousted the gold sovereign, and temporarily undermined the faith of the avaricious in financial stability. The war was costing as much in a week as normal public expenditure in a year. It would double and treble.

An influential section of the newspapers called for a sterner direction of the war effort, and possibly a change of leadership. The Tory Party, well aware of the opportunity greatly to strengthen its position and at the same time to revenge itself upon Churchill, was working busily behind the scenes, directed by Bonar Law, while the enigmatic, gnomish figure of Max Aitken, fast qualifying for a 'Black Belt' in political judo, watched and nudged on the sidelines, fashioning a peculiar political niche for himself.

Finally, the resignation of Admiral Fisher detonated the bomb of political and public feeling. He had never liked the naval action at the Dardanelles, but in a misguided conflict of loyalties had failed to make his views clear in the War Council. His affair with his 'beloved Winston' had steadily cooled, and the disgruntled old sailor, looking like an oriental god, poured out his sorrows into the willing ears of McKenna, never reconciled to his replacement at the Admiralty by Churchill in 1911.

On May 14th the War Council 'sat again for the first time after a long period of coma', but, as Churchill points out, the coma was deliberate, a mark of Asquith's determination to give the operations against the Dardanelles and Gallipoli an uninterrupted chance. He had brushed aside Fisher's ill-expressed fears, and had the support of Kitchener. 'He meant to have the matter put to the proof. After the first repulse he was resolute to continue,' wrote Churchill. But by the middle of May the game was up. Fisher had written anonymously to Bonar Law, but the letter was so typical as to leave no doubt as to its source. On May 15th it was known that Fisher had resigned.

Bonar Law made it clear to Lloyd George that the Tories were resolved to challenge the Government in the House, but agreed that a united front must be preserved if possible. Lloyd George put the situation clearly to the Prime Minister, and literally within the hour Asquith agreed to a Coalition and the formation of a new Ministry. It was, in fact, the beginning of the end of the Liberal Party in Great Britain.

Asquith acted with ruthless energy. He 'did not hesitate to break his Cabinet, demand the resignations of all Ministers, end the political lives of half his colleagues, throw Haldane to the wolves, leave me to bear the burden of the Dardanelles, and sail on victoriously at the head of a Coalition Government,'[1] wrote Churchill.

It is a fair statement, but it was Churchill rather than Haldane who had been thrown to the wolves. Whoever might stay, Churchill must go. Not Asquith, but Bonar Law was 'especially emphatic' about that. Tory hatred was implacable. In the event Asquith did not 'sail on victoriously' for long. An 'agonized nation . . . demanded a frenzied energy at the summit; an effort to compel events rather than to adjudicate wisely and deliberately upon them,' Churchill observed, and in December 1916 the same actors brought about the fall of Asquith, and Lloyd George, the man of colossal energy, the greatest man at getting things done in the history of England, was at the helm.

But Asquith had done great service. He had piloted Britain through the early stages of the unknown with a strong hand. He was, as Lloyd George said, one of the greatest Prime Ministers Britain ever had. When Edward Grey's inept dealings with Italy had plunged that country into a fit of sulks, Asquith 'brushed aside trivialities and brought the negotiations to a stage that led to a speedy decision'. He had prosecuted the war with immense vigour and skill and greatly improved the instrument of the Committee of Imperial Defence. By creating that body Balfour had 'rendered a service to his country which deserves immortality'. The tribute comes well from Lloyd George, for he was the third of the 'Supreme Commanders' who would leave it fully fashioned. Asquith made 'the fullest use of its powers and for further developing its area and scope'.

The baton of command did not drop from the palsied fingers of a weary man, but was seized by the powerful hand of a new runner who would bear it to victory.

Churchill watched these political manoeuvres from the political backwater of the Duchy of Lancaster, and presently from

[1] *The World Crisis*, 1911-14.

the trenches of the Western Front, with particular interest. Twenty years later he wrote:

'I shall never cease to wonder why Mr Asquith, with a large Liberal majority at his back, did not in the crisis of the 1916 winter invoke the expedient of a Secret Session, and seek the succour of the House of Commons. There, is the final citadel of a Prime Minister in distress. No one can deny him his right in peace or war to appeal from the intrigues of Cabinets, caucuses, clubs and newspapers to that great assembly, and take his dismissal only at their hands. Yet the Liberal Government which fell in 1915, the Asquith Coalition which fell in 1916, the Lloyd George Coalition which fell in 1922—all were overthrown by secret, obscure, internal processes of which the public only now know the main story. I am of opinion that in every one of these cases the result of confident resort to Parliament would have been the victory of the Prime Minister of the day.'[1]

This must be one of the most revealing passages Churchill ever wrote, and it is for every man to read into it what he will. Perhaps both Asquith and Lloyd George recognized that it was time to go, that to stay might have been prejudicial to the nation in the circumstances. Their political lives had been strongly based on clear and powerful principles of service. Power was sweet, but it was not the personal dream of either man for its own sake. Their ambitions were greater than power.

When his hour struck Churchill would not make their mistakes—if they were mistakes. He would know what to do.

## IV

With all his great skill and ability to get things done Lloyd George was unable to include Churchill in his War Cabinet. The Tory ministers, with the exceptions of Carson and Balfour, refused to serve with him, and a magnificent chance for Churchill to serve in the Cabinet under a master he admired and respected was lost. No man knew and understood Churchill better than David Lloyd George. Perhaps no other man would have known how to make the best use of him. It was Churchill's personal tragedy—and England's—that the Tory Party denied him the

[1] *Great Contemporaries.*

opportunity. Together in the Cabinet they might have made such a team as would have achieved not only victory, but peace. In a sense Churchill was too young in 1916. In 1940 Lloyd George was too old.

'Here,' wrote Lloyd George, 'his more erratic impulses could have been kept under control and his judgment supervised and checked before plunging into action. Men of his ardent temperament and powerful mentality need exceptionally strong brakes.'

By the time Churchill came to power there existed no man, or body of men, capable of restraining him. He saw to that.

That two such men should have come together at all in the same sphere in the same era is itself a remarkable manifestation of the wealth of personality and talent submerged in the British race. For thirty years one or other of them was at, or near, the head of affairs, and it should be revealing briefly to consider them in contrast. Lloyd George had grown from the sound foundations of a childhood based on the austere simplicities of life in the Welsh valleys. His parents were poor, scrupulously honest, intelligent. He had learned, walking with his grandmother over hill and valley, visiting poor, but honest neighbours, collecting with infinite courtesy small sums owing to his grandfather for the repair of sturdy boots, the arts of social intercourse. He knew the yearning of simple hard-working people for social security. He knew their reverence for earth and sky.

Churchill had no such advantages. Even as a child he had become a misfit, withdrawn, proud and brave, his world peopled with puppets. It had never been necessary for Churchill to get on with children, or to learn the arts of compromise and persuasion. He was without allies or enemies, save for his basic ally, Mrs Everest. He would never learn to 'talk a bird out of tree', nor to persuade a group of highly cultivated and intelligent men that they were persuading themselves. He would dominate or be dominated. He could not allow equals.

Lloyd George had learned to walk on his own sturdy legs, yet not alone. His country, his family, his people were as much a part of him as he was of them. Their aspirations were his. Churchill had missed that vital experience. He belonged only to himself, and to the past.

No man was better equipped for politics than David Lloyd

George. He understood, as Churchill never could, that politics in war or peace is the art of the possible. Churchill challenged the impossible, and committed himself to the unattainable. His tactical and strategic visions seldom provided good alternatives or ways of retreat, nor did they take account of the natural trends of nations. He sought rather to rebuild the past than to establish foundations on which a future might rise, tomorrow or in a thousand years.

Whereas Lloyd George gathered round him, and under him, the finest minds available, supremely confident in his powers of leadership, superb in Council, patient and persuasive, a man who would brook no challenge to his authority, yet fearing no man's wit or brilliance, Churchill was always the slave of his personal likes and dislikes, fearful of the face of innocence, and the brilliant challenging mind. The spotlight was his alone; his the star part, crossing swords on equal terms with no man. Thus he denied himself the chance to be measured against his great contemporaries, and when his great service was done he stood in isolation.

When the First World War at last ended, those closest to all that had happened added up the score, measuring giant against giant, and out of this one man emerged. 'I said to myself —' wrote Hankey, 'Lloyd George was the man who won the war.' Amery and his friends travelling home from the Peace Conference reached the same conclusion. When Churchill's turn came there was no one else on the stage.

It has been said that the ability to pick the best aides is one of the principal keys to success. In this Lloyd George succeeded brilliantly, and Churchill failed totally. Nevertheless it was Churchill's strength in the first phase of his immense career that he could serve such a man as Lloyd George with absolute loyalty. It was his weakness that when supreme power was his he could not find, nor would he have tolerated any man of like stature to serve him.

Together in the First World War these two men were giants in a world not lacking in men of stature. At a critical time in her history Britain accepted one, but not the other. Churchill was sacrificed, not because of the Dardanelles failure, but because commonplace men feared him, because he had walked out of their 'Club', and because in a country regarding mediocrity as a virtue two giants in peace or war is one too many.

G

But it must not be forgotten that politicians, however great their stature, will not ensure wise action or success in war. A third factor or force is essential. This factor in Britain in the First World War was the Committee of Imperial Defence with Maurice Hankey as its Secretary. When the Second World War came the Committee of Imperial Defence was still there, but Hankey was moving into the shadows, to be replaced by Ismay. Hankey's name is very high on the list of those who brought victory in 1918.

# CHAPTER XII

CHURCHILL was hustled out of the Admiralty with the jeers of the Tories and the boos of the multitude in his ears, but with his head held high. He had retained his seat on the War Council, for 'it was on this condition alone that I had found it possible to occupy a sinecure office'.[1] He was resolved to do all in his power to urge forward the whole Dardanelles-Gallipoli venture to a conclusion, but the initiative was never regained after the first disastrous breaking off of the shelling of the Turkish forts. Half measure followed upon half measure, always reacting to the enemy, always too late, always attempting to stuff the holes in a leaky sieve. One hundred and fifty thousand dead lay upon the narrow beaches and the bleak hills before the disastrous end. By that time Churchill was in France, serving with a battalion of the Grenadier Guards. He was then forty-one years old, wonderfully fit and at the peak of his life, his political career in ruins, perhaps irreparable. Yet his zest was unabated. The Asquith Coalition would not last very long, and there could not have been a political future in it for him. Bonar Law and the Tory plotters regarded it as no more than a stop-gap, and would bring it down when the time was ripe. Churchill had few illusions on that score, and was more likely to gain than to lose by resigning his 'sinecure', and going to war. It was consistent with his image in the public and political mind. So be it. Perhaps it was not too late to be a soldier. His attempt to persuade Asquith at the time of Antwerp had been genuine enough—until it failed. He could adapt as swiftly as any chameleon. He had kept himself in good physical condition by regular swimming, and by playing polo whenever a chance occurred. Polo had been for years a true love, and he tended to regard life rather as a polo game, a series of 'chukkas'. If you lost one, there was always the next to win, until the last.

[1] *The World Crisis, 1915.*

And that was not yet. Still, it was difficult to diminish the importance of the 'chukka' from which he had just emerged on the losing side, and with most of the blame on his own head.

'The Duchy' was in any case 'a farce so far as work is concerned,' Edward Marsh had written to a friend, and revealing a concern for Churchill greater than his concern for himself. 'I really don't know how he will occupy himself.' But that he would occupy himself to the utmost none who knew him could doubt. Asquith had most thoughtfully found a place for the faithful Marsh in the 10 Downing Street secretariat. Churchill was free. He did not reproach himself. As for Gallipoli, the responsibility lay squarely upon Kitchener's shoulders, although it would be a long time before any one said so. He was himself to wait more than forty years for the published tribute of a man who knew more about it all than anybody else, and was at the same time completely objective. Churchill did not imagine then that he had forty years to wait. He didn't think much about it, but when he did, it is unlikely that he thought he would make old bones. At his age his father had been very near the end, and had been aware of it. Churchill was, and felt, in the midst of life.

'We owed a good deal in those early days to the courage and inspiration of Winston Churchill, who, undaunted by difficulties and losses, set an infectious example. . . . He may have been rash at times, but he was a tower of strength . . .'[1] Hankey wrote in 1961, and not simply from golden memory. He had all his papers, and the *facts*, at his elbow. He had quoted from Bunyan's *Pilgrim's Progress*:

'What of my dross thou findest there, be bold to throw away; but yet preserve the gold.'

Churchill left the political stage like a lion at bay, delivering a 'formidable apologia' covering the whole of his stewardship at the Admiralty. It was a tremendous epilogue, filling twenty-two columns of *Hansard*, but it was his farewell; at least, for the time being. It was the middle of November 1915, and without more ado he went off to pack his bags for the 'Front'.

It was like old times, then, with Lady Randolph at his side, as well as his 'almond-eyed gazelle' of a wife, as Denis Browne

[1] Hankey, *The Supreme Command*, Vol. II.

called her, to see him off on new adventures. After all, it was only fifteen years since he had returned triumphant from South Africa.

But if Churchill could adapt from one kind of life to another with startling speed, others were slow to accept the metamorphosis. General French, Commander-in-Chief of the British Forces in France, sent a staff car to meet him on landing, not treating him as plain 'Major Churchill', but in Churchill's own words, 'as if I had been still First Lord of the Admiralty'. Even Churchill would find out that he could not have it both ways, and he had meddled too much in French's military affairs to ensure a warm welcome in some quarters. General Sir William Robertson had complained urgently to Hankey, ascribing the friction between French and Joffre as due to the 'unsettling effects' of Churchill's interference. Undoubtedly he had been indiscreet, planting suspicion in French's mind, and suggesting that Millerand and Joffre were ganging up against him. Now his indiscretions were coming home to roost.

The shadows were already on the wall when Churchill dined with the British Commander-in-Chief on his first night in the Chateau Blondecque. 'My power is no longer what it was,' French told him. 'I am, as it were, riding at single anchor. But it still counts for something. Will you take a Brigade?'[1]

Perhaps it was Churchill's dearest wish. In a bound he would regain all the lost ground, and climb all the rungs of the ladder he had neglected. If he handled a Brigade well, and learned his business, a Division would almost surely be his in the course of not too much time.

But it was a dream. Haig soon replaced French, and made it clear to Churchill that in his eyes he was a politician, and Haig abhorred politicians. He had felt an intense dislike of Churchill from his early days. There would not be a Brigade for him. Nevertheless, that major disappointment, perhaps changing the direction of his life, was still some weeks in the future, and weeks in this new world of the trenches and sudden death and slow agonizing wounds had a timeless quality. 'Nowadays we who are alive have the sense of being old, old survivors,' wrote Patrick Shaw-Stewart. And they were old, old in the sense that many of them had not long to live, many to be killed, including Shaw-Stewart, before they had had time to know how young

[1] *Thoughts and Adventures.*

they were; before they had had time to utter their brave and terrible words for the hosts of the inarticulate, as Siegfried Sassoon and Robert Graves were about to do.

Churchill himself was not immune to such depressions. He would help such men as these, inspired to do so by Marsh, and hold out a hand when he could, but it was as well for a man in such conditions to be incapable of seeing life and death in harsh focus. Churchill marched always in a straight line, refusing to be put out by physical danger. It disconcerted him very little when his dug-out was blown up a moment or two before or after he was inside it, or when shells were falling very close on either hand. He held his course, and his timings. It might be more dangerous a foot to the right or to the left, inside or out, a minute sooner or later. Who could tell?

He was with the Guards near Laventie in November when he received the final disastrous news of the Dardanelles campaign. Perhaps it seemed to him that he did a kind of penance, for there is a sense of that in his words. 'It was a comfort to be with these fine troops at such a time, to study their methods, unsurpassed in the army . . . and to share from day to day their life under the hard conditions of winter. . . .'

He did not realize—the onlooker never understands, and he was a born onlooker at war—that it is impossible to share a soldier's life, or a prisoner's life, without being a soldier or a prisoner. It is not enough to march and bivouac with troops day after day, even for weeks, or months, or a year, unless you are truly one of them, and it is your life. If you are a war correspondent or an observer of any kind, you can escape if you wish. Take a few days off. Sleep in a decent bed. Rest. If you are a politician it is an interlude; even if you have dreams that it may not be an interlude. Because it must be an interlude. You have not been a soldier, and you will not be a soldier now. It is too late.

But Churchill's was a salutary and vital piece of experience, even though it, at last, added to his delusions of military competence. One night, as he moved with a small body of men over the soaked and sodden earth and with the flash and shock of gunfire tearing sudden violent holes in the darkness . . . 'the conviction came into my mind with absolute assurance that the simple soldiers and their regimental officers, armed with their cause, would by their virtues in the end retrieve the mistakes and ignorances of Staffs and Cabinets, of Admirals, Generals and politicians—including no doubt many of my own'.

II

Churchill's excursion into soldiering on the Western Front was brief but honourable. It was also exhausting. Although he was extremely fit by normal standards for a man in his forties, the sedentary life of a politician, he lamented, had not fitted him for the severe physical activities which are the lot of a comparatively junior regimental officer in the field. Churchill was never a man to shirk any task. As well as he was able he shared the discomforts of his brother officers. By the end of the year he had prepared a report on the Western offensive at the instigation of General French, and hoped that it would reach the eyes of Lloyd George and Bonar Law. He was an indefatigable writer of lengthy memoranda on almost every activity with which he came into contact. It was impossible for him to divorce himself from the political life. In the trenches the latest secret paper on the development of the 'tank' reached him by post, and was far too close to the enemy for comfort. If he had not access by rank or right to the highest authorities, he assumed that he had, as he had always done, and with the same results. Major Churchill was still Lieutenant Churchill, but several sizes larger, a formidable personage accustomed to authority.

Nevertheless he behaved with restraint, patience and courage. In January 1916 he was given command of the 6th Battalion, Royal Scots Fusiliers. To the true infantry soldier there is, perhaps, no finer rôle than this, for a good army is built upon the quality of its battalion commanders, and it calls forth the very best in a man. Churchill led his battalion fearlessly. His spirit throve on danger and challenge, but he could not at that late hour become a part of a new and confined world, a mere microcosm of the world in which he operated. At forty-two years of age, and committed to politics, the rôle of a battalion commander was not for him. He had missed the military boat for ever. He would never be a general.

Meanwhile his presence in Parliament was missed, not least by Edward Carson who was constantly attempting to bring about his return, but apart from Balfour and men like F. E. Smith, who were not frightened of any man, the Tories, excited by passions of astonishing intensity, were resolved to exclude Churchill from any part in the Government. Nevertheless in the autumn of 1916 Churchill came home and eased himself back into political life, seemingly unaware that many regarded him as the Devil incarnate. A Commission had been appointed to probe to the roots of the Gallipoli disaster, and doubtless the day would dawn when Churchill's part in it would be seen in better perspective. 'What is the use of tormenting myself with these inquiries?' he wrote to Marsh, but he was glad to be able to give his evidence before the Commission. Meanwhile the chance to relax was enjoyable. With Lady Randolph, his imperturbable wife, and Marsh, he sang old songs with Ivor Novello over the brandy and cigars, but his eye never left the ball. Lloyd George, he knew, was destined for power, and Lloyd George was his greatest political friend and admirer, an admirer moreover who knew him and all his faults, and would know well how to use his virtues. Hankey wrote of Lloyd George, the fact that, 'he was never content to rely entirely on the ideas of his own fertile mind and of his immediate entourage adds lustre to Lloyd George's extraordinary achievement'. He feared the rivalry of no man, and had Churchill been in fact the Devil in person Lloyd George would have employed him. His value, given a strong hand at the helm, was incalculable.

Early in December 1916 the machinations of Beaverbrook, aided by Bonar Law, and precipitated to a crisis by Northcliffe with an 'inspired' Editorial in *The Times*, brought about the fall of Asquith, and marked the end of liberalism as a political force. Lloyd George, whose plan for a reconstruction of the War Cabinet had initiated the denouement, at once formed a Government in which Asquith refused to serve in any capacity. It was a remarkable refusal, seeming at first sight out of character, but it is impossible to consider the deeds of public men solely in terms of their public lives. Much that appears irrational and inexplicable becomes clear when something is known of the private background. Both Asquith and Lloyd George were men of sexual passion in whose lives women played powerful parts. Mrs Asquith, a most passionate and opinionated woman, reacted with fury against Lloyd George and the 'conspirators' who had brought about her husband's downfall. The main stream of her venom was always directed against Lloyd George, and it must have influenced Asquith strongly.

Asquith must have realized that the small flame of Liberalism is particularly vulnerable in war, and must be shielded with devotion if it is not to be extinguished. In office the breach between him and Lloyd George would surely have been healed, for they were men of vision, devoid of pettiness, and tempered for years in the turmoil of politics. But it was not to be. When Asquith was again ready, and the anger had cooled, it was too late.

Asquith's wisdom and experience would have been of great value, but above all it was a time for intense drive and clear direction, and apart from Lloyd George himself the outstanding figure who could help to heave the whole nation and its resources at full stretch into the conflict, and keep it there, was Churchill.

Few had any illusions about the nature of final victory, if it were to be gained, for as Balfour remarked drily to Lloyd George after listening with ill concealed disdain to a piece of French rhetoric on the subject of *'Justice, Liberte, et Droit'*: 'He must have strangely misread history if he thinks that *"Justice, Liberte et Droit"* are synonymous.'

At once Lloyd George encountered a resistance to the inclusion of Churchill that was adamant, intense, implacable and various. The *Morning Post* described Churchill as 'a floating kidney in the body politic', and even Beaverbrook, whose liking for Churchill was genuine, and would warm to close friendship over the years, recognized the dangerous nature of Churchill's inner ambitions, and that there were in him the seeds of tyranny. No man's instincts were more delicately attuned to power. But Beaverbrook himself, at that time, was not acceptable to the Tories.

Vainly Lloyd George argued that Churchill would be more dangerous as a critic than as a member of the Government. 'Is he more dangerous when he is FOR you than when he is AGAINST YOU?' he demanded of Bonar Law.

'I would rather have him against us every time,' Bonar Law replied. His distrust of Churchill was 'profound'.

It was clear that any attempt to include Churchill would lead to the 'disruption of the Government at an early date'. Letters poured in. His appointment would be 'intensely unpopular in the Army' ... 'in the Navy'. 'He is a potential danger in opposition. In the opinion of all of us he will as a member of the Government be an active danger in our midst.'[1]

[1] David Lloyd George, *War Memoirs*, Vol. III.

Inevitably Lloyd George's list went forward to the Monarch for approval without Churchill's name. But 'Why,' Lloyd George asked himself, and doubtless others, 'were they so bitter and implacable?' What had caused the outbursts of 'insensate fury', when even a rumour of Churchill's possible inclusion 'threatened the life of the Government'?[1]

It is certainly astonishing even at this long range. Was there then a fatal flaw in his make-up? Was it the recognition of the desire for naked power that lay at the heart of Churchill, which, given something to feed on might become a gnawing hunger? Power combined with total egocentricity, feeding and serving itself alone, must mean tyranny.

It is certain that as First Lord of the Admiralty he had shown himself dangerously irresponsible and had given inner glimpses of himself to shrewd observers, but at that early stage he is unlikely to have revealed himself as he did later to Beaverbrook. Out of power, many have observed, Churchill is a totally different man from Churchill in power. The change is frightening.

'Churchill "up" is quite a different proposition,' Beaverbrook wrote. 'I remember once a terrible scene with him when he was in a position of uncontrolled power and authority in dealing with public affairs which closely concerned me. If any other man living had used such outrageous language to me as he did on that occasion I should never have forgiven him. Churchill on the top of the wave has in him the stuff of which tyrants are made.'

It is certain that as early as 1916 the opposition to Churchill went far beyond any reasonable political dislike or distrust. But whatever it was it did not greatly disturb him, nor did it shake Lloyd George in his balanced assessment of Churchill's talents, and in his resolution to use them. In July 1917 the chance came. The United States was at last in the war at a time when the submarine battle in the Atlantic threatened Britain with starvation. The Ministry of Munitions needed a driving force if the vast appetites of war were to be fed, and Churchill was the obvious —perhaps the only man for the job. Bonar Law was placated. For a moment the Government was 'in jeopardy', but the Opposition had lost cohesion. No one doubted that Churchill was 'a dangerously ambitious man', nor hesitated to say so, yet the nature of his ambitions was not clear. He was not dedicated to

[1] David Lloyd George, *War Memoirs*, Vol. III.

a cause, and his political position must be precarious since he had deserted the only party that could contain him. His cause, of course, was himself.

To understand fully the nature of the Tory hatred and opposition to him one must understand, as I do not, the conception the Tory Party has of itself as the ruling power. It is comparable in its fundamental thinking with such organizations as the Roman Catholic Church, and the Communist Party in Soviet Russia. It regards itself as ruling by 'Divine Right', and if Divine Aid appears to be lacking at any time there is no depth of evil, no artifice of chicanery, to which it will not stoop in order to safeguard and defend itself, and its right to rule. It is not democratic, save in the sense of the Communist Party in Russia: you may argue ways and means within its framework, and no other. All else is heresy. The Tory Party had regarded Lord Randolph Churchill with suspicion and dislike, and at the first sign that the son was even more unreliable than the father, and infinitely more dangerous, it had cast him out. In fact, it had gone to the lengths of 'drumming him out'.

There is much in these early years that is likely to remain speculative. Those who lived through them, and knew the leading actors are certain that Lloyd George was prepared to risk, and did risk, his political career for Churchill. The opposition he faced could have been deadly, and his Government was endangered. In the political sense surely 'no man has greater love than this?' shown by Lloyd George to Churchill. It is the more remarkable because Lloyd George was fully aware that Churchill would not risk his political career for any man, and was congenitally incapable of considering such a course.

One thing must be certain, and that is that Lloyd George needed Churchill as a 'lieutenant' in the great task ahead.

At once the Prime Minister established a Cabinet Secretariat under Maurice Hankey, and thus began to tighten the means of Supreme Command. His Government was further interesting for the emergence of Stanley Baldwin and Neville Chamberlain in junior roles. As a junior Lord of the Treasury Baldwin was able to expand his peculiar talents, but Chamberlain, 'a man of rigid competency', was 'lost in an emergency or in creative tasks at any time'. Such was the verdict of Lloyd George.

When the time came men like Lloyd George and Churchill would be unlikely to appeal to Baldwin and Chamberlain.

## III

Churchill's first deed upon his appointment to the Ministry of Munitions was to rescue Edward Marsh from the dingy basement of the Colonial Office into which the fall of Asquith had tumbled him. Marsh had given his loyalty to Churchill fully aware of the risk he ran, and was prepared to pay the penalty. Toiling away as a clerk dealing with minor and unexciting West African affairs, after being for years at the hub of activity, was disappointing and a poor use of his talents, but he had his wide range of interests in the world of art to sustain him, and his friendships were deep and lasting. He had embarked upon the difficult task of seeing the works of Rupert Brooke through the press, and was publishing the first volume of Georgian Poetry. At the very hour when Churchill's telephone call rescued him from the basement he was attempting valiantly to plead Siegfried Sassoon's case at the War Office, with the help of Robert Graves. In such matters he missed Churchill's influence and prestige sorely.

At once all was well, as though a *genie* had appeared to grant a wish. Later on Sassoon was able to relax in Churchill's room at the Ministry, and to remark wearily, but with feeling, that he wished he had had Churchill as a company commander. It was an accolade.

In Churchill's association with Marsh, and through him with many of the young poets, artists and musicians, he was at his best, most generous in expression, kind and thoughtful, and readily sympathetic. Such men were not in the main stream of his life, but little fish of entirely different strains, seeking the quiet pools wherein to think and to form the words that with their imagery of truth would arouse echoes down the years, and permit the living to share the secrets of the dead. When such men were caught up in the side currents of the torrents of war and politics Churchill could at times rescue them. By this means Churchill himself was enriched and stimulated.

But the task immediately confronting Churchill in the war effort was vast, exciting and complex. It involved the harsh logistics and the 'squalid' problems without which modern warfare could not be waged. It was an essential lesson he was unwilling to learn. He absorbed the detail, but would not add the fundamental truths to his imagination. He observed that the appetites of the armies were voracious beyond supply, that they would consume all and more than the nation could produce, and that industry on which the peacetime prosperity of the nation must depend was being thrown dangerously off course. He was at once wrestling with the almost insoluble problems of priorities. All demands could not be met. Which must come first? Which must be denied, and at what cost? And who would ever know the loss or gain of taking one action instead of another?

Such problems would bulk very large in his life many years ahead. No man would ever know the final answers with certainty, and on the fringe of the major demands were hosts of lesser demands of great importance.

Meanwhile Lloyd George's driving energy at the War Office and as Prime Minister had helped to turn the 'whole island into an arsenal', and it was for Churchill to maintain the momentum, and to see for himself on the ground the most pressing needs of the men in battle. Thus he had opportunities to act as the eyes and ears of the Prime Minister in France, a task very much to his liking.

An incident at the outset of his Ministry was, however, intensely disquieting, revealing a side of his nature that would astonish his contemporaries more than twenty years on. He was curiously unsure of himself. The daring that in the field of physical action was natural to him was sadly lacking in moments of mental and moral decision when his position, and not his life, might be in danger.

Lloyd George had appointed Major Sir Albert Stern to head the department of Mechanical Warfare Supply, a department constantly breaking new ground and fighting the entrenched conservatism of the old warriors. Lloyd George had backed Stern's demands for tanks up to the hilt. They might prove to be the 'secret weapon', and the only means of breaking the deadlock on the Western Front, and putting an end to the appalling attrition. Certain of his political backing and utterly ruthless in his resolution to provide what was needed, Stern had embarked upon a programme to supply 4,000 tanks by early 1918 for the planned spring offensive. Against him were arrayed all the dead and decaying wood of the Military Hierarchy at home and abroad, dedicated to defend the old ways against all innovation. Haig himself was a cavalryman dedicated to the horse.

Very shortly after Churchill's appointment it was discovered that General Sir William Robertson, the CIGS, had cancelled an order for 1,000 tanks signed by Lloyd George in the September of 1916 when Secretary of State for War. Robertson had done this without consulting Stern. In short, the War Office was quietly attempting to sabotage the tank programme, and would thus have sabotaged the spring offensive of 1918. Stern was furious. He went straight to Churchill, confident that the order would be at once reinstated. To his dismay Churchill refused to act. He stated calmly that he had spent twenty months in the political wilderness, and was not prepared to risk his position. In a lesser man such an attitude might have been expected, even if indefensible. In Churchill it seemed impossible.

In vain Stern argued, reminding Churchill that he, as one of the original backers and inspirers of tank production, should be the last man on earth to acquiesce in such a monstrous situation, and to ditch 'his own baby'.

Churchill agreed that all this was true, but the Tory opposition to his inclusion in the Government had shaken his confidence. He was resolved to be careful. He would not resist the War Office.

Thereupon Stern expressed his indignation and contempt in unmistakable terms, accusing Churchill of being nothing more than an unprincipled career politician. Churchill, enraged, demanded an immediate withdrawal and apology, or Stern's resignation. But Stern was disposed to add to, rather than subtract from his indictment, and wrote out his resignation on the spot. Churchill replaced him with an Admiral who knew nothing about tanks.

Fortunately that was not the end of the affair. Stern was not the man to vanish without trace, nor permit the tanks to do so. He went to the Prime Minister, and the order was reinstated. Stern was appointed to head a new production drive which resulted in agreement with the Americans to produce 1,500 tanks, and to provide the armies in France with 5,000 of these machines of victory[1] in 1918.

---

[1] None arrived. 'The light and medium artillery used up to the end of the War by the American Army was supplied by the French. The heaviest artillery was provided by the British. No field guns of American pattern of manufacture fired a shot in the War. The same thing applies to tanks.' David Lloyd George, *War Memoirs*, Vol. V, p. 3067.

There is no mention of Churchill in Lloyd George's comment on this incident. He wrote:

'When I was Secretary of State for War in September 1916, I ordered 1,000 tanks to be manufactured. Sir William Robertson countermanded the order without my knowledge. Thanks to Sir Albert Stern, I discovered this countermand in time, and gave peremptory instructions that the manufacture should be proceeded with and that the utmost diligence should be used in executing the order. We had now a large fleet of these land battleships already completed and many more in the course of construction.'[1]

Churchill maintained silence. There is no note of the affair in *The World Crisis*, nor does the name of Sir Albert Stern appear in the index. It was the kind of incident he could erase from his mind with dangerous facility, and which would deny to his great written canvases of war the reliability demanded by historians.

---

[1] David Lloyd George, *War Memoirs*, Vol. IV. See also Captain B. H. Liddell Hart, *The Tanks, the History of the Royal Tank Regiment*, Vol. I.

## CHAPTER XIII

THE years of Churchill's first return to office from the political wilderness marked significant changes in his attitudes and in the development of his ambivalent nature. As his grandfather Jerome had feared it would prove difficult, if not impossible, to marry in harmony his English and American blood. In Churchill the two were like oil and water. In his early years his English side had been uppermost, but from 1917 his growing contacts with sympathetic elements in the United States, straddled him upon a see-saw of conflicting emotions and aspirations from which he was never to escape. His liberalism faded. He began to see vast and complex problems in terms of black and white. It was a simple world of heroes and villains, a world of childhood innocence and the *Boys' Own Paper*.

But for Churchill it could never be quite as simple as that. Two horses pulled his chariot, and often in divergent ways. His vision of Europe was powerful, sustained by Marlborough; his vision of the United States was romantic, appealing mightily to the Jerome adventurer, an expanding vision of limitless horizons and possibilities. The one was old, the other new. But his visions and dreams were never clear, never based upon a reasoned strategic concept of the possible, and of a genuine social and political aspiration. His longing for power was purely personal. He was not engaged in building any particular social edifice. He built his own life, and 'played his hunches', and his hunches pulled two ways.

As a politician in 1917 he realized that the first flush of his political youth was over. In terms of his father's life, and of his Spencer-Churchill blood, he was already old. He could no longer afford to take liberties, for another sojourn in the wilderness might well prove disastrous. If he had doubts I believe he had them now. He perceived that he had divorced himself from the only possible party that could contain him, and as he remarked many years later, it is comparatively simple to 'cross the floor' once, but twice is a considerable feat even for a political acrobat of exceptional talents. Thus in the five years from 1917 to 1922 he was both cautious and wild by turns.

But 1917 was not only an important year in the life of Churchill; it was a key year in the life of the human race. The revolution which filled the vacuum of chaos following the total collapse of Tsarist Russia, and the entry of the United States into Europe and the war, changed the whole course of European and world history, and brought mankind inevitably face to face with total disaster. On a material plane two mutually exclusive social, political and economic concepts and systems, each worshipping Mammon in its own fashion, were to confront one other with a hatred such as the world had never known even when Charles Martel halted the march of Islam at Tours, and saved Western Christendom from the Infidel.

In Churchill's reactions to these momentous events he gave clear warning of tendencies of grave portent in his own nature, and uttered the first faint, but clear, call to arms in the unholy twentieth century equivalent of the tragic and terrible religious wars that had bathed Eurasia in blood. And although he might not have been aware of Schlegel's 'fervent gratitude' for Martel's 'mighty victory',[1] he would almost surely have detected the note of faint regret in Gibbon, that but for Martel:

'Perhaps the interpretation of the Koran would now be taught in the schools of Oxford, and the pulpits might demonstrate to a circumcized people the sanctity and truth of the revelation of Mahommet.'[2]

Churchill liked to see things in a mighty framework of history, and it seems probable that 'somewhere along the line' he would have drawn the parallel between the tremendous events of the eighth century which saw the birth of Charlemagne, and the present day.

Churchill's gift for words and love of rhetoric, which held within bounds, had served him well, enabling him to expound his ideas and plead causes with virtuosity, evoking images tending to illuminate rather than to conceal, now too often became

[1] Schlegel, *Philosophy of History*.
[2] Gibbon, *Decline and Fall*, Vol. II.

jungles of verbiage in which he chased the shadows of his obsessions. The tragic disasters overwhelming the huge and almost unarmed Russian armies, of which he was to write with distinction some years later, and the collapse of the whole rickety and tyrannical edifice of Tsardom, released a flood of wild and irrational Churchillian nonsense.

Sweeping aside all testimony from unimpeachable sources, ignoring the mountains of Russian dead, the millions of civilians desperate with hunger and cold, and the shameful preoccupations of the Russian monarchy, Churchill announced that Russia 'with victory in her grasp fell upon the earth, devoured alive, like Herod of old, by worms'. According to him the 'ship' that had foundered rudderless in uncharted seas 'sank in sight of port'.

Lloyd George described such outbursts as giving 'A ludicrous picture . . . made attractive only because of the glittering rhetoric in which it is framed by a great colour artist.'[1]

When he came to comment upon the deeds of Lenin and Trotsky Churchill's obsessional hatred was given full rein. Inheriting chaos, these two men, ruthless and brilliant, had sought peace at almost any price, and begun the seemingly impossible task of building Russia in a new image, cordoned off by the world, and starting from scratch.

In 1917 much was obscure, but much was known. For two years the Russian tragedy had been followed with growing anxiety by British and French observers, while the dreadful and diabolic antics of Rasputin and the miserable corruption of the Russian Royal family, had sickened Western statesmen no less than their Russian opposite numbers. In 1915 something might still have been done to avert the terrible crisis which, it was clear, must overtake Russia and its rulers. By the end of that year it was too late. The Tsar and Tsarina were encompassing not only their own destruction, but the destruction of the country over which they had held absolute sway. Nothing could be done without the Tsar's authority; nothing could be done with it. It had ceased to exist, while nothing else existed, nor could exist, while the Tsar remained. The squalid end of Rasputin foretold the death of the Royal family and of old Russia.

While the Tsar and Tsarina mouldered to pathetic and shame-

[1] David Lloyd George, *War Memoirs*, Vol. III.

ful ruin, reduced to the condition of puppets manipulated by Rasputin, and floundering in a morass of mysticism and medieval fears, millions perished of hunger and cold, and millions more died weaponless and almost defenceless on the Eastern Front. To face an enemy, magnificently armed and organized, Russian divisions went into action with three rifles available for every ten men, the remaining seven being ordered to clap their hands to simulate fire. Out of seven million men originally mobilized more than half had been killed in the first year of war. The Western Front was becoming a shambles; the Eastern Front was an *abattoir*.

There was not a political or military group in all Russia that did not seek ways and means of the establishment of a new order throughout the years 1915 and 1916. Even the most mild realized that the Tsar must be overthrown, and a constitutional monarchy established.

On all these matters Britain was exceptionally well informed, thanks in great measure to the quality of Sir George Buchanan, British Ambassador in St Petersburg, and to the careful and balanced analyses of men of the calibre of Lord Milner and Sir Bernard Pares.

From all the information at his disposal Lloyd George wrote: 'The men who gave the Russian Revolution its first impulse were not the bolsheviks, but disgusted aristocrats and bourgeois—princes, merchants and lawyers.'[1] The revolution had become not only 'inevitable—it was imperative'. Soldiers and sailors mutinied. The generals plotted the overthrow of the Tsar. The army resolved to be avenged for its slaughtered millions. Men like Prince Lvov, Rodzianko, President of the Duma, Miliukoff, the lawyer, pressed upon the drivelling Tsar the necessity for immediate change. The days of autocracy were done.

Sir George Buchanan preserved one of the Tsar's final monumental pieces of arrogance:[2]

'Your Majesty, if I may be permitted to say so, has but one safe course open to you, namely to break down the barrier that separates you from your people and to regain their confidence.'

The Tsar replied:

[1] David Lloyd George, *War Memoirs*, Vol. III.
[2] Sir G. Buchanan, *My Mission to Russia*, Vol. II.

'Do you mean that I am to regain the confidence of my people or that they are to regain *my* confidence?'

But it was already too late. Maklakoff had responded to French advice to have patience:[1]

'We've had quite enough patience. . . . Our patience is utterly exhausted! Besides, if we don't act soon the masses won't listen to us any longer.'

None could have described the Tsarist terror more forcibly than Prince Lvov in many discussions with foreign diplomats, and Princess Radziwill wrote: . . .

'the hatred for Rasputin which was openly expressed in the best society of Petersburg and Moscow, was but a blind to hide a campaign for the overthrow of the Emperor himself! A plausible pretext was essential, but the more serious aim was cherished by a considerable number of those sick of the graft, corruption and complete disorder of the administration, and disgusted with the shallow, false and unreliable character of Nicholas II, and the cold-blooded cruelty with which he was trying to suppress every aspiration and movement towards reform. The torrents of blood shed since he ascended the Throne had alienated all respect and affection, and his subjects had come to look upon him as an impediment to the development and the prosperity of Russia.'[2]

With facts such as these readily at his disposal Churchill stated:

'It is the shallow fashion of these times to dismiss the Tsarist regime as a purblind, corrupt, incompetent tyranny.' On the contrary, 'the Tsar was a true simple man of average ability and of merciful disposition'.

It is possible, though improbable, that the deaths at the door of Nicholas II, and the tortures, did not exceed those attributed to the monster Ivan the Terrible, or greatly outnumber the dreadful statistics compiled by Abdul the Damned. But Churchill had discovered a 'Devil' to set against his 'Gods', and

[1] M. Paleologue, *An Ambassador's Memoirs.*
[2] Princess Radziwill, *Nicholas II, Last of the Czars.*

he reserved his hate for those who dared to challenge the sanctity of monarchy or question the right to rule of the traditional ruling class. Lenin, therefore, enjoyed the full force of his invective:

'In the cutting off of the lives of men and women no Asiatic conqueror, not Tamerlane, not Jenghiz Khan can match his fame.'

Lenin dazzled him. He embodied:

'Implacable vengeance, rising from a frozen pity in a tranquil, sensible, matter-of-fact, ·good-humoured integument! His weapon logic; his mood opportunist. His sympathies cold and wide as the Arctic Ocean; his hatreds tight as the hangman's noose. His purpose to save the world: his method to blow it up.'[1]

It may be difficult to follow Churchill on these extravagant flights. Are they passionate outbursts in the heat of the moment, or are they cool and calculated political utterances? I believe they are both. They marked the beginning of the end of diplomacy and the emergence of a world coloured black and white. The attitude was American, revealing that Puritanism that has turned the world into rival camps of good and evil with nothing in between. In 1917 the Devil was born.

Churchill's outburst startled men like Asquith, Balfour and Lloyd George, and induced Lord Esher to remark:

'He handles great subjects in rhythmical language, and becomes quickly enslaved by his own phrases. He deceives himself into the belief that he takes broad views, when his mind is fixed upon one comparatively small aspect of the question.'

Yet it would be a mistake to consider him merely as a frightened reactionary perceiving a new and terrible challenge to long surpremacy. There is a note of envy. Lenin cannot be forgiven even if his slaughters rival those of Tamerlane, for he is not a conqueror. He is a builder, a builder moreover lying low in a neutral land while his country is disintegrating, and only

[1] Winston S. Churchill, *The World Crisis, The Aftermath.*

arriving in time to take command of chaos. Lenin in a new pattern is usurping the sacred rights of monarchy and 'The Barons'.

But it is difficult, and unprofitable, to attempt to fit Churchill into any modern political framework. He is a would-be autocrat of a lost age. His attitudes above all were romantic and sentimental. Thus his visions, whether of Tsarist and revolutionary Russia, of the British Empire, the United States, or France, were based on romantic and sentimental longings for a world of grandeur that never was, a child's world of heroes and villains, with nothing in between but a nurse.

In this period Churchill's images of the United States and France were also fashioned and hardened. Through his contact and friendship with Bernard Baruch he began to understand the portents of the industrial power of the United States, and the peculiar dynamic glamour of American politics and big business. Through the towering figure of Clemenceau he had potent glimpses of the spirit and glory of France.

Whatever the facts, these visions remained constant. He was at once a European, an Englishman and an American. Had he been a Russian or a German the mixture might have mixed.

## II

By making frequent sorties to the Western Front throughout the last year of war, from the autumn of 1917 to the autumn of 1918, Churchill struck a balance of physical action and danger to leaven his work as the Minister of Munitions. In his own right as Minister it was valuable to discover in the field the urgent needs of the men in action, and to supply them. It was also important to know how they were faring. His own exhilaration could not blind him to the fact that an intense weariness pervaded the troops from top to bottom in the middle of 1917. He could understand it but he could not feel it in himself.

The ubiquitous Colonel House, the personal emissary of the President of the United States, commuting easily between the warring capitals, and enjoying the confidence of Foreign Ministers on all sides, had produced various outlines of peace proposals, none of them acceptable. He was not an European, and inevitably aroused suspicions. Nevertheless it had become clear before his country unhappily abandoned its neutral status at a late hour that the struggle should end—before it was too late. There should be an end to the senseless killing.

The expressions of hate, so prevalent on the Home Fronts, were almost entirely absent on the battlefields. Reginald Barnes, a companion of Churchill's youthful soldiering and now a Major-General commanding a division in action, was, as Marsh wrote, 'rather worn and tired by the war, as determined as anyone to make a clean job of it, but very anxious that we should not prolong it unnecessarily. . . . This point of view is pretty general among the sensible fighting men, and it makes me furious with the journalists, shop-stewards, etc., at home who scream about this being the moment to give the Hun bloody socks etc.'

By the middle of 1917 it was too late. The United States, treated with contempt by Germany, and finally pushed over the brink of neutrality by the sinking of the *Lusitania*, was about to destroy Europe's last chance of setting her own house in order. It would go on to the bitter end, and henceforth, inevitably, there would be a new pattern. The writing was on the wall, and Churchill would be one of those to ink it in in the aftermath:

'After immense delays and false hopes that only aggravated her difficulties, Europe was left to scramble out of the world disaster as best she could; and the United States, which had lost but 125,000 lives in the whole struggle, was to settle down upon the basis of receiving through one channel or another four-fifths of the reparations paid by Germany to the countries she had devastated or whose manhood she had slain."[1]

Amery, 'the cleverest bloody fool in Europe', as Balfour called him, underlined it bluntly and coldly. There was no vestige of love-hate in his attitude, for his love was all for his clear concept of Britain, the Empire, and Europe. He did not recall with Churchill's anger and scorn President Wilson's speech on April 2, 1917, in which the President had said:

'We have no selfish ends to serve. We desire no conquest, no dominion. We seek no indemnities for ourselves, no material compensation for the sacrifices we shall freely make. We are but one of the champions of mankind.'

[1] *The World Crisis, The Aftermath.*

When, like Pilate, Wilson washed his hands of the whole affair, his country could settle down to absorb its vast booty, for 'the United States had emerged . . . with an immensely stimulated production, and now found itself transformed from a debtor into the world's greatest creditor, on commercial account alone, as well as on account of the debts due to it from its Allies and as the ultimate recipient of the greater part of the heavy war reparations imposed on Germany.'[1]

It was a harsh lesson to be spelled out miserably over twenty years, and not a line of it learned, least of all by Churchill. It was one of the lessons he disliked. He had been scornful of America for dragging her feet. He had longed for her to enter the European struggle, and in 1917 he was exuberant. He had made good and friendly contact with Bernard Baruch, the Head of the American War Productions Board, and perhaps the second most powerful man in the United States. The tools of war were rapidly coming to hand, and the bill would not be presented until long after the meal was over.

In France the French Government had put the Chateau Verchocq, near Fouquienbergue, at Churchill's disposal, and in his execrable French Fouquienbergue became, Marsh was sorry to say, F— and B—. It was a peak year in Churchill's life. He was back in the political front line and the war front line at the same time. Even the coldness of Haig did not disturb him. Acting often as the eyes and ears of the Prime Minister, Churchill was assured a welcome on the highest levels, and enjoyed every possible facility to see and to learn all that he desired. But he failed to break the crust of Haig's deep-seated dislike.

Nevertheless, always outwardly indifferent to the feelings of others, Churchill's visits to Haig's headquarters were made pleasant by his many acquaintances both old and new. Of these, Major Morton, one of Haig's principal *aides*, was often Churchill's guide and escort on his sorties to the front. It was the beginning of a friendship of great importance in the years to come.

Major Morton had been seriously wounded commanding the last battery to fire at Arras. A bullet, it was found, had lodged in his heart, and miraculously he lived with it. There it remains. He had won a Military Cross, and wore also the *Legion d'honneur avec Palmes*, an honour which carries with it the right of

[1] L. S. Amery, *My Political Life*, Vol. II.

entry to the President of France. Quiet, reserved, yet with a dry humour, and an almost monkish ability to observe the material struggles of men while dedicated himself to service, he was the kind of man to appeal to Churchill's romantic nature, and his needs. Together, often under shell fire, they made many sorties into the dangerous and desolate no-man's lands wherein it was difficult to see aught but squalor, wretchedness and the muddied hopes of men.

Churchill seemed positively to expand, to glow, almost like a man in love in these conditions. It was not that he did not see them as they were, but the squalor did not touch his inner core. His romantic vision of what war 'should be' was so powerful that it affected others while under his spell, even men like Siegfried Sassoon and Graves who had suffered the thing in their very souls. Strangely his humours did not offend. He was like a child protected by a personal armour of dream.

Churchill's sorties to France were spread over a wide field. He travelled frequently with Edward Marsh as his companion, and was almost always in good humour, delighting in simple stories, especially the one about the two women farm workers who failed to persuade the cow to lie down for the bull. He disliked smut, and was seldom bad tempered. He was even patient with bumbling sentries, but could be childishly petulant when Archibald Sinclair,[1] accompanying him, insisted upon reporting back to his Colonel on time, and curtailing a seemingly interminable meander along the front. He was markedly cold, sulking and sticking out his underlip, growling that he would not bother with Sinclair any more. He had been hard to cross as a child, and as a grown man, formidable in temper, such an exercise demanded a high degree of moral courage in his companions, and a sense of detachment. In their very different fashions both Marsh and Morton had such a detachment. Edward Marsh was an ideal companion, caring little for politics, and nothing for power, a source of valuable information on social and literary matters, but Churchill was his hero, *sans tâche*. The desperate issues of power and politics were Churchill's battlefield, not Marsh's. He was but the 'Page', a 'good little boy'.

Major Morton, aloof from the political and power struggles, but keenly observant, was no man's good little boy. He was a

[1] Afterwards Viscount Thurso.

man of exceptional spiritual and moral strength, and of great potential value to an egocentric of Churchill's monumental stature. For Churchill would always need someone with the peculiar authority and integrity of a Mrs Everest in her time, someone whose word could be relied upon at all seasons, who saw him as he was, and to whom, when loneliness cast its fearful shadow, he might speak without fear or favour.

Marsh took Churchill's nonchalance for granted, unable to conceive that fear should touch such a man, and recording his own selfconsciousness. 'I was rather surprised at not feeling the least frightened,' Marsh wrote of an occasion when he was bracketed with his Chief on Wyndschaete Ridge, in the heart of a beaten zone of fire. 'The only thing was that I was a tiny bit selfconscious.'

But on similar occasions Morton was struck by Churchill's extraordinary reactions. He was far from nonchalant. He seemed to glow. This was the food and drink his nature demanded, and even if no longer 'a gentleman's relish', it had been the food of the Gods, far removed from that truly squalid world of factories and the miserable labours of nameless slaves. It remained the most exciting and stimulating activity of man, even though the loved one had become a whore.

Moreover, the greatest man in France shared a comparable vision. The high point of Churchill's visits to France was his meeting with Clemenceau on behalf of Lloyd George, and his short tour with that ancient and magnificent symbol of the spirit of France to the headquarters of Foch, Petain, Weygand, Haig Rawlinson. It had become imperative in the spring of 1918 to know exactly what was happening, and for a little while Churchill warmed himself at that great fire. The needs of the men at the front in that last spring were enormous if they were to escape from their dreadful purgatory, to hold the last mighty surge of the enemy armies, and to throw them back. To those who knew in England present and future were in a fine and delicate balance.

In Clemenceau's intimate company Churchill heard Foch expounding the manner of final victory with words and gestures of astonishing vehemence. At the end, Foch and Clemenceau embraced. France was saved. No man listening to Foch on that March morning of 1918 could doubt it.

'... at that moment the two greatest Frenchmen of this awful age were supreme—and were friends,' Churchill wrote.[1]

After visiting Rawlinson and Haig, Churchill had the honour of conducting the French Premier as near as possible to the scene of battle. He had made a careful study of the war map in Rawlinson's headquarters, and pressed forward urged by Clemenceau, under a violent curtain of shell fire to a 'thin line' on top of a hill. 'What lay beyond that, I could not tell. Rifle fire was now audible in the woods, and shells began to burst in front of us on the road and in the sopping meadows on either side. The rain continued, as always, to pour down, and the mists of evening began to gather. I thought on the whole that we had gone far enough.'[2]

It was the kind of thought often present in the minds of those who had served him as guides, and he is unmindful of himself in a new way, serving the very great man occupying the centre of the stage.

When the time came to take his leave Churchill said:

'This sort of excursion is all right for a single day: but you ought not to go under fire too often.'

The old man looked at him keenly, knowing well the ingredients of war and peace over more than half a century.

'C'est mon grand plaisir,' he said.

Thus was Churchill fortified in preserving an image of war he was not prepared to lose, and which he would not permit the Ministry of Munitions to blur. He believed in 'glory', in the superb 'gamesmanship' of war, and he shut his mind against the harsh arithmetic of the matter, refusing to learn, or perhaps incapable of learning, such lessons.

Nevertheless, through the Ministry of Munitions, and his many visits to factories throughout Britain, he closely observed the dark submerged mass of the industrial iceberg upon which the edifice of modern war must be built, and of which the soldiers were no longer the shining crest. The soldier, coloured drab khaki or drabber grey, had become a dweller in holes in the

[1] *Thoughts and Adventures.*
[2] Ibid.

ground, in warrens of mud, slush, blood and entrails. Tens of thousands of bodies lay like miserable sacks, rotting over acres of pock-marked fields that were fields no more. Churchill saw it all, and did not see it, just as he saw, and did not see the industrial facts which alone made possible the human struggle.

In these attitudes he resembled the overwhelming mass of his countrymen and women, for without the glitter and the glory and the clear purpose war had become a monstrous crime, a manifestation of man's supreme inhumanity to man, to be buried forever, relegated to a barbaric past. Churchill would not permit the truth to destroy his vision, for if a man cannot live with life as it is, and very few can, he must live with illusion. How else to drop our bombs on babies, to shrivel children at play with napalm, to acquiesce in the hunger and misery of millions, to wash our hands of all that?

And why should a man of great talents and opportunities be immune from these tricks and weaknesses of more ordinary men? Thus the Western Front, from which millions prayed for release to a factory, became Churchill's escape from the factory of war. There was no facet of supply of which he was unaware, but he refused to admit its overwhelming significance while being forced to submit to its limitations. Thus when Churchill at last came to power he was to submerge his staff relentlessly in useless toil, to produce all the facts and figures to prove to him that he could not do the impossible. Good soldiers should acknowledge no limiting factors beyond the battlefield. It was a dream. He would not let it die.

Yet by preserving a dream he made life more tolerable for himself, for to look the modern world straight in the eye is to be changed irreparably, to renounce the devil and all his works, to come down from the exceeding high mountain, not to the fabled city, to wealth and power, but to a cross, or to become perhaps a monk, certainly a recluse, derided as a crank. For if men were fully awake to their deeds they would be monsters, and it must be said that few tyrants, however vile and cruel, have satisfied the lusts and insatiable appetites of the mob; no politician is as bad as the majority of those who elect him; no politician would willingly impose upon others, even upon the most terrible and defeated enemy, the miseries demanded by the people.

The Peace of Versailles indelibly underlined this terrible truth.

## III

Three weeks after the conclusion of an armistice, President Wilson became the first President of the United States to embark for foreign soil. He did so against the strong advice of his friends and advisers in America, and in face of the powerful misgivings of the leaders of France, Britain and Italy. He regarded himself as the instrument of an authority that must exceed that of all others present. He would be a 'king' among Prime Ministers.

Wilson had formulated his famous 'Fourteen Points' as a foundation upon which peace could be built. A shrewd and calculating politician on his home ground, he adopted a posture of immaculate idealism in his attitude to 'the lesser breeds without the law', of which Europeans provided barbaric examples. His emissary, Colonel House, had worked indefatigably, gaining the respect and friendship of many European statesmen, as well as an insight into the intricate affairs of Europe. Perhaps he alone in Wilson's entourage saw the pitfalls ahead. For the rest, Wilson was supported by some of the toughest economists and financiers in the world, as well as by sycophantic propagandists whose fulminations would threaten to establish the President as an object of ridicule, even in his own country.

President Wilson's purpose was to set barbaric Europe on a civilized course. He sailed with his 'head in the clouds', and there it remained. He stated that he represented '*the only disinterested people* at the peace conference, and that *the men whom we were about to deal with did not represent their own people*'.[1]

Perhaps the heart of the tragedy about to unfold was that while President Wilson's authority was an illusion, Clemenceau and Lloyd George were driven by the passionate and savage support of huge majorities of their countrymen. While they strove to formulate settlements based on reason and reality, their countrymen howled for blood and gold. Wilson's countrymen merely washed their hands of him, and told him so in unmistakable terms.

'Our allies and enemies and Mr Wilson himself,' said ex-President Roosevelt in a powerful speech, 'should all understand that Mr Wilson has no authority whatever to speak for the American people at this time.'

The President no longer commanded majorities in the Senate

[1] David Hunter Miller, *The Drafting of the Covenant*.

or in Congress, nor would they endorse any agreements to which he might commit himself. Thus, for example, the League of Nations from which it is at least conceivable that a durable peace might have sprung, was crippled and doomed at the hour of its birth. Nevertheless, nothing could prevent the President from taking his seat at the Conference as the most 'exalted' personage present, even though he had to yield the chairmanship to Clemenceau on the soil of France.

At once the Americans were confronted with a 'labyrinth' of secret treaties of which they said they had never heard, but which, in fact, they had chosen to ignore as the manifestations of a wicked cynicism intolerable to an idealistic people living in a clean continent. While the European nations had plundered each other and large tracts of the world for wealth and power, the United States, apart from grabbing the Philippines and Puerto Rico and attempting to establish a 'cordon sanitaire' round the whole of the South American continent, had still not exhausted the plunder of their own vast land.

'The showdown came at the third meeting of the Big Four, as Wilson repetitively voiced his dream of a "permanent peace",' wrote Lincoln Steffens.[1]

Suddenly Clemenceau confronted the President bluntly and ruthlessly with the realities of war and peace. 'We can make this permanent peace,' he roared. 'We can remove all causes of war.' He then went on to state in broad outline the prerequisites of such a peace. France must abandon her African possessions and ambitions, Britain must relinquish India and much else besides, and America could no longer hold the Philippines and Puerto Rico. All nations must have complete access to all markets without hindrance. 'All must throw away their keys to the trade routes, surrender their spheres of influence.'

'Are you willing to pay these prices?' Clemenceau demanded, 'For if not,' and he brought his fist down on the table, 'you don't mean permanent peace. You mean war.'[2]

How, Clemenceau wondered into the anxious and sympathetic ear of Colonel House, can you reach understanding with a man who thinks himself the first man in two thousand years to know anything about peace? It was like talking to 'Jesus Christ', except that Wilson was not remotely like Jesus Christ. But for the

[1] *Autobiography*, Vol. II, quoted by Margaret Coit in *Mr Baruch*.
[2] Margaret Coit, *Mr Baruch*.

presence of the remarkable Maurice Hankey, the guardian and guide of Cabinets and innumerable committees, it is unlikely that the principal delegates would have maintained any coherent contact with the tragic situation. Carefully each night Hankey sought a way through the mazes of spoken words and attempted to discover what there might be of sense or decision. It became a standard joke among those who knew that it was very far from a joke to say, 'Well, we'd better ask Hankey what, if anything, we decided.'

Clemenceau and Lloyd George had both put forward clear outlines of realistic proposals, recognizing that Germany must be brought within the comity of nations and her domestic growth stimulated. France, having suffered a German invasion twice within fifty years, must seek safeguards against a third attempt. The demands of Italy, the collapse of Turkish power and the revolution in Russia, aroused passions often inconsistent with reason while calling for decisions of the most farsighted statesmanship.

At least the Americans were reasonably free from passion, but this was offset by an astonishing simplicity of approach allied to highly developed commercial and financial instincts. The simplicity of approach was manifest in the first of Wilson's Fourteen Points, which stated that the covenants of peace must be openly arrived at. Such a condition was impossible to fulfil. The commercial and financial instincts were represented by the presence of Mr Bernard Baruch.

Inevitably, as it seems now, and to many then, the Versailles Treaty prepared the ground for war, and in condemning Germany to the impossible, destroying her economy and reducing her people to poverty, Europe and America condemned themselves. In order to keep Germany in her place the full force of the blockade was maintained, and it was not until the British General Plumer drew urgent attention to the appalling conditions inside Germany that Lloyd George and Churchill acted at once to send food ships to Hamburg. Meanwhile between one and two million civilians had perished of starvation.

Churchill has been blamed for a piece of inhumanity alien to his whole nature. The responsibility for the maintenance of the blockade beyond war and humanity was on the shoulders of the Cabinet, and of the Allies in general, all of whom were a long way ahead of their electorates in humanity and common sense.

Finally President Wilson went home, disillusioned with everyone but himself, to find his attempts at peace-making and American membership of the League of Nations rejected by Congress and the Senate, while Lloyd George, his government overwhelmingly supported by the electorate, found himself spurred to take steps of which he profoundly disapproved. Germany must be squeezed 'until the pips squeak', the Kaiser 'must be hanged'. He lent his tongue to these slogans, for to have done otherwise would have been political suicide and would have averted nothing. If Asquith had been included in the British Peace Party his influence at Versailles might have had some slight effect. Assuredly, the breach between him and Lloyd George might have been healed and Liberalism might have been preserved in Britain as a political force.

On the sidelines of these great events, absorbed spectators of all that transpired, were Churchill and Bernard Baruch, the one embodying British and European romanticism in its wildest flights of fancy, the other representing an outstanding example of a financial-political tycoon from the New World. While these two men watched the Conference and its principal actors, they also watched each other. While Churchill loved the limelight, Baruch preferred the shadows. While Churchill was outraged by the nauseating cant surrounding President Wilson's performance, Baruch was warning Wilson that 'Lloyd George was trying to seize the moral leadership of the world'.

Meanwhile, Baruch and Churchill were drawn together in a friendship which was to endure. The foundations had been laid in the course of correspondence across the Atlantic dealing with the provision of the means of war. Baruch had been deeply impressed with Churchill's prodigious energies, and had shrewdly appointed him the 'Nitrate King' with the power on behalf of the United States and other interested parties, to seize Chilean nitrates loaded or loading in German vessels in Chilean ports and waters. This had been a buccaneering task very much to Churchill's taste, and he had performed it admirably. At the same time he had had a brief insight into the ways and powers of big business. No one knew better than Baruch that industrial power was the key to war, and therefore to political power. Contemplating the ruin of Europe, he realized that the United States could, and almost surely would, lead the world. She was the great banker, rich in raw materials, the only solvent merchant and manufacturer in the

Western world, the only shop without its windows smashed, its roof stove in, its goods pillaged, and with her factories producing the weapons of war in huge quantity. Given a clear vision the United States could not fail to reap a gigantic harvest of riches.

But the clear vision was lacking, not only in the United States, but everywhere. There was no statesman of the calibre, of the tremendous breadth of outlook, and grasp of history, to understand what had happened in the affairs of men. And had there been such a one he would have been wise to keep his vision to himself. Perhaps it was impossible to see clearly in the aftermath of war. Lloyd George was primarily a home politician, his life dedicated to the establishment of a new kind of social welfare in Britain. Clemenceau, a magnificent old European and French patriot, saw Europe in its age-old terms. Wilson, given the courage of his convictions, might have established a League of Nations with a chance of survival. None saw it in the new terms of the twentieth century; none grasped the nature of war, yet all were uneasy.

What was obvious was that the collapse of Imperial Russia had left a power vacuum in Europe, and into that vacuum the United States had been sucked. Somewhere in these two facts was the heart of the tragedy, and in dispassionate contemplation of those facts lay the solution. But in the aftermath of the most terrible war in history, passion ruled the minds of men. They called it the war to end war, and they were right, but because they did not understand why it must end war the fight must go on. Nothing had been resolved, for the warring powers did not understand what it was they wished to resolve. A world was at an end, and they could not see. Meanwhile, events in Russia were deeply disturbing, exciting new and profound fears, and providing an enemy to distort the view.

Such was the essence of the scene of chaos Churchill and Baruch confronted throughout 1919, and of the two Baruch saw the future more clearly, not as it might be, but as it almost surely would be. As a man whose parents had been refugees from East Prussia to the New World he had a deep distrust of Germany, and did not share the American President's half-baked idealism. He believed that out of the ruin of war would come war again, and that since it would be impossible to ensure peace it would be wise to ensure victory. He saw, as Churchill could not, that British power was threadbare and that America must be the natural heir

H

of Britain's rôle. He perceived also the strategic importance of Britain if American ambitions were to be realized, and to have an ally of the calibre of Churchill in the British camp might be of inestimable value. Besides, Churchill was half American and receptive to American ideas. He did not regard America as a foreign power, and his anger with its shortcomings was the anger of one who wanted to take pride in the deeds of both sides of his family. But America looked westward across the Pacific. Britain was but a bastion to protect her Atlantic flank.

Together the team of Baruch and Churchill combined the financial *panâche* of the new world and the military *panâche* of the old. It was a heady combination. Both men were incurable romantics, both sought power by different routes, and of a different nature. Baruch loved the manipulative power behind the scenes, while Churchill longed for all the trappings in the full glare of the limelight. They were ideal partners, mutually complementary, 'The chief ideologists of the counter-revolutionary International,' Louis Adamic called them.

Both men suffered the peculiar loneliness of the egocentric, arising out of the loneliness of childhood when both had created worlds in which they might dream.

No man observing Churchill as boy or man reading Stevenson, Henty and Haggard, and later Dumas, and much later still Forester's Hornblower stories, could fail to note his total absorption. He did not simply like these books but they were, as one of his close friends put it, 'a draught of wine to a thirsty man'. With these worlds that had never existed outside the dreams of their authors Churchill refreshed himself.

Baruch's early world had not lacked romance. He was born in the little South Carolina town of Camden in 1870, 'in the track of Sherman', a small world desolated by civil war, his childhood filled with stories of 'glory', his heroes Lee and Jackson. With his parents he attended the synagogue, but he had not suffered persecution, and was unaware of being a Jew until he was eleven years old. He was in at the birth of the United States, of the great days when the speculators built their railroads to open up a continent. He had made his first million long before the turn of the century.

A financier and economist of the calibre of Baruch, and with his particular background, could easily appreciate the task confronting Lenin in Russia. What a wonderful challenge it could be to free enterprise! He was ready to lend a sympathetic ear to Lenin's pleas for economic and financial aid, but not on Lenin's terms.[1]

In the spring of 1919 Baruch and Churchill were preoccupied with the situation in Russia. While Baruch shared Churchill's fear and hatred of communism, he was able to see clearly that the old order had brought Imperial Russia to utter ruin and that Lenin, whether you liked him or not, was the only effective authority in the country. The thing to do was to woo him. Churchill would have as soon wooed the devil and would fight him to the bitter end.

Meanwhile, in January 1919, following a General Election in which Lloyd George won an overwhelming personal victory, Churchill had exchanged the Ministry of Munitions for the Ministries of War and Air, and was faced with tremendous problems at home and abroad. Indeed, the problems of peace were seen to be far greater than those of war. Money mattered. Wages could not be maintained at the unprecedented heights reached in war. A sound economic base had to be established. It was clear, too, to the politicians if not to the electorate, that to attempt to extract vast reparations in wealth and labour from the defeated enemy would have been disastrous to the victors.

Inevitably, by facing the country in the hour of victory, Lloyd George was compelled to lend himself to passions of which he deeply disapproved, for to have done otherwise would have been fatal to his government. Few doubted that he was the man to bridge the chasm from war to peace; few doubt now that he would have hesitated to sacrifice himself in the best interests of the country.

The work to be done could not wait. While tens of thousands clamoured for immediate demobilization into an industrial unbalance that might take years to set right, the war-weary millions had been promised 'a land fit for heroes to live in'. Churchill strove to stem the flood of ex-Servicemen into a labour market totally unable to absorb them. That his achievement was slight does not deserve criticism. It was clear that the war industries must be steadily dismantled and return to peace production, that the tragic gaps in the merchant shipping of a nation dependent upon world trade would have to be made good, that markets would have to be regained; that new machinery would have to be

[1] A Pittsburgh firm of consultants advised on the first five-year plan.

designed and made to produce the varied products by which alone trade might flow again. Raw material shortages were acute, and at the heart of Europe itself was the industrial vacuum of Germany, committed to hopeless debt and deprived of the means of paying it.

Only as a single entity could the nations of Europe hope to be re-born, but that would have meant the realization that the war had been essentially a 'civil war', that since Marlborough Europe, if her parts should fight, would fight herself and destroy her own house. But in that house European Russia and Germany had been a vital balance. Germany was ruined and occupied. Russia was cordoned off. The United States was about to cordon herself off, collect the spoils and retreat into isolation. The rump of Europe, hopelessly in debt, her industry in ruins, her peoples weary, starving, millions workless and homeless, their currencies becoming waste paper, became a breeding ground for new nationalisms and new hatreds of a greater virulence than had ever been known before.

It was not surprising that the intricate mechanisms of war could not be instantly dismantled, and that the vast impetus of warfare could not be easily halted. An enemy, and a threat, was essential, and Russia provided the 'Red' bogey ready to hand. There lay justification for the maintenance of armies and armaments.

Meanwhile the prey of the victors was almost devoid of flesh. France, unsatisfied with the return of Alsace and Lorraine, demanded, but did not get, the Saar. The great German war factory of the Ruhr was occupied. Poland was re-born and frontiers manipulated. In Turkey, Kemal Ataturk had arisen to breathe new life and Western ideas into an Oriental people, to regain Constantinople and Western Thrace, and to rap the fingers of Greece.

How impossible, and yet how desperately urgent, to see Europe as a *place*, as the United States was a *place*, but had not been, as 'All the Russias' would be welded into a *place*, a world of continents in place of a multitude of nations and tribes, until from that vision must stem the world as a *place*. For that was the meaning of the world revolution of the twentieth century and the challenge of 'world war'. The war in Europe had been a civil war, and interference from outside could only blur the result, masking both victory and defeat and tending to remake Europe in its old image. Civil wars, in their nature, must be fought out and resolved alone. They are family quarrels.

All this was immeasurably clouded by the collapse of Russia, and the birth of a revolutionary creed regarded as a malignant cancer menacing the economic and social basis of the outside world. Churchill was dedicated to the smashing of this creed. He saw it as an abomination, threatening to destroy the imagery and glory of his world, and evoking in him nostalgic dreams of the Congress of Vienna. How different things had been! Imperial Russia had maintained a 'glittering façade' to mask the horrors and miseries of a colourful and terrible régime. It had presented an exuberant mass of brilliant flower and foliage upon an immense dung heap of suffering and squalor. Now the dung heap was revealed for all to see. A group of ruthless and dedicated men prepared to wrestle with the problem of driving 160,000,000 men, women and children, 98 per cent illiterate, unfed, unshod, unsheltered, and spread over a land area nearly three times as large as the United States of America, lacking in communications and more than the rudiments of industrial power, through five hundred years of history in the shortest possible time. There would be little aid from any quarter.

Nothing was more natural than that Churchill should do all in his power to support the various groups of 'White' Russians fighting under Deniken and Koltchak to give substance to a liberal form of government under Kerensky. Churchill had inherited a situation which he could not in any case dismantle. French and British armies were already deeply committed, holding a stretch of strategic railway line in the south from Odessa, and an area in the region of Archangel in the north. With the full agreement of Sir Henry Wilson, Chief of the Imperial General Staff, Churchill supported all these endeavours with arms.

He could not forgive the Bolsheviks the Treaty of Brest-Litovsk; nor could he understand that to strip Russia to the bone was a sign of strength, not weakness, for only by concentrating on what he might hope to hold and consolidate was Lenin able to defeat the counter-revolution, at last to regain all that he had lost.

In February 1919, a month after his appointment to the War Office, in a speech at the Mansion House, Churchill referred to,

'The aid which we can give to these Russian armies ... who are now engaged in fighting against the foul baboonery of Bolshevism . . . can be given by arms, munitions, equipment and technical services raised upon a voluntary basis.'

Before the end of the year when the tragic, ill-conceived and half-hearted British and Allied intervention petered out, 100,000 tons of arms and equipment had been landed by the British at Vladivostok and the total bill to Britain had reached £100,000,000. Yet, as Churchill saw it, the effort had not been in vain.

The energies of the Bolsheviks had been wholly contained throughout all 1919 in meeting and defeating the White Russian armies. 'A breathing space of inestimable importance was afforded to the whole line of newly-liberated countries which stood along the western borders of Russia. . . . By the end of 1920 the "Sanitary Cordon" which protected Europe from the Bolshevik infection was formed by living national organisms vigorous in themselves."[1]

Above all, Poland had been resurrected and secured.

Churchill could not abide a grey world, and if Lenin was constructing a world at all it would be indubitably grey, if not black in Churchillian terms. He could not compromise with it, and in his sustained efforts to aid the forces of counter-revolution to the last he alienated a section of the British working class.

Before the props of World War I were cleared away the stage was being set for the second instalment of the European civil war.

---

[1] *The World Crisis, The Aftermath.*

# CHAPTER XIV

CHURCHILL was never more likeable than in his periods of innocent bewilderment in the political wilderness. Until he regained his wind and organized his forces, he paused in his pursuit of power and gave his mind and energies to a variety of social and cultural activities. He relished the conversation of artists and poets, and basked in the warm companionship of his wife and his faithful, witty, Auguste, Edward Marsh.

In the winter of 1922-3 he found himself, as he put it, 'without office, without a seat, without a party and without an appendix'. He had been rushed to hospital three days before the election on the downfall of the Lloyd George Coalition. New and disturbing patterns were appearing in the political firmament, and he did not like the portents. But experience soon taught him that he could not blame the loss of his parliamentary seat upon the loss of his appendix. True, he had been out of action at a crucial moment, but his wife had fought for him valiantly at Dundee in his absence, and when, towards the end, he had attempted to address a huge crowd from his wheel chair, he had been howled down. Had he been on his feet he might have suffered physical assault, for he was 'struck by the looks of passionate hatred on the faces of some of the younger men and women'.

Clearly he was in an unenviable position, and the way ahead politically—if there were a way ahead—was obscure. With the fall of Lloyd George his own political house had foundered, yet it had not been a decision of the electorate, nor even of Parliament. Lloyd George had been the victim of the revolution of the Tories to regain power freed from his 'great dynamic force'. 'That force,' as Baldwin pointed out in a passionate speech at the Carlton Club, 'had already broken up the Liberal Party. He did not want it to break up the Conservative Party.'[1]

Beaverbrook, meanwhile, had persuaded the ailing Bonar Law

[1] L. S. Amery, *My Political Life*, Vol. II.

to lead. The backing of *The Times* was assured. But Lloyd George was also the victim of a newspaper vendetta pursued over four years with remarkable virulence by Lord Northcliffe's newspapers. The Prime Minister had refused Northcliffe's request to be included in the British Peace Delegation in 1918, and Northcliffe had dedicated himself to vengeance.

But it was Liberalism itself that had become a casualty of war, Churchill realized, and that was a calamity. The war and the long, unfruitful negotiations in the aftermath had put Lloyd George and Churchill himself off course. While their stature had increased as statesmen, they had diminished as domestic politicians. While they had been preoccupied with genuine attempts to create a possibility of peace, listening sympathetically to the appeals of Botha and Smuts for moderation, Tory mediocrity in Britain, always myopically suspicious of talent, and terrified of genius, had closed its ranks and was reaching for the helm.

It was a dismal prospect, at home and abroad, for Lloyd George was probably the only man who might have piloted Britain through the dangerous years. But he had made grave mistakes in foreign policy. Enamoured of Venizelos, he had backed Greece against the 'run of the play', and would have done much better to trust the instincts and emotions of Churchill and his liking for Turkey. The problems looming and insistent on every hand defied solutions acceptable to all the parties concerned. It had been urgently necessary, for example, to establish stable governments in the Middle East and to settle the affairs of Ireland. Churchill had played a leading part in these difficult transactions, and could look back with some pleasure and pride on his performance.

Evidently the electors had their minds on other things. Furious crowds taunted him savagely and loaded him with the entire responsibility for the tragic failure of the Dardanelles. He was unpopular on all sides. His departure from the Air Ministry had drawn a severe comment from *The Times*:

'He leaves the body of British flying well nigh at that last gasp when a military funeral would be all that would be left for it.'

His record at the War Office had been equally dismal, for he had turned the clock back to 1914 to the chagrin and dismay of the young officers, especially of the Royal Tank Corps, who had believed he would be a potent ally. Without a wicked enemy clearly in his sights, Churchill had seemed to lapse into dreary mediocrity, or at best an old-fashioned orthodoxy.

It became increasingly clear that he had not given satisfaction in many quarters at home. At Walthamstow some fanatic threw a brick through the window of his motor car, while foot and mounted police held back angry crowds, many men shaking their fists. 'They were more like Russian wolves than British workmen —howling, foaming and spitting, and generally behaving in a way absolutely foreign to the British working classes,' he told the *Evening News*. Churchill had found his enemy. His violent hatred of Russia and its new rulers hardened swiftly into a hatred of British socialism. He refused to compromise or to listen to reason.

J. C. Squire, writing to thank Marsh for introducing him to Churchill in 1918, had been fascinated but perceptive:

'He has enormous qualities, especially the primary quality of courage; one defect—the defect of romanticism—or rather, since romanticism may be good, of *sentimentalism*. You don't sum up Russia by calling Lenin a traitor, or by calling munition workers well-fed malcontents.'

But Churchill did, and began to rant with increasing violence. Communism and socialism had struck at the very roots of aristocratic privilege, and the right of his class to rule. His whole dream of knight errantry, crusades and the good against the wicked, glory and romanticism was threatened. He saw the growing strength of labour as a threat to the Constitution, promising the overthrow of established order. He was progressively overcome by the extreme exuberance of his verbosity as he allowed his mind to paint vivid pictures of the imagined British Terror. His sense of humour dried up completely when friends joked of the 'revolution', and imagined him qualifying for a promiment 'lamppost'. He didn't think it was at all funny.

Forced to convalesce through the winter of 1922-23 in the South of France, Churchill had not yet come to grips with his political future, or with his new enemy. It was impossible for him to brood for long. He was mercurial in his moods; 'but with Winston,' a friend wrote to me, 'these "moods" were those of a very great actor playing different stage rôles and could not be called "moods". He was no Charles Hawtrey, superb in a single sort of character only; but he was like Charles Hawtrey in that you knew that each character was (Hawtrey) Winston unmistakably. Yet he was not completely versatile. There were rôles and characters he was quite unable to portray. He could never be a clown or portray a madman, like Irving in *The Bells*. He had no interest in comedy, seeking always grandeur and magnificence....'

Painting had opened up a new visual world for him, giving him a new dimension for his great powers of observation. He loved bold and brilliant colour, and in painting found his best relaxation, as bold with his paints as with his words. But, above all, he loved words. For some years he had been planning a personal historical panorama of the war, and had embarked upon the writing of the first two volumes. He dictated with enormous zest, savouring the words and the wonderful flexibility of the English language in his mouth, delighting in its sounds, and all its marvellous life. But it was a long time since he had been a writer, thinking with pen or pencil in hand, and his work suffered. He had become a talker. Edward Marsh, of course, at once detected the orator when he read the drafts and put in the commas, not without many gentle arguments. There was in his work something of the quality of a play, the pauses for applause clearly discernible. But the real fault was that he was no longer 'thinking writing', but wilfully on the lower level of 'thinking-talking'. The words, the flow, were magnificent, but the 'think' had fallen below the high standard of *The River War*, and his life of his father. Nevertheless it was tremendous stuff.

Churchill and Marsh had worked together on the first volume in the summer of 1921 at Biarritz when Churchill had been Colonial Secretary, and in one of his phases of high romanticism. He could look back on that period with pure pleasure and pride, and something more than either of these words convey. He had been inspired by T. E. Lawrence, and had come as near as he would ever come to a genuine love and admiration for a fellow man. For Lawrence in Paris in the full panoply of his Arab robes, his grave face tranquil and strong under the headdress, had seemed to Churchill to be the living proof of his dreams. There were such men, and here at last was such a man alive!

After that meeting Churchill had wooed Lawrence, striving to tempt him away from the modest life he looked for. 'The greatest employments are open to you!' And, he reflected with boyish pride, 'Governorships and great commands were then at my disposal.'

Lawrence made him glow. 'What! Wilt thou bridle the wild ass of the desert?' his friends exclaimed in unbelief. And Churchill had not been wholly unsuccessful. Together they had set Feisal on the throne of Iraq, and had striven to lay a foundation upon which the deep antagonisms of Jew and Arab in Palestine might be adjusted. They had established the Emir Abdulla in power in Trans-Jordania, and had sited the Royal Air Force in a sound and strong position in an arm of the Euphrates, thus releasing a body of troops from service. And Churchill drank in Lawrence's dream of the Middle East, and with it one of those 'twopence coloured' pictures of the Arab that became fixed and indestructible in his mind, and upon which he would dilate to his startled friends and advisers as romantically as Ethel M. Dell. Thus the Arab was always for Churchill a courageous, courteous, urbane individual, superbly masculine, terrible in his wrath, living an ascetic life in company with Allah, a camel, a spear and rifle, an Arab mare and a Saluki dog, jealous of his honour above all, like a medieval knight of chivalry.

It had been a brief but fruitful partnership, but Lawrence would not be persuaded to go on. His dreams were not of power, and only some new catastrophe might have launched him again in the mainstream of affairs. I believe that in no words Churchill has written, save only in *Savrola*, did he so deeply and truly reveal the brave, dreaming boy in himself, longing to be a hero, at times a Lancelot, more often, perhaps, a D'Artagnan—or a Lawrence. Of the meeting in Paris Churchill wrote:

'From amid the flowing draperies his noble features, his perfectly chiselled lips and flashing eyes loaded with fire and comprehension shone forth. He looked what he was, one of Nature's greatest princes.'

Reluctantly Churchill had to accept Lawrence's statement that all personal ambition had died in him before he had entered Damascus in triumph.

'He was indeed a dweller upon the mountain tops where the air is cold, crisp and rarefied, and where the view on clear days commands all the kingdoms of the world and the glory of them.'

In his friendship with Lawrence, in expressing his admiration to the point of reverence, Churchill had his own vision 'on the road to Damascus', and came alive more vividly himself. He was confirmed in his imagery and faith by this visitation. His world was true. But he continued to the end to worry at the proposition that Lawrence would really fade away, that he *wanted* to fade away and to find himself in anonymity and obscurity.

'While Lawrence lived one always felt—I certainly felt it strongly —that some overpowering need would draw him from the modest path he chose to tread and set him once again in full action at the centre of memorable events.'

But there are no facts about a man. We can only speculate, and strive with such intuition and such springs of sympathy as we may possess to discover and to understand. Perhaps something should always remain hidden at the core of an individual, some inner core of truth that should never be invaded, nor even probed. No one can say us nay, that this is right or wrong. But I believe that his meeting with Lawrence provides a key to Churchill's life and nature, and to his crowning achievement in the summer of 1940. Lawrence fused Churchill's faith in his inner vision of what life could be and should be. It was not simply romance. It was true. Men could be larger than life size. Had Lawrence lived, Churchill might—it is just possible—have found the one man with whom he would work, with whom he would share a dream, and more than a dream, to whom he would have been loyal as nearly as he could come to equality. Churchill could be loyal to a man set in authority over him, as he was loyal to Lloyd George and Neville Chamberlain. But he would not tolerate a rival, and no man would share his throne.

Liddell Hart believes that Churchill would have made Lawrence his 'super-Lindemann'. There was no one else. There never would be until, in the end, like Richard on Bosworth Field, he would cry away his kingdom for a horse. But there was no kingdom, and no horse.

Looking back on the years as he convalesced at Cannes, nearing his fiftieth year, and living again the war and its aftermath, meeting Lawrence, Sassoon, Graves, meeting and mourning Rupert Brooke, Churchill walked in Elysian fields. These men had added to him, and expanded his growth. For he too was an artist in paint and words, and in life itself, for his life must be above all his story, his monument, a creation out of time.

But he was troubled when he thought of his lost seat in Parliament. For more than twenty years it had been his stage, and had become his temple. It could not throw him out. He repaired his strength and prepared to do battle. The death of his great grandmother, Lady Londonderry, had brought him financial security. The royalties from his *The World Crisis* would bring him new fame and fortune. But politics was his life. The prospect looked bleak, but he would prevail. He would be St George for England, and sally forth against the Socialist Dragon, breathing enough fire for the two of them.

## II

In the early summer of 1923 the resignation of Bonar Law, followed soon afterwards by his death, presented Churchill with his first chance, and he fought West Leicester as a Liberal against Pethick Lawrence, the Socialist. It still seemed that a miracle might fuse the broken Liberals, and provide him with the kind of political platform best suited to his talents in a time of peace. He had mistaken his father's natural rebellious spirit and cast of mind, as well as his own, for Liberalism whereas in truth both were born independents who could only flourish in attacking rôles, and were hamstrung by party discipline. He had never thought out his liberal attitudes, and had been attracted by the personality of Lloyd George.

Churchill's assault upon the electors of West Leicester was not only in vain, it was ludicrous and barren. He had nothing constructive to offer when not only England, but all Europe, was crying in growing agony and dismay, which might turn to despair, for men with the imagination, skill and courage to rethink the economic and social structures of their countries in new terms, and with the faith to rebuild. It was a challenge that politicians everywhere would ignore at their peril. Doubtless, when all the rubble of war was cleared away, there would be much (or little) of good to preserve out of the past on which to lay sound foundations. To attempt to rebuild upon the rubble must prove disastrous. Lloyd George was busy working out proposals for a 'New Deal' which might breathe new life into Liberalism and the community. The Socialists had a plan.

Churchill had nothing except violence. Any kind of 'New Deal' was anathema. His savage attacks against Socialists and Socialism sounded absurd in face of an opponent of the quality of Pethick Lawrence, and aroused the people to anger against himself. The pretensions of the working class touched him on the raw, and evoked irrational responses swiftly becoming obsessional.

Perhaps Churchill did not see clearly that his political home, if he had one, must be with the Tories, but he shared with them their belief in their right to rule, and their resolve, at whatever cost, to do so. The steady rise of the Labour Party as a political force made this truth doubly true. By making a fierce and sustained attack against Labour at every opportunity he might find his way back to the Tory fold. Perhaps it was the only way back for him, and however tortuous the road he must perform the necessary political contortions. There were many who shared his hatreds while lacking his courage and his brilliant demagogic gifts, or deprecating his honest approach. His friend, F. E. Smith, Lord Birkenhead, in whose conversation and company he found his greatest pleasure at the time, but of whose caustic tongue he was also afraid, carefully prepared a more acceptable Churchill image. He was, wrote Birkenhead, 'a restive young thoroughbred' whose loyalty to the 'stately continuity of English life' was part of him. His violence was also a part of him, and was misunderstood.

Early in 1924 a by election in the Abbey division of Westminster gave Churchill his second chance. Balfour, Birkenhead, Austen Chamberlain, the *Daily Mail*, and a circus of 'Bright Young' and 'Gaudy Old' things, supported him against the official Tory candidate, Captain Nicholson, a nephew of the deceased Member. Throughout February and early March controversy raged in the Press. The local Conservative Association stuck to their candidate, and Baldwin, the new leader of the Party, withheld his message of support for Nicholson for so long that Amery in desperation stepped into the breach at the last moment.

Churchill labelled himself an Independent Anti-socialist and plunged into action to attack Nicholson's candidature with a piece of brazen effrontery and political humbug it would be difficult to equal. He protested himself in no way hostile to the Tory Party, and its leaders, and that he saw clearly that it must be the obvious spearhead of the attack against Socialism. He was their obvious champion. He objected to Nicholson, however, on the grounds that his family had held the seat, and that a constituency should not be passed on from 'father to son, or uncle to nephew', as in this case, 'as if it were a piece of furniture!' His true views were the complete opposite, and he expressed them clearly some years later in supporting Lord Hartington, son of the Duke of Devonshire, for a safe family seat.

The Abbey election was a nine days' wonder, a wild circus of talent supporting Churchill in his violent and exciting demagogy. Rivers of blood would surely flow in Britain if such men as Ramsay Macdonald, Philip Snowden, Arthur Henderson and J. H. Thomas held power. They would never restrain their followers. But Churchill's policy, apart from the maintenance of rule by the privileged and 'the stately continuity of English life' did not emerge. Serious Tories observed that he had supported Free Trade all his life, and had crossed the 'floor' twenty years earlier on that issue. The Tory policy was Protection, and the 'Amerys' of the Party were acutely aware of the tremendous social and economic issues demanding clear thinking, rational attitudes and urgent attention at home, while great challenges, not least in the Dominions and Colonies, loomed abroad. Like Bonar Law they regarded Churchill as, at best, a doubtful ally, recognizing that he was incapable of the many changes of attitude that would prove vital to Tory survival.

By a narrow margin the Abbey division elected Captain Nicholson, and Churchill had performed a 'knockabout' turn as near as he would ever come to a comic part. He had done more: he had performed the first difficult contortion on his way back. A few months later an electorate, a prey to desperate hopes and even more desperate fears, was stampeded by the 'timely' production of the infamous 'Zinoviev' letter by the Foreign Office to vote the Tories into power. Churchill was returned to Parliament as a 'Constitutionalist' for Epping with Tory support, and to find to his utter amazement that by a miraculous swing of the political trapeze he had lodged in the seat of the Chancellor of the Exchequer. He had expected very little or nothing, and when Baldwin offered him the job he thought at first that he meant the Duchy of Lancaster. He would have been well satisfied with that, as a new beginning. The appointment was the more remarkable in that Churchill supported Free Trade, and was a mere tyro in the world of economics or finance. Apart from hating Socialism he had not taken an interest in domestic affairs since his translation from the Home Office to the Admiralty in 1911. Churchill was amazed. I am not sure that he was, when he thought about it, happy. Perhaps it seemed to him too much like destiny, a destiny he had hoped to avoid. He had already outlived his father's years, and now he had his father's old job, and would wear his father's robes.

However these things may be, the chance had arisen out of Tory fears, and they had embraced him in an attempt to split the probable enemy forces. They feared the brilliance of Birkenhead as a potentially dangerous outsider, and disliked Austen Chamberlain's Francophilia. They were deeply suspicious of the efforts of such men as Briand and Brüning to discover a *modus vivendi* for Europe in which Britain must play a part. The only man in Britain of the stature to do so was David Lloyd George, the only man 'whose knees had not been knocking' in 1919, as Churchill had testified. Above all things the Tories feared the possibility of a comeback by Lloyd George, at that time adrift like a Leviathan on turbulent seas. A Churchill in the wilderness would be certain, they believed, to forge a new alliance with the man he had served and admired above all others; moreover, the one man who might even now grip the British imagination and persuade an anxious public that with him remedies might be found for their fearful ills.

Thus the Tories reversed the Bonar Law view, and preferred Churchill with them rather than against them, and wisely, having decided upon such a course, Baldwin went the whole hog. By this strange providence Churchill wore his father's robes.

### III

It must be doubtful whether Britain has ever had a more dreary Chancellor than Churchill. Neither the times nor the job were suited to his talents. Moreover he belonged to the past, the last man on earth to rethink the economic present. He adopted not only his father's robes but his father's policies, lapsing into a dreary, unimaginative Victorian orthodoxy, not to be disguised by the sparkling wit and presentation of his pedestrian-and crippling budgets. In their happiest moments, which were rare, some called him the merriest tax collector since Robin Hood, but the times were not for merriment. He cut the Service estimates to the bone, hamstrung the Air Force, and crippled the Navy.

Yet when the Americans at the peace conference had sought to deprive the British Navy of its power, Churchill had stood proudly by as Lloyd George, supported by Clemenceau, had called their bluff. The American Colonel House 'was rapidly losing his self-control', Hankey wrote, when Lloyd George told him that even if the United States made a separate peace we should go on fighting. 'We could not,' Lloyd George continued, 'give up the power which had enabled the American troops to be brought to Europe. That was a thing we were prepared to fight through. Britain was not really a military nation. Her main defence was her Fleet. To give up the right to use her Fleet was a thing to which no one in England would consent.'[1]

A few years later Churchill was succeeding where the United States had failed. At the same time as Chancellor he embraced the dangerous slogan of no war for ten years, and went on repeating it almost up to the last moment when it had become almost exactly true. No one seemed to realize, except perhaps old Clemenceau, and outcasts like Lenin and his lieutenants abroad, Litvinov and Maisky, that peace, like war, was indivisible.

While Baldwin and Montagu Norman embarked for the United States in an attempt to have the interest rate reduced on the British debt of $1,000,000,000, Churchill returned to the Gold Standard as a matter of pride to look the dollar in the eye, as if such a miracle could come about by the mere manipulation of words, or of figures. Lloyd George, bitterly attacking this early return to the Gold Standard, had evolved a 'New Deal' very much on the lines Franklin Roosevelt would follow a decade later in the United States. Churchill was as hostile to this kind of liberalism as any 'Republican', and far from the progressive wing of his own party. Confronted with his ancient Elizabethan attitudes to India, the emerging Commonwealth and Colonies, which he expressed in his father's words, progressive Tories tore their hair, and by 1927 Amery was writing in desperation to the Prime Minister:[2]

'I feel myself daily more and more out of touch with a Cabinet which under the influence of day-by-day work, and above all of Winston, is becoming steadily little England, and even anti-Imperial, as well as hopelessly negative on fiscal policy. Possibly

[1] Lord Hankey, *The Supreme Command, 1914-18*, Vol. II.
[2] L. S. Amery, *My Political Life*, Vol. II.

the best thing would be that we should be beaten. I confess I cannot at this moment see any other way of getting that "old man of the sea", Winston, off our shoulders.'

By that time Baldwin was beginning to wonder whether he had chosen the lesser of two evils, and to find Churchill's rabid views on India particularly indigestible. Certainly he had prevented an alliance between Churchill and Lloyd George—which might have spelled the death of both of them, as easily as their re-birth—and in the meantime the Labour Party had grown to offer the people an alternative government.

Churchill had clearly become the wrong kind of champion to set against that challenge, for he had done much to alienate the great reservoir of goodwill in the working classes, themselves basically Tory, and without which the Tory Party could not hope to survive.

Churchill in his nature, and in the nature of his dreams, was incapable of seeing or meeting the grim challenge of the 1920s. It was a time for the boldest methods if Britain's economy was to be made to work, and if the people were to achieve some measure of social and economic justice. Above all, new methods were demanded. There was no way back; the present was a limbo; the way forward was obscure. Miserably the country drifted into near revolt, arising out of the dreadful inertia of the executive. Unemployment grew steadily, and the bitterness of the hungry, ill-clad and workless hundreds of thousands, condemned to futility and a dole, destitute of dignity, came near to utter despair.

As a politician, in what might well prove to be the last phase of his active political life, Churchill had plumbed the depths of unimaginative mediocrity, from which he might only emerge to be charitably forgotten in quiet retirement. It would have made a dismal last chapter to an uneven story. It was the story Churchill could not write, could not live, and could not play. Yet it would have been a bold man who would have ventured to prophesy any very different future for him.

In his book, *The Economic Consequences of Mr Churchill*, J. M. Keynes contributed a sorry epilogue, revealing the Chancellor's responsibility for the dire condition of the coal industry. Coal had provided the Chancellor with his most vivid and most dubious episode. On May 4, 1926, an accumulation of strikes and protests from the four quarters of the country, from stricken coal miners, shipyard and railway workers in particular, culminated in the General Strike. To Churchill this seemed the opportunity for which he had watched and waited. He could see it only in black and white, a form of war. At once he proclaimed himself 'For King and Country' as though confronted with revolutionaries instead of hungry and desperate people asking for work and wages. He did not even suggest 'cake'. At the same time he occupied the editorial chair of the *Morning Post*, from which to direct operations and publish a Government news sheet, *The British Gazette*.

This was the kind of situation in which Churchill revelled, and in which he could display his talents even to appal and alarm his friends. Confronting him was the honest and towering figure of Ernest Bevin, the head of 'The Dragon'. But it was not 'King and Country' against revolution. It was not a dragon. It was the heart cry of the core of a nation, of men promised 'a land fit for heroes to live in' ready to settle for wages, food and shelter on a bare existence level.

Churchill has been blamed by many, not his enemies, that there was a strike at all. Virginia Cowles, summing up the evidence with admirable impartiality, acquits him of the charge of deliberately precipitating the crisis following the refusal of the *Daily Mail* printers to set up a leader 'For King and Country'. There is always a spark for war, and often it is almost irrelevant. Churchill's responsibility lay in his nature, and in his ignorance of the times he lived in. By denying the leadership of the 'Miners' Council', by refusing from the beginning to believe that the socialist leaders could lead, he deprived them of the chance to prove that they could.

'If Lloyd George had been in Churchill's shoes it is probable that the whole disaster would have been averted,' wrote Miss Cowles.[1] Lloyd George had defended the Union leaders in the House in a speech of moderation and humanity. 'I know a great many of the people responsible. They are as little revolutionaries as any men in this House,' he said. And it was true. Amery described it as 'the mildest mannered revolution that ever tried to coerce a constitutional government'. On May 12th it petered out, to leave behind the dregs of a bitterness that lives still. The Unions were almost destitute of funds. It cost the miners £60,000,000 in wages, and for months added half a million unem-

[1] Virginia Cowles, *Winston Churchill, the Era and the Man*.

ployed to a huge 'standing army' of workless. A first estimate of the cost to the country put it at £160,000,000. In the final analysis it topped £800,000,000. Half such a sum, plus a gleam of imagination, could have solved the whole problem of the mines.

It is the dreary record of a dreay time with as dreary a Government as Britain ever suffered, and all its members earned badges of shame as the country wallowed in disillusion to the financial collapse of 1929-30 which plunged the whole Western world into panic. In the aftermath of that disaster it soon became clear that a new and worse world was in the making.

## IV

Through those years it seems that the Mr Churchill in public life was little more than a 'robot' pilot, a stand-in while the real Mr Churchill performed on a stage more to his liking. The first volume of his great war saga, *The World Crisis*, had been acclaimed in April 1923, to be followed by a second volume in the autumn. Henceforth the royalties were a golden stream. By 1929 he had completed and published *The Aftermath*. With these books he had carved a new niche for himself. No one had done anything comparable. It was a unique personal record of war, an autobiography and a war report disguised, as Balfour said, as 'a history of the universe', but not history. It was certainly a *tour de force* of wonderful dimensions, and a tremendous success.

At the same time he had purchased his estate at Chartwell in Kent, and was developing and expanding the house and grounds with exciting unorthodoxy. Marsh's stepmother had once purchased her vegetables from Chartwell garden, and Marsh, who had joined Churchill as his right hand upon his appointment as Chancellor, convalesced at Chartwell in 1927, wishing 'there were a God I could thank for those who love me'.

The nature of Marsh's complaint must have been peculiarly haunting to Churchill, reminding him constantly of the last tragic years of his father's illness. But he had not hesitated for a moment to carry off the stricken Marsh to the shelter, peace and care of his home, and—if not to nurse him—to ensure that he was nursed back to health under a roof where he would feel assured of affection, and where he was 'one of the family'. It had been a long and fruitful association, relaxed and happy in all its aspects, and since 1910 almost a *ménage à trois*. Since 1924 Marsh's task for Churchill had been almost wholly personal and literary, and they had become virtually collaborators. Thus Marsh's official retirement a few years in the future would be unlikely to affect their association.

In 1927 Marsh had been visiting a niece in Corsica and, attempting to take a short cut through thick hillside scrub when out walking, had lost direction and finally, overcome by exhaustion, had collapsed at the foot of a cliff in a pool of brackish water. He lay for nineteen hours before search parties found him. He could barely speak, and his whole body was lacerated by thorns. General paralysis of the insane was suspected, and finally his breakdown was complete. Soon after he had been moved to London, Mrs Churchill fetched him to Chartwell by car, and there he regained his strength.

Marsh's condition was acutely depressing, not only for the patient but for those who nursed and cheered him. It did not occur to Churchill to shirk his duty, nor did he flinch to live with a grisly reminder of the past. He was, moreover, in a state of change natural to men in their fifties, and of peculiar portents in his own case. He had remarked some years earlier to Harold Nicholson that 'the Churchills damp down at forty', and he had lived life broadly on that assumption. If he had not precisely expected to die 'young', he had equally not expected a long life. All the evidence seemed to be against such a possibility, and when he wore his father's robes as Chancellor it had seemed to confirm an end pattern. He had failed to reach the top, and was out of sorts with his time. He believed that the kind of power at which he had aimed, and for which he had believed himself destined, must be now a chimera. The idea was growing in his mind to leave politics, and to devote himself to the many literary tasks challenging his imagination, and to make money.

As for Marsh, weak, barely able to speak or hold a pen, he was surely reaching an end, if not of life, at least of effective contribution, literary or political. Thus I believe that it demanded fortitude and compassion from Churchill to succour Marsh under his roof at such a time. By doing so he dispelled his father's ghost, and crossed a rubicon. He was, for a year or two, between two lives, the first not yet quite done, the second not begun. It was certain that he could not simply continue in the old pattern. He would need to re-think the future and, with all the varied experience of the past, plan his course to power. And Marsh steadily regained his health and strength, ready for the new literary collaborations working in Churchill's head.

It is through Edward Marsh that an outsider may catch an occasional glimpse of Mrs Churchill as a gay and affectionate woman, and not merely as a paragon of all the virtues. Marsh observes her and adores her, 'radiant and beautiful' at Churchill's side as the bells ring out for victory on Armistice Day 1918. When Churchill's car overturned in the war, 'Clemmie' ended up gracefully on Marsh's lap, and with not a hair out of place. Churchill, of course, is always up with the driver on all occasions, and these two, constant companions, witty, gay, unfailingly agreeable, in the back. As a tower of strength at her husband's side, or hovering in the background, Mrs Churchill is always emerging, but rarely to life. Most of those who have had the privilege of knowing her, however well, say simply 'Clemmie is wonderful'.

Churchill's private life has remained very properly a thing apart, nor should one wish to probe, even if it were not both improper and distasteful to do so, for in itself the absence of a revealed private life is in its own fashion revealing. It is certain that his private background enhanced his public strength.

Apart from Lady Churchill's immense resources of uncommon sense, her remarkable equability, her flawless devotion, a little more is discernible. Her sympathy and delight in the many facets of her husband's nature was profound. She understood him. Her hand was ever on the helm, but never obtrusive. She did not steer, but many times she held the craft steady when it threatened to cavort dangerously.

I think that the marital relationship of the Churchills was as near to 'Darby and Joan' as it is likely the male and female may achieve. It was entirely rewarding—for both of them. In its fashion their married life was a genuine idyll, and it was not for nothing that Churchill wrote: 'I married in 1910 and lived happy ever after.' It was the simple truth.

It would be absurd to look for passion, for the dark tumults in the blood, the dreadful anguish attendant upon the love of a Tristan and Isolde, of Romeo and Juliet. Such loves are of a different order, destined for tragedy.

The easy relationship of the Churchills was manifest in their use and choice of 'pet names'; that she was 'Dear Cat' and he

'Dear Pig'. In their mouths these words became endearments endowed with the deepest affection, a private code. Norman McGowan[1] tells of how, often, Lady Churchill returning home would cry out with a loud 'wow-wow' in the hall at Chartwell, and await her husband's answering bark.

Edward Marsh for many years was the intimate third party in this enviable partnership, the essential hero-worshipper and follower in an adventurous triumvirate that has echoes of schooldays.

'Sir Winston is all nature and one never comes to the end of him,' wrote John Raymond. Neither his wife, nor Marsh, ever came to the end of him. Few men were less inhibited in their private behaviour. He would indulge in long monologues in his bath, not in the least put out to be overheard by valet or anyone else. 'At first I used to think he was talking to me,' wrote Norman McGowan, but when he answered what he thought was his master's call, Churchill said:

'I wasn't talking to you, Norman. I was addressing the House of Commons.'

And so he would continue, twiddling the taps with his toes until his wife, or some new urgency, induced him to move on to the next phase.

I do not know at what stage of life Churchill developed his passion for fish and birds. 'He was crazy about fish,' McGowan noted. His study was lined with small tanks in which the brilliant creatures darted and lazed through the intricate choreography of their lives, revealing to the quiet observer extremes of behaviour, ferociously barbaric, exquisitely gentle. Out of doors, Churchill would visit his fishponds to lure the carp to take maggots from his hand.

Yet it is difficult to think of Churchill as a married man, and almost impossible to consider him as a family man. Twenty-four hours a day appear to be always at his disposal to live his own life. He can, and often does, devote his entire energy to the varied works in hand, political, literary, artistic, even bricklaying, and discussions far into the nights, good eating and good drinking with his cronies, Birkenhead, Beaverbrook, Baruch prominent among them. The unforgiving minute is always filled, and no

[1] *My Years with Churchill.*

spectre of boredom is ever visible. As he awakens to a new day secretaries are at his bedside, newspapers and bulletins read, memos, essays, articles, books, ideas, dictated. Unobtrusively his physical needs are ministered. He is free. Life is for him.

There are children; but where? Do they ever intrude? Do they play with their parents? Are they within or without all this activity? Are they loved? And do they *know* that they are loved?

### V

The 1920s are a dark limbo of frustration in the aftermath of war, and by their end a turning point had come, not only in the life of Churchill but in the world. There had not been peace, and now only the blind and the ignorant could believe that there would not be war. The financial collapse had revealed the political and economic bankruptcy of the Western world, and while a dreadful inertia pervaded Britain the figures of Hitler and Mussolini loomed over Europe. When the General Election came in the early summer of 1929, and Lloyd George was striving boldly to inspire the country with the challenge of a 'New Deal' and a new outlook, it was Baldwin and his pipe that more closely reflected the mood of the British people. 'The heroic remedies,' proposed by Lloyd George, he told a gathering of City men at the Mansion House, 'were unnecessary.' Unemployment would be helped by the decline in the birth rate! There was no need, really, to do anything at all.

Amery had appealed to Baldwin time and again to face the facts:

'We are confronted by a problem of appalling difficulty which calls for an immense effort at the reconstruction of the whole base of industrial and financial system. It is the solving of that problem which can alone save this country and the Empire.'[1]

All appeals were ignored. Labour found itself in office without power, and the Liberals irrevocably split. Nothing was solved; nothing would be solved. Simply the way was paved for a series of 'caretaker' governments to live with the country through a period of lethargy until the inevitable war should once again stir men's hearts.

[1] *My Political Life*, Vol. II.

## THE APPRENTICESHIP TO POWER 249

It would have been a form of political suicide for a man like Churchill to associate himself with such governments, even if they would have had him. He held his parliamentary seat, and virtually contracted out, to wait and see. His England had become barely discernible beyond the corridors of his mind, still lit with vivid imagery and dreams. The steady moves towards building a Commonwealth of Nations, towards Dominion status for India, and the final emergence of independent colonies, struck at the roots of his mid-Victorian faith. Those who worked to such ends were traitors to the 'Empire', to the King-Emperor's most glorious majesty. India was 'the brightest jewel' or nothing. Irwin, Samuel, Amery and their kind were traitors, or at best deluded fools without vision—for vision in Churchillian terms went only backwards to forgotten splendours. His India was the India of Gungha Din, and never of Ghandi. He became increasingly violent and offensive in his utterances, and a speech to the West Essex Conservative Association revealed his cast of mind. In it he described Ghandi[1] as

'a seditious Middle Temple lawyer, now posing as a fakir of a type well known in the East, striding half naked up the steps of the Vice-Regal Palace, while he is still organizing and conducting a defiant campaign of civil disobedience, to parley on equal terms with the representative of the King-Emperor.'

His bankrupt attitude towards India, and almost everything else, offended his friends and finally divorced him from Baldwin, and set him squarely in the political wilderness. When his tenure of office as Chancellor had ended in 1929 there had been a kind of power vacuum in Churchill. His long official association with Marsh had also ended, but the literary association would continue. He had devoted himself more and more to his literary and private affairs, and the rewards of the material world had pulled his imagination steadily in the direction of the United States. He had expected to be 'damped down', possibly dead, and he was vitally alive, between two worlds, and perhaps two Churchills. Churchills died young, but Jeromes lived. He was at least half tycoon in his nature and half American in his blood. His friendship with Bernard Baruch had flourished, and whenever they met there was an ease between them neither had known, or knew,

[1] Viscount Templewood, *Nine Troubled Years*.

with any other man. They delighted to show each other the excitements of their own countries with pride and prejudice, and entertained each other like princes.

Through Baruch Churchill orientated towards his mother's country. Frequently Baruch was able to steer Churchill into profitable investments with an acumen that enabled him to ride the worst financial storms unscathed. It was clear, too, that the United States having ransacked Europe for the last of its nineteenth century treasure, leaving it threadbare, would inevitably inherit the Western future, whether she liked it or not. Loathing 'Imperialism' and 'Colonialism' she practised both with outstanding hypocrisy, and an evangelical zeal that would have nauseated a hard-bitten general of the Salvation Army. Her idea of freedom was the 'American way of life', and the sooner the Filipinos, or anyone else, learned to get up and walk and talk in the American image, the better it would be for all concerned. Above all the United States was still living in the nineteenth century.

In November 1929 Churchill was on his way across the Atlantic to seek his fortune. L. S. Amery was a fellow passenger. The differences between them, apparent in their schooldays at Harrow, had deepened, Amery, the scholar, Churchill, the reporter. They would never be close friends, but it was unlikely that they would ever be enemies. They had clashed daily in Cabinet, Amery fighting Churchill every yard of the way in vain. Amery believed in the future; Churchill believed in the past, and Churchill as Chancellor had 'held the purse strings'. It had been the more exasperating to Amery because in his writings Churchill had displayed a wisdom and awareness seldom evident in counsel. Perhaps he found it impossible to believe in 'peace', or genuinely to work for it.

The last pages of *The Aftermath* are both sombre and wise. He knew that mankind could 'unfailingly accomplish its own extermination. That is the point in human destinies to which all the glories and toils of men have at last led them. They would do well to pause and ponder upon their new responsibilities.'

But there was no time to 'pause and ponder'. The people of France and Britain, surging behind Clemenceau and Lloyd George, screaming for revenge, had swept their leaders on their vengeful course, helpless. 'Deep in the soul of France, and the mainspring of her policy and of almost her every action, lay the fear of German revenge. Sombre and intense in the heart of the powerful classes in Germany brooded the resolve that their national history should not be finally determined in accordance with the Treaty of Versailles; and in the pulses of her multiplying and abounding youth throbbed the hope that they might live to see, or die in advancing, a day when victory should once again light the standards of the Fatherland."[1]

Against these portents was 'Locarno', the Dawes plan, the half-hearted efforts to rebuild, to reintegrate Europe. There was no faith, no constant or concerted effort. Such parts as such a 'peace' offered were not those to stimulate the talents of a Churchill, and there was an appalling fascination in the prospect of a war that might mean the end of civilization. It was a vision in the back of Churchill's mind that would not be dispelled. Perhaps it was in too many minds, a sombre spectre in the wings, inhibiting performance, standing in the way of growth, in the building of peace. In effect the world waited.

Amery's diary notes of his shipboard encounters with Churchill in November 1929, reveal, I believe, the bankruptcy of Churchill as a peace-time politician.

'On essentials,' Amery wrote, 'he is still where he was twenty-five years ago.... He just repeats the old phrases of 1903 and no argument seems to make any difference to him. He can only think in phrases, and close argument is really lost on him; the only way to get home to him would be by equally striking counter-phrases.... He can only talk in terms of political manoeuvre. He had been all he ever wanted to be short of the highest post which he saw no prospect of, and anyhow politics were not what they had been.'

One night as Churchill began to undress for bed, putting on his night shirt and 'a woolly tummy band over it', Amery fired a last exasperated shot: 'Free Trade, a mid-Victorian statesmanship and the old-fashioned nightshirt, how appropriate a combination!'

But the shaft did not touch Churchill. He felt the sap rising in him, a man revitalized and free, untrammelled by the limitations of high office, almost a youth again but with a vast experience behind him, and high adventure ahead. The United States suited his mood and his temperament, but he was soon as contemptuous of Franklin Roosevelt's 'New Deal' as he was of Socialism at home, and wrote a paper to prove the 'futility' of

[1] *The World Crisis, The Aftermath.*

such measures. To give 'the lowly a feeling of equality', as Baruch expressed it, was to misunderstand the nature of man, and it was useless for Baruch to reason that the 'New Deal ... was a part of the world-wide demand for a more equal distribution of the good things of life. On the wisdom with which this demand was met depended the welfare of man.'[1]

Nevertheless the United States was exciting, and a world for financial swashbucklers to live in. It was more Churchill's world than twentieth-century England, and it might be true to say that at the end of the 1920s he began to see himself as a 'Yankee' and a 'Marlborough'. For Marlborough was very much in his thoughts, and he had had written the draft of the opening chapters for Marsh's comments. M. P. Ashley was already working on research at Blenheim, and his mind teemed with visions.

By the time Churchill returned to England his literary programme was itself prodigious, involving Marsh and others, whatever their official duties, in exhaustive research, careful reading of manuscripts and proofs, and detailed planning. The ideas burgeoning from Churchill's mind in profusion all must be followed up by someone, often for no reward beyond the satisfaction of serving such a man. He was irresistible. Keith Feiling advised and helped constantly on many aspects of Marlborough; Pakenham Walsh was a willing aid while Marsh, serving in his official capacity as secretary to J. H. Thomas, read proofs with meticulous care and made precis of a dozen stories Churchill might or might not build his books upon. These included *Monte Cristo, The Moonstone, She, Ben Hur, Thais, Uncle Tom's Cabin, A Tale of Two Cities*, and probably *Faust*, for luck.

Despite all these activities of which Churchill was the tireless hub and dynamo, a social life urbane, witty and well informed, and of great diversity flourished round him at Chartwell and his house in Sussex Square. He delighted in the company of elegant and well-dressed women, and was singularly at home in feminine company of which his wife was the centre. With them his affectionate nature found expression, but with men there was always a lack of depth in his relationships. As Boothby once said of him, and many others have confirmed, one must be either his servant, indifferent to him, or his enemy. 'The full truth, I believe,' Desmond Morton said, 'is that Winston's "friends" must be persons who were of use to him. The idea of having a friend who was of

[1] Margaret L. Coit, *Mr Baruch*.

no practical use to him, but being a friend because he liked him, had no place.'

Most of those attracted to his orbit knew this perfectly well, and were glad to be with him to share in his immense vitality, and for life to be quickened. Again Desmond Morton commented, 'he certainly gave all who knew him at least as much pleasure as they may have given him use or interest. He owes them no debt.' Few gave him more 'use or interest' than Desmond Morton from 1930 to the end.

Thus Churchill's wilderness was luxuriant and fruitful. He had definitely become a 'bad boy' in Baldwin's eyes, and it suited him very well. Arthur Ponsonby was among those who feared his 'lust for war', and believed that 'politically he is a great danger, largely because of his love of crises and faulty judgment'. He had not forgotten Churchil's boast some years earlier, 'I like things to happen, and if they don't I like to make them happen.'

In 1930 and the years that followed no man needed to make things happen; they were happening thick and fast, and by the middle of the decade it seemed beyond the wit of any man to halt the steady march to war. Ponsonby's fears were the hopes of many others. 'He's a good fighter, and will do better out than in, and will come back in a stronger position than before,' T. E. Lawrence wrote.[1] 'I want him to be P.M.' Marsh hoped so too, but thought the hope forlorn. He was nearing the end of his service, and had moved out of the main stream of his master's life.

Churchill watched and waited, the centre of his own stage, content to utter his sombre and potent warnings and asides to confound the figures fumbling their lines. His hour would strike. He had discovered his destiny, and was not alone. From 1930 onwards he prepared himself diligently for his task.

---

[1] In a letter to Marsh: See *Edward Marsh*, p. 565.

# PART FOUR

# THE WARRIOR

## CHAPTER XV

❧❈❀❧

AGAINST the backcloth of the first half of the twentieth century men appear as a species of furious dwarfs bent upon self extermination and the destruction of their civilization. The great are not great enough; the small lack grace, humility and integrity. Yet slowly, it had seemed that the curse of Babel was being overcome, and at the end of the nineteenth century the struggles of Europe had become clearly domestic. War had been the solvent of a family learning painfully to live together. The ambitions of Louis XIV had united a great variety of European peoples under the genius of Marlborough, and the Napoleonic wars had been unable to undo the work. In 1870 the rise of Germany had been curbed by Bismarck short of disaster, but the seeds of hate and fear had been sown, and the dragon's teeth sprouted.

Nevertheless war in the twentieth century could have, and should have, meant a resolution—perhaps a final resolution—of ancient problems, leading to a wider understanding and integration of peoples, the inheritors of a common culture, of interwoven racial streams, of language patterns in common, proclaiming one family. All European wars had become civil wars.

But in 1914 and again in 1940 the nature of European war was not understood. The pride of nations remained excessive, threatening a relapse into barbarism, a new dark age of unreason from which man armed with his new means of destruction would be unlikely to emerge. Left to settle its own disputes Europe could have become whole. The time had been used up, and the lessons unlearned.

Much of all this Churchill saw clearly. He blamed the people. 'The peoples, transported by their sufferings and by the mass teachings with which they had been inspired, stood around in scores of millions to demand that retribution should be exacted to the full. Woe betide the leaders now perched on their dizzy pinnacles of triumph if they cast away at the conference table what the soldiers had won on a hundred blood-soaked battlefields."[1]

Woe, indeed! The leaders foreswore their leadership in the crucial hour. But neither the blame nor the woe may be evaded. Passions had been aroused in the peoples by their leaders, commanding all the means of propaganda. Thus they had created Frankensteins.

Churchill saw the portents. In 1928, in the last volume of his *The World Crisis, The Aftermath*, he wrote:

'It was not until the dawn of the twentieth century of the Christian era that war began to enter into its kingdom as the potential destroyer of the human race.... All the noblest virtues of individuals were gathered to strengthen the destructive capacity of the mass.'

How tragic, for if this be the rôle of the noblest virtues, what then of the most ignoble?

Yet up to 1917 there had been a chance, and chances, doubtless growing more perilous with the years, were to present themselves, never to be taken. In 1917 hate between the opposing troops, if not between the leaders, had begun to evaporate. A situation approximating stalemate had arisen. Left to settle its own domestic dispute Europe would have been forced to come to terms with its members, without victors or vanquished. The moves towards peace growing through 1916 must have succeeded. A limit would have been set to German ambitions, and her vital place secured in the European family. French honour had been sustained, and her integrity assured.

But the domestic quarrel had alarmed others far beyond Europe, and British and French, longing for victory overwhelming and complete, had sought to lure outside aid rather than to abjure it. Thus a people who had properly turned their backs upon Europe, and had been gravely warned by their great President Washington never to look back, rushed into Europe for the kill, grabbed the loot, and rushed out again, leaving the contestants to stew in their own bitter juices. No decision had been reached.

Of the European family nearly nine million men had been

[1] *The Gathering Storm.*

killed, and more than twenty million maimed. Throughout all Europe men and women who had survived the holocaust found themselves homeless, starving, denied the dignity of labour. It was a mere foretaste of things to come. In Britain the toll of unemployed rose to the huge figure of three million, matching the numbers of the British casualties of war. In Germany it was far worse. Even in the United States of America the ranks of the workless were swollen, and the river would become a torrent.

It was believed that blood and hate could be paid for in cash, and national debts had become astronomical. Europe's only chance would have been to wipe the slate clean, especially of guilt, and to have seen herself as a continental entity. It was not even a dream. France, above all, could not entertain such a feeling. She had been invaded five times in a century, her country laid waste and drenched in blood. Her fears of a resurgent Germany were real and terrible, and they grew.

Meanwhile the absurd payments demanded from Germany as reparations in the first years destroyed her currency and made it difficult to begin to rebuild her industry. In the following years more money was poured back into the country than had been taken out, but the insane work had been done. French fears impelled her into the Rhineland, and the occupation of the Ruhr, but as Churchill points out:

'Up till the year 1934 the power of the conquerors remained unchallenged in Europe, and indeed throughout the world.'

Nevertheless British power had been gravely curtailed, and her position in the Far East undermined by American insistence that she should break off her alliance with Japan. It was an alliance based upon strategic realities. It had worked well. When it was crudely broken a potent move had been made on the road to war, and the loss of the British Empire in the Far East. Britain had made an enemy in an arena where she would urgently need a friend.

By 1930 the pause in the struggle had passed the halfway stage, and it had become clear that the defeated were gathering new strength. The last feeble efforts of the most far-sighted statesmen to solve the European problem had petered out. But there had been decisive changes. Soviet Russia, the only nation whose strategic interests were easily reconciled with those of France and

Britain, had been declared a pariah and an outcast. Thirteen times in little more than a hundred years she had been invaded from the west, until at last her rotten house had fallen apart. She was striving to rebuild in a new pattern inimical to capitalist society. It was the unforgivable sin. Her brilliant Foreign Minister, Litvinov, and her Ambassador, Maisky, failed to establish the alliances which alone might have given security to France and Central Europe.

But it was not only loathing and fear of Russia that deterred Western statesmen from making a close and clear alliance, but a refusal to admit the substance of the shadow of war. They wanted to speak in whispers.

Thus France and Britain strove to hide, to set up a defensive wall which they imagined to be impregnable, and to provide a cover shield for an offensive. But offensively and defensively their military leaders lived in the past.

Meanwhile unemployment was by far the greatest and most urgent of the domestic problems facing politicians, and they failed to solve it. But in Italy and Germany dictators had arisen to flout the conventions of Western capitalism and monetary policy, to put all men to work, and with appalling ruthlessness and barbarity to rouse national spirit and pride to a dangerous intensity. The portents were obvious and ominous.

Britain, it seemed, had learned nothing from her tragic experiences, except to fear. She preferred illusion to reality. She had lost the place, and unable to follow the text, floundered, terrified of war and peace, unable to cope with either, an ostrich withdrawn behind her ditch, and suspended from numerous hooks which had ceased to exist. Politically, morally, socially, economically, her condition was deplorable.

The Tories had successfully isolated the most brilliant men in Britain by the end of the 1920s. Lloyd George, producing plans to defeat unemployment and establish a 'New Deal', was irreparably in the political wilderness, as also was Asquith. Both commanded splinter groups of Liberals which would fail to cohere, and would fail therefore to act as a balance of political power. Baldwin and Neville Chamberlain, ill-matched and ill-starred 'ugly sisters', the one benign, lethargic, shrewd; the other arrogant, a political accountant, bigoted and lacking in humility, contrived with ease to hamstring a Labour Government under Ramsay Macdonald, and to manipulate the first Labour Prime

Minister like a puppet. By way of an uneasy coalition with themselves in the ascendant they finally gained the political saddle. Steadily England sank beneath their weight to the bottom of a stagnant pond, like a body with a millstone round its neck.

There were, of course, individuals of vision, integrity and energy in all parties, and these, desperately aware of the new and sinister powers risen Phoenix-like in Central and Southern Europe, cast about to discover a focal point from which England might rally before it was too late. The League of Nations failed miserably in the face of determined threats and contemptuous deeds. Europe had become a continent wherein the gangster flourished, and in Germany and Italy the march of civilization was halted.

No man knows, nor will ever know, how greatly Europe had been impoverished by its gigantic losses in flesh and blood. Among the multitudes of the dead there must have been those who, had they lived, would have demanded and helped to fashion a new Europe. In every warring country the finest men had died, and a vast swathe had been cut out of the age-group of men who would have been between twenty and thirty years old at the war's end. Thus a vacuum lay between the middle-aged and the young. It was a loss beyond compute. It should have mantled the survivors in humility and resolution, and given courage to the middle-aged and ageing. It did nothing of the sort.

For such a climate Churchill was made. He stood alone, himself a kind of survivor, a throw-back to a glorious and imperial past, a kind of 'Chieftain', and because many men of all kinds were dismayed by all that they saw and knew, and much more that they suspected, they found themselves drawn to him. He was on the side-lines of the political scene. He was not involved with these dismal men who were not even bothering to steer the national ship, and who tended to deny the existence of the terrifying rocks ahead.

## II

The ten years from 1929 to 1939 are the years of assessment in Churchill's life, of maturing, and of preparation for his tryst with destiny. He thought and planned with a conscious deliberation he had seldom, if ever, shown before. In 1930 he was fifty-six years old. He had lived dangerously, an adventurer, an opportunist ready to grasp every hand and foot hold on the way. But the way had not led to the pinnacle of power he looked for; nor, if one sees him clearly, could it have done so, for there was nothing in him of the conventional traveller.

For a year or two, released from high office, he cast about, travelling, lecturing, endlessly discussing, and at last considering the nature of the present and the future. For suddenly there was a future. He was not tying up the abundant loose ends of a full life. He was at a new beginning. He had lived one life, and now perhaps twenty years of high endeavour lay ahead, a twenty years in which he might not only reap the harvest of his past, but build upon his experience. He surveyed the whole course of his route, and discovered his position. He remained an adventurer, and an opportunist, but now he had to look upon the play from the wings, preparing himself for the great adventure and the great opportunity when, and if, it should come. He learned his lines assiduously.

In January 1931 he divorced himself from the inner councils of the Tory Party, and placed himself squarely in the political wilderness. From this position, freed from party loyalties, he could choose his moments to dash on to the parliamentary stage, to steal the limelight from the dreary principals. He recognized that whatever else he might be, however much he might fill his life with literary works, painting, discussing, even bricklaying, he was overwhelmingly a politician.

But what kind of politician? An independent, a monarchist, at once a 'Little Englander' and an 'Empire Loyalist', an antisocialist and a romantic reactionary. Politics provided his arena, and parliament his great stage. But what torch did he carry? And what part, above all others, must he play?

If he had ever seriously considered following any other course but politics, it was but a temporary aberration. No sooner had he said aloud that he had a mind to give up politics, and make money than he knew the falsity of that. He would be true to himself, and his dreams. But he had to think right through his position, discover himself, his strengths and his weaknesses, and this, in these ten years, he achieved, in as much as it is possible for a violently romantic and sentimental man to do so.

Churchill's interest in domestic politics was never more than superficial or forced. His heart was not in it. He had inherited his policies from his father, and his father's friends, obediently read

Cobden and John Bright, and clothed worn-out themes in glowing words. But in all his nature, all his instincts, all his thoughts from childhood he was profoundly moved by the inextricably woven patterns of war and peace. This was politics!

Churchill had observed clearly that peace had been dealt a blow at Versailles that might well prove mortal, but he was not then aware of the nature of that blow, and of its tragic implications for mankind. For if peace were destroyed, war must also lose its meaning.

1929 is one of the most clearly marked of the signpost years. Until the middle of that year it was possible for optimists to believe that Europe showed signs of settling down. The huge sums withdrawn from Germany in reparations were flowing back again in loans. The great ships *Bremen* and *Europa* from German yards had won the Blue Ribands of the Atlantic. Once more by such tokens the world must know that they were a great people. The Treaty of Locarno had temporarily quietened French and German fears, and the problems of Poland, Danzig and Germany's eastern frontiers did not appear pressing. The well-informed knew of the brilliant efforts of General von Seeckt to maintain the continuity of the German General Staff, but he was forced to make do with TEWTS and EWTS.[1] The menace of Hitler was not yet sinister beyond the German frontiers, nor was the menace of German militarism.

But if it was not easy to understand in 1929 and 1930 the nature of the calamity that threatened the human race, it was easy to see that the embers of war were smouldering, and were almost certain to burst once more into flames. Perhaps the only possible means of preventing war would have been an immediate and urgent recognition of this situation on the parts of the British, French and United States Governments. It would be the last thing they would do.

Churchill was fully aware of these trends. He was aware, too, that peace had not followed the great outbreak of 1914-18, and that, therefore, the struggle had been abortive, an exercise not in war but in murder. There would not be a new war, but a continuation of the struggle. The implications were not realized. The conditions of peace, and the purposes of war were not thought out.

Yet it was for this struggle that Churchill urgently and

[1] Tactical exercises without troops.

thoughtfully prepared. He was not alone. A small group of distinguished politicians shared his fears. They met constantly for discussion, and with Churchill increasingly the focus of their orbit. Those who needed him aided him in whatever capacities they could; those he needed he attracted with a fascination few could resist.

Soldiers, sailors, airmen, strategists, diplomats, journalists, all in well-placed positions collected information for him with enthusiasm, and a deep sense of purpose. He established powerful contacts in France and the United States, and a small inner core of dedicated men served him devotedly at home, almost as a personal staff. Of these, Professor Lindemann, a man of immense driving force and gnawing ambition, bigoted, dogmatic, humourless and dedicated, a man of obsessional hatreds, especially for Germans, became his 'Witch Doctor' as scientific adviser. Brendan Bracken was his eyes and ears, his devoted servant, diligent, talented, a perfect public relations man. Desmond Morton, alarmed at the nature of the growing threat of war, provided the kind of information normally available only to the most senior ministers of the Crown, and enabled him to make his brilliant pyrotechnic attacks on the Tory Front Bench in Parliament. Ralph Wigram, a shining light of the Foreign Office, clung to Churchill like a drowning man to a spar, and these few, together with a handful of politicians, knew clearly the part he might be called upon to play, and were resolved to help him to prepare.

Churchill lived life so fully in these years that it is difficult to unite all his trails into a coherent whole. It is like watching a superb juggler nonchalantly spinning a dozen or so plates with one hand, performing some virtuoso feat with the other in a different *genre*, while engaging in intricate discussion. Yet he always appeared relaxed, even in 1932 writing to Marsh to come down to Chartwell for a rest:

'Clemmie says you *must* come. Just vegetate—as I do. Love from W.'

In 1929 he was present in New York with Baruch when financial disaster plunged Wall Street and half the world into near ruin. He had observed the 'frenzy' in the New York Exchange on 'Black Thursday', October 24th. On the 23rd 'a final cataclysmic break . . . sent a shudder of apprehension through the

Street.'[1] And on the next day Churchill watched from the visitors' gallery as 'panic swept the floor of the Exchange, by that time a frantic madhouse'. It made a deep impression. He observed that the 'greed of gain' had 'outstripped the great achievement' of production and progress, and commented:

'The whole wealth so swiftly gathered in the paper values of previous years vanished. The prosperity of millions of American homes had grown upon a gigantic structure of inflated credit, now suddenly proved phantom.'

The ghost of his grandfather Jerome walked that unheroic battlefield, but it was not for him. It had not been enough in itself even for his grandfather. His friend, Baruch, was in any case the supreme performer on that stage, and there was no comparable rôle to be played in London. In the United States, Baruch also occupied a unique position, the intimate and confidante of the highest servants of the State, including the President.

It was all grist to Churchill's mill, and Baruch would almost certainly prove a valuable ally, whatever might befall. In 1931 Churchill was back again in New York for personal consultations with his friend and for a lecture tour. He had found time to do some painting in the South of France, complaining of the poor light that had denied him the bold primary colours he loved. At the same time he had not neglected his literary production. *The Eastern Front*, the final volume of *The World Crisis*, had brilliantly crowned that achievement, and his book *My Early Life* was delighting a numerous public. Written, more or less, from a 'subaltern's point of view', he had taken great care with it, sending its parts to Marsh for comment and haggling over the use of hyphens, and his preference for 'and' wherever possible instead of a comma. Two rough draft chapters of *Marlborough* were already in Marsh's hands, and other literary projects were on the stocks.

But his eye and mind were already focusing steadily on the main chance, diminishing the rest of his prodigious activities to the status of 'hobbies'.

Meanwhile, Churchill suffered an enforced rest. Stepping out of his taxi on the wrong side in Fifth Avenue on his way to Baruch's apartment, he was knocked down and badly injured.

[1] *Bernard Baruch*, autobiography.

Recuperating in the Bahamas, the avalanche of his labours continued unabated, and he was soon fit to give forty lectures throughout the United States before returning home to 'vegetate' at Chartwell.

There are some who believe that his *Life of Marlborough*, which he wrote in these years, 1932-37, was of major importance in equipping him for his great task as war leader, but this I think is to assume that he was capable of changing his nature. Amery believed that in the writing 'he discovered that fusion of political and military ideals, as well as the inspiration of family piety, for which all his life had had been groping'.

I doubt it. But it was the most difficult and disciplined mental exercise he had ever undertaken, and as such it 'rounded off' his education, and brought him as near to maturity as he could come. He increased his awareness of the inner fabric of nations, and of the means whereby they might be held together in alliances, and constrained to fight in a common cause. He saw, and clearly recognized, the supreme virtues of patience and foresight deployed by Duke John, but these were qualities, however desirable, alien to his headstrong nature. No mental, spiritual or physical exercise or experience could long quench his ferocious 'itch', his determination to 'make things happen'. It might, however, have made him more conscious that he was not only an Englishman, and half an American, but also, if he were a Marlborough, a good European.

Two passages from the preface to Volume III make painful and instructive reading in the light of all that we now know:

'When British generals of modern times feel themselves hampered by the tardy or partial action of allies, or embarrassed by the political situation at home, let them draw from the example of Marlborough new resources of endurance, without losing his faculty of "venturing all".'

Such an example would not have sufficed to save Wavell, whose patience, resource and endurance made him the nearest to Marlborough of all the commanders of the Second World War. And Marlborough, unlike Wavell, was not on the receiving end of a barrage of cables, telephone calls, exhortations, reproofs, acid criticisms, and demands for explanations. Had Marlborough lived and served under, and within reach of, a Churchill it is

THE WARRIOR 267

unlikely that his great campaigns would have reached their fulfilment. He might well have gone the way of Wavell and Auchinleck.

A few pages on, Churchill wrote words which would serve as an epitaph to the war in which he held the highest power in the State:

'his (Marlborough's) tale is rich in suggestion and instruction for the present day; for it illustrates what seems to have become a tradition of Britain—indomitable in distress and danger, exorbitant at the moment of success, fatuous and an easy prey after her superb effort had run its course.... Here in foretaste we may read the bitter story of how in the eighteenth century England won the war and lost the peace.'

But it is clear, I think, that Churchill, whatever he may have learned from his profound study of the life and times of his ancestor, could not apply that knowledge to the times he lived in. Nor could he have sustained for a week that sweetness of temper, that enduring patience which, allied to genius and strategic vision, enabled Marlborough to reshape Europe. Churchill's genius was of a different order, and he was on the threshold of old age before his prodigious energies were channelled into a single course.

The production of ten books in the course of the ten years 1929-38 were among the least important of his activities in that period.

III

In *The Gathering Storm* Churchill pays tribute to some of those who, inside and outside of Parliament, combined to prepare him for power, and enabled him to mount his powerful and consistent attacks on the Government. The virtue of these attacks, well known to any reader of *Hansard* throughout these years, is that in as much as they related to the military developments of our probable enemies abroad, they were accurate.

From 1932 onwards Churchill was dedicated above all to the task of arousing Britain to the rapidly growing menace of war, and the startling state of unpreparedness of the country. For this unpreparedness he was as much to blame as anyone, for he had been in the van of those who had dismantled the Services and the industrial organization supporting them. It was not so much that Britain had disarmed and pared her Services to the bone, but that she had done so without a practical policy for peace. It had not been even a worthwhile gesture. Her leaders had not thought out her position in peace or war, nor defined a sane foreign policy. Their actions, including Churchill's, had been dictated by the worst kind of political opportunism, and were tardily made abundantly clear by Baldwin in his speech of 'appalling frankness' in 1936:

'Supposing,' he said, 'I had gone to the country and said that Germany was rearming, and that we must rearm, does anybody think that this pacific democracy would have rallied to that cry? ... I cannot think of anything that would have made the loss of the election from my point of view more certain.'

It must be as clear and unequivocal a statement of Tory principles and policy as has ever been made, but it revealed also a lack of understanding of the condition of the people. Britain was not a 'pacific democracy', but a demoralized democracy, incapable of being inspired by a bankrupt régime to brandish weapons it did not possess.

From the inhibitions of government Churchill in 1931 had wisely freed himself. He knew as much about the trends and the preparations for war on the continent of Europe as the successive Prime Ministers and the senior members of their Cabinets and Armed Services. Indeed, it is ironical that his inside knowledge was due to the magnanimity and foresight of Ramsay Macdonald, a man he cruelly dubbed 'the Boneless Wonder'. On achieving office without power in 1929, Macdonald had sent for Maurice Hankey and had been told the worst. Broadly, of some 30,000 factories that had been fully geared into the war effort by 1918, barely a round dozen remained. If this wild dismantling had been allied to careful planning and organization it would have been at least a noble, if quixotic and premature, gesture. Instead, it had been done haphazard and without benefit to the country's tottering economy, nor to its growing army of unemployed.

But in one respect the country had prepared. Lloyd George had clearly understood that the ability to wage modern warfare rested squarely on industrial power and production. It would be no longer a true guide to study the growths of the armies, navies and air forces of potential enemies, nor even of their actual war production in terms of weapons. The 'iceberg' of war potential was no longer visible above water. The future would inevitably belong to the big battalions backed by industrial power, to the nations '100 million strong'. Accordingly, with the help and advice of Hankey and Sir Eyre Crowe, Lloyd George had established a foreign intelligence organization under Major Morton with the task of watching foreign industry. The main target had been Soviet Russia in the early years, but the focus had shifted to Germany, becoming Nazi Germany.

While Britain and France remained in their states of palsied torpor, fearful of shadows, disgruntled with themselves and the world, and complaining of a lack of inspiration in their peoples, even the 'piano factories' of the Third Reich were being equipped with the jigs and machine tools which would make possible a rapid turnover from peace to war. Such a metamorphosis would take Britain months, possibly years.

This kind of information was available to British heads of Government and the Services. No one wished to hear, nor to believe, and to press it home was to court unpopularity, even to the point of losing seniority. Cynicism, frustration, and even corruption began to pervade those, including journalists, concerned with such developments. Attempts at objective observation and reporting were harshly discouraged. Inevitably the public was less and less well informed, and demoralization grew.

Fortuitously Major Morton and Churchill were near neighbours, but it was only the deliberate and definite agreement given in writing by Ramsay Macdonald, and later confirmed by Baldwin and Chamberlain in turn, that enabled Morton to arm Churchill with his vital statistics. Thus in all his years of skilful and accurate sniping in Parliament, Churchill was using ammunition provided by those he was attacking, and equally available to them.

Prominent among his supporters in the House, many of them powerful attackers in their own right, were Leo Amery, Austen Chamberlain, Sir Robert Horne, Robert Boothby, Sir Archibald Sinclair, Capt. F. E. Guest, Lord Winterton, Sir Edward Grigg and Sir Henry Page Croft. Frequent visitors to Chartwell included Ralph Wigram, Robert Vansittart, F. E. Smith, Duff Cooper, Lord Willingdon, J. H. Thomas, Alexander Cadogan and H. A.

Gwynne of the *Morning Post*. From time to time T. E. Lawrence or Basil Liddell Hart would put in an appearance and join in discussion, and Ian Colvin of the younger journalists was a useful source of information.

Chartwell, therefore, became an outlet for many of those who knew themselves increasingly hemmed in and frustrated. Soldiers, sailors, airmen, Foreign Office officials and journalists, were all finding it unprofitable, and even dangerous, to speak their minds. To bring back news from Germany that the 'boss' didn't want to know could mean the loss of a 'K' on a CMG, or the sack, while a cynically contrived lullaby would gain advancement.

The rottenness permeating the Government and most of the newspapers spread through the blood stream of the whole country, and it is likely that without Churchill to cling to as a hope or a bastion some would have resigned in despair. In December 1936, Ralph Wigram, one of the most brilliant young men in the Foreign Service, died with a *cri du coeur* on his lips.

'I have not been able to make them understand. Winston has always, always understood, and he is strong and will go on to the end,' he said to his wife.

Churchill had often visited the Wigrams in North Street. 'My friend ... took it too much to heart,' he wrote. He took it deeply to heart himself, but his own heart was unbreakable, and his course was becoming clear.

### IV

It may be that the decade of the 1930s will be seen as the graveyard of European liberal democracy. Perhaps if men had acted with courage and decision in the earlier years of the aftermath, all might have been well. But to act with courage and decision demands a clear concept of aims, and an equally clear concept of the condition of one's country. It would have been asking more from men than history has taught us to expect. In the 1930s it was too late. Communism had bred its reactionary opposite of fascism and nazism, and between these two dynamic creeds *laissez faire* liberal civilization foundered, as it was bound to do unless it could formulate a dynamic of its own, and act upon it. Instead, Britain dithered like an old nanny, accustomed to the best households, urging alien hooligans of extreme vulgarity to behave themselves. France, meanwhile, was burrowing herself in behind 'impregnable' fortifications, and sunk in a torpor of political corruption and cynicism.

It was useless for Britain to protest that 'war settles nothing—cures nothing' in a world dominated by the belief that war would settle everything and cure everything. To Hitler, Tojo and Mussolini, with their dreams of conquest and empire, such protestations were transparent hypocrisy, and utterly contemptible. Britain and France had 'had enough', content to rest on their laurels, and trying to declare that all legitimate adjustments could be achieved by peaceful negotiation.

In such a world it was criminally foolhardy to attempt to sit on a fence that was not there. The courses open to Britain were clear: she could continue to regard herself as a European and world power, contract the necessary alliances, and build up her naval and military strength. She could decide to maintain her world position, wash her hands of Europe, and build up her maritime strength to 'hold the ring' while the volcano erupted. Or she could divest herself of power, trust to peaceful trade, and defend her island.

She did none of these things. She merely drifted, ill-prepared, towards full engagement in world war at the timings of her enemies. The third course would have been, at that time, difficult to maintain, for the United States would almost certainly have regarded the maintenance of Britain as an Atlantic base, essential to her security.

The lot of the citizens of Britain and France throughout this period was an unhappy one. To Western 'big business', fascism and nazism offered certain attractions, even if their methods were unpleasant. Wealth and privilege would be likely to survive in the same hands. The German and Italian dictators, it was observed, were the only rulers with an answer to unemployment, and with the ability to control labour. Communism, on the other hand, meant the extinction of private profit, and was a threat to established order. In the main, men of all persuasions shied away from a distasteful choice, and clung to ill-founded hopes that less harshly organized systems might survive by some kind of miracle.

But it became more and more difficult to compromise. Wherever one was, in the Far East, in Germany, in Russia, in Abyssinia or Spain, observers found it increasingly difficult not to take sides. At home, politicians and the purveyors of news and opinion, all with their private hopes and fears, frowned upon reports which contradicted such hopes or confirmed such fears.

Finally, in Spain, European and world civil war had its bitter, bloody and terrible rehearsal. By the middle of the 1930s the most reliable correspondents and observers in the world were being 'smeared' as Reds or Blacks. In Britain the 'Left' read and believed the stories of the growing terror in Germany, the ghastly persecution of the Jews, the strong-arm 'castor oil' methods of Mussolini in Italy, mustard gas in Ethiopia, and supported the Spanish Government cause. The 'Right', with the exception of a small reactionary fringe as dedicated to fascism as their counterparts to communism, was uneasy, equivocal, brooding and barren.

Spain was the heart of the matter, and not only inside Spain, but in France and Britain, men and women found themselves facing the ultimate struggle in their own hearts and minds. In Spain, and about Spain, it was necessary to choose. The choice was not for long between the elected government, liberal in its inception, or the Monarchy, or Franco. The choice was between communism and fascism. Yet thousands of men and women, Europeans and Americans, who supported neither of these creeds, and even loathed them, fought and died in the struggle. In doing so they shamed the governments of their countries who dared nothing, and believed in nothing.

It must be almost impossible for those who lived through those years, acutely aware and inevitably involved, to look back even now objectively. I cannot. Yet one had to believe that those young English men and women who fought on the Government side in Spain were overwhelmingly liberal in their attitudes. They fought—God rest their souls!—for a dream of freedom; for it was, even then, a dream.

Churchill himself was not immune from these stresses of the spirit. His position of privilege insulated him against the smears damaging lesser folk, and prevented him from suffering the indignities attendant upon travel, or knowing the steady erosion of 'Freedom'. His aristocratic background, his mystical attitude to Monarchy, and his wholehearted dislike of socialist trends, inclined him to support Franco. His liberalism and his admiration for the courage of the Spanish Government troops, and especially for the British fighting in the 'International Brigade', pulled him the other way.

In 1936 and 1937 his utterances reflected the conflicts in his mind.

'This Spanish welter is not the business of either of us (Britain and France),' he said in August 1936. 'It seems certain that a majority of Spaniards are on the rebel side.... It is certainly to be hoped that, even if Germany and Italy on the one hand, and Soviet Russia on the other, send help to their respective factions ... France will nonetheless adopt the same attitude of detachment as Great Britain.'

As a strategist he knew that an alliance must be made with Russia and France if the march of Nazi Germany was to be contained in war or peace. Long before the outbreak of the Spanish Civil War he had been acutely aware that time was running out. In the Far East Japan, bursting with population, had been the first to embark upon conquest, savaging China and creating the State of Manchukuo, at the same time threatening Hong Kong by land and sea. In Africa and the Mediterranean, Mussolini's delusions of grandeur had led him to embark upon the conquest of Abyssinia, and the establishment of a new Roman Empire. The Mediterranean, he boasted, would become an Italian lake. Even in the Gran Chaco a bitter war raged between Paraguay and Bolivia, seeming irrelevant in the general theme, but with its own dark connotations in the 'Siamese-twin' American continents.

Nothing had more powerfully revealed the moral bankruptcy of the Western world than the contempt with which the dictators of Japan, Italy and Germany treated the platitudinous threats and appeals of the League of Nations. Palsied with fear that the dictators would embrace each other in hard alliance, Britain and France failed to condemn their dreadful excesses, and failed even to defend themselves while they could.

None of these sideshows caused Churchill's hard stare to waver from the principal enemy.

'Until the middle of 1934 the control of events was still largely in the hands of His Majesty's Government without the risk of war,' he wrote. 'They could at any time, in concert with France and through the agency of the League of Nations, have brought an overwhelming power to bear upon the Hitler Movement, about which Germany was profoundly divided.'

In the face of Hitler's fast-rising power and clear intentions, the British Government continued to urge the French to disarm, while assuring them of British support! A Russian alliance, which alone might ensure a balance of power in Europe and safeguard France, was ignored. Nothing that Churchill could say inside the House, or out of it, aroused the Government.

'There is something to be said for isolation; there is something to be said for alliances,' Churchill observed bitterly. 'But there is nothing to be said for weakening the Power on the continent with whom you would be in alliance, and then involving yourself more (deeply) in continental tangles in order to make it up to them.'

Nevertheless, when Hitler occupied the Rhineland and kicked the Treaty of Locarno into the waste paper basket, France still had more than enough power to act alone. She did nothing. Henceforth Hitler knew, even if his generals did not, that he could do as he pleased. Distrusting each other profoundly, as well they might, Britain, France and Russia would never commit themselves in concert.

Slowly Britain had begun to prepare. The demands of Churchill and his friends for a Ministry of Supply were not to be answered until the beginning of 1939, but in 1936 Sir Thomas Inskip became Minister of Co-ordination of Defence, 'The most remarkable appointment,' Churchill commented, 'since Caligula made his horse consul.' The observation, like so many very bright remarks, was not wholly merited, and Churchill should have been grateful that his own considerable claims to the job had been ignored. A premature minor rôle might well have ruined him.

Meanwhile, without prejudice to his political freedom, he accepted Baldwin's invitation to sit on the Committee of Imperial Defence on Air Defence Research, and with his personal adviser, Professor Lindemann, at his elbow. He had discovered that he was an unreliable gauge of popular feeling in the abdication crisis. The predicament of Edward VIII had aroused all the natural Royalist in him, but when he rose to make his final plea for the King in the House, he was howled down, receiving, according to

*The Times*, 'The most striking rebuff of parliamentary history.' Similarly, he had completely misunderstood the clamour of youth for peace.

Baldwin had known in his very bones, in a way that Churchill could not know, that Parliament and people were Monarchist without being 'Royalist', and that a clamour for 'peace' meant a profound discontent with peace.

Commenting twenty-five years later, John Raymond wrote:[1] 'The Baldwins will always beat the Beaverbrooks—and even the Churchills—except at times of national disaster . . . as the Lion beat the Unicorn all over Town.'

The Baldwins and Chamberlains were beating the Beaverbrooks and Churchills all along the line in the last fatal phases of the 1930s. Chamberlain, like some arid and arrogant schoolmaster, had rebuffed an approach by Roosevelt on the eve of Hitler's rape of Austria, and at the same time treated the advances of the Russians with calculated and cold disdain.

'That Mr Chamberlain, with his limited outlook and inexperience of the European scene, should have possessed the self-sufficiency to wave away the proffered hand stretched out across the Atlantic leaves one, even at this date, breathless with amazement,' Churchill wrote ten years later.[2]

I believe that it was at this time that Churchill began to doubt his destiny. The leading actors were already on the stage, and where on earth, but for him, was there a man to match them? One felt that half the world watched and waited in growing anguish for the entry of the Hero. The climax was approaching. There was no sign.

Britain and France were not only becoming isolated, but ineffectual, and in February 1938 Anthony Eden resigned the Foreign Secretaryship, no longer able to stomach the Government's negative attempts at appeasement without purpose. When he heard the news Churchill reached his lowest ebb, and 'for a while the dark waters of despair overwhelmed me'. For the first and last time in his life he could not sleep, for Eden had seemed to him the 'one strong young figure standing up against the long,

[1] *The Sunday Times*, December 3, 1961.
[2] *The Gathering Storm*.

dismal, drawling tides of drift and surrender, of wrong measurements and feeble impulses.'

'I watched the daylight slowly creep in through the windows,' he wrote, after his long wakeful night, 'and saw before me in mental gaze the vision of death.'

He and Britain had reached their lowest ebb together.

# CHAPTER XVI

IT IS unlikely that Churchill's sudden descent into despair was simply the result of the undignified and weak dealings with Italy that had led to Eden's resignation, nor even to the imminence of Hitler's violation of Austria, and all that that implied. Rather was his mood the culmination of an unease and confusion of thought that had been growing through the years. He had been slow to realize the nature and extent of the Nazi menace, and it was not until 1932 that he had become fully aroused. Even then his thinking was confused. The pattern was new, and he did not like it. The guilt of Versailles sat heavily upon France and Britain, inhibiting corrective actions of which they were fully capable. But the inhibitions lay far deeper than Versailles, revealing a struggle in the very bowels of once liberal and aristocratic cultures. Political, social and economic evolution had broken down, and the world was faced with total revolution. Half the world refused to look. Britain especially tended to see the political justice of Hitler's moves in outworn terms, and failed to assess the clear military and strategic threats.

The once simple strategy of maintaining a balance of power in Europe, and the need for Britain to prevent any one nation becoming predominant, was bedevilled by the great political and ideological growths of Communism and Fascism. If forced to choose between these two creeds which denied the fundamental tenets of Christendom, and submerged the individual in the body of the Corporate State, Churchill would have reluctantly chosen Fascism. But it was a loathsome choice. Neville Chamberlain, lacking Churchill's aristocratic background and violence of temper, found both creeds merely distasteful. For France the choice was more simple, but she needed Britain to cement her alliance with Soviet Russia. Meanwhile the dictators acted with speed and growing boldness, as they watched the obstacles crumbling miraculously before their trumpets.

In the Mediterranean, Britain allowed herself to be frightened by Mussolini's air force, and permitted the Italian dictator to lay the foundations of his 'Roman Empire'. In Spain she watched the basic issues joined, and washed her hands of the affair. Joyfully Hitler engulfed Austria, gaining a common frontier with his ally, Mussolini, and outflanking Czechoslovakia. In the Rhineland he consolidated his ability to make war, and attack France. With the absorption of Czechoslovakia he opened the way to the East, and enveloped Poland's southern flank.

Then, and only then, Britain and France at last acted with an insane guarantee to Poland, provoking Hitler to inevitable action and forcing him into a temporary *mariage de convenance* with Russia.

'Never,' wrote Liddell Hart, 'has there been a more astonishing case of collective self-delusion under the influence of righteous indignation.'

Against this strategic absurdity only Lloyd George raised his voice, while Churchill, unable to resist a warlike gesture, however ill-timed and fatuous, subscribed to it. Indeed, Churchill's attitudes throughout these dismal years are only marginally better than those of the Tory Government.

He had drawn wrong conclusions from the many rehearsals of war in progress. He thought the submarine had become obsolescent and said so firmly. In disagreement with most observers, he believed that the air weapon had been over-estimated on land and sea. His statements leave no room for doubt.

Early in 1937 he was persuading himself that the German menace was fading, and in January he declared that 'judged by every standard, Germany is bankrupt'. By March he had come to the conclusion that the steel shortage, coupled with the tremendous rise in the costs of war metals, was seriously hampering German rearmament. In the following months he committed himself to the grave statement:

'I will not pretend that, if I had to choose between Communism and Nazism, I would choose Communism.'

By that time the persecution of the Jews and the horrors perpetrated inside Germany were beyond all doubt. But Churchill's choice was emotional, not political, nor strategic, and arose out of the hope that the whole business would prove a nightmare from which we should all soon awake. In the late autumn of 1937 he had almost convinced himself that his earlier fears of Germany were groundless:

Three or four years ago I was myself a loud alarmist,' he said. 'In spite of the risks which wait on prophecy, I declare my belief that a major war is not imminent, and I still believe that there is a good chance of no major war taking place in our lifetime.'

It was from such dreams as these that he awoke following Eden's resignation, and in the tragic second week of March 1938, which saw the Nazi triumph in Austria, he was back on his true course. Chamberlain had rejected his plea for a 'grand alliance' with France and Russia, almost with a patronizing sneer. He had mentioned it to Halifax and the Chiefs of Staff, and dismissed it as quite impracticable. But Churchill, deeply moved by the Austrian tragedy, challenged him in the House:[1]

'Europe is confronted with a programme of aggression nicely calculated and timed, unfolding stage by stage, and there is only one choice open not only to us but to other countries, either to submit like Austria, or else to take effective measures while time remains....'

He went on with bitter irony to draw attention to the strength of the 'Little Entente', Roumania, Yugoslavia and Czechoslovakia and their considerable resources in oil and armament. Of Czechoslovakia he said:

'No doubt they are only a small democratic State, no doubt they have an army only two or three times as large as ours, no doubt they have a munitions supply only three times as great as that of Italy, but still they are a virile people, they have their rights, they have their treaty rights, they have a line of fortresses....'

None of this had the slightest effect on Chamberlain. Writing to his sister a week later on March 20th, he observed:[2]

[1] *The Gathering Storm.*
[2] Keith Feiling, *The Life of Neville Chamberlain.*

'You have only to look at the map to see that nothing that France or we could do could possibly save Czechoslovakia from being overrun by Germans, if they wanted to do it. I have therefore abandoned any idea of giving guarantees to Czechoslovakia, or to the French in connection with her obligations to that country.'

There was still a faint chance that France and Russia might act alone in support of the Czechs, and the bare threat gave Hitler pause. But not for long. Chamberlain soon left the Nazi dictator in no doubt that he could have his way, and by the spring of 1939 he had consolidated his position in Central Europe beyond his dreams, and greatly strengthened his ability to make war.

Yet Neville Chamberlain was a strong man in his fashion, moved by a cold and ruthless 'evangelism', empty of real passion, and overriding the moral scruples of the French and British alike, incapable in his monumental arrogance of considering the proposition that he might be wrong. When he returned from Munich, waving his pitiful piece of paper, and declaiming 'Peace in our Time', no one asked him what he meant, for peace, like war, as Litvinov had said, was indivisible and it did not exist.

'The Municheers seemed actually to believe in peace,' wrote Leo Amery, and there can be no other excuse for them, or for us. But what did peace mean? What kind of peace, and what for? To conquer unemployment, to build a stable and fruitful society, to distribute food to the hungry?

Or was it simply that they believed in the absence of war; imagining that all the ills of mankind would adjust themselves, perhaps by some miraculous intervention of the Deity? Did they believe that the wronged, the hungry, the homeless, the workless, would acquiesce indefinitely in their dreary condition? For such was peace, and there was no strength in it to defy the powerful dynamic of war.

The failure of the Western democracies in the years between was the failure to make peace, and because of that the embers of war smouldered, subject to postponement, but never to be avoided.

## II

The differences between the Government and its critics were not so wide as they appeared, and were in great measure the natural expressions of those whose task it is to govern, and those who are

## THE WARRIOR 281

in little danger of being called upon to reinforce their words with deeds. The facts were not in dispute. The official Opposition, floundering between war and peace, and without an incisive policy for either condition, had been led by the Tories to the knacker's yard, and emerged emasculated of their socialism. Macdonald had succumbed to the Londonderry House treatment, and had gone down in a mist of euphoria.

With the coming of Neville Chamberlain no new light appeared upon Britain's domestic or foreign horizons, but the appointment of Leslie Hore-Belisha to the War Ministry brought a wind of change to blow through the stale and dusty corridors of the whole military machine. At this time Churchill had begun to move away from his outside position, and would have liked to come more into the line of power. In an endeavour to soften his savage attacks on the Government, Baldwin had offered him the seat on the Air Defence Committee. The result was unfortunate. Churchill was not muted, and Lindemann joined the Tizard committee with serious results.

'Almost from the moment that Lindemann took his seat in the committee room,' wrote C. P. Snow, 'the meeting did not know half an hour's harmony or work undisturbed.'

Lindemann was a man prone to extreme dislikes, and was devoid of charm. His dislike of Tizard was at once obsessional, and it was enough for an idea to emanate from that source to damn it in Lindemann's mind. Unable to stomach Lindemann's diatribes, which were borne with great patience by Tizard, P. M. S. Blackett and A. V. Hill resigned. Fortunately Tizard's position and great talent enabled him to prevail, and when the committee re-formed, with Blackett and Hill again in their places, Lindemann was absent.

Unhappily Churchill shared Lindemann's dislikes, and gave his ear exclusively to Lindemann's advice. But for that the strategic bombing of Germany might never have been carried out, for Lindemann's estimates of the probable results proved wildly inaccurate, while Tizard and Blackett were very near the mark, and extremely unpopular.

'The story goes,' wrote Blackett, 'that at that time in the Air Ministry it was said of anyone who added two and two and made four: "He is not to be trusted: he has been talking to Tizard and Blackett".'

Churchill had always disliked that kind of simple arithmetic, and never more so than in war. It precluded the impossible.

Meanwhile, at the end of 1937, Hore-Belisha's wind of change had blown through the War Office like a tornado. He was a man of great energy, charm, talent, enthusiasm, and moral courage, nevertheless he was of a type to be regarded by hoary military relics as a 'bit of a bounder'. He was doomed from the outset to be blown away by his own endeavours, but not before he had played a brave part in putting Britain's military house in order.

Immediately after 'sacking' the Army Council in December 1937 he was warned by Major-General Sir Fabian Ware, a distinguished educationist, that the entrenched military hierarchy would not tolerate him, and that the mysterious and 'invisible' forces of 'The Establishment' would get rid of him.

'Nothing will happen at once,' he told Belisha, 'but you will find in the months ahead attacks on you from various quarters. There will be whispering in drawing-rooms, and words will be dropped in influential ears. They will get you out."

When Hore-Belisha asked Fabian Ware how long he thought the process would take, he was given the accurate estimate of eighteen months to two years. Undismayed, and with the acclamation of the newspapers in his ears, Belisha tackled the immense task of revitalizing the army with an energy and enthusiasm that spread swiftly throughout the whole military body. But the rust of years had bitten deep, especially at the top. It was called tradition.

Churchill was among those who appeared to admire the new War Minister and to welcome his deeds, but in his position he must have been fully aware of the fate in store for him. He was himself a difficult mixture of traditionalist and progressive, and had proved a disappointment to Fuller and Liddell Hart, the chief exponents of armoured warfare and mechanization. Whatever the reason, and it may not have been formulated in Churchill's mind, he nursed a resentment against Hore-Belisha. The Sandys case was almost certainly a factor.²

---
[1] R. J. Minney, *The Private Papers of Hore-Belisha*.
[2] See *The Private Papers of Hore-Belisha*, etc., etc. The embarrassment caused by leakage of A.A. Defence information.

Perhaps Churchill wanted the job for himself. Certainly he was ready and anxious to serve under Chamberlain, and had asked Belisha to sound out the Prime Minister. Chamberlain had been adamant in his refusal to consider Churchill as a colleague.

'If I take him into the Cabinet he will dominate it. He won't give others a chance even of talking.'

Belisha persisted, but with no better fortune. It might have been unpleasant to inform Churchill of this attitude, but it would have been wise. In the event, Belisha kept his own counsel, and from that time 'a coolness developed', wrote R. J. Minney.

Finally, when Belisha was sacked by Chamberlain almost two years to the very day after his appointment, and after having been assured less than a fortnight earlier that he enjoyed the Prime Minister's full confidence, Churchill was one of the very few to whom Chamberlain had disclosed his intention.

By the good offices of Beaverbrook and Bracken, both of whom liked Belisha, a telephone call was put through to Churchill, at that time in Paris, asking him to telephone Belisha's number. The ensuing conversation was curiously reserved. Churchill, believing that Belisha had been offered the Ministry of Information, which had been Chamberlain's intention earlier in the day when Churchill left for Paris, advised him to accept. But Belisha had been offered the Board of Trade, and was unaware of Chamberlain's original intention. He refused.

The sequel to these somewhat indefinite attitudes occurred in June 1941 following a debate in the House. Belisha had voiced criticisms which had drawn Churchill's fire. When he left the chamber he heard Churchill following him. He was piloted to the Smoking Room, told to sit down, as though he were a schoolboy called to the Head's study, and grimly warned. Churchill stood glowering over him:

'If you fight me I shall fight you back,' he said. 'And remember this: you are using a 4.5 inch howitzer, and I am using a 12 inch gun.'

Churchill turned and walked away without another word. It was at this time that he had suddenly become aware of his immense armament of power, and like a child with a new toy was anxious to try it out. Belisha had caught the mere fringe of a hurricane that would cut down Wavell in the desert a month later. This was a new Churchill, deeply disturbing to those nearest to him, and causing at least one of them to begin to see in him a likeness to Henry VIII, rather than to Marlborough, or Napoleon, the models of his choice.

All this was still a long way off in 1938 and 1939, but Churchill's attitudes to power in these last years of his preparation caused his close advisers some uneasiness. His many-sided personality, particularly the Yankee-opportunist in him and the Marlborough visionary with the backward look, made him subject to unpredictable moods. Apart from Mrs Churchill, whose position was unique, and whose influence was wholly good, only Baruch, and possibly Beaverbrook, enjoyed a friendship with him which was not directly dependent upon value given.

Perhaps Baruch knew Churchill better than anyone else. From 1932 until the outbreak of the Second World War he paid visits to England as an unofficial emissary of the President of the United States, a prototype version of Harry Hopkins. Churchill had no doubt that Baruch was one of the powers behind the American scene, the 'Elder Statesman No. 1', while Baruch saw Churchill not only as the main hope of Britain, but as of great potential value to US strategic interests, which Churchill's blood would enable him to identify as his own. He shared none of Churchill's illusions in regard to the relative strengths of their two nations. Britain, he knew as well as any living man, had been bankrupted by the First World War, and would surely be totally ruined by the Second, while her Empire existed mainly in the imagination of dreamers. The United States, on the other hand, had become the most powerful country in the world.

Baruch was four years Churchill's senior, and their relationship was based upon an intricate mutual admiration of each other's qualities. They were a strange couple, the one a Jewish-American financier coveting power behind the scenes, the other an Anglo-American aristocrat-politician coveting power in the limelight. In theatrical terms they were only interested in scripts which gave them such parts. Both were incapable of working with others as part of a team, although Churchill saw himself as a kind of captain of school whose word was law.

But Baruch was all American and his vision whole. His friendship towards Britain, provided socialism could be held at bay, was based upon the recognition that she was vital to American security in the Atlantic, an essential base and bastion. Churchill must be the instrument of Britain's preservation in the great clash which seemed to both men unavoidable.

Baruch had passed through some trying times in the 1930s. When he had faced Alger Hiss, his prosecutor in the 'Merchants of Death' trial in 1935, he had emerged with his reputation unscathed, thanks to his brilliant defence by Senator James Byrnes. He had been damned as 'Public Enemy No. 1', and smeared as a 'Dirty Jew', a target for Nazis on the one hand and Communists on the other. Hitler, it is said, frothed at the mouth at the mention of Baruch's name, for Baruch's influence was great with the American President, and his hatred of the Nazi régime absolute. Some of his family had already suffered under Hitler, and others were doomed to perish in the gas ovens.

In March 1938 Baruch sailed for England avowedly to 'back Winston Churchill for leadership', but Churchill did not share American confidence in his future. He was emerging from his black time. 'I'll be on the side-lines over here: you'll be running the show over there,' he said to Baruch as they parted. The reverse would prove true.

Back in the United States, Baruch urged Roosevelt to move faster towards a war posture than was politically possible. 'You put a burr under their (the public's) tail, Bernie,' Roosevelt said. 'And if I hear 'em holler, I'll know you're doing all right.'

In 1939 Baruch worked out the Industrial Mobilization Plan to enable the nation 'to move smoothly from peace into war'. It proved quite inadequate when the time came, but was none the less a useful preliminary. In the meantime the mere mention of possible US involvement in war would have brought a dangerous storm about the President's ears.

Churchill was aware of these sympathies and developments. In his mind the United States was not a foreign country, bitterly opposed to Britain's colonialism, and resolved to 'free' the remnants of her Empire, but the great submerged mass of the iceberg, whose vast industrial and financial power would support and nourish the glittering pinnacle of Britain. The seed of his dream of a union of the English-speaking peoples, the union of his own two halves, had begun to germinate.

Yet equally strong in him was his eighteenth-century Englishness, and the powerful streak of Europeanism derived from his study of, and kinship with, his great ancestor, Marlborough. These strains were never to be reconciled. He was neither a Yankee nor a Marlborough, nor did he bear the slightest resemblance to either, but these were the ingredients within him, endowing him with a duality of dreams, incompatible and impossible to harmonize on his terms.

In the year 1939 there were other dualities more relevant than these, and of concern to his advisers. Liddell Hart, a member of Churchill's 'Focus' group, and its adviser on strategic aspects of the developing situation, was uneasy about what General Monash called 'the Churchill way of rushing in before we are ready, and hardly knowing what you are going to do next'. He 'was fostering the growing sense of concern and just indignation, among our people, with a recklessness and jack of judgment that was bound to precipitate the war. . . .'[1]

Liddell Hart further observed,[2] 'that while he (Churchill) listened, in a sense, he did not really take in a point except in so far as it fitted in with his own thought, and could be transmuted into words of his own of which he might make effective use.'

These worries were fully justified by events, but Churchill's most dangerous obsession in the last year concerned his attitude to France and French military power. A carefully prepared memorandum on the condition of the French Army aroused him to a violent outburst of rage. He would have none of it.

In April 1938 he had stated:

'Those who know France well, or have long worked with French statesmen and generals, realize the immense latent strength of France. They see what is not apparent to the casual observer. They see the French Army always on the watch. Part of it mans the ramparts round their country. The rest constitutes the most perfectly trained and faithful mobile force in Europe.'

This statement was pure rubbish, but he clung to it. The French Army was to prove itself as mobile as a bog, and those who feared these things in advance strove to inform Churchill in vain. Their memoranda were 'vile calumnies'. Magnificent phrases evoking the glory of France burst from him. He could move himself to tears, or to anger 'terrible to behold'.

[1] L.H. Private Paper, 1941. Letter addressed to John Brophy, Esq., 7.9.41.
[2] Points supplementary to an estimate of Winston Churchill, 12.4.42.

Such aberrations were not to be confined to his attitude to France, and would prove dangerous and costly. Nevertheless, as Europe and the world moved with terrifying speed towards disaster, it was manifest that Churchill was built in the heroic mould of a champion of whom England might be in sore need. As his blood responded to the challenge of war there was a ring in his voice that began to evoke echoes even in the dulled spirits of his countrymen. His shadow in the wings had begun to darken the stage. Between him and Chamberlain there was very little common ground. Chamberlain did not dislike the Germans: he had no quarrel with them.

Churchill found it difficult to make a distinction between the Germans and the Nazi régime, and his nature responded to the 'glory' of France. As a student of war he knew that without Russia there could not be a balance of power in Europe, and Germany could not be contained. His hatred of Communism was probably greater than Chamberlain's, but still he remembered that the object of war must be peace, and that the demands of war made strange bedfellows.

'Why should you shrink from becoming an ally of Russia now?' he demanded in the House.

For without that alliance Britain and France could not challenge Nazi Germany. Between these poles of Germanophilia and Francophilia, confused by the fear and hatred of Soviet Communism, Britain faltered and dithered through the years. Without Russia, Britain's only sane policy was to hold the ring with her sea power, and never to come to grips with great continental armies. But honour—what there was left of it—and frustration and a lack of clear aims would not permit such a course. Thus France and Britain, having finally estranged Soviet Russia, were miserably united in a crusade against evil for which they were spiritually and morally, as well as militarily, unprepared. Certainly the Nazi régime was the most shocking and terrible stain ever to disgrace the human story, but France and Britain had been ready to turn blind eyes to many of its worst excesses, and were even envious of its deeds. At best they were nations in limbo, and sorry champions of civilization.

Inevitably pure strategic issues were clouded. The Ottoman Turks and Tsarist Russia at their atrocious worst had not put themselves beyond the pale of alliances with nations accounting themselves civilized. Now Nazi Germany and Soviet Russia and their irreconcilable creeds had done so. There were few who could regard this situation objectively; few whose emotions were not deeply involved. Finally, with Hitler demanding Memel and Danzig, it was Chamberlain, furious to find himself Hitler's dupe, who rushed into his insane guarantee of Poland, and sparked off the conflict.

Hitler's strategic vision was clear. Knowing that only Russia could make good such a challenge, and perceiving that a rapid conquest of Poland would present him with an initiative he need never lose, he shelved his hatred of Bolshevism and his dreams of Eastern conquest to await their hour, and sent von Ribbentrop to Moscow to negotiate an immediate agreement for the partition of Poland. Neither Stalin nor Hitler harboured illusions about the real intentions of the other, but for Russia the opportunity was not to be missed. It was a shotgun wedding in hell.

On September 1st Hitler's armour, devastatingly supported from the air, crossed the Polish frontier and raced on with a speed never before known. On September 3rd Britain, with France lagging some six hours behind her, declared war on Germany, simply to watch and wait. Long before France could put herself into an effective war posture Poland was laid waste. On the 17th the Russians moved into Poland from the east. In the first week of October Hitler blandly offered peace to the West while the tragic funeral pyre of a brave people sent its acrid fumes to heaven.

Yet Germany was not ready for war. With only six armoured divisions in readiness, and with only eleven fully trained divisions out of a total of forty-three divisions, facing the eighty-five divisions France was slowly deploying on the Western Front, she had demonstrated the new technique of the *Blitzkrieg* in the hands of Guderian. It was a British invention, a trail blazed by Liddell Hart and Fuller.

### III

The period from September 3, 1939, to May 10, 1940, known as 'The Phoney War', was the natural consequence of these emotional declarations and commitments. Once war had been declared and a state of war was in being, the nations involved, equally incapable of major offensive actions, prepared for the contest that must, perforce, take place. Normally such preparations are completed in advance of declarations of war, but in this case it was otherwise.

There were other curious features. Those passions which must be aroused in the people for the successful prosecution of armed conflict, and from which the leaders must be aloof, and therefore capable of clear judgment and lucid strategic and political planning, were aroused in the leaders, while the people remained relatively calm. Indeed the general mood of the country was of relief, rather than excitement. They had reached their climacteric of war expectation at the time of Munich, and thereafter the passion had ebbed. The description of 'The Phoney War' was a verdict of the people.

It is arguable, and probably always will be, which of the contestants made the best use of the period of waiting. Chamberlain, with his unfortunate phrase to the effect that Hitler had 'missed the bus', had somehow persuaded himself that the period of comparative calm had been to Britain's advantage. But if this were true it must imply a remarkably wise use of resources, for while the British people had barely been asked for sacrifices, and were supporting a war expenditure of a mere £2,000,000,000 a year, Germany was spending the equivalent of £3,200,000,000 backed by a dedicated public.

Throughout the period of gestation Germany concentrated on building up her oil reserves to feed her armour and air force, and brought her divisions up to strength and a satisfactory state of training. Britain transferred a small infantry force, startlingly deficient in armour, into France. The Tizard Committee, freed from the violent disturbances caused by Professor Lindemann, improved the radar defences against the air attacks Britain greatly feared. France, deep in her 'impregnable' Maginot Line, furbished up her 'soixante-quinze', twiddled her thumbs and waited. It was clear that in spite of the sustained efforts of a few brilliant young soldiers, she had learned little or nothing about the uses of armour. Her tanks, of which she had a great quantity, surpassing the numbers available to the enemy, were parcelled out, and could not be concentrated in defence or attack. The effect of a German armoured division upon the Austrians, as well as Guderian's handling of his armour in the *Blitzkrieg* on Poland, appeared to have escaped her notice.

K

But by the time 'The Phoney War' gave birth to total war, few could deny Germany's strategic gains. Largely thanks to Churchill, she had occupied Denmark and Norway, and secured for herself the Swedish iron ore Churchill's efforts had attempted to deny.

Throughout the whole period there was a growing feeling—less than a real hope—that war might not 'break out' at all. Hitler had made his offers of peace soon after the digestion of Poland, and absolved himself from any warlike designs against Britain and its possessions. That these statements were genuine was beside the point.

'In this war,' Chamberlain stated, 'we are not fighting against you, the German people, for whom we have no bitter feeling, but against a tyrannous and foresworn régime.'

The feared air attacks against British cities failed to develop. Everywhere fire brigades, swollen by volunteers, waited for 'the bells to go down'. Barrage balloons sailed gracefully in the September skies, and no less gracefully in the still untroubled skies of spring.

It remained for Churchill, at once recalled to his old seat at the Admiralty, and soon stimulating the Military Co-ordination Committee, to provide such fireworks as were possible, and to quicken the blood. What Churchill said was not very different from Chamberlain's sober pronouncements, but it sounded different, for it was clear that while Chamberlain had never heard 'the sound of the trumpets', Churchill heard very little else.

'We are fighting to save the whole world from the pestilence of Nazi tyranny, and in defence of all that is most sacred to man.'

In such words Britain recognized its war leader when the hour should strike. Yet in the months of 'The Phoney War' many feared that if the hour should be too long delayed he would destroy himself. It was clear at once that his ferocious itch for action was unabated. 'Winston is back', the Admiralty signalled to all hands, as soon as he took his seat as First Lord, and it was the same 'Winston' of a quarter of a century earlier, seemingly at sixty-six untouched by time. Soon there were no doubts about it. Norway would be his Antwerp; Greece his Dardanelles.

But in 1939 and 1940 no one could regard him or resist him

with the tolerance and wisdom of an Asquith. He had become a very formidable personage indeed.

## IV

Less than a week after taking office Churchill focused his attention in the north, seeking opportunities for adventure. He wanted the naval planners to find a way of forcing a passage through to the Baltic, and 'to establish a battle squadron which the enemy heavy ships dare not engage.' By this means he would be able to threaten Germany's Baltic coast, and at the same time establish a line of communication with the Russians. He had called this plan Catherine, after Catherine the Great. Russia exercised for him a strange fascination, at times irresistible. He was at once a potential ally and an implacable enemy, unable to comprehend the Marxist dialectic. Russia remained for him, as he put it: 'A riddle wrapped in a mystery inside an enigma.' In short, they spoke a different language, not only Russian, but Communist.

In mid September the Russian invasion of Poland from the East switched Churchill's target. He had been entranced with a a tentative outline plan to destroy the railway line linking the Swedish iron ore mines with Norwegian ports. It was an idea by which a large profit might be obtained at small cost, but the essence, underlined by planners, was speed. The memorandum was marked not later than October.

It was from this modest suggestion that after many months the Norwegian adventure slowly grew to its dismal, and inevitable, debacle. The mining of the Norwegian leads was agreed upon. Land and sea operations were argued. The objectives changed frequently; the object lost clear definition. The forces available, or to be made available, were never welded into a coherent whole, nor was a combined operation of land, sea and air clearly conceived.

Meanwhile Hitler had been provoked to occupy Denmark, invade Norway, and confront our forces with an opposition against which they could not hope to prevail without a major operation, properly led, and adequately supported in the air. At the same time only the fortunate chance of a Finnish surrender to the Russians in mid-March saved Britain from a desperate and useless involvement in Finland that would not have availed Finland, and might well have added Russia to our enemies.

As a war reporter Churchill could state with precision the prime causes of failure, but he was also a principal executant:

'now after all this vain boggling, hesitation, changes of policy, arguments between good and worthy people unending, we had at last reached the simple point on which action had been demanded seven months before. But in war seven months is a long time.'

Yet it was his own reluctance to abandon an idea, however dated, his own insistence on examining and re-examining all possibilities, that had contributed greatly to the delay, to the unwieldy growths on the original simple idea, and the final obscuring of objectives and object. Moreover, the strategic blunder of insisting on Narvik, and clinging to it after it had become militarily untenable and useless, was his. Trondheim had offered better opportunities. Finally half-hearted efforts aimed at Trondheim, via Namsos and Andelsnes petered out, and on May 1, 1940, the King of Norway embarked for England with the Norwegian gold reserve and the remains of the force.

The comments of the official historians properly provided the last word:

'The measures adopted to secure the traditional object of decisive encounter at sea, which was not secured, deprived us of our best chance to restore the position on land.'

A laconic summing up does justice to the failure:

'Because we had no airfield we could not mount the air strength to secure one; because we had no proper base we could not assemble the men and material to capture one; because we had no consistently held objective no one of our objectives had been achieved.'

Nine days later the Germans had invaded Holland, and their armour, having moved without difficulty through the Ardennes and crossed the Meuse, was sweeping like an avalanche through France. In Britain Churchill had become Prime Minister and Minister of Defence. The power was his. 'Churchill was a man cast in the heroic mould,' wrote General Fuller, 'a berserker ever ready to lead a forlorn hope or storm a breach, and at his best when things were at their worst.'

Churchill and the British people had arrived at a climacteric together, a trysting place, an appointment with destiny. It was a simple act of recognition. In all the excitements, the alarums and excursions of those crowded days, it seems, looking back, striving to feel again the essence of those hours, that he and they alone were calm, confident, knowing their hour. The tremendous political excitements, the fervent and anxious comings and goings, the urgent manoeuvres behind the scenes, the committees sitting in the Carlton Club and the Reform, passed them by.

In the midst of the storms surging round him Churchill maintained an unusual calm, a remarkable decorum. He defended his colleagues, shouldered their blame, and scorned to defend himself. His champions were numerous, and he was aware of them, as though from afar off. He heard old Lloyd George rise to his defence, and Duff Cooper's eloquence. He heard the words of Cromwell in Amery's mouth, and Greenwood speak for England. But he, Churchill, had become England.

Yet in those first nine days of May it often seemed that only a miracle could save Churchill for his rôle. The Norway fiasco had been the last paragraph in a long chapter of botcheries, as Lloyd George described them. Chamberlain, plain for all to see, save only himself, was not the man for war, but he clung to his position with the tenacity of a man shipwrecked clinging to a life raft. He could not lead. He could not arouse the people to the perils they must face; nor could he call them to the sacrifices they must make. At last the enemy had done that.

Leo Amery wrote in his diary:

'It is all terrible, and must mean the end of the Government and perhaps of Winston as well. But if so, what on earth have we left? My only conclusion is that we cannot do worse than with the present lot, and that if we only change often enough we shall end by finding someone who can lead us to victory.'

Amery himself might have been that man. Beaverbrook thought so, and he was acceptable to the Labour leaders. He was also a strategist, and would have made a fine Minister of Defence. But it is doubtful if Amery had any real illusions about that: he wanted the job, but in his heart he knew that no man would run in double harness with Churchill. His memory went back a very long way. Churchill had lived for power. The stage would be his, and his alone.

So Amery worked for Churchill, and so did Clem Davies, the Liberal leader, persuading the cautious Attlee not to oppose. Both men were untiring, knowing that there would not be a reward. But above all Brendan Bracken, the most devoted of Churchill's men, bore his master's torch boldly throughout the country, swaying the doubters by his eloquence and faith.

In the last meeting at No. 10 Downing Street Churchill stood with Lord Halifax at the Prime Minister's side confronting Attlee and Greenwood, knowing well the intense dislike and distrust these men had for Chamberlain. He spoke quietly, paying tribute to Chamberlain's stewardship. For himself he said nothing. He allowed Halifax to excuse himself from the Premiership. He would not serve under Halifax,[1] and this was known to the Labour leaders. Bracken had made sure of that. So Churchill stood calmly at ease, one with himself, waiting for the ceremony to arrive at its fore-ordained conclusion.

At six o'clock on the evening of May 10th Churchill saw the King, and returned at once to the House, his temple, with his offering of blood, toil, tears and sweat.

Seldom has a burden sat less heavily upon a man. He had plucked the sword from the stone as easily as it were embedded in butter. It was his. He would wield it alone.

---

[1] *My Political Life*, Vol. III p. 371.

## CHAPTER XVII

❧❀❦

FEW who lived through those summer days of 1940 in Britain are likely to deny that when Churchill took command it was like emerging from a long and debilitating illness, when suddenly the body awakens, becoming one with its spirit, knows itself pristine, and torpor falls away from mind and limb.

Nothing that went before; nothing that comes after may sour the taste of that brief honeymoon. In that summer Churchill saw himself mirrored in the pool of England. The nation gave him back his image. No man was an island, for each one had become a part of a larger life, and Churchill its symbol. He was its voice, clothing its secret longings in romance and glory, awakening echoes, stimulating its passions, giving it an illusion of Elizabethan splendour. He could move himself to tears, or laughter; chuckle, or rasp himself to scorn or rage, and with careful mispronunciation load simple words with ridicule or loathing.

Were he sentimental, England was sentimental with him; was he brave, all were brave. Perhaps never before had such an actor declaimed upon such a stage, his entry uncontrived, yet a miracle of timing, his audience, soon embracing more than half the world, spellbound. For a little while he fanned the bright flame of a candle lit by Elizabethan England. Churchill put words to the music of war. He did not choose the great themes, for these, Dunkirk and the Battle of Britain, were already on the conveyer belt of war, challenging him to his part. He responded gloriously. Dunkirk of itself, and in its nature, gave him strength, consummating his marriage, for even without a Churchill England would have responded to that triumph and disaster. It is in such trials that the people have always discovered the best in themselves.

Shakespeare, in those days, seemed to live again to storm our ears,

> Come the three corners of the world in arms,
> And we shall shock them . . .

And if this, we knew, to be the bombast of a David without a stone to his sling, no matter, for England had become in truth—or illusion,

> This royal throne of kings, this scepter'd isle,
> This earth of Majesty, this seat of Mars,
> This other Eden, demi-paradise;
> This fortress, built by nature for herself,
> Against infection, and the hand of war;
> This happy breed of men, this little world;
> This precious stone set in the silver sea,
> Which serves it in the office of a wall,
> Or as a moat defensive to a house . . .

Through the months when invasion was a genuine expectation the 'moat' held, and stirred by Churchill such a heritage became a simple truth, an old currency reminted. Never before had words proved such potent instruments of war. They were more deadly than the sword, the ammunition in fantastic profusion of friends and foes, flowing inwards and outwards, and for many purposes. But they were also two-edged. While Hitler's demagogy inspired the Germans, they helped to consolidate England's will to win, and Churchill's words, so stimulating to ourselves, cemented the resolution of the enemy to fight on, beyond defeat, to the bitter end.

Words were also potent in a different context, for it became a war in which conferences were, in the final analysis, as General Fuller has remarked, more decisive than battles.

Churchill's words, fortunately, may be separated without great difficulty from his deeds, yet his words and deeds were baked together in the same hot oven. In June 1940, while tragedy overwhelmed France and the smoke rose from the bonfires burning the archives of the Quai d'Orsay, Churchill, 'Crowned like a volcano by the smoke of his cigars' indulged his imagination to the dismay of his hosts.

'Until one in the morning he conjured up an apocalyptic vision of war,' wrote Paul Baudouin. 'He saw himself in the heart of

Canada directing, over an England razed to the ground ... and over a France whose ruins were already cold, the air war of the New World against the Old dominated by Germany.'[1]

He had begun the bombing of Germany in May, like a boy in a glasshouse throwing stones, unable to resist, in his frustration, in his desperate hunger for action, from throwing something. And there was no other powerful means of hitting back. Stimulated by Lindemann and Arthur Harris he embraced a bombing policy that in his heart he hated, and which grew to vast proportions, consuming between forty and fifty per cent of the war production of Britain.

'The Fighters are our salvation, the Bombers alone provide the means of victory,' he wrote.[2]

And no man can measure the starvation effects on other battlefields, on the great battlefield of the Atlantic where the war was nearly lost and won, in the Middle East, and in Malaya.

'But, for a long time, he continued to believe that the war would be won by aircraft,' wrote Sir John Kennedy. 'So sure was he of this that the bombing policy of the Air Staff was settled almost entirely by the Prime Minister himself in consultation with Portal, and was not controlled by the Chiefs of Staff.'[3]

At the same time he steadfastly denied that the army might 'play the primary rôle in the defeat of the enemy'.

Nevertheless, America was the overwhelming card with which he proposed to fill his Royal Flush. His firm resolve from the outset was to bring the United States into the war, and he had promised the President at all costs to preserve the Home Fleet.

His confidence that the United States would come to Britain's aid was unshakable. 'They are moving into the war by sentiment,' he said to Kennedy at Dytchley. 'I could make out a very strong case to show why it would pay America to keep out.'[4] Certainly there was no sentiment for them in business and they would have scooped the financial pool. Britain's entire

[1] From the Private Diaries of Paul Baudouin, Secretary to the French Cabinet.
[2] *The Second World War*, Vol. II.
[3] Kennedy, *The Business of War*.
[4] Ibid.

accumulated wealth in the United States, standing at some $5,000,000,000 was swiftly drained to pay for essential supplies at enormously inflated prices on a 'Cash and Carry' basis.

In August 1940 Britain yielded the first of her sovereign rights in exchange for fifty obsolete destroyers, and Admiral Leahy, at that time US Ambassador to Vichy, was jubilant. It was a harsh deal, and Winant wrote:

'It was a great thing for sovereignty over British Territory to be surrendered to another power—the first action of its kind for 300 years.'

The pains of this loss to Britain are clear in the US Ambassador's full text. But to Churchill the United States was his maternal home, his other country, and these were stakes he must be prepared to lose in order to coax America fully into war. This aim dominated his thinking throughout 1940 and 1941, and in this light many of his early deeds must be judged, notably his attack on the French Fleet at Oran, and the abortive attack on Dakar. For Roosevelt, with all his ignorance of foreign affairs, was a former Assistant Secretary of the Navy, and therefore 'sensitive to the danger of German power being established in Africa'.[1] Churchill harried the President with 'pointed little reminders' throughout 1940 and 1941, arousing him to the danger of the French Fleet becoming available to the enemy:

'the control of West Africa would pass immediately into their [enemy] hands . . . and also affect Dakar and of course thereafter South America.'[2]

In fact, however, Churchill's action at Oran had thrown Vichy France into the arms of Germany.

Again, after the disaster in Greece, Churchill telegraphed Roosevelt: 'You alone can forestall the Germans in Morocco.'[3] At the same time he confided his hopes to Smuts. He knew well Roosevelt's domestic difficulties, but he would not rest (of course, he would never rest!) until he had the United States completely committed.

[1] Pamela N. Wrinch, Dept. of Gov. Boston Univ., *The Military Strategy of Winston S. Churchill.*
[2] *The Second World War*, Vol. II.
[3] Ibid.

Meanwhile, with France defeated Churchill welcomed de Gaulle to Britain as the Constable of France, an act of inspired recognition. Perhaps very few would have seen, then, in that sombre, austere man, junior in rank, coming in poverty, a refugee destitute of men and arms, and soon to be condemned to death by Vichy, the living spirit and slender hope that France might live again. The Americans, on the other hand, regarded de Gaulle with ill-disguised irritation, for he confronted them with a truth they would have preferred to deny. He remained for a long time, even after the Japanese attack on Pearl Harbour, the doubtful leader of the 'so-called' Free French, and the occupation of the French Islands off Newfoundland was denied to him as long as possible. Cordell Hull seemed to see de Gaulle through the wrong end of a telescope, as well as upside down.

The truth is that the Americans were deeply shocked by the fall of France. It defaced an image stemming from Lafayette, and they would have been much less surprised to see Britain vanquished, and less hurt. But for Churchill's American blood they would not have given Britain a good chance throughout 1940. It was their ambition to liquidate the British Empire, of which they puritanically disapproved and greatly envied. As Amery remarked, the ghost of George III still lingered, and it was Roosevelt's strong desire to put all British Colonies under trusteeship. Meanwhile they dallied with Vichy, and snubbed de Gaulle.

But Churchill and de Gaulle were concerned with the fundamental problems of survival; all else must wait. De Gaulle himself bore the United States attitude with dignity, observing that they 'bring to great affairs elementary feelings and a complicated policy'. He saw too, 'the ambition of Roosevelt to make law and dictate right',[1] and was aware, as Amery later put it, of

'the ruthless determination with which, both during the Second World War and afterwards, they [USA] made acceptance of their principles the condition of political and economic support....'[2]

It was Churchill's task, as he saw it, to attempt to inspire American confidence, and get all the aid he could. It gratified him to have become the 'Protector' of the embryo of 'Free France', and to know that in de Gaulle's eyes both he and his country

[1] General de Gaulle, *The Call to Honour*, 1940-42.
[2] L. S. Amery, *My Political Life*, Vol. III.

were a tower of strength. It was a strange partnership, and it is a tribute to Churchill's innermost nature that when all the skins were peeled away there at the core was an unblemished aspiration, not alone for power, but for true greatness. For de Gaulle was a kind of chalice, a mystic vessel in which the soul of France found sanctuary, to rise again, as it were from the dead. He was utterly dedicated, not to himself, nor to power, but to an idea of 'Glory', even if it may be a delusion, but of such a nature as to change the course of history.

While de Gaulle rallied Free France round him from four meagre rooms overlooking the Thames Embankment, Churchill, a stone's throw away, sat on a pinnacle of power no Englishman since Cromwell had ever assumed for himself.

## II

There were some who saw the hand of a benign Providence in the fact of Dunkirk. Before it could be grappled into a dance of death with the enemy the British Army had been hurled out of the ring, miraculously to survive. The appalling spectre of attrition that had haunted the survivors of the First World War was laid, and disaster turned into triumph. Much valuable equipment, the product of Hore-Belisha's ministry, had been abandoned to the enemy. Nine destroyers and scores of little ships had been lost, and twenty-three destroyers had limped into port for repairs. But nearly 200,000 men, no longer raw by virtue of this adventure, had been scooped up from the open beaches to be re-equipped, re-fashioned, and to provide the hard core of new British Armies, to fight again.

By this fortune the future became singularly uncomplicated. There was little room for manoeuvre. There would be time for Britain to remember that she was a maritime power, and that by the time the enemy had digested his conquests, the existence of Britain must threaten 3,000 miles of enemy-held coastline, open to unpredictable attack at scores of points. Through the months the ring would be tightened round Europe from the Eastern Mediterranean to the North Cape.

But the immediate business was to survive, and Churchill's immense buoyancy of spirit and belligerence banished all other possibilities from the public mind. Disaster, however ominously near it at times appeared to those at the head of affairs, seldom entered the heads of the people. The entry of Italy into the war forced British shipping to the long haul round the Cape, and confronted the defenders of Egypt and the Nile Delta with an enemy fired with grandiose ambitions and outnumbering them ten to one. At the same time the enemy U-boats operating in the Atlantic had begun to arouse memories of 1917, threatening the slender lifeline with the arsenal of the United States. The island was clearly beleaguered, and invasion appeared imminent through the months of summer.

In these circumstances the strategic and tactical blunders of the year seemed almost trivial, and even the hard-driven planning staffs understood the temper of their driver, and forgave him his rashness. Doubtless, when the first excitement had begun to wear off, there would be breathing space for the hard strategic and tactical planning out of which alone victory and peace might might come.

Meanwhile Churchill's first sorties into the field of military command had been ominous. On May 20th he had urged the army to 'furious unrelenting assault', a feat of which the French Army was incapable, at a time when the waterlines might have been held, and would have assuredly gained valuable time. Thus Churchill 'cast away the remaining chance of blocking the enemy by a defence based on natural obstacles that still lay across his path', wrote Liddell Hart.

Moreover, the only Tank Brigade available to Britain in France had shown its mettle by punching the enemy to a halt at Arras. This, coupled with King Leopold's brave decision to remain with his troops, and inspiring the Belgians to hold out until May 28th, made Dunkirk possible. Yet Churchill condemned the Belgian King.

Swiftly there followed the attack on the French Fleet at Oran, and soon afterwards the ill-starred, inadequately appreciated and planned, expedition to Dakar. The strategic importance of Dakar would have been difficult to over-estimate, and risks were justified. In the event only a miracle could have brought success, and as Anthony Irwin wrote,[1]

'no British-inspired combined operation was ever again launched with such complete political disregard for the minimum requirements of the military forces involved.'

[1] *RUSI Journal*, August 1961.

And had the landings been pushed forward after the Naval defeat,

'the consequences might well have been as grave as those suffered by the Allied Armies at Suvla Bay, Anzac Cove, or Cape Hellas.'[1]

The root of the trouble was that in England,

'The idea that any French commander outside the group of "Vichy Traitors" could willingly co-operate with the Germans was beyond comprehension.'

The tragic disintegration of France and the lack of morale of her troops at home had warped the judgment of observers. It did not seem to occur even to de Gaulle that overseas units and Colonial troops might give their loyalty to their local commanders.

Throughout 1940 opportunities for offensive action were severely limited, and could nowhere be decisive. The great actions were defensive in the skies above the Island, and in the waters of the Atlantic. In December Churchill boldly reinforced Wavell in the Middle East despite the meagre reserves available in Britain. A breathing space had been gained, and the future had begun to lose its look of pure chance. Steadily the industrial might of the United States was being lured into the struggle. It was a time for the patience and steadfast courage of a Marlborough, focusing his mind clearly on strategic objectives, completely aware of the tactical planning and timings which alone would make success possible, and refusing to be lured, or tempted by wayward chances, one hairsbreadth from his course.

At home General Sir Bernard Paget was competently training new armies. In the Middle East Wavell's foresight and organization had provided a sound base from which his generals could move with confidence to shatter Italian dreams. In the Far East the defences of Singapore and Malaya demanded urgent attention, the first priority after the defence of Britain itself. And, miraculously, there might be time.

Unhappily Churchill revealed none of the characteristics of his great ancestor. The fact that strategy and tactics must go hand in hand, and that both must be thoroughly worked out from

[1] *RUSI Journal*, August 1961.

every angle, was, in the words of one of his chief planners, 'quite beyond Winston'. He indulged in 'delectable' strategic visions with no idea whatever how these might be attained, and his 'rage', to quote a senior member of his staff, 'was wonderful to behold, when some horrible staff officer pointed out that the idea might be grand, but for some stupid reason, such as there was not enough transport to keep the divisions in shot and shell, impossible'.

It was not wonderful to experience, as Sir John Dill and his staff discovered. No argument, however unanswerable, counted at all.

In December 1940 however Churchill was still the Churchill all those who had worked for him and struggled for him knew. His zest was boundless, but he was still rewarding simply to strive for, glorying in his position. There were no signs, nor would there be, of mellowing. His body had, of course, grown older, but he was able to conserve his energies from 1940 onwards. Vast horizons opened before him, and wherever he looked on his maps, 'ships and men all were his'. He was the Captain-General, the Supreme Commander, and at his whim men would move against the enemy by land and sea and in the air, from the North Cape to the Nile. That was his ground, within the embrace of his outstretched arms, his battlefield. The Far East was visible only out of the tail of an eye. 'I confess,' he wrote, 'that in my mind the whole Japanese menace lay in a sinister twilight.' And because of that, Singapore was doomed, and the great ships, the *Prince of Wales* and *Repulse*, and much more besides, would be lost.

Even as First Lord of the Admiralty there had been severe limitations upon his actions; now, there was none, save only the possible. He could order life to his own timings, and all must march to his personal tune. He could sleep through the afternoons, and talk far into the nights with men who had laboured, often in difficult conditions, through twelve or more hours of the long days, and whose nerves were strained. Whenever a thought occurred to him someone was at hand to take it down. Without moving a muscle, other than those necessary for speech, he could preserve every idea, good, bad or indifferent, entering his head. He ceased to evaluate in his own mind, even briefly. There was no need to wait for morning, to seek pencil or paper, or tape recorder. He had simply to utter.

Planning staffs were deluged hour after hour, day after day, with memoranda, and finally bludgeoned mercilessly. Yet he would have been startled, shocked and incredulous, had he been informed of this. He was no more—and no less—merciless than a child in the nursery. As it was, spates of telegrams, more deadly than his demands on his planners, poured forth directly to his commanders in the field, his lieutenants everywhere.

There was no possible means of abating this torrent. General Sir John Dill, perhaps the finest soldier in Britain, had replaced Ironside as Chief of the Imperial General Staff after Dunkirk, but Churchill did not like him. It was said that he never went against his Chiefs of Staff, but he never went with them, or heeded advice. Sir John Dill, too weak in protest, was steadily worn out and destroyed.

Nothing could be discarded without explanation, argument, 'proof' of impracticbility. 'Even then he was not done,' wrote a senior member of his staff.

'He would set his brain to work out further suggestions as to the general way (never in detail) how this might be overcome, and the staff officer would then have to work out a lot more facts and figures, in which W. was quite uninterested, being interested only in the conclusion. If this last was hopelessly unfavourable to his plan, he might easily produce another, and yet another, set of ideas to which no one could give an immediate answer....'

Early in January 1941 the planning staffs from the C.I.G.S. downwards knew that they were no longer being driven, but ridden by an 'Old Man of the Sea' with a stranglehold. He had arranged to see the efforts of the Joint Planners at least at the same time, if not before their own Chiefs, and had short-circuited the usual channels, demanding immediate and direct information from any source. It was only the loyalty of the Joint Planners to their Chiefs and the General Staff at the War Office that saved them from becoming poor relations.

Perhaps the heart of the tragedy was that the harassed planning staffs were unable to give their full attention to the initiation of ideas and plans of their own based on the strategic and tactical realities. In January Sir John Dill had received a detailed appreciation and plan from Amery, which at least justified Amery's short-lived ambition that he might be Minister of

Defence. A few months earlier, while at home the planners were fully occupied with batting to Churchill's furious bowling, Brigadier Eric Dorman Smith had published a carefully prepared appreciation and plan of campaign based on the strategic and political realities, and by which British power might have been preserved.[1]

It would have been impossible to implement any plan that did not arise first in the mind of Churchill, already becoming deeply committed to the bombing offensive which would deny long-range bombers to support the operations in the Far East, the Middle East, and in the Battle of the Atlantic. In his heart, I believe, Churchill hated the bomber, for nothing could be further away from the charge at Omdurman, and the kind of warfare he had dreamed and lived from the nursery. Yet the attrition of the First World War haunted him, and the bomber would (Harris and Lindemann assured him) prevent a repetition of that. There would be no need for a Second Front. It was the bomber, therefore, that squatted upon the mind of Churchill, frustrating him, for having accepted this means of defeating Germany, no other major offensive effort was possible. He could not calm his mind, nor master his ambitions to emulate both Marlborough and Napoleon, and to consider those many actions that were both possible and profitable.

Nevertheless until 1941 Churchill had worn the garment of power with a kind of innocence, a veritable St George for England, undivided within himself, and entirely unself-conscious. And then, suddenly, as some said, he 'realized his power', as though before he had been unaware of it, as Adam had been unaware of sin. It had to be used, to be demonstrated, to the full.

It may be true to say that to become aware of power is at once to begin to lose it, to feel its limitations, to be anxious to try out this invisible, and terrible instrument, to be corrupted.

The old Churchill was gone, that infinitely fascinating and various man, always formidable, usually unpredictable, invariably exciting and rewarding to work with and for, even at rare moments seeming lovable. A tyrant reigned in his stead, ominous, moody and threatening, browbeating Sir John Kennedy, and snarling at Sir John Dill about the Middle East, where Wavell and his generals had won their magnificent victories, 'What you need out there is a Court Martial, and a firing squad!'

[1] *RUSI Journal*. India, January 1941.

In that January of 1941 he was already resolved on his expedition to Greece, to snatch away from Wavell in the hour of triumph in North Africa, the very means of victory. It was an extraordinary and tragic metamorphosis.

Churchill's mercurial and childlike moods, as well as his grave limitations as both strategist and tactician have been amply commented upon by many, notably Lord Alanbrooke, General Sir John Kennedy, and Lord Ismay.

'He is a mass of contradictions,' wrote General Lord Ismay, 'he is either on the crest of a wave, or in the trough: either highly laudatory, or bitterly condemnatory: either in an angelic temper, or a hell of a rage: when he isn't fast asleep he's a volcano. There are no half measures in his make-up. He is a child of nature with moods as variable as an April day . . .'[1]

Compare this with Napoleon's dictum:

'The first quality in a general in chief is to have a cool head, which receives exact impressions, which never gets excited or dazzled by good or bad news. . . . There are men who, due to their physical and moral constitution, create a picture out of everything . . . nature has not intended them either to command armies or to direct the grand operations of war.'

It would be difficult to discover a man, if Napoleon's formula is a guide, less equipped than Churchill for the enormous task he had grasped for himself.

'He is like a child that has set his mind on some forbidden toy,' wrote Sir John Kennedy. 'It is no good explaining that it will cut his fingers or burn him. The more you explain, the more fixed he becomes in his idea. . . .'

And again:

'Everybody realized and appreciated Churchill's great qualities. But there were few who did not sometimes doubt whether these were adequate compensation for his methods of handling the war machine. . . .'[2]

[1] Quoted by John Connell in *Auchinleck*.
[2] Kennedy, *The Business of War*.

He was, in the words of another, like the general manager of a vast railway network who insists on playing with the toy railway in the garden. But perhaps most dangerous of all was his conviction 'that he had inherited all the military genius of his great ancestor, Marborough', and that he was incapable of seeing 'a whole strategical problem at once. His gaze always settles on some definite part of the canvas and the rest of the picture is lost,' wrote Field Marshal Viscount Alanbrooke.

It was in January 1941 that Harry Hopkins, the personal emissary of President Roosevelt, arrived to make his first contact with Churchill. He was at once impressed that whereas 'tranquillity prevailed' round Roosevelt,

'Churchill, on the other hand, always seemed to be at his command post on the precarious beachhead and the guns were continually blazing in his conversation; wherever he was, there was the battlefront—and he was involved in the battles not only of the current war, but of the whole past, from Cannae to Gallipoli.'[1]

Hopkins also remarked Churchill's working habits, and that he

'was getting full steam up along about ten o'clock in the evening; often after his harassed staff had struggled to bed at 2 or 3 a.m. they would be routed out an hour or more later with an entirely new project for which a plan must be drawn up immediately....
'Churchill's consumption of alcohol ... could be described as unique, for it continued at quite regular intervals through most of his waking hours without visible effect on his health or on his mental processes.... His principal aides—General Sir Hastings Ismay, Professor F. A. Lindemann, Commander Charles Thompson, Sir Desmond Morton, J. M. Martin, and Bracken—made no attempt to keep up with him in consumption of champagne, whisky and brandy (he detested cocktails), and they had to summon reserves of energy to be able to keep up with him in work.'[2]

It may have been that the visit of Harry Hopkins expanded Churchill's horizons of power beyond England, wherein he alone

[1] *The White House Papers*, Vol. I.
[2] Ibid.

was Caesar, to the prospects of an infinitely greater throne upon which he might sit jointly, or even not sit at all.

'I suppose you could say that I've come here to try to find a way to be a catalytic agent between two prima donnas,' Hopkins told Ed Murrow.

Hopkins then believed, wrote Sherwood,

'that the formidable egos of Roosevelt and Churchill were bound to clash, and, in anticipation of that he said: "I want to try to get an understanding of Churchill and of the men he sees after midnight."'[1]

### III

The men Churchill 'saw after midnight' were beginning to worry many of those in high places, who were not in frequent personal contact with this inner group.

'Often I wondered during the war where Churchill got some of his more outrageous strategic ideas from,' wrote General Sir Bernard Paget. 'He much preferred to seek and take advice from people like Cherwell, Harris, Wingate . . . than of the C. of S.'[2]

Such fears were becoming widespread and many were especially distrustful of Beaverbrook. Churchill produced his own ideas, and was never open to the ideas of others unless he could be induced to believe they were his own. He loved an audience, especially if it could be relied upon to applaud at the right moments. The mutter was heard that the 'Croney war' had replaced the 'Phoney war'.

General Paget, whose great task was to prepare the British army at home for its future rôle, and to plan the cross-channel re-entry into France under the code name of 'Skyscraper', found Harris and Lindemann particularly disturbing.

'Harris was not interested in anything but bombing. He had no use for airborne troops and I was never allocated more aircraft

[1] *The White House Papers*, Vol. I.
[2] Private correspondence.

than for the lift of a battalion, though in "Skyscraper" I envisaged five airborne divisions (two British, three US) as in fact we had available on D-Day. Harris told me it was useless to drop troops since they did not explode when they hit the ground. He had the full support of Churchill for his reckless bombing."[1]

Cherwell (Lindemann) was believed to be the real danger by many. Of him, Paget wrote:

'Cherwell was an amateur who thought that military problems could be solved by means of a graph. He produced an album of of them which gave Churchill an almost childish pleasure to peruse. But when I told him how misleading some of them were, he did not show me any more!'

Finally Churchill never forgave Paget for his refusal to assault and capture Trondheim in 1941 without air cover.

Yet in the main Churchill could be deterred from his most outrageous military ideas by sustained opposition from the Chiefs of Staff. He would rage furiously, often for three days, only to emerge suddenly 'all sweetness and light'.

'Fortunately for us,' Paget commented, 'unlike Hitler, he did not in the last resort go against the advice of the C. of S.'

Far more dangerous than any personal influences was the map room in 'The Hole', next to Churchill's sleeping quarters beneath the Cabinet Offices. Often in the small hours of the morning he would rise from his bed, and enter the map room alone, a holy of holies, and gaze upon the war maps, and the dispositions of all his forces. Here, alone in the night, he could stage his battles, not the campaigns of Marlborough, or Majuba Hill or Maiwand over again, as some believed, but new battles of his own.

The 'small boy of Anglo-American parents playing with soldiers on the nursery floor' was nevertheless alive in him. There were names to conjure with, arising out of a nearer past, out of those early jaunts with Asquith on the Admiralty yacht before the First World War. Valona, Pantelleria, Rhodes, the Dodecanese, all the furnishings of those exotic seas, the Adriatic, the

[1] Private correspondence.

Tyrrhenian, the Aegean, were spread before him, under his hands and eyes. Ideas concerning all of them sprang into his mind, demanded attention, and died hard.

Facing his maps he saw himself as a boxer, 'I have always thought,' he said, 'that the Western democracies should be like a boxer who fights with two hands and not one.' He continued to think in those terms, conceived and richly imagined in his lone vigils. He wanted to 'unroll the Nazi map of Europe from the top', and strike simultaneously in the Mediterranean. There was his decisive theatre of war. 'We should be able to rip at Hitler's mouth (France),' he told General Mark Clark, 'at the same time we are ripping at the Axis belly (Mediterranean).'

Before the 'Torch' landings in North Africa he wrote:

'If it had been in my power to give orders, I would have settled upon "Torch" and "Jupiter" properly synchronized.'

'Jupiter' was his plan for an attack against North Norway, 'to lay our claw on French North Africa and tear with our left at the North Cape'.

Churchill thought consistently on these lines, always to strike the enemy on the flanks, and to make the fullest use of sea power. But in the early days of 1941 he brooded darkly on the Middle East, lashing himself into a fury of frustration that would bring disaster upon many. Napoleon warned against the dangers inherent in browsing over maps. The area of the Middle East early in 1941 was especially dangerous, the flags indicating Army, Corps, divisional and other headquarters giving a false impression of the number of troops available. It seemed to Churchill that here was his striking power, and what was everybody doing? His long memoranda in early January, especially those printed in Appendix F to *The Grand Alliance*, reveal a growing frustration with the proportion of fighting troops to the 'tail'. The administration and 'two' sides of the Army in conflict gave cause for disquiet. He could not reconcile himself to the logistics of modern war, and that it required more and more men back to keep one man forward. When the outward bound convoys arrived in the Middle East there would be '370,000 men, on pay and ration strength. From this enormous force the only recognizable fighting military units are the following:'

Churchill then lists seven divisions, two of them incomplete, and one infantry brigade.

His exasperation grew steadily, and the desire to act became overwhelming. He changed the defence priorities, banishing the Far East into a 'sinister twilight', and advanced the Middle East in its stead. Since the inception of the Committee of Imperial Defence in 1904 the defence priorities slowly emerged as, the British Isles, the Far East, the Middle East, in that order.[1] In slightly more detail the Chiefs of Staff list in 1940 read:

i The British Isles
ii Malaya and Burma (covering India and Australia)
iii Persian Gulf (Iraq, Syria and Persia, if possible)
iv Gibraltar and Malta
v Delta Egypt

Churchill moved Delta Egypt into second place, and with the defence of the Island reasonably secure this became his focus.[2] From early January he subjected General Wavell to a stream of directives, exhortations, demands and inquiries adding up to a sustained pressure without parallel in military history. He was resolved to go to the aid of Greece whether 'the gallant little Greeks' wanted aid or not, whether indeed it was possible or not.

The idea, distasteful to the Greeks, was sheer military lunacy, especially in the context of the time. Wavell's generals were on the eve of complete victory. On January 10th Churchill telegraphed Wavell:

'Destruction of Greece (by Germans) will eclipse victories you have gained in Libya, and may affect decisively Turkish attitude, especially if we have shown ourselves callous of fate of allies. You must now therefore conform your plans to larger interests at stake. . . . Nothing must hamper capture of Tobruk, but thereafter all operations in Libya are subordinated to aiding Greece. . . . We expect and require prompt and active compliance with our decisions, for which we bear full responsibility. . . .'

For two months his mind leapt about in the region like a grasshopper. Valona appeared to fascinate him,

---

[1] Not to be confused with policy. See Hankey, Vol. I. 'A policy? . . . The politicians would sooner have a tiger. . . .'
[2] Directive, April 28, 1941, and D.M.O.'s comment. See Kennedy, *The Business of War*.

'All accounts go to show that a Greek failure to take Valona will have very bad consequences....'

He believed it was more important for the Greeks to take Valona than for Wavell to take Benghazi,

'It is quite clear to me that supporting Greece must have priority after the Western flank of Egypt has been made secure.'

But there is neither a hope, or intention, in the Greeks to attempt to take Valona. Churchill convinces himself that it will be the key to determining the attitude of Yugoslavia. He is full of 'ifs',

'If Yugoslavia stands firm and is not molested, if the Greeks take Valona and maintain themselves in Albania, if Turkey becomes an active ally, the attitude of Russia may be affected favourably....'

Then all at once Valona is forgotten. Meanwhile on February 7th General O'Connor gained a spectacular victory at Beda Fomm, and Wavell telegraphed for permission to press on to Tripoli. On the night of February 11th Dill, supporting Wavell to the hilt, saw

'the blood coming up his (Churchill's) great neck and his eyes began to flash.
'I gave it as my view,' said Dill, 'that all the troops in the Middle East are fully employed and none are available for Greece.'[1]

The Prime Minister lost his temper, and on the following day, the 12th, telegraphed Wavell:

'We are delighted that you have got this prize (Benghazi) three weeks ahead of expectations, but this does not alter, indeed it rather confirms, our previous directive that your major effort must now be to aid Greece and/or Turkey. This rules out any serious effort against Tripoli ... concentrate all available forces in the Delta in preparation for movement to Europe....'

[1] Kennedy, *The Business of War*.

It is an extraordinary situation, for Churchill was fully aware of the importance of Tripoli, as his desire to capture Pantelleria two months earlier showed. Yet, after Beda Fomm, with O'Connor roaring to press on, the Naval Force H, consisting of *Renown, Malaya, Ark Royal, Sheffield* and supporting destroyers, set off to bombard Genoa, when by joining with Admiral Cunningham off Tripoli enemy reinforcement could have been cut off, and Rommel would not have been heard of in the Western Desert.

While all this was going on Wavell's generals were unaware that victory was about to be snatched from their hands. On February 7th Brigadier Dorman Smith, Wavell's emissary, agreed with General O'Connor to continue the pursuit of the enemy to Tripoli, and on the 8th Dorman Smith saw General Sir Henry Maitland Wilson at Barce, finding him in complete agreement. Dorman Smith at once telegraphed Wavell from Tobruk, and pressed on himself back to Cairo. 'I saw Wavell about 10 a.m. on February 11th,' wrote Dorman Smith. 'He said, "Glad to see you," and waving his hand at his office hung with new maps of Greece, "you find me busy with my spring campaign."'

That was the day in England when Churchill told Dill:

'What you need out there is a Court Martial and a firing squad.'

The die was cast, and nothing, not even a last minute change of heart by Churchill, could halt the tragic march of events. On March 6th he telegraphed to Anthony Eden in Cairo:

'Difficult for Cabinet to believe that we now have any power to avert fate of Greece unless Turkey and/or Yugoslavia come in, which seems most improbable.... We do not see any reason for expecting success, except that of course we attach great weight to opinions of Dill and Wavell.... We must liberate Greece from feeling bound to reject a German ultimatum.... Loss of Greece and Balkans by no means a major catastrophe for us provided Turkey remains neutral. We could take Rhodes and consider plans for *influx* (descent on Sicily or Tripoli). We are advised from many quarters that our ignominious ejection from Greece would do us more harm in Spain and Vichy than the fact of submission of Balkans, which with our scanty forces alone we have never expected to prevent.'

Whatever this may be it is not leadership, and Churchill was in complete command.

'I believe,' he wrote, 'I had as much direct control over the conduct of the war as any public man had in any country at this time.'

It was too late. The British force had sailed for Greece when Eden received the Prime Minister's telegram. Eden had been a poor and dangerous counsellor, for he lived in a rarified political air of his own, incapable of relating political ends to military means, a condition that would bring him to ruin. Of course, the soldiers should have stood firm, but they were subject to sustained political pressures against which, in the end, they could not stand.

The US Ambassador heard Wavell remark to Dill:
'I hope you'll be sitting on my court martial, Jack.'
Why Wavell gave in remains for most of us a mystery.[1] Four precious British divisions, the very means of complete victory in the desert, were on their way to experience a second Dunkirk on the shores of Greece, followed by a devastating blow upon them from the airborne enemy in Crete. 15,000 men were lost with all their valuable equipment, and the naval resources in the Mediterranean were dangerously extended in the work of rescue. Through the port of Tripoli Rommel built up his army to bring Wavell's successor to the brink of disaster before the brilliant strategic victory of First Alamein turned the tide.

In July Churchill sacked Wavell, and made a bitter attack upon him which deeply shocked Sir John Dill, and many others. But Dill was to be the next victim. He was already a very tired man. His long letter to General Auchinleck, Wavell's successor in the Middle East, and destined to be Churchill's third great victim, is revealing of the situation, and is printed in full in *Grand Strategy*, Vol. II.[2]

If the tragic events unfolding from January 1941 until the autumn of 1942 were a true guide to the character and deeds of Churchill he would be in danger of being convicted as a megalomaniac and a tyrant. He was, in fact, neither of these, although both ingredients were powerful in his make-up. Before examining

---
[1] John Connell's biography will doubtless supply the answer.
[2] HMSO, also cited in *The Business of War*, Kennedy.

the sound and practicable strategic aims which his restlessness and tactical itch have obscured, his sacking of Wavell, Dill and Auchinleck demand attention.

'I think that the first time I ever deeply disliked Winston and realized the depths of selfish brutality to which he could sink, was when he told me not only that he was getting rid of Wavell from the Middle East, but why,' wrote one of the Churchill's staff.

The 'why' was simply to show his power: if he could sack Wavell he could sack anyone. Churchill prowled about his room like a disgruntled lion, growling away to himself. He had never forgiven Wavell for a personal telegram after the evacuation of Somaliland, but Wavell had produced an unanswerable case for a fighting retreat, and carried it out brilliantly. Churchill demanded to see the casualty list, and remarked that the losses of the troops involved 'only' totalled 1,800. This made him feel that Wavell had in some way cheated him, and he sent off a furious cable accusing him of breaking his word, and much else besides.

When Wavell replied briefly, 'Butchery is not the mark of a good tactician' Churchill raged. He knew that his accusations against Wavell were unforgivable, yet Wavell 'forgave' him without a thought: it would not have occurred to him to bear resentment. This aggravated Churchill's sense of injury. Moreover he was far from callous in the matter of casualties, and did all he could to avoid them.

I owe the following brief analysis to one who was an associate of all those concerned over many years. Churchill heartily disliked any person whose personal character was such that he could not avoid, most unwillingly, feeling respect for that person. His overwhelming desire to dominate resulted in a feeling of inferiority in regard to anyone who was not in the least afraid of him, nor ever would be, and in whose character he could not detect a flaw. Were there such a flaw, Churchill would attack it, whatever his victim's other qualities.

Sir John Dill, for example, was a man whose personal character was as high as Wavell's, but he was greatly disturbed by Churchill's unjust criticisms. Churchill took full advantage of this weakness and destroyed him.

Naturally, to Churchill, any such person as Wavell must be

either a rival or in a position to do him some potential harm. That such a person would never dream of doing Churchill harm never entered his thought processes.

('If you have power, you use it,' would be his unalterable expectation.)

Wavell was an adult of stature; Churchill was the eternal child. It would have been inconceivable to Wavell to consider himself a hero; Churchill was always playing a hero's part, identifying himself with Marlborough and Napoleon on the one hand, and d'Artagnan or Hornblower on the other. Undoubtedly the part of the 'swashbuckler' suited him best. He 'adored funny business', and delighted in the company of Mountbatten and Wingate, rating them more highly than the greatest of his commanders. He wanted to replace General Sir William Slim and make Wingate Commander-in-Chief, Burma.[1] In his telegram sent from Ottawa to this effect he referred to Wingate as the 'Clive of Burma', and said that 'everyone was calling him that' when, in fact, no one was. Providence intervened in Wingate's death, and Slim survived.

## IV

In July 1942 Churchill had reached the nadir of his Supreme Command. 'Prime Ministers need luck as well as Generals; Prime Ministers who usurp the rôle of Commanders-in-Chief need a double dose of it,' wrote Sir John Kennedy. It seemed to Churchill that he had been short of luck. He had refused to shed so much as a particle of the immense load he carried. Power, for him, was indivisible. He held it. He walked alone.

The efforts of Lord Hankey, with his very great prestige, of R. G. Menzies, the Australian Prime Minister, had failed to move him one millimetre from his course, or to cause him to modify his position. He had faced a storm building up in Parliament and weathered it with ease. In the Upper House Lord Chatfield had supported Hankey:

'It is much better to do away with the extraordinary position as it had grown up and to merge it into the War Cabinet, so that the brains of several men can be applied to the task of making these very vital decisions, which are going to affect us for all

[1] Ottawa, 1944—Since confirmed by Official History.

time, instead of the burden resting so largely on a single pair of shoulders, however broad, however able, whatever confidence we may have in these shoulders. . . .'

After the fall of Singapore and the loss of Malaya he had been accused of losing the Empire in 100 days; and what would happen in the next 100 days? Hore-Belisha demanded. The account was heavy. He had sent the great capital ships, *Prince of Wales* and *Repulse*, to their doom. The Japanese were rampant in the Pacific, and the German Afrika Corps led by Rommel was rampant in the Western Desert. Churchill must have known in his heart that with his Greek tragedy, and by throwing away Tripoli, he had let them in, and his obsession with Rommel had grown into a blend of admiration and fear. He gave way to 'protracted, and often calculated rages,' as Hopkins observed, noting in July that, 'The Prime Minister's powers of emotional endurance were now being tested to the limit after six months of mortification.'[1] It had been longer than that. Since the new year of 1941 he had lived at a high pitch of emotional intensity, and very little had gone right.

Churchill had been at the White House with President Roosevelt when the news of the fall of Tobruk had been brought to him, and the next day he saw the New York newspapers with their 'flaring headlines', ANGER IN ENGLAND, TOBRUK FALL MAY BRING CHANGE IN GOVERNMENT? CHURCHILL TO BE CENSURED.

Tobruk had become a symbol in the public mind, a symbol with which even Churchill had become entangled. Its loss should not have been a surprise to him, for it had been agreed in Whitehall, but the news filled Churchill's bitter cup to overflowing. He described himself as the unhappiest Englishman in North America since Burgoyne—but Burgoyne had been made a scapegoat after Saratoga, and Churchill would provide scapegoats other than himself. He would have done better (at least in his own mind) to compare himself with George Germaine.

But the power to direct the main war effort was moving rapidly out of Churchill's hands, as he had known it would after his meeting with President Roosevelt at the Arcadia conference in January. The Combined Chiefs of Staff Committee had been formed. In due course the United States would take command.

[1] *The White House Papers*, Vol. II.

He had hastened to dub himself the President's First Lieutenant. The nature of the war had changed mightily. In June 1941 Hitler's tremendous assault upon Soviet Russia had changed the shape of the future, and six months later the Japanese attack on Pearl Harbour had precipitated America into the conflict.

None of this had eased the lot of Britain in the first half of 1942; rather had it increased the burden upon her, for she still fought the Battle of the Atlantic virtually alone, and provided more aid to Russia than she received. In July Churchill knew that he had but a little time to go, and he would make what use of it he might. He wanted one last prize of his own: Rommel must be destroyed. Nothing else would suffice.

'During this month of July, when I was politically at my weakest and without a gleam of military success, I had to procure from the United States the decision which for good or ill, dominated the next two years of the war.'

He fumed at his position, and when Roosevelt's emissaries, General Marshall, Admiral King and Harry Hopkins, arrived at Prestwick aerodrome on July 18th, and went straight through to London without calling on the Prime Minister at Chequers, as he had asked, he 'threw the British Constitution at me with some vehemence', wrote Hopkins. He did his best to placate the Prime Minister, to persuade him that 'no rudeness had been intended'; the President had instructed them to go direct to London to confer with Eisenhower ... in Churchill's England![1]

In that gloomy July Rommel was at the gates of Egypt with a wealth of glittering prizes almost, it seemed, within his grasp. In dire emergency, General Auchinleck, leaving his Chief of Staff to act for him as best he could in Cairo, had gone into the desert with his Deputy Chief of Staff, Major-General Dorman Smith, to take command of the weary army his generals had brought within a hairsbreadth of utter defeat and despair. These two men were probably the finest team to command an army in the Second World War, combining 'great powers of leadership united with a brilliant and original intellect'.[2] The presence of Auchinleck, his appearance of indestructible calm, put heart into troops who had imagined themselves at the end of the tether.

[1] *The White House Papers*, Vol. II.
[2] Barnett, *The Desert Generals*.

At a place called El Alamein, in July 1942, was fought one of the great decisive battles of the Second World War, and there Auchinleck and his army halted Rommel's march to the Nile Delta, and saved Egypt.

'It is, perhaps, the measure of the Prime Minister's distress,' wrote Major-General Dorman Smith, 'that he was at that time, and still remains, quite unable to assess the strategic importance of the July Battle of El Alamein.'

For Churchill nothing less than the swift and total destruction of Rommel and the Afrika Corps would satisfy his need.

But for Roosevelt it was otherwise. He saw clearly the decisive nature of the struggle in the Middle East, and his directive to his Chiefs of Staff in London, dated July 16, 1942, must rank as one of the most important of the war. It reads, in part:

7. If SLEDGEHAMMER is finally and definitely out of the picture, I want you to consider the world picture as it exists at that time and determine upon another place for US troops to fight in 1942.
8. The Middle East should be held as strongly as possible whether Russia collapses or not. I want you to take into consideration the effect of losing the Middle East. Such loss means in series:
    (i) Loss of Egypt and the Suez Canal.
    (ii) Loss of Syria.
    (iii) Loss of Mosul oil wells.
    (iv) Loss of the Persian Gulf through attacks from the north and west, together with access to all Persian Gulf oil.
    (v) Joining hands between Germany and Japan and the probable loss of the Indian Ocean.
    (vi) The very important probability of German occupation of Tunis, Algiers, Morocco, Dakar and the cutting of the ferry route through Freetown and Liberia.
    (vii) Serious danger to all shipping in the South Atlantic and serious danger to Brazil and the whole of the East Coast of South America. I include in the above possibilities the use by the Germans of Spain, Portugal and their territories.
    (viii) You will determine the best methods of holding the Middle East. These methods include definitely either or both of the folowing:

(a) Sending ground forces to the Persian Gulf, to Syria and to Egypt.
(b) A new operation in Morocco and Algiers intended to drive in against the back door of Rommel's armies. The attitude of French Colonial troops is still in doubt.

(Point ix concerns Japan, and I omit it here: author.)

(x) Please remember three cardinal principles—speed of decision on plans, unity of plans, attack combined with defence, but not defence alone. This affects the immediate objective of US ground forces fighting against Germans in 1942.

(xi) I hope for total agreement within one week of your arrival.[1]

No testimony could more clearly underline the decisive nature of the struggle at El Alamein. Coupled with the great US naval victory at Midway, it marked a turning point of the Second World War,

'but it was left to the enemy to put Auchinleck's achievement in true proportion and be first in paying him due tribute,' wrote Liddell Hart. 'An ironical sequel to his removal was that the renewal of the British offensive was postponed to a much later date than he had contemplated, and an impatient Prime Minister had to bow to the new High Command's determination to wait until satisfied that preparations and training were complete, even though the delay meant leaving the initiative to Rommel.'[2]

During the first week in August Churchill visited Auchinleck's Eighth Army headquarters in the desert. It was a sombre visit, for his purpose was to get rid of his great general together with his senior staff, Lieut.-General T. W. Corbett, who had held the fort in Cairo during the Commander-in-Chief's absence directing the battle, and Major-General Dorman Smith, whose plan had paved the way to victory, and whose appreciation would form the basis for final victory.

Auchinleck lived simply like his troops. Fried bread, bacon and sausage eaten in a kind of 'meat safe' to keep out the flies was not much to Churchill's taste, and it must be doubtful whether

[1] *The White House Papers*, Vol. II.
[2] *The Tanks*, Vol. II.

he grasped the nature of desert warfare. It was a long way from Omdurman. He barely said a word, and left to find better fare with Air Vice-Marshal Coningham and his senior officers of the Desert Air Force.

'The food had all been ordered from Shepheard's Hotel,' Churchill records. 'A special car was bringing down the dainties from Cairo.... This turned out to be a gay occasion in the midst of care—real oasis in a very large desert.'[1]

Auchinleck's insistence on keeping his tactical headquarters close to Alamein and his corps commanders, had irritated Coningham, and it is probable, Dorman Smith thought, that 'the last nail was driven into Auchinleck's coffin on that day'. Coningham was a man of power after Churchill's own heart, and Auchinleck's dedicated soldierly austerity irked him sorely.

In November Rommel was trapped between the overwhelming force built up through the months by the British, and by the Anglo-American landings in the rear. With his supply route gravely threatened he fought one of the great losing battles of his life at Alamein, inflicting heavy losses in men and destroying six hundred tanks, a total three times greater than the German strength.

'The new (British) commanders were fortunate, for they came upon the scene just as the balance was swinging decidedly in the British favour,' states the Official History.[2]

Throughout England the bells rang out. At the same time the Russians launched a tremendous counter-offensive against the German Sixth Army under Von Paulus at Stalingrad, and the grand climacteric of the Second World War had come.

So, at the last, Churchill had his Pyrrhic victory. He had found some solace in the great bomber offensive well under way since May, with the '1,000 bomber' raid on Cologne. The raids would fail signally to undermine civilian morale, but in the front lines of battle soldiers feared for their wives and families, knowing that the homelands they sought to preserve by their courage were being destroyed in their rear. While the German armies

[1] *The Hinge of Fate.*
[2] Playfair, *The Mediterranean and Middle East,* Vol. III. HMSO.

went down to utter defeat before the Russians, a power vacuum was forming in the heart of Europe.

Henceforth the direction of the war moved out of British hands, and beyond her power greatly to affect. For the United States, coming back into the old world from the new, an era of vast opportunities and tremendous responsibilities lay ahead, barely to be foreseen. For Churchill there remained the most difficult part he had ever had to play. He played it bravely, but the forces arrayed against him were too strong, and he perceived their courses too late. The power to shape the destinies of mankind in general, and of Europe in particular, was clearly in new hands.

## CHAPTER XVIII

CHURCHILL's attitude to war, and his conduct of war, derived from his broad historical sense. It was not for nothing that he discoursed interminably on war, from 'Cannae to Gallipoli', as Hopkins observed, for war was his political life. He knew war for what it was, the ultimate political weapon, a breaking off of diplomatic contact, and a resort to the intimate contact of violence. Peace and war were not distinct states of man. The business of politics, extending into the international field, was constant throughout the whole history of mankind, the arts of war and peace, growing, as Byron sang, in the Isles of Greece, confined within the framework of the possible. This was the music of life, a tremendous symphony 'Pathetique' compounded of the movements of war and peace; peace providing the weaving of the strings, the sweet music of flutes; war the thunder and beat of drums, the roar of brass.

Thus to regard peace as some distinct and positive state of man, existing of itself, was misleading, and must lead to war and peace becoming meaningless and without form, an end of politics, catastrophe. For Churchill to regard war as anything but a political instrument, guided by intelligence, a means of gaining political ends, or maintaining a position when all other means had failed, would be absurd. Indeed, it would have been absurd for any European, Eurasian or Asiatic citizen of the 'old' world, to hold otherwise. But in the 'new' world it was different. The United States had enjoyed a brief and unique history, peculiarly its own and broadly untouched by international political struggles. Its knowledge of warfare derived from its self-liberation from the burdens of vassalage to the England of George III, and a civil war of great intensity through which it had welded its several states into one nation, one people, however various.

Thus the United States of America had come to regard peace as a natural condition of mankind, and war as a crime and

L*

disaster. The great spaces and areas for development within its wide frontiers absorbed its energies, satisfied its passions, and fired its imagination. In its great Military College at West Point the study of war was therefore divorced from politics. If war should break out, the 'generals' would take over (under the Supreme Command of the President of the nation), extinguish the conflagration, and punish the criminals responsible. And this attitude was strengthened by a puritan background, leading men to accept a simple conception of 'good and evil', right and wrong, black and white. Such attitudes, if a situation should arise to bring the United States into war on a world stage as a dominant force, would inevitably write an end to political history as it had been from the beginning.

Churchill's attitude to warfare was, in my view, wholly sound, and his regrets for the passing of an old order, when war had been, as he called it 'a gentleman's game', revealed a nostalgia for a more civilized attitude to a barbaric side of life. His own brief experiences in Colonial wars and punitive expeditions, retaining (at least on the winning side!) illusions of 'glory', tended to strengthen his backward look, and at the same time urged him to attempt to reconcile these with his knowledge of the slaughter of 1914-18. In short to build a bridge between one kind of war and another.

In *The World Crisis, 1915* he wrote:

'Battles are won by slaughter and manoeuvre. The greater the general, the more he contributes in manoeuvre, the less he demands in slaughter. The theory which has exalted the *bataille d'usure* or "battle of wearing down" into a foremost position is contradicted by history and would be repulsed by the greatest captains of the past. Nearly all the battles which are regarded as masterpieces of the military art, from which have derived the foundation of states and the fame of commanders, have been battles of manoeuvre in which very often the enemy has found himself defeated by some novel expedient or device, some queer, swift, unexpected thrust of stratagem. In many such battles the losses of the victors have been small.'

Further down the same page he observes,

'The distinction between politics and strategy diminishes as the point of view is raised. At the summit true politics and strategy are one. *The manoeuvre which brings an ally into the field is as serviceable as that which wins a great battle.'* [My italics.]

The influence of Marlborough is clear, and the suggestion that he was fighting Marlborough's battles over again is not without truth. This could be a virtue if one lived in the right century, but it is probable, I believe, that Churchill dwelt too much in the eighteenth century, the age of reason, and the wars of kings. In those days wars were fought by mercenary armies, and the great commander was at pains to preserve them. Thus Frederick of Brunswick was conceded first place in his time for his almost bloodless victories in Holland.

Dumouriez brought this era to a close with his cannonade at Valmy, which led Goethe to remark on the battlefield:

'From this place and from this day forth commences a new era in the world's history, and you can all say that you were present at its birth.'[1]

One hundred years later Marshal Foch commented:

'The wars of kings were at an end; the wars of peoples were beginning.'[2]

Napoleon had introduced the 'peoples' as war's plentiful cannon fodder, and Napoleon also greatly influenced Churchill's thinking. Yet war, although increasingly lethal, retained its clear political content, formalized by Karl von Clausewitz in the second quarter of the nineteenth century:

'The subordination of the political point of view to the military would be contrary to common sense, for policy has declared the war; it is the intelligent faculty, war is only the instrument, and not the reverse. The subordination of the military point of view to the political is, therefore, the only thing which is possible.'[3]

The arrival of the United States upon the World War stage re-

---
[1] Creasey, *The Fifteen Decisive Battles of the World.*
[2] Ibid.
[3] *On War,* Vol. III.

versed the military and political and made of war a 'lethal game' played to a vast audience, with the 'stars' cheered and applauded, and 'big hitters' like Patton regarded as dangerous versions of 'Babe Ruth', the MacArthurs idolised. It was an infectious disease.

Thus recognizably in 1917 a new era had begun, and in the autumn of 1942 this era was sealed beyond a doubt. The thread of politics no longer threaded the needle of war, and the needle could not repair: it could only destroy. This dreadful fact was underlined in two words at the Casablanca conference in January 1943, when President Roosevelt announced that the 'object' of the gigantic struggle was nothing less (or more!) than the 'Unconditional Surrender' of the enemy. There were no 'terms' to ponder. Nothing. A fight to the finish.

The point has been laboured, but never too much. Many strategists and historians have underlined this turning point in the affairs of men, and Captain Liddell Hart was among those very few who realized that there would be '. . . . millions more lives needlessly sacrificed, while the ultimate peace merely produced a fresh menace and the looming cloud of another war'.

At once the growing opposition to Hitler inside Germany was silenced, and the leading figures who had striven to establish contact with Britain since the beginning, were reduced almost to despair. Goebbels was jubilant, and Soviet Russia knew that if she could win the race to Berlin, her most ambitious politico-strategic dreams would be fulfilled. But there was not to be a race, and for Britain it could only mean disaster. The Turks and Spaniards, at least, were without illusions, and all Churchill's hopes of bringing Turkey into the war were shattered by the unconditional surrender statement. In November 1942, Jordana, the Spanish Foreign Minister, had said to Sir Samuel Hoare, 'If Germany did not exist, Europeans would have to invent her.' It was clear to many that if Germany were destroyed the vacuum of Central Europe would be filled by Soviet Russia, and 'All the defeated countries would become Bolshevik and Slav', as the Turkish Prime Minister told Churchill.

It is only possible to guess at Churchill's reasons for his outwardly calm acceptance of the President's almost casual statement. Some say that he shared fully in the President's view; others that he was taken completely by surprise in that euphoric haze of brandy and cigar smoke attendant upon such meetings;

still others that he did not take them at their face value, for, in a sense, they are meaningless. The words, one feels, should have acted as a cold douche.

As the toboggan of war gathered speed towards the inevitable pause marked by Hiroshima and Nagasaki, by way of the destruction of Germany and the vast fire raids upon Tokyo, Churchill would say that he would put things right later on. But there would be no later on, for him.

Yet it is impossible to acquit Churchill of being attracted to the view of war as a lethal game, and himself as a star performer, courting the cheers of the multitude. He shared President Roosevelt's obsessional hatred of Hitler, and unlike Stalin, he could not say, 'history shows that the Hitlers come and go, but the German people and the German state remain'.[1] Moreover he was blinded by the immense industrial power of the United States, and saw himself as a partner in the most powerful alliance the world had ever seen. For a little while the Yankee in him dominated the Marlborough.

II

Churchill's agonizing restlessness, which led him to bludgeon his planning staffs, and harass his advisers, has obscured the clear and coherent purpose of his strategy. He saw Britain clearly as 'the great amphibian', and sought to use sea power to the greatest possible advantage. Secondly, he sought allies by every manoeuvre open to him.

'A maritime state is a neighbour of every country accessible by sea,' Sir Eyre Crowe had said before the First World War, and Churchill agreed with that estimate, even when in 1912 he assured the Germans that 'we cannot menace the peace of a single Continental hamlet'.[2]

Churchill's problem was that he had too many neighbours. All the seas and indentations of that vast coastline within the Mediterranean, and the immensity of the Atlantic seaboard of Europe (and even of Africa), seemed to bristle with opportunities he was loath to miss, and unable to take. No enemy could hope to provide defence everywhere, and Britain's maritime strength, properly applied, could force the enemy to move large forces to

[1] Cited by Major-General J. F. C. Fuller in *The Conduct of War*.
[2] *The Times*, February 10, 1912.

vulnerable points he believed to be threatened. In *The World Crisis* Churchill had elaborated the delectable possibilities.

'Moreover, the selection of these points would remain a mystery to the enemy up to the last minute. He would no doubt learn that the expedition was preparing, and that transports had assembled. But whether they would go North or South could not be known till after they had put to sea. Against such uncertainties it was impossible to prepare with precision beforehand. The amphibious assailants , , , need not decide till the last moment. . . . They might pretend to be going North, and then go South. . . . They might practise every feint and deception known to war. . . .'

One of his difficulties in dealing tactically with his American ally was to overcome their distrust of his 'feints' and 'menaces', especially in the Mediteranean. In fact Churchill's strategy in the Second World War was almost exactly the same as he had desired in the first, and had lacked the power to apply. Again in *The World Crisis, 1915*, he wrote:

'The essence of the war problem was not changed by its enormous scale. The line of the Central powers from the North Sea to the Aegean and stretching loosely beyond even to the Suez Canal was, after all, in principle not different from the line of a small army entrenched across an isthmus, with each flank resting upon water. As long as France was treated as a self-contained theatre, a complete deadlock existed, and the Front of the German invaders could neither be pierced nor turned. But once the view was extended to the whole scene of the war, and that vast war conceived as a single battle, and once the sea power of Britain was brought into play, turning movements of a most far-reaching character were open to the Allies.'

Churchill then named the 'three salient facts' of the war situation in 1915:

'. . . first, the deadlock in France, the main and central theatre; secondly, the urgent need of relieving the deadlock before Russia was overwhelmed; and thirdly, the possibility of relieving it by great amphibious and political-strategic operations on either flank.'

In the middle of 1941 the situation was comparable. The 'deadlock' was real enough, and so was the need to relieve pressure on Russia. France was no longer the 'central theatre' in the First World War sense, but neither was the bulk of British manpower being swallowed up in an appalling stalemate of attrition.

This was Churchill's theatre of war, and all the rest remained in a 'sinister twilight', subject to after-thoughts, usually disastrous. He had to see his battlefield whole, within the embrace of his arms, from the Eastern Mediterranean to the North Cape. The rest was 'behind his back'. In the First World War Japan had been an ally; in the Second, Churchill relied upon the United States to take care of her. At his first meeting with President Roosevelt at Placentia, Newfoundland, he had been promised that 'the United States, even if not herself attacked, would come into the war in the Far East and thus make final victory sure'.

Together they had agreed an embargo against Japan, denying her oil and machine tools, and freezing her credits, in the resolve to force her to war. 'Our joint embargo is steadily forcing the Japanese to decisions for peace or war,' Churchill wrote in early November 1941, and on the 25th of the month General Marshall and Henry Stimson, Secretary of War, discussed the position with the President in the White House. The President expected an attack almost at once, 'The question was how we should manoeuvre them into the position of firing the first shot without allowing too much danger to ourselves.'[1]

When, on December 7th, the Japanese struck with devastating effect at Pearl Harbour, 'it completely solidified the American people', and Churchill had gained his great ally. 'I went to bed,' he wrote, 'and slept the sleep of the saved and thankful.'

Inasmuch as the defeat of Germany and Japan were assured, he had reason to feel both saved and thankful, but he was soon to discover that it was no part of Roosevelt's intention to preserve British Imperial power east of Suez. On the contrary, the American President became convinced of a community of interests existing between the United States and Soviet Russia, and Churchill would be the 'Cinderella' in a partnership loaded heavily against him. At the great conferences of the three powers, Roosevelt found time to discuss world affairs with Stalin in private. By the time they reached Teheran in November 1943, 'The US Chiefs of Staff . . . prepared themselves for battles . . . in which

[1] US Congress. Hearings before the Joint Committee in the Pearl Harbour attack.

the Americans and Russians would form a united front.'[1]

In a private talk with Stalin, 'Roosevelt referred to one of his favourite topics, which was the education of the peoples of the Far Eastern colonial areas ... in the arts of self-government. ... He cautioned Stalin against bringing up the problems of India with Churchill, and Stalin agreed that this was undoubtedly a sore subject. Roosevelt said that reform in India should begin from the bottom and Stalin said that reform from the bottom would mean revolution.'[2]

On being assured by Stalin that he need have no fear about the Pacific 'in gratitude and without Churchill's knowledge ... discussed with Stalin the question of a common front against the British, and proposed that he and Stalin should back Chiang Kai-Shek against Churchill on the question of Hong Kong and Shanghai. ...'[3]

Churchill's major strategic blunder in reversing the Far East and the Middle East in the defence priorities, could not be undone. It had arisen out of his 'most remarkable failing', noted by Alanbrooke, of being unable to 'see a whole strategical problem at once. ... This failing is accentuated by the fact that often he does not want to see the whole picture especially if the wider vision should in any way interfere with the operation he may have temporarily set his heart on.'[4]

This appears to explain Churchill's attitude conclusively, and his intense concentration upon the war theatre of his choice.

### III

From the outset Churchill's search for allies was a binding thread running through the fabric of his strategy, and powerfully influencing his tactical ideas. The three allies he sought with unremitting energy were Soviet Russia, the United States of America, and Turkey, and Russia's *alliance de convenance* with Nazi Germany did not modify his intentions. When Nazi Germany invaded Russia in June 1941, and six months later Japan attacked Pearl Harbour, his main search was over. He continued to woo Turkey almost to the end.

[1] *The White House Papers*, Vol. II.
[2] Ibid.
[3] Fuller, *The Conduct of War*.
[4] Bryant, *The Turn of the Tide*.

In seeking Russia and Turkey as allies, and even in seeking co-operation with Vichy France whenever opportunity offered, Churchill was thinking of war in its traditional European pattern. The United States itself was viewed primarily as the great industrial power and arsenal, rather than a military power ready to commit armies in Europe. He did not regard her enlistment of 10,000,000 men with enthusiasm. In this thinking he had not properly grasped that the new ingredients of Communism and Fascism would make of it a religious war with new complications, and new portents. For it would not be a war of a 'true faith' against an abominable heresy, clearly realized, but a clash of two heresies, fundamentally opposed, yet with superficial likenesses, and each more, or less, abominable according to the point of view of the outsider. Of the two Fascism inspired the greatest obsessional hatred in capitalist democratic societies because they knew that it was a cancer ever present in their own bodies, whereas Communism, equally distasteful, was alien and would require revolution for its establishment.

Out of the inevitable clash between these two faiths could emerge the triumph of what is loosely termed democracy, a true faith in the value of the individual and the freedom of man, expressed in religious and ethical values by Christianity.

It must be evident now—I believe it was evident then—that the only possible rôle for Britain in such a struggle was to hold the 'ring', to avoid deep entanglements with either 'devil', while seeking to prevent the overthrow of one by the other by all means in her power, and attempting to ensure that they would cancel each other out. Thus she would work to the end that out of the exhaustion of 'purgatory' a more 'liberal' condition might grow and prosper: in short, that the devils would be 'cast out'.

In such terms, Roosevelt's embrace of Soviet Russia, his remarkable faith in her idealism and good 'democratic' intentions, at least in the international field, is the only excuse for 'Unconditional Surrender'. If he decides to destroy one devil and preserve the other, he must convince himself either that the one he preserves is not a devil at all, or able to be redeemed, moreover, one of which he is not afraid.

For Churchill there was no such easy way out. At Casablanca in January 1943, when unconditional surrender was announced as the Allied object, he was caught in a period of aberration and ambivalence, between his eighteenth century 'Marlborough' conceptions of war and the nature of Europe, which was deeply rooted, and the new flames his Yankee blood had lit in him. With his strategic bombing policy, his one potent weapon, he, too, had embarked upon the destruction, not merely of Hitler and Nazism, but of Germany itself and her civilian population. He had embraced Russia, almost with indecent haste, while loathing but not fearing her creed. He had supplied her military needs from the outset at frightful cost, against all the advice of his Chiefs of Staff, and had failed to understand the strength of his position.

Long before Casablanca it had become vital to formulate a clear and unequivocal 'Object' of war. It meant a great deal of honest thinking and heart searching: it meant clearing away an immense undergrowth of emotions, defining clearly a faith, and the kind of society worth preserving, or seeking to establish, with the lives of men and the wealth of nations. Such a faith could not be expressed by an 'Atlantic Charter', a meretricious and 'high falutin' piece of jargon, of which the best that can be said is that it might have been 'well meaning', and very properly became acutely embarrassing to its sponsors.

Casablanca began a new era, more decisive than any battle. Up to that time Churchill, in almost unquestioned control, had with much justification pursued at first a policy of survival, and thereafter had sought to establish a non-losing, if not a clear-winning, position. In that context I want to consider briefly his search for allies.

Churchill's desire for an alliance with Soviet Russia had turned his thoughts towards the Baltic long before the outbreak of war.

'A British fleet in mastery of the Baltic,' he wrote, 'would hold out a hand to Russia in a manner likely to be decisive upon the whole Soviet policy and strategy.'[1]

He had visualized such an alliance,

'implemented by a British battle squadron joined to the Russian Fleet and based on Cronstadt.'[2]

Four days after taking office as First Lord, Churchill had in-

[1] *The Gathering Storm.*
[2] Ibid.

structed his naval planners to work on plan 'Catherine'. In his minute, Appendix G, *The Gathering Storm*, dated September 12, 1939, he wrote:

'The arrival of this fleet in the theatre and the establishment of command would probably determine action in the Scandinavian States. They could be brought in on our side. . . .'[1]

Indeed, without the co-operation of Soviet Russia, not at once to be expected, since the manoeuvre was a bait, a Swedish port would be an essential requisite of the operation, and in the event of an alliance with Russia, a supply route would be opened. Yet he had risked war with Russia in his desire to intervene in Finland.

Similarly much of Churchill's Balkan preoccupation, and his pursuit of Turkey, was inspired by his search for an alliance with Russia. In a broadcast on October 1, 1939, he said:

'It cannot be in accordance with the interest of safety of Russia that Germany should plant herself upon the shores of the Black Sea, or that she should over-run the Balkan States and subjugate the Slavonic peoples of South Eastern Europe. That would be contrary to the historic life-interests of Russia.'

At that moment Soviet armies faced the Germans in the midst of Poland.

Churchill hoped that Russia would think on these 'rational' and historic lines, but he could not be sure. A few months later he developed this theme:

'Anyone can see how obnoxious, and indeed deadly, a German advance to the Black Sea or through Bulgaria to the Aegean must be to Russia. Fear only will restrain Russia from war, and perhaps a strong allied front in the Balkans.'[2]

'But,' he adds, 'we cannot count on this.'

When, six months later, Germany attacked Russia, Churchill was soon haunted by fears that Russia would make a separate peace, inspired by his memories of the First World War, and the

[1] *The Gathering Storm.*
[2] PM to General Ismay for COS *Committee*, January 6, 1941.

peace of Brest Litovsk. To forestall such a possibility, and to allay his fears, upon which the Russians played skilfully, he promoted the Murmansk convoys at the expense of urgent demands elsewhere, notably in the deadly Battle of the Atlantic, and sought to encourage his new ally by every means in his power. Even as late as September 1942 he dreaded to inform Stalin that the North African 'Torch' landings would mean a break in the convoys, and 'at one point he even suggested postponing "Torch" long enough to allow just one more convoy to be sent'. His desire was to open staff talks with the Russians on his longed-for North Norway operation, plan 'Jupiter', 'to help offset the effect on the Soviet Government of interrupting the convoys.'[1]

Churchill's tragic insistence on intervention in Greece may be traced in part to his desire to please Russia and lure the Turks. The Italian attack on Greece, and the German entry into Roumania and Bulgaria had stimulated his fears that the enemy would drive through the Balkans to the Aegean. It heightens the tragedy that Germany was on the very eve of launching 'Barbarossa' against Soviet Russia, and Churchill's intervention precipitated a German invasion of Greece she had not, otherwise, intended. By that his cup was filled. He had hoped also that British intervention in Greece might induce Turkey to join with Yugoslavia in defending the Balkans, but instead his suit with Turkey was fatally prejudiced. Geographically Turkey was compelled to a harsh realistic view, instigated by present fears rather than future hopes. When the time came she had no doubts whatever of the end meaning of 'Unconditional Surrender'. The last chance was lost that a supply route might be opened to Russia with Turkish aid, or even that an airfield might be made available to Britain.

Spain and Vichy were also unfavourably impressed at a time when it was feared that Spain might permit, or be unable to prevent, the passage of German troops. Earlier Churchill had hoped that British success in Cyrenaica might hearten Spain 'to fight for her neutrality'. Similarly he had hoped thereby to gain a bloodless victory in French North Africa.

On the last day of 1940 Churchill had sent a message to Marshal Petain:

[1] Dr Pamela N. Wrinch, Dept. of Gov., Boston Univ., *The Military Strategy of Winston Churchill*; and War Dept., Washington, D.C., *Strategic Planning for Coalition Warfare, 1941-2, US Army in World War II.*

'If at any time in the near future the French Government decide to cross to North Africa or resume the war against Italy and Germany we should be willing to send a strong and well-equipped Expeditionary Force up to six divisions to aid in the defence of Morocco, Algiers and Tunis.'[1]

On the 23rd of the month he had minuted General Ismay for COS Committee in similar terms, adding:

'We are willing to enter into staff talks with General Weygand, or any officers nominated by him.'

It irked Churchill that there were no French leaders ready to set up a French Government in North Africa. Surely there was an opportunity, 'the most splendid ever offered to daring men'. But the daring men of that kidney were already with de Gaulle, far from the infections of Vichy France. Even Wavell's victory at Sidi Barrani, of which Churchill had entertained great hopes, failed to evoke an echo in French North Africa.

These Churchillian assaults upon Vichy's neutrality were closely intertwined with his pursuit of the United States, and his constant attempts to arouse Roosevelt to the dangers to the United States of a German occupation of North or West Africa. As early as June 9, 1940, he had tried to stimulate American fears, and particularly to annul any false impression inspired by his great 'We shall never surrender' speech of June 4th. He telegraphed the Marquess of Lothian, British Ambassador in Washington:

'If Great Britain broke under invasion, a pro-German Government might obtain far easier terms from Germany by surrendering the Fleet, thus making Germany and Japan masters of the New World. This dastard deed would not be done by His Majesty's present advisers, but if some Quisling Government were set up it is exactly what they would do, and perhaps the only thing they could do, and the President should bear this very clearly in mind. You should talk to him in this sense and thus discourage any complacent assumption on United States' part that they will pick up the debris of the British Empire by their present policy.'[2]

[1] *Their Finest Hour.*
[2] Ibid.

This was his bargaining 'ploy' in the destroyer deal, for if the destroyers were sent Britain's chances of fighting on would be greatly improved. He then tried to lure America in to sending a force to Northern Ireland, and after the debacle in Greece his message to the President on May 4, 1941, is in the nature of a genuine *cri de coeur*:

'... if you cannot take more advanced positions now, or very soon, the vast balances may be tilted heavily to our disadvantage. Mr President, I am sure that you will not misunderstand me if I speak to you exactly what is in my mind. The one decisive counterweight I can see to balance the growing pessimism in Turkey, the Near East, and in Spain would be if United States were immediately to range herself with us as a belligerent power. If this were possible I have little doubt that we could hold the situation in the Mediterranean until the weight of your munitions gained the day.'[1]

Of course, it was quite impossible, and Churchill knew very well that the President would not have a hope of persuading Congress to war. Already the immense British losses of Merchant tonnage in the Atlantic had inspired 'Lend-Lease', an overt act of war in itself, and the denouement was near. In December the Germans had ground to a halt before Moscow, and Churchill was on his way to Washington for the first Anglo-American war conference, and the foundation of the Combined Chiefs of Staff.

The heavy burdens of the year had lifted for him and he felt sure of the 'all-conquering alliance of the English-speaking peoples'. The signal honour of addressing the US Congress awaited him, and he rose magnificently to the opportunity. He had never addressed a foreign Parliament before, as he said, 'Yet to me, who could trace unbroken male descent on my mother's side through five generations from a lieutenant in Washington's army, it was possible to feel a blood-right to speak to the representatives of the great Republic in our common cause.'

And, of course, he had far deeper roots than that on his mother's side. He felt quite at home, 'more sure of myself than I had sometimes been in the House of Commons', and perhaps there was a hint of something missed in his reflection that 'if my father had been American and my mother British, instead of the other way round, I might have got here on my own'.

[1] *Their Finest Hour.*

## THE WARRIOR

For a little while he seemed to have the best of both worlds, feeling genuine pride in the vast industrial and military potential of his 'second country', thrilling to the proposition that together, in union, they—his parent Nations—could face and challenge the world.

Triumphantly, as he wheeled the President in his special chair, he taunted his old friend Baruch, who had previously enjoyed the rôle, 'He's my baby now!' But the President was nobody's baby, and swiftly made it plain that he was the senior partner, a master politician, Commander-in-Chief by right of all the forces of the United States, moreover a Patrician of his country, a match for Churchill in guile if not in rhetoric, ruthless and resolute, confiding intimately in no man or woman, not even his wife, an enigma, neither realist nor idealist, a man as volatile as David Lloyd George, and perhaps not unlike that other master of Churchill in his political manoeuvres, and ambitions.

Those who have written directly about Roosevelt from years of contact, serving him in personal capacities, particularly in the drafting of his speeches, and thus having some access to his mental processes, as well as to his humours, reveal genuine admiration and devotion. Yet the inner man never appears. When he relaxes, and jokes with these 'his friends' he appears as a 'God' playing with the children. From the record of Sam Rosenman it does emerge that Roosevelt thinks in terms of 'people', that in a broad sense he 'loves' people, and seeks human welfare. The 'New Deal' must bear out the truth of this.

But it is, I think, from Robert Sherwood, also a close collaborator with Rosenman and Roosevelt as a speech-drafter, and the architect of Hopkins's *The White House Papers*, that one catches a glimpse of the man: he was, wrote Sherwood, 'gloriously unpompous', and a man of 'unconquerable confidence, courage, and good humour'.

'Frances Perkins has written of Roosevelt that he was "the most complicated human being I ever knew". Henry Morgenthau, Jr, has written: "Roosevelt is an extraordinarily difficult person to describe ... weary as well as bouyant, frivolous as well as grave, evasive as well as frank ... a man of bewildering complexity of moods and motives." Miss Perkins and Morgenthau were members of Roosevelt's Cabinet and knew him far longer and better than I did. But I saw enough of him, particularly in hours when he was off parade and relaxed, to be able to say "Amen!" to their statements on his complexity. Being a writer by trade, I tried continually to study him, to try to look beyond his charming and amusing and warmly affectionate surface into his heavily forested interior. But I could never really understand what was going on in there. His character was not only multiplex; it was contradictory to a bewildering degree. He was hard and he was soft. At times he displayed a capacity for vindictiveness which could be described as petty, and at other times he demonstrated the Christian spirit of forgiveness and charity in its purest form. He could be a ruthless politician, but he was the champion of friends and associates who for him were political liabilities, conspicuously Harry Hopkins, and of causes which apparently competent advisers assured him would constitute political suicide. He could appear to be utterly cynical, wordly illusionless, and yet his religious faith was the strongest and most mysterious force that was in him. Although he was progressive enough and liberal enough to be condemned as a "traitor to his class" and "that Red in the White House", he was in truth a profoundly old-fashioned person with an incurable nostalgia for the very "horse-and-buggy era" on which he publicly heaped so much scorn. He loved peace and harmony in his surroundings and (like many others) greatly preferred to be agreed with, and yet most of his major appointments to the Cabinet and to the various New Deal and War Agencies were peculiarly violent, quarrelsome, recalcitrant men. He liked to fancy himself as a practical, down-to-earth, horse-sense realist—he often used to say "Winston and Uncle Joe and I get along well together because we're all *realists*" —and yet his idealism was actually no less empyrean than Woodrow Wilson's. Probably the supreme contradiction in Roosevelt's character was the fact that, with all his complexity, he achieved a grand simplicity . . .'

But it must not be forgotten, and could never for a moment be forgotten by Roosevelt himself, that he bore ten pounds in weight of iron upon his legs, that in the midst of his virile maturity, he had been stricken with infantile paralysis, and that thereafter a dagger was sharpened within him, poised Heaven knows by what slender thread, to kill at a stroke. No man may know, I imagine, what depths of the psyche a man must plumb to survive such an ordeal, what new strengths—and weaknesses

—he must discover in and to himself by such a challenge, both awful and deadly.

Roosevelt was a man who dearly loved the sea, the earth, the sky, the very feel of living. He would often say, pinioned to his wheelchair by his iron limbs, and wishing to break off some interview, 'Well, I must run along now,' as if he would do, simply, that impossible feat, as other men.

Some say that they never saw cruelty so deeply written on a face when caught off guard—cruelty, it may be, bears the same countenance as pain, akin to pain. That he would have been a match for Churchill on equal terms, I believe, is sure, but the dice were heavily loaded in his favour. He envied Churchill his ebullience: Churchill envied him his power. Together they knew who they were, each a confirmation of the other's strength, or weakness. Kings consort with kings; presidents with presidents; tycoons with tycoons, only then do they truly know themselves in their condition. There is a communion, but no trust.

One thing is certain; neither Roosevelt nor Churchill was a match for the Oriental Potentate and real realist, referred to as 'Uncle Joe', the third member of this unique triumvirate.

In December 1941, whatever else may be true, or false, the most momentous alliance in history thus far was sealed in Washington, at the conference named 'Arcadia'.

## IV

From Casablanca to Teheran, by way of Washington and Quebec, Churchill fought a series of rearguard actions for British influence, prestige and power. These conferences, which fixed the grand strategy of the Second World War in its final phases, and decided the fate of Europe, spaced the year 1943 from January to December. At their end British power had become a tattered garment, and the terrible future belonged, inevitably, to the United States and to Soviet Russia. Europe, with all its tragic faults the greatest civilizing and balancing force in the world for 3,000 years, had had its long day.

In 1943 Churchill was in his seventieth year. He had been geared to a tremendous pace from the beginning, and although he thrived on the alarums and excursions of war, the pace had begun to tell. At this time, too, the strong and beneficent influence of Lady Churchill began to fail. He had been like a rocket, and once the fuse was lit there had been but one way and one speed to travel. Field Marshal Smuts, his old enemy and comrade, feared that he would not 'stay the course'. He was often ill, running temperatures that might lead to pneumonia, suffering occasional 'heart flutters', but refusing to lie down. Even when he did lie down his activities of mind were not greatly curbed; the cables and memoranda flowed on, an inexhaustible stream of exhortation and suggestion, probing every department of war. He had the constitution of an ox.

Churchill had at last shot up into the 'stratosphere' of power and world politics only to find two planets of overwhelming magnitude dominating that rarified firmament. His bargaining power had ebbed away through two exhausting years, and perhaps only a miracle could save his country a real stake in the future. His two companions in that remote wilderness of which he had dreamed from the cradle were devoid of sentiment. It could not be otherwise, for such is the nature of power.

Yet there was between the three at the top a curious intimacy, for only in each other could they see themselves reflected, confirming the reality of their positions beyond their frontiers.

In January 1943 when Churchill went into the grossly unequal contest he was always aware that his authority as Prime Minister of Britain did not match the authority enjoyed by the Dictator of Soviet Russia or the President of the United States. He was a delegate; they were not. In the industrial and military field Britain was nearing its peak, and must thereafter wane. The sombre shadow of diminishing returns loomed darkly, less than two years ahead, and the future beyond that point must be in pawn to the present. The inexorable logic of the logistics Churchill had always loathed, and which he had invariably omitted from his calculations, threatened Britain with exhaustion. For her, victory must come in 1944, or she might find herself powerless to influence the course of events. By the middle of 1944 British forces in Europe would be outnumbered in an ever increasing ratio by the forces of the United States, and her island would have become, perhaps irrevocably, a great military base of American Atlantic power. Beyond the middle of 1944, such authority as Britain might still possess by virtue of her military capability in the field to bring about a decisive victory, or greatly to influence the decisions of military command, would be impaired.

But for the United States, coming in a tremendous crescendo to her full strength, time was plentiful. And for Soviet Russia, at last with the upper hand over her enemies, and grinding them down with her immense weight and strength, patience was a necessity. Time was on her side, and the more deeply the Western Allies would be committed to a Second Front mounted through France and the Low Countries, the more certain she would be that her dreams would be fulfilled.

Before the meeting at Casablanca, and the fatal after-luncheon 'Unconditional Surrender' statement of President Roosevelt, there was a chance, however slight, not only for Britain, but for Europe. At Teheran in December of the year the Grand Strategy was determined, and thereafter pursued its course to the end. Thus Churchill's failure to challenge 'Unconditional Surrender' and to insist upon the formulation of a policy and a clear object, must be written down as the most tragic blunder of his life. Within a few months not only Churchill himself, but the great majority of responsible soldiers and politicians, deeply regretted it but could not change it. Only the Russians were jubilant for, as Herbert Feis[1] wrote, the United States had begun to woo them with ideals.

It is clear, I believe, that by the end of 1942 a change of note could be detected in the 'dynamo' driving Churchill. He had begun to weary, if not to mellow, and the battles he fought, even with his own Chiefs of Staff, had lost their original edge. In November 1941 he had appointed General Sir Alan Brooke as Chief of the Imperial General Staff in succession to Sir John Dill, and had, in a sense, found his 'Katherine Parr'. No more heads would fall on that level.

Sir Alan Brooke was a sensitive man, with much of the schoolmaster in his nature. He understood Churchill more by instinct than intellect, and discovered ways to coax, if not to manage, him. The combination of Brooke and Churchill in the military sphere at once eased the tensions at home, and convinced serious critics, notably Lords Hankey and Chatfield, that all might yet be well. With Brooke ever at his side, patient and firm, knowing when to meet anger with anger, and when to soothe, Churchill found the brake he had lacked since Mrs Everest. Moreover, Brooke could be as dogged as a mule in defence of a principle or vital issue, but he lacked the vision of a Dill or a Wavell, and while he was able to temper many of Churchill's wilder tactical

[1] *Churchill, Roosevelt, Stalin*, Princeton University Press.

ideas, he could do nothing to avert the calamitous Grand Strategy to which the Western Allies were ever more deeply committed.

At the Quebec Conference in August 1943, the US Joint Chiefs of Staff, backed by the President, were in no mood to bandy words with their British opposite numbers. They were resolved upon a showdown, to make the British understand once and for all that they were dictating the military pattern. From the moment that they had announced their decision at Arcadia of 'Germany first', they had been impelled by an urgent desire to come to grips with the enemy. They ignored the physical difficulties, the enemy sinkings of merchant shipping in the Atlantic at twice the British and American combined rate of building. They ignored the desperate shortage of landing craft, due not only to the demands on all fronts, but also to the determination of Admiral King to supply the Pacific at all costs and to starve the Atlantic. Moreover, those who believed, against much popular and official pressure and the violently expressed views of Admiral King, that Germany first was the correct policy, had cause to fear that if they didn't get into the fight in Europe speedily they might be forced to abandon that priority.

In 1942 they had accepted British assurances that 'Sledgehammer' was impossible, with bad grace, in spite of the almost total absence of US troops in Britain and that fact that the disastrous Dieppe raid represented very nearly the limits of British capability that summer. They believed that 'Torch' in November 1942 had not only prevented a cross-Channel attack in 1943, but had been deliberately calculated to do so by their Machiavellian allies. They saw the Mediterranean as the graveyard of all their hopes, and Churchill's 'soft under-belly' plans gave them the creeps.

When Churchill pointed out that the invasion of Italy, coupled with his threats and feints in the Balkans, immobilized many German divisions which would have been otherwise available on the Eastern Front, and that the defeat of Italy would make it possible to advance through the Ljubljana Gap upon Vienna, their worst fears were confirmed. They were ill-disposed to gather even the fruits of victory almost at once ripe in Italy, while they disputed, and then threw victory away by arguing too long with the Italians about the meaning, or lack of meaning, of 'Unconditional Surrender'.

The fact that the steady build-up of forces in Britain, and the constant invasion exercises, observable by the enemy, held upwards of sixty enemy divisions in readiness from Brest to the Skagerrack, leave alone Norway, and constituted a 'Second Front', with Italy and the Balkans a 'Third Front', convinced them of British perfidy, and determination to sabotage the cross-Channel attack upon which they had set their sights from the outset.

Convinced that they were being deliberately thwarted and subtly lured into the Mediterranean 'graveyard', they had used the threat of switching their main effort to the Pacific in an endeavour to keep the British in line. They had always been out-talked, for the British came to the conference tables with their arguments well rehearsed and their plans thoroughly worked out, and to be presented lucidly, drily and pedantically by Field Marshal Sir Alan Brooke. The United States Chiefs of Staff were, on the other hand, often at loggerheads among themselves; far from resolved on the course they wished to pursue. In addition, they believed that Churchill could and would get at the President behind their backs, and have his way.

The Americans came to Quebec in what they called 'a fish or cut bait' mood. There was, of course, some substance in their fears. The idea of a frontal assault upon the enemy across the Channel was not popular with Churchill, Smuts, or the King. Alan Brooke himself was not keen. They all hoped that their maritime strategy would prevail and enable them in the end to walk in almost without firing a shot. In addition, they had an aversion to holding troops inactive when opportunities offered, and to abstain from assaults on the enemy flanks for the sake of a future that must be problematical. In short, the British wanted to strike at targets of opportunity, always within the framework of 'holding the ring', while the Americans wanted to set up a major target at a definite date, and hit it.

It was in a sense a fundamental difference between the approach to a military problem of a sea power and a land power. But it was also deeply political, for whatever the means none had foreseen the end to be desired.

But there had been no need for anything but frankness. The hard facts were that a cross-Channel attack was not possible before 1944, and in August 1943 the British went to Quebec with the plans for it—for 'Overlord'—in their pockets. When they realized that the Americans were ready to reverse their whole strategy and abandon 'Germany first', they were dumbfounded. In the event, the Americans did not change their minds, but they did impress upon their fast weakening ally that henceforth they were the masters and would call the tune. At Teheran, three months later, they underlined their decisions and dispelled Churchill's last hopes of Italy and the Balkans by producing a plan to assault in the South of France in concert with the assault on Normandy, and thereby making any other adventure impossible.

Stalin's delight was marked. He had found a great ally, and nothing short of a miracle could stop his armies filling the vacuum of Central Europe.

'The ultimate effect of this distrust,' wrote Professor Trumbull Higgins, 'appeared at the Teheran Conference in November-December 1943, when after the United States joined up with the Russians to push through the cross-Channel invasion, this policy of Russo-American military collaboration tended to continue in the even more delicate realm of politics, a realm in which Mr Churchill was a true master, a master solidly based on Clausewitz. But by 1944-45 the British Prime Minister had misled the Americans too often on the military end to expect to be respected and heeded on the political.'[1]

This, I believe, is grossly unjust, but it is what happened that matters, and Higgins underlines it:

'... General Marshall, who had made no public speeches concerning his many "difficult scenes" with President Roosevelt in 1942, had so won the latter's confidence by 1944-45 that there was no debate "whatsoever" between them in this era in which political considerations should have dominated the scene.'[2]

The tragedy of Europe, therefore, arose in part at least from the distrust between the British and American allies, and it is difficult to achieve even a glimpse of this distrust in the making. The records of the meetings of the combined Chiefs of Staff do not convey an impression of the heat and feeling frequently

---

[1] Trumbull Higgins, *Winston Churchill and the Second Front*. New York, Oxford University Press.
[2] Ibid.

generated. At times, all secretaries were excluded, and perhaps only Admiral King of those directly concerned behind closed doors has given more than a hint of the acrimony. Professor Higgins has a passage of interest in regard to the Quebec meeting, which confirms the

'fundamental distrust of the sincerity of the military policies of Mr Churchill' at that time, a 'distrust which at the Trident[1] and Quadrant[2] conferences Stimson and Marshall had finally succeeded in conveying to President Roosevelt. After the middle of 1943 the President could not longer be induced to believe that his British colleague was driving deeper and deeper into the Mediterranean for the sake of a cross-Channel invasion. When this American disillusionment was accentuated by the apparent alienation of the Russians at this time, it is not surprising that in Mr Churchill's careful language: "There was emerging a strong current of opinion in American governmental circles which seemed to wish to win Russian confidence even at the expense of co-ordinating the Anglo-American war effort." [3]

Churchill was worried about many things at Quebec, apart from military strategy. Britain needed a loan, and in order to get it Churchill agreed to the Morgenthau plan to turn Germany into a 'potato patch'. This was economic and political absurdity of a deadly kind, but with Professor Lindemann at his side, driven by his obsessional hatred of Germany, the British Treasury was suddenly alarmed that the Prime Minister might agree. H. E. Brand,[4] then in Washington, rushed to Quebec in an endeavour to prevent the signing, but when he reached Quebec he was not admitted to Churchill. The deed was done. It was too late.

The British have always been reticent about the conduct and atmosphere prevailing at these meetings, and it is only from the Americans that an insight may be gained. James Gould Cozzens, in *Guard of Honour*, had carefully observed:

'their human plights, their various mental and physical predicaments. He would, perhaps, observe that the Protagonist of the

[1] Trident, Washington, May 1943.
[2] Quadrant, Quebec, August 1943.
[3] Trumball Higgins, *Winston Churchill and the Second Front*.
[4] Later Lord Brand.

Bulldog Breed was often grumpy, half a mind on his brandy-soured stomach and throatful of cigar-flavoured phlegm. Grimacing, Mr Churchill must taste, too, the gall of his situation. Fine phrases and selected words might show it almost a virtue that, far call'd our navies melt away; that, on dune and headland sinks the fire; but those circumstances also kept him from the leading position. Except as a piece of politeness, he did not even sit as an equal. His real job was to palter. His field and air marshals, on short commons of men and machines, his admirals of the outclassed Fleet, all nerves bared by close to four years of war in the main unfortunate, supported him, courageous and proud, but also at the last word impotent.

'Across the table . . . the Union strong and great, was in a pleasanter position; justifiably cockier. They had the ships, they had the men, they had the money, too! However, the Champion of the Four Freedoms was, in cruel fact, not free to leave his chair; he could not do it unless somebody helped him. His top military chiefs, shown able enough as far as they had gone, were disadvantaged because they had never waged any war to speak of, fortunate or unfortunate. And then, too, though they had so much of everything else, they faced what they called their opposite numbers with only four, instead of five, stars.'

In this unfruitful atmosphere,

'agreement was ordinarily resisted by mutual misrepresentations, and obtained by a balance of disguised bribes and veiled threats.'

It was necessary to observe these things with

'calculated detachment—not underrating these persistent children, nor even despising them. They were boys in mind only. They had the resources of man's estate. They were more dextrous and much more dangerous than when they pretended they were robbers or Indians; and now their make-believe was really serious to them. You found it funny or called it silly at your peril. Credulity had been renamed faith. Each childish adult determinedly bet his life and staked his sacred pride on, say, the Marxist's ludicrous substance of things only hoped for, or the Christian casuist's wishful evidence of things not so much as seen.'

In late November, by the time Churchill and Brooke reached Teheran for the great conference with the Russians, the old man was showing signs of strain. The American passion for the Chiang Kai-sheks, and their curious belief that these two adventurers were the rulers of China, did nothing to lighten Churchill's brooding anxieties. The private conversations between Roosevelt and Stalin, from which he was excluded, were a presage of the shape of things to come.

'Not enough heed was paid to the way in which military developments could affect political possibilities,'

wrote Herbert Feis in one of the classic understatements of our times.

'No one suggested that military strategy be adjusted to serve the political purposes and settlements in mind.'[1]

Churchill made such suggestions with all his remaining energy to the war's end, but in American eyes to confound military strategy with politics was heresy. The old man was very tired. His star was long past its meridian, and the twilight was upon him.

V

Through all the tremendous comings and goings, the exhausting journeys by sea and air, the long and often bitter controversies, the formal and informal dinners and banquets, Sir Alan Brooke, the CIGS, served Churchill with a quiet devotion beyond the demands of his office, confiding to his diary some of the extreme stresses he himself suffered. In October he recorded: 'I can control him no more. He has worked himself into a frenzy.' Churchill could not abandon his dreams, and his desire to 'storm Rhodes' consumed him. The President was adamant, proof now against all the arguments of the 'Former Naval Person', a long time ago, or so it seemed.

By December Churchill was more than weary, and on the nineteenth of the month Lord Moran, his personal physician, feared pneumonia. There was some heart flutter, pulse 130, temperature 102. Brooke would have moved heaven and earth to

[1] *Churchill, Roosevelt, Stalin.* Princeton University Press.

bring comfort to the old man. As he lay prostrate at Carthage his mind would not rest. He 'felt we were at one of the climaxes of the war', and sent off his desperate plaint to Roosevelt, lest we 'sabotage everything we could have in Italy'. The ghost of 'Anvil', as Alexander called the proposed assault against the South of France, threatened everything:

'What can I do, Mr President, when your Chiefs of Staff insist on casting aside our Italian offensive campaign, with all its dazzling possibilities, relieving Hitler of all his anxieties in the Po Basin and when we are to see the integral life of this campaign drained off into the Rhone Valley in the belief that it will in several months carry effective help to Eisenhower so far away in the north?'

They were deaf to his pleadings, but wherever he was remained 'the vortex'. Immediately after Christmas he was moved to Marrakesh—'my beloved Marrakesh, a haven where I could regain my strength.' There he had the news of the sinking of the German battleship *Scharnhorst*, a wonderful tonic. He had forced through his plan to mount a flank attack at Anzio to open the road to Rome. He would fight to the last ditch.

Early in 1944 he was back again in England, waiting for D Day, praying that all would be well, for the die was cast. He was quickly tired, ready to take offence, and giving it freely. 'I should have to resign at least once a day,' Brooke wrote, if he had taken offence each time the old man insulted him, or said that he had lost confidence.

When after some minor upset between them, Ismay came to Brooke saying that Churchill thought Brooke hated him, the CIGS answered quietly, 'I don't hate him, I love him.'

Slowly through 1944 the hopes of early victory in the West petered out, the armies chained to the slow pace dictated by the gigantic logistics of modern war. Even, it sometimes seemed, that if the enemy were to disappear the pace would barely quicken. In the last days of March 1945, while Montgomery waited on the banks of the Rhine with his enormous build-up of strength for the assault, first Hodges with the American First Army, and then Patton with the American Third Army, bounced the river, and the race was on into the heart of Germany.

General Patton's announcement of his Rhine crossing reveals

all the bitterness of the rivalries between the allies in the field:

'Without benefit of airborne drop, without benefit of the United States or the British Navy and *not* having laid down the greatest smoke-screen in the history of modern war, and without either a three months' build-up of supplies or a whole extra American army, and with no preliminary bombardment, and finally without even a code word, Lieutenant General Patton and the Third United States Army crossed the Rhine yesterday.'

The end game was about to unfold, while in the north Montgomery staged his pyrotechnic display and air circus to dazzle the eyes of the privileged spectators, and to give Churchill his last close-up of the din and smoke of battle. Politics and war were by that time indissolubly mixed in the minds of all save Eisenhower and his generals. No consideration of the future shape of Europe, of the feared occupation of all Central Europe by the Russians, would cause Eisenhower to change by so much as a comma his military plans. For nearly three weeks the great city of Prague lay open while Patton waited on the arrival of the Russians, and for Eisenhower, the Supreme Commander, Berlin was nothing more than a 'geographical abstraction'.

Ralph Ingersoll wrote:

'They (the British) must have wondered, sometimes, whether history had not committed them to an alliance, at worst with madmen and at best with congenital optimists, the corner stones of whose faith were ignorance and vanity."[1]

For Churchill the conferences held at Yalta in February 1945 and at Potsdam in July, were the last battlefields. The two great potentates of the East and West, his 'partners' in the long struggle, impatient with his hopes and fears for the Europe they had 'tidied up', and whose future they had arranged, were preoccupied with the Far East, and with the war with Japan which they expected might go on for eighteen months beyond the death of Germany. In their anxiety to gain the certainty of Soviet participation in the war against Japan, the Americans presented Stalin with a powerful bargaining counter he was swift to use. As soon as Germany was defeated he would join in against Japan,

[1] *Top Secret.*

and establish his territorial claims in the Far East, making good the losses of Russia in 1904.

In all this Churchill was not asked to have a say, nor did he attempt to. 'To us,' he wrote, 'the problem was remote and secondary.' The Far East remained for him in that 'twilight' it had occupied in his mind from the beginning. At Potsdam, Britain would be granted the right to join in the invasion, while the sour American General Stillwell casually by-passed Mountbatten's Supreme Command and indulged in direct communication with Washington. All that Churchill could do was to struggle for better things in Europe.

In those months from Yalta to Potsdam, Churchill was deeply troubled in a way he had never known before. A task to tax to the limits the genius of a Marlborough confronted him, for he alone was the champion of the old world against the new, and the grave incursions of the East. Bravely he pursued his almost private battle for the integrity of Poland, for 'free elections', for the feeding of landless, Stateless, starving multitudes already milling in the wastelands whose future boundaries were unknown. Above all, perhaps, he fought for the dignity of France, and for her recognition as a great European power with a voice in the councils. Without France, Western Europe would become a mere rump.

Churchill had failed to generate warmth in that strange, dedicated Frenchman, Charles de Gaulle, but de Gaulle's passion had generated some new fire in Churchill himself, kindling an aspiration to transcend his extreme egocentricity. Charles de Gaulle, Churchill knew, bore the lamp of France within him, sheltering it, as young Tom of Warwick bore north and sheltered the tiny candle of hope lit by Arthur's dreams. Without a human sanctuary such a flame must die; without a human sanctuary such a flame would not be lit.

And this, I swear, Churchill knew, or felt in his bones. With Eden, his 'squire', he fought like a tiger for France, and was thereby a greater man than either of his powerful allies. They were bemused by material power, believing themselves able to mould the world in the image they desired, knowing best the forms of government and behaviour alien peoples should adopt. Churchill knew otherwise.

General de Gaulle, himself excluded from these conferences and high debates, was not greatly troubled at the 'slight' upon him, and was careful not to give the impression that he was 'vexed or angry'. 'Later on,' he wrote to Georges Bidault, his Foreign Minister,

'we shall be in a far better position to discuss the European imbroglio from without, if we have not participated in the rigmarole to come, which may well end in rivalries between those present.'[1]

At Yalta and at Potsdam, Churchill was a fighter for lost causes that were never lost while men believed in them. He gained for France a grudging recognition, and the control of one of the zones of occupation to be established in Germany. Between January and July of 1945 all was won and lost in the West, for the armies in the field had been shorn of their political meaning and purpose and had become mere weapons of destruction. Again and again Eisenhower, the Supreme Commander, reiterated, patiently, as though to recalcitrant children, that his business was to destroy the German Army, and that Berlin was meaningless, even as a symbol. Yet had his armies occupied Prague, and had he permitted the drive through to Berlin for which Churchill pleaded to the last, who shall deny that Soviet Russia, her armies weary and at the end of enormous lines of communication reaching back over a thousand miles of 'scorched earth' to her bases, must have accepted a situation she would have been powerless to undo?

It was not to be. As Churchill walked the old battlefield of Balaclava after Yalta, having said his last farewell to Roosevelt on his way home to die, he looked back with nostalgia upon a glorious fragment of that 'gentleman's game' for which he had always yearned, and at which he had longed to excel. In this quiet valley 'of the shadow of death' he could hear in his mind the thunder of hooves bearing men on in wild and dreadful ecstasy into the cannons' mouth. It was all over, and less relevant than the ancient Peloponnesian War his rival Thucydides had recorded 'to last for ever'. On that old battlefield of Balaclava Churchill stood, and knew that he stood, at the threshold of a new age, to be shaped by other hands and minds than his, or perhaps not shaped at all.

At Potsdam there was a new man to meet, a new President of the United States, a 'plain dealer' shrewd in plain dealing, and about to be caught up in affairs of an awful complexity, which

[1] *Salvation, War Memoirs of General de Gaulle,* 1944-46 Documents.

were an inheritance not easily to be understood, except perhaps in the very bowels of men who knew, and counted themselves, European. To understand one had not only to think, but to feel, to lay the mind—even the soul—open in the prayer that upon these matrices might be made known the way.

The clangour of power had become so great that the growing pleas of Japan for peace, at almost any price but the loss of their Emperor, went unheard, and 'Unconditional Surrender' was to be writ indelibly upon two pieces of earth scorched by the fire of 'ten thousand suns'. It was not understood that the forces that shape the destinies of men are not to be seen, added up, calculated in material symbols; they reside in the human heart, held within the inexpressible framework of faith and aspiration. The only eye leading men on beyond physical vision is an eye within, and all the great and lasting victories of men have been won by those striving for visions seen by this inner eye alone.

These men who believed at Yalta and Potsdam that they could mould men and nations as they desired, usurped the prerogatives of the gods. The vision within de Gaulle, and the small flame of faith and mystery alight in Churchill, was more important than all that could be seen or known of France, and Britain, and of defeated Germany. Beneath all the rubble, forces as yet unknown still lived and would presently revive to build—no man knew what.

Nothing but uncertainty is certain, and the genius of living and politics is improvisation in the service of aspiration and faith. The greatest casualty of war had been the image men call God, and in that image the dignity of individual man. The worship and supreme power of materialism had been proclaimed, and in that dark shadow people would become nameless pawns.

Churchill had never been in touch with 'the people'; had never understood the 'mysteries' of their thinking and their choices, except in those brief days of deadly physical peril when he had given tongue to the voices echoing in their hearts. Until he awoke suddenly 'with a sharp stab of almost physical pain' just before the dawn on July 26, 1945, he had believed that the people of Britain would elect him to lead them into peace. At Yalta, Stalin had reassured him with the words, 'since the people would understand that they needed a leader, and who could be a better leader than he who had won the victory?' he had no reason to fear, and so far as he knew he had not feared. He had forgotten his own words, written long before power came upon him:

'Those who can win a war well can rarely made a good peace, and those who could make a good peace would never have won a war.'[1]

The death of his old chief, David Lloyd George, in February of the year, might have reminded him, for with all his great talents for peace Lloyd George had failed successfully to bridge the gap, unable to disengage himself from the drives and passions generated by war, not in himself, but in the people. Churchill pronounced his tribute in the House of Commons they both had loved through half a century:

'As a man of action, resource and creative energy he stood, when at his zenith, without a rival. His name is a household word throughout our Commonwealth of Nations. He was the greatest Welshman which that unconquerable race has produced since the age of the Tudors. Much of his work abides, some of it will grow greatly in the future, and those who come after us will find the pillars of his life's toil upstanding, massive and indestructible.'

These were noble words, nobly thought and nobly spoken, but could it be said with equal truth that the 'pillars of his own life's toil' would be indestructible? Had the locusts not eaten the years of maturity when alone such foundations of the future must be laid? It might be so. He had fought the great fight with all his might, but it had been always—or nearly always—his own fight. He had stayed the course.

Out of office the illusion of power still clothed him, not only in his own mind, but in the minds of millions throughout the word. At Fulton he fired his last great broadside to warn the Western world of Russian ambitions, and to make his plea for union of the English-speaking peoples; at Strassbourg he abandoned an idea barely out of the womb. Soon, when his old friend Bernard Baruch met him on Pier 90, New York, it was 'Old Man England' meeting 'Old Man America'. They were both very old men, and they had had their long day. Reporters no longer buzzed about them, wondering what they 'were up to'.

[1] Churchill, *My Early Life*.

In these years of the aftermath of war, Churchill crowned his immense literary achievement with the six volumes of his *Second World War*, again, as Balfour had said of his earlier work, his 'Autobiography disguised as a history of the universe'. He was a soldier who always wanted to be a politician; a politician who always wanted to be a soldier. Perhaps as a very old man he would still look back, as he had done in 1930, on those great years 'from twenty to twenty-five', when he had ridden in the charge at Omdurman, when he had written *The River War*, a superb piece of war reporting, and when he might still have been a soldier. I believe that he might have exchanged all else to have been, simply, General Sir Winston Churchill, VC, GCB.

He was a great complex of a man, compounded of warring ingredients, and full of passion, as well as sentiment. For a little while with him we became dangerous children pursuing visions of glory. In England's desperate need he renewed her youth and fortified her spirit. For him it was never England right or wrong, but simply, England!

He was a man 'magnificently unprepared for the long littleness of life'.[1]

*Belchamp Walter*
*February 1962*

---

[1] de Quincey.

# BIBLIOGRAPHY

Amery, Rt. Hon. L. S. *My Political Life.* Three volumes. London, Hutchinson, 1953.
Asquith, Hon. Herbert *Moments of Memory.* London, Hutchinson, 1937.
Lord Oxford and Asquith *Memories and Reflections, 1852-1927.* London, Cassell, 1928.
Asquith, Margot *Autobiography.* London, Butterworth, 1937.
Asquith, C. and Spender, J. A. *Life of Lord Oxford and Asquith.* London, Hutchinson, 1935.

Barnett, Corelli *The Desert Generals.* London, Kimber, 1960.
Bartlett, Ashmead *The Uncensored Dardanelles.* London.
Baruch, Bernard M. *The Public Years.*
Baudoin, Paul *The Private Diaries, March 1940 to January 1941.* London, Eyre & Spottiswoode, 1948.
Bryant, Arthur *Turn of the Tide.* London, Collins, 1957.
— *Triumph in the West.* London, Collins, 1959.
Butler, Sir James (Ed.) *History of the Second World War.* London, HMSO.
— Vol. II, *Grand Strategy,* J. R. M. Butler. London, HMSO.
— Vol. V, *Grand Strategy,* John Ehrman. London, HMSO.
— Vol. VI, *Grand Strategy,* John Ehrman. London, HMSO.
— Vols. I, II, III, *The War at Sea,* S. W. Roskill, London, HMSO.
— Vols. I, II, III, *The Mediterranean and Middle East,* I. S. O. Playfair and others. London, HMSO.
— Vols. I, II, III and Appendix vol., *The Strategic Air Offensive,* Sir Charles Webster and Noble Frankland. London, HMSO.
Byrnes, James F. *Speaking Frankly.* London, Heinemann, 1947.

Chatfield, Lord *It Might Happen Again.* London, Heinemann, 1942.
Churchill, Randolph *Lord Derby.* London, Heinemann, 1960.
Churchill, Rt. Hon. Sir Winston *The World Crisis.* Five volumes. London, Four Square, 1960.
— *The Second World War.* Six volumes. London, Cassell, 1948-54.
— *Savrola.* London, Longmans, 1900.
— *The Story of the Malakand Field Force.* London, Longmans, 1898.
— *The River War.* London, Eyre & Spottiswoode, 1933.
— *London to Ladysmith via Pretoria.* London, Longmans, 1900.
— *Ian Hamilton's March.* London, Longmans, 1900.
— *Lord Randolph Churchill.* Two volumes. London, Macmillan, 1906.
— *My African Journey.* London, Hodder & Stoughton, 1908.
— *Liberalism and the Social Problem.* London, Hodder & Stoughton, 1909.
— *My Early Life: A Roving Commission.* London, Butterworth, 1934.
— *Thoughts and Adventures.* London, Butterworth, 1933.
— *Great Contemporaries.* London, Butterworth, 1938.
— *Arms and the Covenant.* London, Harrap, 1938.
— *Step by Step: 1936-1939.* London, Butterworth, 1939.
— *Into Battle.* London, Cassell, 1941.
— *The Unrelenting Struggle.* London, Cassell, 1942.
— *The Unknown War.*
— *The End of the Beginning.* London, Cassell, 1943.
— *Onwards to Victory.* London, Cassell, 1944.
— *The Dawn of Liberation.* London, Cassell, 1945.

— *Victory, Secret Session Speeches*. London, Cassell, 1946.
— *Marlborough, His Life and Times*. Four volumes. London, Harrap, 1948.
Clausewitz, Karl von *On War*. London, Routledge, 1908.
Coit, Margaret L. *Mr Baruch*. London, Gollancz, 1958.
Connell, John *Auchinleck*. London, Cassell, 1959.
Cooper, Duff, Viscount Norwich *Old Men Forget*. London, Hart Davis, 1953.
Cowles, Virginia *Winston Churchill, the Era and the Man*. London, Hamilton, 1953.
Cozzens, James Gould *Guard of Honour*. London, Longmans, 1949.
Cornwallis-West, Mrs George *Reminiscences of Lady Randolph Churchill*. London, Edward Arnold, 1908.
Creasy, Sir Edward *Fifteen Decisive Battles of the World*. London, Nelson's Classics, 1913.
Cunningham, of Hyndhope, Viscount *A Sailor's Odyssey*. London, Hutchinson, 1951.

Dalton, Hugh *The Fateful Years*. London, Muller, 1957.
Driberg, Tom *Beaverbrook*. London, Weidenfeld & Nicolson, 1956.

Eade, Charles (Ed.) *The War Speeches of Winston Churchill*. London, Cassell, 1952.
— *Churchill by His Contemporaries*. London, Hutchinson, 1953.
Eden, Sir Anthony *Full Circle*. London, Cassell, 1960.

Feis, Herbert *Churchill, Roosevelt, Stalin*. Princeton, Oxford, 1957.
Feiling, Keith *The Life of Neville Chamberlain*. London, Macmillan, 1946.
Fuller, Major-General J. F. C. *The Conduct of War 1789-1961*. London, Eyre & Spottiswoode, 19
— *The Second World War, 1939-1945*. London, Eyre & Spottiswoode, 1948.

Garvin, J. L. (Ed.) *These Eventful Years, the Twentieth Century in the Making*. Two volumes. London, Eyre & Spottiswoode, 1955.
Gaulle, de, General *War Memoirs of* . . Four volumes, London, Collins, 1955.
George, David Lloyd *The War Memoirs of* . . Six volumes. London, Ivor Nicholson & Watson, 1933-36.
Grigg, Sir James *Prejudice and Judgement*. London, Cape, 1948.
Guedalla, Philip *Mr Churchill*. London, Hodder & Stoughton, 1941.

Harris, Seymour E. (Ed.) *Foreign Economic Policy for the United States*. Harvard, Oxford, 1948.
Harrison, G. A. *Cross-Channel Attack*.
— *US Army in World War II*.
Hart, Liddell, Capt. B. H. *The Tanks, the History of the Royal Tank Regiment*. Two volumes. London, Cassell, 1959.
Hassall, Christopher *Edward Marsh*. London, Longmans, 1961.
Higgins, Trumbull *Winston Churchill and the Second Front*. New York, Oxford University Press, 19
Hull, Cordell *The Memoirs of Cordell Hull*. Two volumes. London. Hodder & Stoughton, 1948.
Haldane, General Sir Aylmer *A Soldier's Saga*. London, Blackwood, 1948.

Ingersoll, Ralph *Top Secret*. London, Partridge, 1950.
Ismay, Lord *Memoirs*. London, Heinemann, 1960.

Johnson, Franklyn Arthur *Defence by Committee*. Oxford University Press, 1960.

Kennedy, Major-General Sir John *The Business of War*. London, Hutchinson, 1957.
Kruger, Rayne *Goodbye, Dollie Gray*. London, Cassell, 1959.

Leahy, William D. *I Was There*. London, Gollancz, 1950.
Leslie, Anita *The Fabulous Leonard Jerome*. London, Hutchinson, 1954.

MacGowan, Norman *My Years With Churchill*. London, Souvenir, 1958.
Marlborough, Consuelo, Duchess of *The Glitter and the Gold*. London, Heinemann, 1953.
Marder, Arthur J. (Ed.) *Fear God and Dread Naught*, the correspondence of Admiral of the Fleet, Lord Fisher. Three volumes. London, Cape, 1952-59.
Minney, R. J. (Ed.) *Private Papers of Hore-Belisha*. London, Collins, 1960.
Morgenthau *Secrets of the Bosphorus*. London, Hutchinson.

Neilson, Francis *The Churchill Legend*. London, Nelson.
Nicolson, Harold *King George V*. London, Constable, 1952.
North, John *Gallipoli, the Fading Vision*. London, Faber, 1936.

Pogue, Forrest *The Supreme Command*.
— US Army in World War II.

Raymond, John *The Doge of Dover*. London, MacGibbon & Kee, 1960.
Rosenman, Samuel I. *Working With Roosevelt*. London, Hart Davis, 1952.

Sherwood, Robert (editor) *The White House Papers of Harry Hopkins*. Two volumes. London, Eyre & Spottiswoode, 1948.
Sommer, Dudley *Haldane of Cloan, His Life and Times*. London, Allen & Unwin, 1960.
Spears, Sir Edward, Major-General *Assignment to Catastrophe*. Two volumes. London, Heinemann, 1954.
Smuts, J. C. *Jan Christian Smuts*. London, Cassell, 1952.
Stettinius, Edward R. Jnr. *Lend-Lease, Weapon for Victory*. London, Penguin Books, 1944.
Stimson, Henry L. and McGeorge Bundy *On Active Service in Peace and War*. London, Hutchinson, 1949.

Taylor, A. J. P. *The Origins of the Second World War*. London, H. Hamilton, 1961.
Templewood, Viscount *Nine Troubled Years*. London, Collins, 1954.
Thomson, Malcolm *David Lloyd George*. London, Hutchinson, 1948.
Truman, Harry S. *Years of Decision*. London, Hodder, 1955.

Wells, H. G. *Men Like Gods*. London, Cassell, 1923.
Williams, Francis *A Prime Minister Remembers*. London, Heinemann, 1960.
Wilmot, Chester *The Struggle for Europe*. London, Collins, 1952.
Winant, John G. *A Letter from Grosvenor Square*. London, Hodder & Stoughton, 1947.
Wrinch, Pamela N. *The Military Strategy of Winston Churchill*. Dept. of Gov. Boston Univ.

# INDEX

Agadir crisis (1911), 158-9
Air Defence Committee, 274, 281
Aitken, Max, see Beaverbrook, Baron
Alamein: First, 319, 320; Second, 321
Alanbrooke, F.M. Viscount, 29; as C.I.G.S., 341-2, 343, 347-8
Algeciras Conference (1906), 157
Amery, L. S., 58-9, 98, 241-2, 248, 250-1, 269, 293-4
Arcadia Conference (January 1942), 317-18, 339, 342
Ashmead-Bartlett, W., 184, 187
Asquith, H. H. (Earl of Oxford and Asquith): forms government (1907), 145, 148; relations with W.S.C., 165, 175; lacks dynamism, 186; agrees to Coalition, 190; falls, 190-1, 200-1
Asquith, Margot (Lady Oxford), 166, 200
Atlantic Charter, 332
Attlee, Clement (Earl Attlee), 294
Auchinleck, F.M. Sir Claude, 29, 314, 318-19, 320-1
Austria, Nazis absorb, 279
Avon, Lord, see Eden, Sir A.

Baldwin, Stanley (Earl Baldwin), 203, 231, 240, 248, 260-1, 275; speech of 'appalling frankness' (1936), 268
Balfour, A. J. (Earl of Balfour), 70, 134, 152, 190; attitude to W.S.C., 97, 191, 199; pierces his armour, 147
Balkans, 157-8; Balkan Wars, 161-2, 165-6
Baruch, Bernard: friendship with W.S.C., 29-30, 73, 214, 249-50; heads War Production Board, 216, 224-7; at Versailles, 223; influential position of, 265, 284-5
Beaverbrook, first Baron: association with W.S.C., 29, 202, 308; Bonar Law his tool, 152, 189; plots Asquith's downfall, 200
Berchtold, Count Leopold von, 162, 171
Beresford, Lord Charles, 149
Berwick, Duke of (James Fitz James), 44-5
Bevin, Ernest, 243

Birkenhead, Lord, see Smith, F. E.
Blackett, P. M. S., 281-2
Blood, Gen. Sir Bindon, 71, 82
Boer War: condemned abroad, 104, 113; W.S.C.'s escapades: train ambush, 106-9; escape, 109-12; British military methods out of date, 112-13; W.S.C.'s part in peace terms, 135
Boothby, Robert (later Baron), 269
Bourchier, J. D., 161
Bracken, Brendan, 29-30, 264, 294, 307
Britain: 'the great amphibian', 136-7, 327
British Navy: Fisher's reforms, 67, 163; Prince of Wales and Repulse, 303, 317
Brooke, Sir Alan, see Alanbrooke, Viscount
Buchanan, Sir George, 211-12

Cadogan, Sir Alexander, 269
Cambon, Paul, 170
Campbell-Bannerman, Sir H., 127
Carson, Sir Edward, 191, 199
Casablanca Conference, 326, 332
Cassell, Sir Ernest, 125
Chamberlain, Sir Austen, 269
Chamberlain, Joseph, 105
Chamberlain, Neville, 203, 260-1; rebuffs Roosevelt's offer, 275; Munich, 279-80; refuses to have W.S.C. in the Cabinet, 283; guarantee to Poland (1939), 288
Chartwell, 35, 244
Chatfield, Admiral Lord, 316
Cherwell, Viscount (Prof. Lindemann), 29, 264, 274, 281, 307, 308-9; strategic bombing policy, 297, 305
China: U.S. policy towards, 347
Churchill, Lady (Clementine), 29, 38, 144, 166, 196-7, 246-7, 339
Churchill, Jack, 47
Churchill, Lady Randolph, 31; memoirs, 49-53; marriage, 53, 54, 56-7, 106; relations with W.S.C., 68-9; second marriage, 144
Churchill, Lord Randolph, 31, 36-7; marriage, 53-4; political career, 54-7, 96

# INDEX

Churchill, Sir Winston (b. 1620), 44-5
Churchill, Sir Winston Spencer. THE CAREER. Nursery days, 27-9; schooling, 30-1, 56, 58-9; development, 33-5; Hussars, 61-7; Cuban War, 72-9; India, 79ff.; Malakand, 82-3; Tirah campaign, 83-7; Sudan, 89-91; contests Oldham, 96; Boer War, 97-114; wins Oldham, 113; early political education, 117ff.; U.S. lecture tour, 125; joins Liberals, 128-9, 141-2, 173, 208-9; Under-Secretary of State for the Colonies, 135; meets Marsh, 138; marriage, 144; African trip, 144-5; President of Board of Trade, 145; Home Secretary, 145; 'Battle of Sidney Street', 146; Curragh mutiny, 147; First Lord, 147-8, 149-51, 163ff.; Mediterranean cruises with Asquith, 164-6; prepares for war, 169, 174-6; sends naval division to Antwerp, 177-8; Dardanelles campaign, 183-4, 186-8; backs the tank, 186; Duchy of Lancaster, 190, 196; excluded from Lloyd George's War Cabinet, 190, 191-2, 201-2; fighting in France, 195, 196-9; Minister of Munitions, 202, 204ff.; reaction to Russian Revolution, 209-10, 212-14, 226-8, 233; more visits to the Front, 216-20; Ministries of War and Air, 227, 232-3; intervention in Russia, 229-30; in the wilderness, 231; Chancellor of Exchequer, 239-41; General Strike, 243-4; divorced from Baldwin, 249, 253, 262; 'Focus' group, 264, 286; snipes Front Bench with ammunition they give him, 269; First Lord, 290; botches Narvik expedition, 292; Prime Minister, 292ff.; starts bombing Germany, 297, 305; woos Roosevelt, 297-8, 335-7; Oran, 298; backs de Gaulle, 299; reinforces Wavell, 314; becomes a tyrant, 305ff.; Greek expedition, 311, 334; Crete, 314; dismisses Wavell, 314, and Auchinleck, 320; accepts 'unconditional surrender' policy, 326-7, 341; his strategy, 327-36; address to U.S. Congress, 336-7; begins to weary, 339-41, 347-8; appoints Alanbrooke C.I.G.S., 341; to Marrakesh, 348; Yalta and Potsdam, 349ff.; electoral defeat, 352; Fulton speech, 353.

THE MAN. Yankee v Marlborough, 21, 29-30, 42-3, 47, 208, 325, 327, 331-2, 336-7; the 'nursery thread', 27, 28-30, 81-2, 94, 217; relations with mother, 68-9; family and friends, 70-1; egocentricity, 21, 36, 37, 69-70, 92-102; arrogance, 28, 36-7, 120; tyrannical streak, 134, 201, 202, 305ff.; corrupted by power, 283-4; without compassion, 94-5; attitude to women, 40, 67-9; 'Puckish' charm, 132; irked by social formalities, 43, 74; energy, 74, 122; not an intellectual, 96, 123; tastes in reading, 80-1, 124, 143-4, 226; phrases rather than thoughts, 188, 213; sense of destiny, 33-5, 47, 129, 253; military ambitions, 179, 354; no strategist, 42, 184-5, 302-3, 309-11, 330; direction of war, 303-4; vacillation in command, 313-14; misjudgments and illusions, 220, 274, 278-9, 286, 301; uninterested in domestic politics, 262-3; archaic romanticism, 26, 121, 129-30; views on Empire, 126, 129-30, 249; relations with other power-seekers, 119-20; belief in the Secret Session, 191; causes of unpopularity, 93-4, 98, 99-102; comparison with Lloyd George, 191-3.

HIS WRITINGS. *The World Crisis*, 35, 234, 244, 250-1, 265; *Marlborough*, 35, 99, 252, 266-7; *Great Contemporaries*, 38; *Malakand Field Force*, 84; *Savrola*, 84-5; *The River War*, 92-6, 97; *Lord Randolph Churchill*, 126-7; *My Early Life*, 265; *The Second World War*, 354.

JUDGMENTS OF CONTEMPORARIES. Alanbrooke, 307, 330; Amery, 98, 241-2, 250-1; Asquith, 131; Balfour, 97, 132; Beaverbrook, 202; Begbie, 131; Joseph Chamberlain, 105, 132; Neville Chamberlain, 283; Virginia Cowles, 243; Sir A. Haldane, 89, 108-10; Hankey, 196; Harcourt, 131; Hopkins, 28, 307-8; Ismay, 306; Sir John Kennedy, 306; Keynes, 242; Liddell Hart, 286; Lloyd George, 131, 192; Dowager Duchess of Marlborough, 56; Morley, 131; Sir Bernard Paget, 308; Rosebery, 132; J. C. Squire, 233; H. G. Wells, 37

Clausewitz on war, 325
Clemenceau, Georges, 218-19, 221-3
Cockran, Bourke, 73-5, 125
Cologne, '1,000-bomber' raid, 321
Committee of Imperial Defence, see Hankey, Maurice
Communism, 228-9, 233, 270-3, 331
Coningham, Air Vice-Marshal, 321
Cooper, Duff, 269
Corbett, Lt.-Gen. T. W., 320
Cowles, Virginia, 243
Cozzens, James Gould, 345-6
Crete, 314
Croft, Sir Henry Page, 269
Cromer, first Earl of, 95
Crossman, R. H. S., 167
Crowe, Sir Eyre, 269, 327
Czechoslovakia, 279-80

Dakar, 301-2
Dardanelles, 183-4
Davies, Clement, 294
Delcassé, Théophile, 156
Depew, Chauncey, 125
de Robeck, Admiral, 183, 188
Dieppe raid, 342
Dill, Sir John, 29, 304, 314-15
Dorman Smith, Maj.-Gen., 313, 318-20

Eden, Sir Anthony, 275-6, 314
Edward VIII, King, 274-5
Eisenhower, Gen. D. W., 318
Enver, Bey, 155-6, 165
Esher, first Viscount, 70, 136, 146, 153-4, 213
European politics: nineteenth-century, 32; at 1900, 61-5; British attitude towards (1906), 136-7
Everest, Mrs (nurse), 26-8, 56-7, 59

Far Eastern policy, 311, 329-30, 349
fascism, 270-3, 331
Finland, 291
Fisher, Admiral Lord, 67, 128, 153; relations with W.S.C., 29, 149, 163-4; resignation over Dardanelles, 186-9
Foch, Marshal Ferdinand, 218-19
France: relations with Germany, 156, 158-9; W.S.C.'s preoccupation with, 286, 350-1; Vichy government, 334-5; landing in southern France, 344; and see Gaulle, Charles de
Free Trade, 127, 128, 141-2

French, Gen. Sir John (later Earl of Ypres), 197
Frewen, Clara, 27, 52, 56, 60
Fuller, Maj.-Gen. J. F. C., 282, 288

Gallipoli, 183-4, 196
Gandhi, Mahatma, 249
Gaulle, Gen. Charles de, 299-300, 350-1, 352
General Strike (1926), 243-4
George V, King, 152-3, 171
German Navy: *Goeben* and *Breslau*, 176-7
Germany: challenge of, 149-50; ultimatum to Russia, 158; warned by Lloyd George (1911), 159; post-war treatment of, 223-4, 259; rise of nazism, 270 ff.; invasion of Poland, 288; not ready for war, 288; takes Denmark and Norway, 290, 291-2; destruction of Germany would let in Russia, 326; Morgenthau plan, 345; and see *France*; *Wilhelm II*
Goethe on Valmy, 325
Gold Standard, return to, 241
Greece, expedition to (1941), 306, 311-14, 317
Grey, Sir Edward (Viscount Grey of Fallodon), 151, 170, 186, 190
Grigg, Sir Edward (Lord Altrincham), 269
Guest, Capt. F. E., 269
Gwynne, H. A., 269-70

Haig, F.M. Earl, 197, 216
Haldane, Gen. Sir Aylmer, 86-9, 106-11
Haldane, first Viscount, 150
Halifax, first Earl of, 294
Hamilton, Sir Ian, 81, 83, 85-6
Hankey, Maurice (first Baron): Committee of Imperial Defence, 136, 146-7, 153-4, 174, 185, 186, 187, 194, 196; Cabinet Secretariat, 203; Versailles, 223; foreign intelligence organization, 268-9
Harris, Marshal of the R.A.F. Sir A. T.: strategic bombing policy, 297, 305, 308-9
Henry of Prussia, Prince, 171
Higgins, Prof. Trumbull, 344-5
Hill, A. V., 281
Hitler, 32, 274
Hopkins, Harry, 28, 307-8, 318
Hore-Belisha, L., 281, 282-4

Horne, Sir Robert, 269
House, Col. E. M., 214, 221
Hozier, Blanche (Lady Churchill's mother), 27

Imperial Preference, 127, 128
India, military potential of British, 136-7
Industrial Revolution, 24-6
Inskip, Sir Thomas (Lord Caldecote), 274
Ismay, Gen. Sir Hastings (Baron), 29, 307
Italy: demands Tripoli (1911), 160; takes Abyssinia, 273; enters war (1940), 301; victory thrown away in, 342

Japan, 273, 329, 349; and see *Russo-Japanese War*
Jerome, Camille, 51
Jerome, Clara (*née* Hall), wife of Leonard; ancestry of, 47, 49; life, 50-2; and see *Frewen, Clara* (daughter)
Jerome, Clarita, 49
Jerome, Jennie, see *Churchill, Lady Randolph*
Jerome, Leonard (grandfather of W.S.C.), 31, 47, 48-9, 50-1, 53-4
Jerome, Leonie, see *Leslie, Leonie*
Jerome, Travers, 74

Kerensky government, 229
Keynes, J. M. (Baron), 242
King, Admiral E. J., 318, 342
Kitchener, F.M. Earl, 82, 89-91, 93-4, 154, 196

Law, Bonar, 152; and W.S.C., 179-80, 189-90, 201; becomes Prime Minister, 232; dies, 237
Lawrence, T. E., 35, 38, 234-6, 270
League of Nations, 222, 224, 273
Lend-Lease, 336
Lenin, 213-14
Leopold of the Belgians, King, 301
Leslie, Leonie, 27, 51, 56-7
Liberalism: a casualty of war, 232, 260
Liddell Hart, Capt. B., 270, 288; on 'unconditional surrender', 326
Lindemann, Prof. F. A., see *Cherwell, Viscount*

Litvinov, Maxim, 260
Lloyd George, David: relations with W.S.C., 29, 129, 131, 173, 203, 206-7; Chancellor of Exchequer, 148; warns Germany (1911), 159-60; advocates 'weak under-belly' strategy, 186; becomes Prime Minister, 190, 200 ff.; comparison with W.S.C., 191-3; reaction to Russian Revolution, 210-11; at Versailles, 221, 223; chooses between political suicide and advocating revenge, 224; electoral victory (1919), 227; fall of Coalition, 231; his 'New Deal', 241, 248; death, 353
Louis of Battenberg, Prince, 174-5
Lytton, Pamela and Constance, 137-8

MacArthur, Gen. Douglas, 42
Macdonald, Ramsay, 260-1, 268-9
McGowan, Norman, 247
McKenna, Reginald, 149, 189
Malaya, loss of, 303, 317
Marlborough, John Churchill, first Duke of, 40-3, 45-7
Marlborough, eighth and ninth Dukes, 60
Marlborough, Frances, Dowager Duchess of, 31-2, 56
Marsh, Edward: W.S.C.'s attitude to, 29, 118; first meeting, 137-42; East African trip, 144-5; refuses promotion, 147-8; to 10 Downing Street, 196; returns to Ministry of Munitions, 204; trips to the Front, 217-18; illness, 244-6, 252, 253
Marshall, Gen. George, 318, 344
Martin, J. M., 307
Menzies, R. G., 316
Milner, first Viscount, 211
Montenegro, 158
Montgomery, F.M. Viscount, 29, 321
Morgenthau, Henry, 155-6; Morgenthau plan, 345
Morton, Sir Desmond, 216-18, 252-3, 264, 269, 307
Mountbatten, first Earl, 316, 350

nazism, see *Fascism; Hitler*
Nicholas II, Tsar, 153, 210-12
Northcliffe, first Viscount, 200, 232
Norway, expedition to (1940), 292
Norwich, first Viscount, 269

O'Connor, Gen., 312-13
Oran, 298
'Overlord', 343-4
Oxford and Asquith, Earl of, see Asquith, H. H.

Paget, Sir Bernard, 308-9
Pares, Sir Bernard, 211
Patton, Gen. G. S., 348-9
Poland, guarantee to, 278, 288
Ponsonby, Arthur (Baron), 253
Portal, Marshal of the R.A.F. Viscount, 297
Potsdam Conference, 349-53
power and authority, 133-4

Quebec Conference, 342, 345

Rasputin, 210-11
Roberts, F.M. Earl, 82, 98
Robertson, F.M. Sir W. R., 206-7
Rommel, F.M. Erwin, 314, 318, 319, 321
Roosevelt, Franklin D.: 'New Deal', 251-2; rebuffed by Chamberlain, 275; 'unconditional surrender', 326; regards Middle East as decisive, 319-20; Roosevelt and Stalin v Churchill, 329-30; character of, 308, 337-9
Rosebery, fifth Earl of, 127-8, 132
Russia: and Germany, 156-8; Bolshevik Revolution, 209-14; and see Nicholas II; U.S.S.R.
Russo-Japanese War, 136, 156

Sarajevo, 170
Serbia, 158
Sherwood, Robert, 337-8
Sinclair, Sir Archibald, 269
Singapore, loss of, 303
'Sledgehammer', 319, 342
Slim, F.M. Sir William, 316
Smith, F. E. (Lord Birkenhead), 199, 269
Somervell, R. (Harrow master), 59
Spanish Civil War, 272-3
Spencer family, 45
Squire, J. C., 233
Stalin: birth, 33; and Roosevelt, 329-30, 339, 344
Stalingrad, 321
Steevens, G. W., 96, 97
Stern, Maj. Sir Albert, 205-7
Stilwell, Gen. J. W., 350

tank, invention of the, 185-6
Teheran Conference, 329-30, 341, 344, 347
Thomas, J. H., 269
Thompson, Cmdr Charles, 307
Tizard, Sir H. T., 29, 281
Tobruk, fall of, 317
Tory Party, 203
Tripoli: taken by Italy (1912), 160; sacrificed to Rommel for Greece, 314
Truman, Harry S., 351
Turkey: key position of, 155; Young Turks' revolt, 157; effect of 'unconditional surrender' policy, 326, 334; and see Balkans

'unconditional surrender', 326, 331, 334, 341
unemployment, 243-4, 248
U.S.S.R.: 'White' Russian revolt, 229-30; Western fears of, 260; need of France and Britain to ally with, 287; agreement with Nazis, 288; British aid to, 318, 334; W.S.C. seeks alliance with, 330-4; agrees to declare war on Japan, 347-50; allowed to take Prague and Berlin, 351; and see Russia
U.S.A.: FIRST WORLD WAR. Provided no tanks or artillery, 206n; financial results of participation, 215-16, 258-9; Britain's natural heir, 224-6; anticolonialism, 250; insists that Britain end Japanese alliance, 259; Wall Street crash (1929), 264-5; and see Wilson, Woodrow
SECOND WORLD WAR. Financial results of participation, 297-8; anticolonialism, 299, 329; U.S. Joint Chiefs of Staff, 317, 342-5; takes over direction of the war, 322, 325-7, 339; community of interests with U.S.S.R., 329, 331; Churchill's wooing of U.S.A., 297-8, 335-7; and see Roosevelt, F. D.

Valmy, Dumouriez' cannonade at (1792), 325
Vansittart, Sir Robert, 269
Versailles Treaty, 220-3

# INDEX

war, nature of: W.S.C.'s and American views contrasted, 323-7
Ware, Sir Fabian, 282
Wavell, F.M. Lord, 311-14; dismissal, 314-16
Welldon, Dr (Harrow Headmaster), 88-9
Wells, H. G., 37
Wemyss, Admiral, 183
Wigram, Ralph, 264, 269, 270
Wilhelm II, Kaiser, 153; 'shining armour' speech, 158; Willy-Nicky letters, 156-7, 172
Willingdon, first Marquess of, 269
Wilson, Woodrow, 215-16, 221-4
Wingate, Gen. Orde, 308, 316
Winterton, first Earl, 269
World War, First: statesmen blind to its approach, 167-9; British equivocation, 170, 171; outbreak, 172, 176; British strategy, 184-5, 186; munitions shortage, 185; morale at the Front, 214-15; demobilization, 227-8; reparations, 259; the missing generation, 261
World War, Second: Britain unprepared, 267-8, 287; the Phoney War, 288-92; invasion of France, 292; Oran, 298; Dakar, 301-2; Malaya, 303, 317; strategic bombing, 305; Greece, 306, 311-14, 317; Crete, 314; fall of Tobruk, 317; Alamein, 319, 321; Stalingrad, 321; direction of war passes to U.S., 322, 325-7; Hodges and Patton cross the Rhine, 348-9

Yalta Conference, 349-53

'Zinoviev' letter, 239

For Product Safety Concerns and Information please contact our EU
representative GPSR@taylorandfrancis.com
Taylor & Francis Verlag GmbH, Kaufingerstraße 24, 80331 München, Germany

www.ingramcontent.com/pod-product-compliance
Lightning Source LLC
Chambersburg PA
CBHW071233290426
44108CB00013B/1395